# Researching Language in Schools and Communities

## Functional Linguistic Perspectives

Edited by
Len Unsworth

CASSELL

London and Washington

Cassell
Wellington House, 125 Strand, London WC2R 0BB
370 Lexington Avenue, New York, NY 10017–6550

First published 2000
© Len Unsworth and contributors 2000

**British Library Cataloguing-in-Publication Data**
A catalogue record for this book is available from the British Library.

ISBN 0 304 70244 7 (Hardback)
    0 304 70245 5 (Paperback)

Typeset by Textype Typesetters, Cambridge
Printed and bound in Great Britain by T J International Ltd, Padstow, Cornwall

# Contents

# Contributors

**Frances Christie** is Professor of Language and Literacy Education at the University of Melbourne.

**Carmel Cloran** is an independent consultant and researcher in systemic functional linguistics and socio-semantic variation.

**Suzanne Eggins** is a senior lecturer in the School of English at the University of New South Wales.

**Linda Gerot** is senior lecturer in language and literacy education at the Queensland University of Technology.

**J. R. Martin** is Associate Professor of Linguistics at the University of Sydney.

**Clare Painter** lectures in English and linguistics at the University of New South Wales.

**Gillian Perrett** lectures in the teaching of English as a second and as a foreign language at the University of Sydney.

**Louise Ravelli** lectures in linguistics at the University of New South Wales.

**Joan Rothery** is an independent consultant and researcher in systemic functional linguistics, literacy and learning.

**Maree Stenglin** is Manager of Education Services at the Australian Museum in Sydney.

**Len Unsworth** is a senior lecturer in the Faculty of Education at the University of Sydney.

**Geoffrey Williams** is a senior lecturer in the Department of English at the University of Sydney.

# Introduction

*Researching Language in Schools and Communities* is a resource for developing research projects in these areas. It shares with readers the catalytic influence of systemic functional linguistics (SFL) on the development of new perspectives and productive transdisciplinary approaches in a variety of fields of applied language research. As applied language research using SFL has become more widely known, people working with and studying language in a range of areas, with varied experience and from different linguistic and research traditions, are beginning to explore the application of SFL in their own fields. This book is a resource for such explorations.

The first chapter explains the model of language and social context underlying SFL and argues that SFL is particularly suited to applied language research because it is premised on the complete interconnectedness of the linguistic and the social. The meaning-making systems of language that SFL describes are based on how people actually use language in different social contexts, so the descriptions of systems of language are integrally related to descriptions of these social contexts.

Chapter 2 introduces some basic concepts of functional linguistic analysis, simultaneously showing how to use the grammatical analyses to explicate the ways in which texts both construe and are construed by social context. This is illustrated through analyses of two texts appearing in the *Sydney Morning Herald* on 7 March 1992 which deal with efforts of the St. George Building Society, to convert to the status of a bank. In order to do this, St. George required the permission of its members. The grammatical analyses illuminate the ways in which these texts played their different roles in relation to this process of conversion.

The subsequent chapters demonstrate the value of incorporating SFL perspectives into the design of studies investigating language in use in many different contexts including young children's first language development, everyday talk, second and foreign language learning, socio-semantic variation in language use, the language of classroom interaction and learning, literature for children, reading processes, interpretive responses to literature, school subject-specific literacies and critical discourse analysis. The first two chapters provide sufficient background to enable those new to SFL to make productive critical use of the research reviewed, the studies described and the advice on project design provided in subsequent chapters. Nevertheless, the book is an introductory resource and therefore provides clear references to more elaborated accounts.

Although SFL is the principal theoretical orientation informing the research approaches described, a very significant feature is the articulation with other disciplinary approaches. We recognize the complementary contributions of different research perspectives on the complex issues addressed. The particular advantage of SFL for interdisciplinary studies of children's first language development is pointed out in Chapter 3; the SFL conception of language necessarily implicates issues of social and cognitive development. From the point of view of SFL, developing linguistic understanding is concomitant with developing social and cultural understanding, so a study of children's language development is a way of exploring their development as social subjects. This is further demonstrated in the account of socio-semantic variation in mother–child talk in Chapter 7 which explores the interface between SFL and the sociology of Basil Bernstein. The relationship between SFL and other aspects of Bernstein's work is addressed in Chapter 8 in analyses of the language of classroom interaction and learning. Bernstein's notions of regulatory and instructional discourse have been adapted in defining and identifying the regulatory and instructional registers that together build pedagogic discourse.

Aspects of Vygotsky's work, especially his theory of the ontogenesis of higher mental functions, are of central theoretical significance to the investigation in Chapter 5 of the use of SFL in exploring literary texts with primary school children. The research concerns primary school children's development and use of functional grammatical concepts as metalinguistic tools in assisting them to describe patterns of relations among characters and the significance of changes in those patterns as the text evolves.

The complementary contribution of SFL research in foreign and second language development in relation to other approaches is discussed in Chapter 4, while Chapter 6 shows that from an SFL perspective, researching everyday talk can reveal how we jointly construct the social reality in which we live. The very encounters we think of as most trivial turn out to be instrumental in constructing and maintaining the social identities and interpersonal relations that maintain our social lives.

Chapters 9, 10 and 11 indicate the ways in which SFL has been deployed in investigating school literacies. In exploring reading processes in Chapter 9, SFL is used to investigate some problematic aspects of testing reading comprehension by explicating the linguistic 'integrative work' necessary to relate different kinds of questions to the cues about answers provided in the test texts. The role of students' knowledge of genre and register in comprehending texts is also explored.

What counts as an effective interpretation response to literary texts in secondary school English examinations is the subject of Chapter 10. It is argued that what is ostensibly required is often not what is actually rewarded by markers. Student answers from two public examination questions are analysed using SFL to make explicit what differentiates high and low scoring responses and how successful answers deploy linguistic resources for constructing interpersonal meaning.

Chapter 11 deals with some of the major findings of extensive SFL research into the linguistic characteristics of the kinds of texts students are required to read and write as part of their subject area learning in primary and secondary schools. The main genres in a number of subject areas are noted. Then some of the principal differentiating features of the discourses of school history and school science are discussed, and a comparative study of school science text book explanations is outlined.

The final chapter reflects the relevance of SFL to applied language research across school and community contexts and demonstrates the interrelationships among SFL and other theoretical approaches by extending the relationship between critical discourse analysis research and SFL. Texts ranging from a picture book for children, the U2 song 'Sunday, Bloody Sunday', answers to secondary school English examinations, excerpts from the movie script of *Educating Rita*, a poem by an Aboriginal leader and a speech by a politician, are analysed using different aspects of SFL to show how functional linguistics provides a tool for addressing the key concerns of critical discourse analysts about inequality in society and the ways in which texts are used to realize power and ideology.

The contributors hope that this book will facilitate the further engagement of applied language researchers with SFL perspectives and encourage complementary if not more collaborative transdisciplinary efforts across different fields of study and theoretical approaches in projects of mutual concern.

*Len Unsworth*
*Faculty of Education*
*University of Sydney*

# Acknowledgements

The author and publishers gratefully acknowledge the following for granting permission to reproduce their texts:

St. George Building Society, NSW (Chapter 2); Australian Council for Educational Research ('The Creature' from ACER Primary Reading Tests, Chapter 9); Mushroom Group of Companies ('Took the Children Away' by A. Roach, Chapter 12); Shortland Publications ('Who Will Be My Mother?', Chapter 9).

Every effort has been made to trace copyright ownership. The publishers will be happy to hear from copyright owners and to make the necessary additions in future printings and editions.

# 1 Developing socially responsible language research

*Frances Christie and Len Unsworth*

## 1.1 Choosing systemic functional linguistics as a research tool

If you have little or no experience of systemic functional linguistics to date, you may wonder why language researchers in areas such as children's literature, reading development, classroom discourse, social class and literacy, and language and gender would turn to systemic functional linguistics (SFL) in investigating their own fields. That this is increasingly the case is evident in the range of research areas addressed in the chapters of this volume and the references in these chapters to the growing number of other scholars in these fields also using SFL. The purpose of this book is to illustrate how linguistics can contribute to 'applied' language research and to provide access to the concepts of SFL as a potential research tool in your area of study. This first chapter will explain what SFL is and how its descriptions of language are completely interconnected with descriptions of the contexts in which language is used. Chapter 2 outlines some key aspects of grammatical analyses that can be used when investigating spoken and written texts. The subsequent chapters indicate the application of SFL to a broad range of areas of inquiry, illustrate research that has been done and suggest research methods and questions to pursue.

## 1.2 Distinguishing systemic functional linguistics

There are many traditions of linguistic research. SFL is distinctive in that the theory has always been developed in response to questions about language in applied contexts: educational (how is a language best taught and learned?); computational (how should language be modelled for automatic text generation?); sociological (what is the role of conversation in the creation and maintenance of self and society?); and literary (how does a text mean what it does and come to be valued as it is?). The seminal work on SFL was begun by its foremost theorist, Michael Halliday, in the 1950s and 1960s and ongoing work by Halliday and other scholars is continuing its development (Halliday and Hasan 1976; Halliday 1994; Martin 1992a; Matthiessen 1995).

The variety of questions raised in applied language research in SFL differs from other traditions in several respects. We outline three here and then explain them more fully in Section 1.3 on modelling language and social context. First, SFL argues that all languages have to manage three major functions: to represent experience ('ideational' or 'experiential' function); to set up and sustain interaction between people using language ('interpersonal' function); and to create connected and coherent discourse ('textual' function). All languages are internally organized into these three components or 'metafunctions': ideational, interpersonal, textual.

A second distinguishing feature of the SFL model is that it describes a language in terms of sets of choices of meaning. A set of options – such as singular/plural number, past/present/future tense, postive/negative polarity – is called a system, hence the name 'systemic' linguistics. When language is described in this way, every choice embodied in an utterance or text carries meaning in terms of the potential choices *not* made.

Thirdly, SFL theory proposes that the object of language study should be a whole text (meaningful passage of language), not a decontextualized sentence or utterance. Putting these three aspects of SFL together – functions, choices, whole text – we can characterize SFL theory as having a strong commitment to the view that language study should focus on meaning and on the ways in which people exercise choices in order to make meaning.

Much traditional language study, including traditional school grammar, has no comparable commitment to the study of meaning in language. If you have studied traditional school grammar you will probably have learned about the categories or classes of words found in English, such as nouns, verbs, adverbs and the like. Some use of these word class labels is retained in SFL, but as you will see in Chapter 2, the theory also uses many other terms that are functionally more relevant. Functional terms like 'Actor' or 'Theme' are essential because they are part of the general enterprise of exploring how people construct and negotiate meanings in the many contexts in which they interact.

Systemic functional descriptions of language are not lists of rules based on what powerful social groups prescribe as 'correct' usage or on what language structures it is neurologically possible to produce.

> Instead of seeing 'what people actually say or do' as somehow deviating from or not being able to be accounted for in an idealised theory of code, Halliday's systemic approach turns this around and sees the system as being determined by behaviour. (Schirato and Yell 1996: 45)

SFL is concerned to describe 'meaning potential' – the linguistic options or choices that are available to construct meanings in particular contexts.

The next step in elaborating the nature of SFL is to understand how the systematic description of language is theoretically linked to a systematic description of the social contexts in which language is used.

## 1.3 Modelling language and social context in systemic functional linguistics

A fundamental premise of SFL is the complete interconnectedness of the linguistic and the social. The focus is on how people use language to make meanings with each other as they carry out the activities of their social lives. They do this through their selections from the sets of choices that are available in the language systems. The choices individuals can actually make from these systems are, however, constrained by two factors. The first is that meaning is always constructed within a context and context limits the range of meanings that can be selected. There are meanings that are expected and appropriate to contexts of all kinds, ranging from what you would expect in a classroom to what you would expect in a disco bar or in a picture book. The second factor that constrains individuals' linguistic choices is that not everyone within a culture or community has access to all of the possible contexts and therefore all the possible ways of speaking or writing. Because of their sociocultural positioning, some people would find it very difficult to communicate with participants at a literary luncheon; others would find a community barbeque in a country town difficult; some people would know exactly what to say and do if they were arrested, while others would be very ill-equipped to negotiate such a situation. Since the meaning-making systems of language that SFL describes are based on how people actually use language in different social contexts, the descriptions of the systems of language must necessarily be related to descriptions of these social contexts.

SFL approaches the description of social context by interpreting it as two inter-related levels: context of situation and context of culture. The context of situation is the immediate context in which the language is used. The 'same' context of situation may be very different in different cultures. For example, buying food in a Western-style supermarket where prices are not negotiable is quite different from buying fresh food in a market in Bangkok or Singapore, where bargaining is expected. Some contexts of situation are culture-specific. The context of culture can be thought of as the full range of systems of situational contexts that the culture embodies.

Any context of situation is described in terms of the three main variables that influence the way language is used: FIELD is concerned with the social activity, its content or topic; TENOR is the nature of the relationships among the people involved; MODE is the medium and role of language in the situation – whether spoken or written, whether accompanying or constitutive of the activity. These situational variables are related to the three overarching areas of meaning already referred to – the 'ideational', the 'interpersonal' and the 'textual' (Table 1.1).

**Table 1.1** Relating contextual variables to metafunctions

| Variable within context of situation | Component of language system (meta-function) |
| --- | --- |
| FIELD: social activity, topic | Ideational: to represent experience |
| TENOR: social roles and relations | Interpersonal: to enable interaction |
| MODE: medium and role of language | Textual: to achieve coherence and connectedness |

Thus there are three components of the context each relating to one of the three areas within language. In Chapter 2 you will see how there are in fact particular kinds of grammatical structures relevant to each metafunction and hence to each component of context. In this way SFL analyses of an actual text necessarily link its language choices to its context of use; grammatical analyses in this sense can be said to be 'socially responsible'.

But the ways in which language is structured for use are influenced not only by the immediate context of situation. Language choices are also influenced by the context of culture. Cultures evolve recognizable ways by which members can achieve their social purposes in the range of situations they typically experience. These ways may involve language to a greater or lesser extent. Everyday routines like buying goods are not heavily dependent on language while other practices such as a university essay, a department store policy on shopping bag inspections or a character reference are entirely constituted by language. Any such culturally recognized practice, or 'genre', entails its own characteristic text structure. The next sections will elaborate the ways in which context of situation and context of culture influence the structuring of language for use, illustrating these with sample texts. (For further explication of text/context relations see Halliday and Hasan 1985, Martin 1992a: 493–46, Eggins 1994: 1–80, Matthiessen 1995: 33–44.)

### 1.3.1 Interfacing language and context of situation

For people whose mother tongue is English, Halliday (Halliday and Hasan 1985: 37) points out, it is possible to make certain inferences about the situation in which quite short text fragments such as the following might have occurred:

once upon a time
this is to certify that
on the blackboard, Miss
four hearts
on your marks
it's on Channel nine
just a trim, is it?
rail strike threat averted

We can infer *ideational* meanings (i.e. participants like the people or objects involved in some process or event and the relevant circumstances of place, time, etc.). For example, 'on the blackboard' suggests an instructional situation in a classroom, and 'four hearts' suggests card play. We can reconstruct the nature of the social activity in which the language plays some role. This is the aspect of the context of situation which Halliday (Halliday and Hasan 1985: 12) refers to as the FIELD:

> The FIELD OF DISCOURSE refers to what is happening, to the nature of the social action that is taking place: what is it that the participants are engaged in, in which the language figures as some essential component?

But we can also infer *interpersonal* meanings or the nature of the relationships among the participants. We know from 'on your marks' that the speaker has the power to command other participants in this social context. We can tell from forms of address such as 'Sir' or 'Miss', or the use of participants' surnames or first names, something of how well the participants know each other, and perhaps even how they feel about each other (from the use of diminutives, nicknames, etc.). Such meanings relate to the relative power or status of the participants, the extent of their contact and affect. These dimensions are part of what Halliday (Halliday and Hasan 1985: 12) calls TENOR – the second of the three key variables in the context of situation:

> The TENOR OF DISCOURSE refers to who is taking part, to the nature of the participants, their statuses and roles: what kinds of role relationships obtain among the participants, including permanent and temporary relationships of one kind or another, both the types of speech role that they are taking on in the dialogue and the whole cluster of socially significant relationships in which they are involved.

From the text fragments above we can also tell whether they were spoken or written. The vocative 'Miss' in 'on the blackboard, Miss', as well as indicating the differential status in relation to tenor, also indicates this is a spoken text in relation to mode. In addition we can tell whether the text fragments were ancillary to events in the situation ('30 please'; 'four hearts') or whether the full text was actually constitutive of the context of situation, being a story or document ('once upon a time'; 'this is to certify'). These are *textual* meanings and relate to the third contextual variable – MODE (Halliday and Hasan 1985: 12):

> The MODE OF DISCOURSE refers to what part the language is playing, what it is that the participants are expecting the language to do for them in that situation, the symbolic organisation of the text, the status that it has, and its function in the context, including the channel (is it spoken or written or some combination of the two?) and also the rhetorical MODE, what is being achieved by the text in terms of such categories as persuasive, expository, didactic and the like.

We can see that the three contextual variables – FIELD, TENOR and MODE – are related to the three different dimensions of meaning – ideational, interpersonal and textual. These overarching functional regions of meaning in language, or metafunctions, have been glossed in various ways. One way reported by Martin (1991a: 104) is to say that ideational meaning construes 'reality', interpersonal meaning 'social reality' and textual meaning the 'semiotic reality' that manifests itself as text as meaning is made. The 'hook-up' between these metafunctions (and their glosses) and the contextual variables is summarized in Table 1.2, after Martin (1991a) and Iedema *et al.* (1994).

**Table 1.2** Contextual variable and metafunction 'hook-up'

| Contextual variable | Metafunction (meaning) | 'reality construal' | 'work done' |
|---|---|---|---|
| FIELD | ideational | reality | representing our experience of reality |
| TENOR | interpersonal | social reality | enacting our social relations |
| MODE | textual | semiotic reality | presenting messages as text in context |

All situations are characterized by the particular values of the three contextual variables – field, tenor and mode, to which Martin (1991a: 123) assigns the umbrella category *register*.[1] Correspondingly, the three dimensions of meaning (metafunctions) are always constructed simultaneously. If we take the text 'Helen Murson has given out some very detailed lecture notes in her classes', we can easily construct the ideational meanings – who is doing what to whom; and we can infer the contextual variable field as university or college education. Similarly, we can infer interpersonal meanings and the contextual variable, tenor, noting that the speaker has the role of information-giver and that Helen Murson has both higher status than, and less contact with the speaker and addressee (as suggested by the inclusion of the surname). We know the interactional roles of the participants, and something of the relative status and contact among them. The textual meanings are related to the contextual variable mode – the part that language is playing. This text is probably spoken; is more likely to be constitutive of than ancillary in the situation; and presents Helen Murson as the speaker's focus or point of departure in the structuring of the utterance.

There is a consistent relationship, then, between particular aspects of the context of situation and the metafunctions of language. The relationship is bi-directional because one can infer the values of the contextual (register) variables from the language of the text and one can also predict the meanings likely to be constructed in language from the values of the register variables. This bi-directional relationship between language and context of situation is indicated in Figure 1.1.

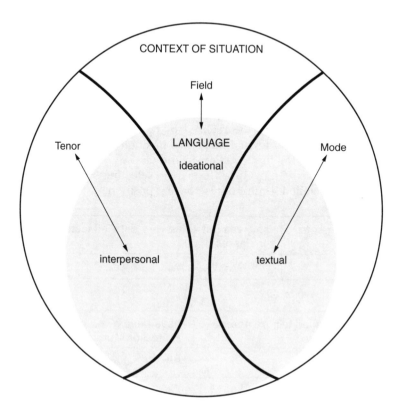

**Figure 1.1** Field, tenor and mode realized as ideational, interpersonal and textual metafunctions in language (Martin 1992a)

If the text discussed above is changed to 'Professor Murson has given out some very detailed lecture notes in her classes', the experiential meanings are essentially the same – the same participants involved in the same process and the same locational circumstance. The textual meanings are also the same in that 'Professor Murson' is the speaker's focus for the ensuing utterance, but the interpersonal meanings have changed: the status difference between Professor Murson and the speaker is now much greater and the relationship is now more formal. 'Has Professor Murson given out very detailed lecture notes in her classes?' also changes the interpersonal meaning because the speaker is now demanding rather than giving information and there is a concomitant change in role for the listener. If the text was changed to 'Some very detailed lecture notes were given out by Professor Murson in her classes', we would again see that the experiential and interpersonal meanings are the same as the original version, but by putting 'Some very detailed lecture notes' first, the focus or textual meaning has changed. The speaker's orientation in the utterance is to the lecture notes and not so much to the professor. Similarly, if the text were 'The giving out of very detailed lecture notes by Professor Murson . . .', we would note, as previously, that, in this segment of the text, the experiential and interpersonal meanings are the same, but the textual meanings are again different because this is clearly a text which is written rather than spoken.

The different areas of meaning – the ideational, the interpersonal and the textual – each tend to be realized by particular systems within the grammar. For example, textual meanings in English are realized in part by what is selected for first position in the clause – the Theme/Rheme system – as we have seen by the difference in selecting 'Professor Murson' or 'Some very detailed lecture notes' for first position.

| Professor Murson | has given out some very detailed lecture notes in her classes |
|---|---|
| Theme | Rheme |

| Some very detailed lecture notes | have been given out by Professor Murson in her classes |
|---|---|
| Theme | Rheme |

On the other hand, to change the ideational meanings we would change the participants, processes or circumstances involved (known as the TRANSITIVITY system), so we could change 'Professor Murson' to 'Professor Chang', or we could change the process 'gives out' to 'asks' or the participant 'very detailed lecture notes' to 'complicated test questions'.

| Professor Murson | has given out | some very detailed lecture notes | in her classes |
|---|---|---|---|
| Participant | Process | Participant | Circumstance |

| Professor Chang | asks | complicated test questions | in her classes |
|---|---|---|---|
| Participant | Process | Participant | Circumstance |

Changing interpersonal meanings may involve a different choice from the MOOD system in the grammar. It is the position of the subject which changes to realize the difference between giving and demanding information:

| Professor Murson has | given out some very detailed lecture notes during classes |
|---|---|
| Subject | |

| Has Professor Murson | given out very detailed lecture notes in her classes? |
|---|---|
| Subject | |

We can summarize the relationships among the variables in the context of situation, the metafunctions and the grammatical systems by extending Table 1.2 to include the grammatical systems as shown in Table 1.3.

**Table 1.3** Context, metafunction and grammar

| Contextual variable | Metafunction (meaning/ semantics) | 'reality construal' | 'work done' | Grammatical system |
|---|---|---|---|---|
| field | ideational | reality | representing our experience of reality | TRANSITIVITY |
| tenor | interpersonal | social reality | enacting our social relations | MOOD |
| mode | textual | semiotic reality | presenting messages as text in context | THEME |

Here we have simply introduced the lexicogrammatical systems of TRANSITIVITY, MOOD and THEME. We will describe and explain these and other systems in detail in Chapter 2.

### 1.3.2 Construing context of culture: Genre, Register and Language

We have briefly outlined the interconnectedness between language and the contextual variables of field, tenor and mode, for which Martin adopts the cover term register.[1] We have said that this interconnectedness is bi-directional, in that we can infer the context from the language and also predict the likely language choices if we know the contextual variables. You will probably find it quite easy to construe the register variables from the following text collected by Christie (1993), especially if your early childhood education occurred in an English-speaking culture.

**Text 1.1**

| | |
|---|---|
| T: | Good morning everyone. |
| C: | Good morning, Mrs P. |
| T: | Let's sing our morning song. |
| | (they all sing together) |
| T: | That's good, thank you. |
| | Okay, it's newstime. News? Who's got some news? |
| | Now let's hear from you Joseph. |
| J: | Good morning, Mrs P, good morning girls and boys. |
| C: | Good morning, Joseph. |
| J: | There's a horse next door and it always jumps over the fence. |
| T: | Gosh, so what do you do? |
| J: | Chase it home again. |
| T: | Well, thank you Joseph. |
| | Now your turn Mandy |
| | . . . (several children then contribute news in this manner) |
| | . . . |
| T: | That's all we'll have time for today. |

The field, tenor and mode variables in this context of situation can be summarized as follows:

field:    Announcements of personal 'news' by children as nominated by their teacher in an early childhood classroom.

tenor:    The teacher exercises power in directing the interaction. She is addressed formally by the children as Mrs P. She addresses the children informally by their first names. The contact has been sufficiently frequent that the participants know each others' names. The affect seems to be neutral.

mode:    The channel is aural and the medium is spoken language. It is the language of face-to-face interaction, so feedback is immediate. The language is constitutive of the social activity rather than ancillary to it.

But this 'morning news' text also proceeds through a number of clearly differentiated stages, which have been named by Christie as indicated in Figure 1.2.

This structuring at the level of genre is referred to as the 'schematic structure' of a text (Martin 1992a: 105). Christie (1985, 1993) has shown that the kind of structuring described in Figure 1.2 is generally consistent across different occasions of 'morning news' in infant classrooms.

| | | |
|---|---|---|
| T: | Good morning everyone. | |
| C: | Good morning Mrs P. | |
| T: | Let's sing our morning song. | |
| | (the all sing together) | Lesson Initiation |
| T: | That's good thank you. | |
| | Okay it's newstime. News? Who's got | |
| | some news? | |

| | |
|---|---|
| Now let's hear from Joseph. | Nomination |

| | | |
|---|---|---|
| J: | Good morning, Mrs P, good morning | |
| | girls and boys. | Greeting |
| C: | Good morning Joseph. | |

| | | |
|---|---|---|
| J: | There's a horse next door and it always | |
| | jumps over the fence. | |
| T: | Gosh, so what do you do? | Giving |
| J: | Chase it home again. | |

| | | |
|---|---|---|
| T: | Well thank you Joseph. | |
| | Now your turn Mandy | Finish |

\* . . .

| | |
|---|---|
| T:    That's all we'll have time for for today. | Closure |

\*The Nomination, Greeting, Giving and Finish stages are recrursive as several children give their news

**Figure 1.2** Schematic structure of morning news genre

As well as the schematic structure of different teaching/learning situations, or 'curriculum genres' (Christie 1993, 1997, 1998) it is possible to describe the schematic structure of texts in all situation types. The structuring of sales encounters, for example, has been described by Hasan (Halliday and Hasan 1985), using the term 'generic structure' rather than Martin's term 'schematic structure'. Figure 1.3 shows the elements of structure in a sales encounter:

This kind of fairly consistent organising of texts into stages in a range of situation types is another way in which the social context influences how language is structured for use. As well as the influence of the register variables of field, tenor and mode, texts are also shaped into predictable stages by their cultural purpose.

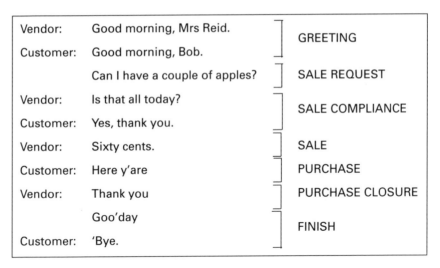

**Figure 1.3** Schematic structure of a sales encounter

So far we have mentioned only a few genre examples, but the context of culture can be thought of as the vast repertoire of genres by which members of the culture seek to achieve their goals through social processes. The genre potential of a particular culture is the possible configurations of register variables, i.e. the acceptable combinations of field, tenor and mode. The concept of genre addresses the fact that values of field, tenor and mode do not freely combine and that the systematic combinations that are allowable in a given culture at a particular time are, at least theoretically, able to be accounted for by genre networks. As Eggins (1994:35) explains:

> the following configurations of register variables give us genres which are accepted in Australian culture:
>
> field        cars
> tenor        salesperson/customer
> mode         face-to-face
>
> Thus, our culture recognises this register configuration by institutionalising the transactional genre of buying and selling cars.
>
> field        shorthand
> tenor        lecturer/student
> mode         face-to-face
>
> This register configuration can be achieved through the pedagogic genre of 'lecture'.
>
> However, the following configurations of register variables are not acceptable genres in most Western cultures:
>
> field        babies                        shorthand
> tenor        salesperson/customer          lecturer/student
> mode         face-to-face                  telephone
>
> We do not as yet recognise the transactional genre operating within the field of 'babies', nor can we as yet undertake a course in shorthand over the phone.

Genre is realized by combinations of different values of the register variables. The register variables are realized by language. Language is the means by which we 'read' both register *and* genre. (Figure 1.4).

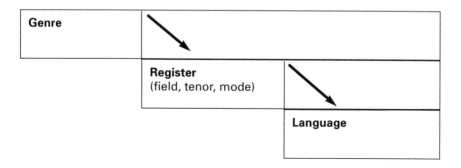

**Figure 1.4** Genre realized by register and register realized by language (after Martin 1991)

The genres we have mentioned have all been 'spoken' genres, but, of course, structuring also applies to written texts. The generic structure of nursery tales, for example, has been detailed by Hasan (1996). Although there are some structural differences among nursery tales, we would have no difficulty in recognizing stories such as *The Three Little Pigs*, *Henny Penny* and *The Three Billy Goats Gruff* as being of the same genre. To take account of this, Hasan proposed the notion of a Generic Structure Potential (GSP). The GSP describes the total range of textual structures available within a genre. It is designed to highlight both the variant and invariant properties of these structures. To do this a GSP must be able to specify:

1. the elements of structure which are obligatory if the text is to be regarded as a complete instance of the genre;
2. all elements of structure which are optional, so that while their presence or absence might affect the actual structure of the text as a whole, the recognition of the text as an instance of a particular genre is not affected;
3. the obligatory and optional ordering of the elements with respect to each other, including the possibility of iteration.

A text is a complete instance of a particular genre if it realizes all of the obligatory elements of structure. The optional elements of structure and options for the ways in which all elements may be ordered account for text variation. Texts may be structurally different because they are different genres or they may be different versions of the same genre.

Hasan's GSP for nursery tales indicates the obligatory and optional elements as shown in Figure 1.5.

| Optional | Obligatory |
|---|---|
| Placement | |
| | Initiating Event |
| | Sequent Event |
| | Final Event |
| Finale | |
| Moral | |

**Figure 1.5** Optional and obligatory elements of a GSP for nursery tales (after Hasan 1996: 54)

Her GSP for nursery tales is illustrated for the tale of Henny Penny (Galdone, 1968) in Figure 1.6. The optional structural elements of Placement and Moral are not found.

Although the analysis of texts into stages of generic structure appears very straightforward, it is important to note that these analyses are neither intuitive nor ad hoc. Objective justification for distinguishing the separate stages must be established. Since each stage makes its own particular contribution to the overall purpose of the text, it is possible to identify the distinctive meanings defining each stage. These distinctive meanings are revealed in analyses of the differing patterns of lexicogrammatical choices that characterize the generic stages. For example, the lexicogrammatical patterns of the Placement stage of nursery tales are different from those of the Initiating Event; both are different from those of the Finale. (For examples of detailed analyses relating generic stages to lexicogrammatical patterns see Hasan (1996) and Eggins (1994: 41–6).) Even a basic knowledge of functional grammar and discourse (such as that provided in Chapter 2) will enable you to establish the distinctive grammatical patterns that characterize the stages of generic structure in the genres of concern in your work. Subsequent chapters will address the application of genre analysis in different areas of language research. For example, Perrett (Chapter 4) considers the role of genre in interviews in the context of second language development; Eggins shows how genre theory is adapted to the study of everyday talk in Chapter 6; Christie dis-

| | PLACEMENT |
|---|---|
| One day when Henny Penny was scratching among the leaves, an acorn fell on her head. 'Goodness gracious me!' said Henny Penny. 'The sky is falling! I must go and tell the king.' | INITIATING EVENT |
| So she went along and she went along and she went along, until she met Cocky Locky. 'Cock-a-doodle-doo! Where are you going, Henny Penny?' asked Cocky Locky. 'Oh,' said Henny Penny, 'the sky is falling and I am going to tell the King.' 'May I go with you, Henny Penny?' asked Cocky Locky. 'Yes, indeed,' said Henny Penny. So Henny Penny and Cocky Locky went off to tell the King that the sky was falling. | SEQUENT EVENT |
| They went along and they went along and they went along, until they met Ducky Lucky. 'Quack, quack, quack! Where are you going, Henny Penny and Cocky Locky?' asked Ducky Lucky. . . . | SEQUENT EVENT* * The Sequent Event is iterative. In this case two additional sequent events result in Goosey Loosey and Turkey Lurkey joining the party travelling to tell the King that the sky had fallen in. |
| They went along and they went along and they went along until they met Foxy Loxy. 'Where are you going, Henny Penny, Ducky Lucky, Goosey Loosey and Turkey Lurkey?' asked Foxy Loxy. 'Ah, ha!' said Foxy Loxy, 'But this isn't the way to the King. . . Come with me and I will show you a short cut . . .' They went along . . . until they reached Foxy Loxy's cave. In they all went after Foxy Loxy. | FINAL EVENT |
| From that day to this Turkey Lurkey, Goosey Loosey, Ducky Lucky, Cocky Locky and Henny Penny have never been seen again. And the king has never been told the sky is falling. But Foxy Loxy and Mrs Foxy Loxy and their seven little foxes still remember the fine feast they had that day. | FINALE |
| | MORAL |

**Figure 1.6** Generic structure of the nursery tale *Henny Penny*

cusses her work on classroom discourse in terms of 'curriculum genres' in Chapter 8; Gerot (Chapter 9) discusses differences in children's reading of narrative and 'report' genres; Rothery and Stenglin (Chapter 10) investigate 'response' genres in students' interpretations of literature in the secondary school; and written genres in school subjects such as history and science are discussed by Unsworth in Chapter 11.

## 1.4  Researching and theorizing language as social practice in SFL

Those principally involved in theorizing SFL do not see linguistics, socio-linguistics or applied linguistics as dichotomous categories. At the same time that Halliday (1973, 1978, 1985, 1994, Halliday and Hasan 1976) was developing systemic functional linguistic theory, he conducted an intensive longitudinal study of a child's language development from the earliest months to facility in using the mother tongue (Halliday 1973, 1975, 1979). He also directed literacy education research at University College London, which began as a Nuffield Project in the mid 1960s and continued up to 1970 as the Schools Council Project on Linguistics and English Teaching (Halliday 1978, Keith 1990). This concomitance of the theoretical and the applied has remained a hallmark of Halliday's work. The publication of the second edition of *An Introduction to Functional Grammar* (Halliday 1994) paralleled his publications addressing issues such as language education (1991), problems of literacy practices in science (1993a), a challenge to applied linguistics (1993b) and contemporary issues such as technologizing literacy (1996).

Similarly, Hasan, another prominent SFL scholar, has said that her work is motivated by 'an idea that there is a continuity from the living of life on the one hand right down to the morpheme on the other' (Cloran *et al.* 1996). Her work ranges from 'semantic networks' and 'lexis as most delicate grammar' to investigations of the role of everyday talk between mothers and children in establishing ways of learning (Cloran *et al.* 1996) and 'Literacy, everyday talk and society' (Hasan 1996). Likewise, alongside Martin's (1992a) *English Text: System and Structure* are a raft of publications linked to genre-based literacy research (Martin 1991, 1993a, b, c, d, e, 1994), which Martin guided, largely in collaboration with the New South Wales, Metropolitan East, Disadvantaged Schools Program at Erskineville in Sydney. In the United Kingdom, language researchers who work with SFL, such as Carter and Berry at Nottingham University, continue to carry out research in educational linguistics (Berry 1987, Carter 1997, Carter and McCarthy 1997); at the City University of New York, Lemke has published SFL influenced studies: *Talking Science* (1990) and *Textual Politics* (1995). Doctoral students in SFL come from and continue to work in other discipline areas. The range of discipline backgrounds represented by the contributors to this volume reflects something of the breadth of utility of SFL in advancing diverse aspects of language research.

*1.4.1 SFL in partnership with a range of disciplinary approaches to language research*

The kinds of complex social issues which applied language research needs to address today require the complementary contributions of a range of disciplinary perspectives. Current studies in linguistics, education, sociology, psychology and related areas now tend to be more integrative in developing research across disciplines. Here we will illustrate briefly SFL contributions to such research by addressing three current areas of concern:

1. Why do education systems disadvantage working-class children?
2. How are gendered subjectivities created and maintained through the language of interaction?
3. How can people learn to be critically aware of the ways they are socially positioned in the texts they read?

Basil Bernstein's work addresses the first question. From his early work in the 1950s on the apparent differences in school performance of students of different social classes, Bernstein developed, over more than three decades, a detailed sociological theory addressing questions of social structure, power relations, the differential ways in which power and knowledge are distributed and the mechanisms by which such distribution occurs. Central to this enterprise is his theory of codes. He describes a code as a 'regulative principle which controlled the form of the linguistic realisation' of speakers in different socializing contexts (Bernstein 1971: 15).

Researchers have been able to use SFL to show how the variation in language use among different socioeconomic groups is related to different coding orientations among these groups in particular social contexts. Hasan used SFL to map the meaning choices taken up by mothers and their pre-school children in their spontaneous talk. She was able to show evidence of systematic semantic variation in the ways mothers talked to their children which was clearly related to the social class of the family and to the sex of the child. Williams (1995) used this work on 'semantic variation' to analyse ongoing talk between mothers and young children during joint book reading at home. He showed that the nature of family linguistic interaction varied as a function of social class location. Cloran (1994) also addressed coding orientation in her investigation of variation in the use of 'decontextualised' language in mother–child interaction across different social groups. The work Hasan and her associates have done on semantic variation provides powerful support for Bernstein's formulations with respect to coding orientations (see Chapter 7). An extended account of a range of SFL-based language research projects linked to the sociology of Basil Bernstein is available in Christie (1999).

Work on gendered subjectivities is addressed by a number of

contemporary researchers of language in schools and communities. Many incorporate their expertise in SFL into a conjunction of 'interdisciplines', approaching their work from multiple perspectives with mutual critique. For example, Poynton (1985, 1990) in her work on gender relations positions herself at the conjunction of 'linguistics, feminist theory and post-structuralist social/critical theory' (Poynton 1993). In a major work concerned with the inter-connectedness of literate practices in secondary school geography and what counts as student success, Lee (1996) uses feminist and post-structuralist theory to argue that different literate practices not only produce different kinds of knowledges but also produce gendered subjects differently positioned in relation to those knowledges. And as the series editor's preface notes (xiii), in developing 'readings' of geography curriculum documents, textbooks, student talk, student writing, teacher talk and so forth, Lee's 'principal approach is to selectively use the lexicogrammatical analysis of systemic functional linguistics'. Similar use is made of SFL in concert with complementary feminist/post-structuralist theory in Wright's (1991, 1993) work on the contribution of teacher talk to the production and reproduction of gendered subjectivity in physical education classes.

Work on critical language awareness (CLA) 'highlights how language conventions and language practices are invested with power relations and ideological processes which people are often unaware of' (Fairclough 1992: 7). Fairclough notes the influence on current critical language study of various groups and approaches, including social theorists such as Bourdieu, Foucault and Habermas, while acknowledging that the most important group in Britain has been the 'critical linguistics' group (Fowler *et al.* 1979, Kress and Hodge 1979). This group used SFL as it was being developed at that time attempting 'to make explicit the ideological meanings of texts' (Hodge 1993: 19). Fairclough's associates (Wallace 1992, Clark 1992, Janks and Ivanic 1992) who are concerned with developing CLA in schools and communities make explicit use of SFL in their work. This is usefully summarized by Janks and Ivanic (1992: 325–6) in the context of developing 'resistant' reading:

> A central aim of CLA is to uncover the choices which have been made in the creation of a text. At a macro level this includes the selection of a particular language, a particular variety of that language, a particular genre or mixture of genres, and a particular register or variety of registers. At the micro level this involves the selection of specific linguistic items and linguistic structures in a selected order. Because language is a system it can be seen as 'a network of interlocking options' (Halliday, 1985). Choice of one option necessarily implies rejection of other options. Because any selection directs our attention 'to what is present . . . and away from what is no longer there' (Kress and Hodge, 1979), it is useful to consider the range of options from which a linguistic feature has been selected, thus highlighting what might have been selected but was not. Attention to what was and was not selected is a useful starting point for resistance.

The significance of SFL influence on literacy education was further emphasized in a paper in the *Harvard Educational Review* by ten academics (from the United Kingdom, the United States and Australia), who called themselves The New London Group.[2] They proposed 'a pedagogy of multiliteracies' intended to facilitate access to and critique of 'the evolving language of work, power and community'. Any semiotic activity, including using language to produce or consume texts, was treated as a matter of 'Design' and the ideational, interpersonal and textual metafunctions of SFL (Halliday 1978) were specified as 'the different functions of Available Designs' (New London Group 1996: 75). The authors further indicated that teachers and students need a language to describe the forms of meaning that are represented in Available Designs. What is required is

> an educationally accessible functional grammar; that is, a metalanguage that describes meaning in various realms. These include the visual, as well as the multi-modal relations between different meaning-making processes that are now so critical in media texts and the texts of electronic multi-media. (77)

The SFL model of text/context relations, outlined in this chapter, clearly underlies the group's summary of the role of this metalanguage in their enterprise:

> the primary purpose of the metalanguage should be to identify and explain differences between texts, and relate these to the contexts of culture and situation in which they seem to work. (77)

### 1.4.2 Dialoguing with other disciplinary approaches in SFL research

SFL researchers of language in schools and communities seek to articulate their work with developments in other research traditions. Here we can only briefly note articulations relating to teaching and learning, and to theorizing language and ideology. In respect of teaching and learning, Christie (1994: 109) noted that the general conclusions arising from SFL work both support and are supported by some of the more recent trends in the psychological theorizing of Bruner (1986) and the revival of interest in the work of both Luria and Vygotsky (e.g. Vygotsky 1986, Hickman 1987, Wertsch 1985). The facilitative role of SFL in informing pedagogies of access to specialized literacies was linked to the social psychology of Vygotsky in a detailed account by Wells (1994) of the complementary contributions of Halliday and Vygotsky to a 'language-based theory of learning'. In discussing the explicit teaching which characterizes genre-based approaches to literacy derived from SFL research, Martin (1993a) draws on Bernstein's distinction between 'visible' and 'invisible' pedagogies and relates the visible genre-based literacy to that outlined by Bourdieu:

> a rational and really universal pedagogy, which would take nothing for granted initially, and would not count as acquired what some and only some of the

pupils had inherited, would do all things for all and would be organised with the explicit aim of providing all with the means of acquiring that which, although apparently a natural gift, is only given to the children of the educated classes. (Bourdieu 1974: 133, quoted in Freebody 1991: 108)

The way SFL work on pedagogy relates to other research traditions is further taken up in several of the chapters that follow. (See also Hasan (in press) for an SFL-based critique of Bourdieu's view of language as a point of departure for pedagogic action.)

The theorizing of language and ideology in SFL as discussed by Martin (1997) proposes a re-articulation with the work of Lacan, Foucault and Derrida. As Martin points out, the semiotic interpretation of how social subjects are positioned within the culture involves modelling the meaning potential available to them and the different ways they draw on this potential as they interact with each other. He therefore makes use of Halliday and Matthiessen's (to appear) framework for modelling semiotic change according to the time depth involved (logogenesis – unfolding of language in a text; ontogenesis – development of language in the individual; phylogenesis – developments in language over long periods of history). Martin (1997: 10) proposes approaching subjectivity dynamically, making it possible to

> foreground the ways in which subjects engage dynamically with texts as they unfold (logogenesis), the ways in which they are positioned and re-positioned socially throughout their life (ontogenesis) and the ways in which a culture reworks hegemony across generations (phylogenesis). . . . In these terms, language, register and genre constitute the meaning potential that is immanent, from moment to moment as a text unfolds, for the social subjects involved, at the point in the evolution of the culture where meanings are being made.

Looking at meaning from the perspective of social change in this way clearly facilitates further dialogue across different theoretical orientations, including Critical Discourse Analysis (Fairclough 1995). (See Martin, Chapter 12.)

### 1.4.3 Expanding dimensions of the theory: functional semiotics

Recently fundamental principles of SFL have been extrapolated to develop functional semiotic analyses of images, that is visual grammar (O'Toole 1994, Kress and van Leeuwen 1990, 1996, van Leeuwen 1996, Lemke 1998). These accounts indicate how ideational, interpersonal and textual meanings are realized visually by the selections made from systems such as horizontal angle (frontal, profile or somewhere in between), vertical angle (above, eye level, below or some position intermediate between these), whether the represented participant(s)' gaze is directed to the viewer or not, and so on – all of these choices combining, as they do in language, to simultaneously construct different aspects of meaning.

This SFL perspective on visual semiotics features strongly in contemporary texts on English and literacy (Goodman and Graddol 1996), curriculum area learning (van Leeuwen and Humphrey 1996) and communication and cultural literacy (Schirato and Yell 1996).

## 1.5 Making the most of this book

A major goal of this book is to alert you to the potential of SFL to expand and enhance the perspectives you are developing on your chosen area(s) of study so that you can approach the development of your own research from the vantage point of intersecting and complementary theoretical orientations. The strategy employed is one of providing starting points. The book does provide a stand-alone introduction to the basic concepts of SFL and their application to researching various parameters of language in use in schools and communities. This requires a close reading of the first two chapters in conjunction with the subsequent chapters dealing with particular fields of interest. But there is much to be gained by exploring the chapters beyond the actual focus of your present concerns. In some cases there will be clear links among chapters which could benefit your work. For example, there are obvious connections between Chapter 3 where Painter deals with children's language development and Chapter 7 where Cloran discusses social class and semantic variation in children's home language practices. Similarly, useful links are to be made between Eggins in Chapter 6 on everyday talk and Christie's study of spoken interaction in the classroom in Chapter 8. This is also the case with Gerot's Chapter 9 on exploring reading processes, Chapter 11 by Unsworth on subject-specific literacies and Chapter 4 by Perrett on second language development. Chapter 5 by Williams dealing with literature for children can be productively related to Chapter 10 by Rothery and Stenglin dealing with students' critical response to literary texts. Chapter 12 by Martin reminds us of the significance of critical discourse analysis across all fields of applied language study. It is also likely that the nature of your interests will enable you to construct other links among chapters. Beyond this, the book energetically promotes further related reading by providing relevant references. You can supplement these by surfing the Internet and visiting sites such as *Network*:

    http://minerva.ling.mq.edu.au/Resources/Network/Network.html,
which provides a host of information about SFL including recent PhD, dissertations and bibliographies. It also provides access to related sites such as Mick O'Donnell's systemic web page:

    http://www.dai.ed.ac.uk/staff/personal pages/micko/systemics.html,
also containing a variety of current systemic information, including a link to the following site which focuses on systemic linguistic applications to education:

    http://cirrus.dai.ed.ac.uk:8000/systemics/Education/index.html

## Notes

1. Martin (1991, 1992) regards the contextual variables of field, tenor and mode as semiotic systems in their own right which are realized by language (connotative semiotic). He uses 'Register' rather than 'context of situation' to emphasize a discursive view of context rather than the materialist reading which the term invites. Halliday uses the term *register* to refer to the effect of context upon language:

> I would see the notion of register as being at the semantic level, not above it. Shifting in register means re-ordering the probabilities at the semantic level . . . whereas the categories of FIELD, MODE and TENOR belong one level up. These are the features of the context of situation; and this is an interface. But the register itself I would see as being linguistic; it is a setting of probabilities in the semantics. (Halliday quoted in Thibault 1987: 610)

   Despite the terminology difference, Martin and Halliday have a common view of the relationship between context and language – one of interdependency based on correspondences among field, tenor, mode and Ideational, Interpersonal and Textual metafunctions respectively.

2. Courtney Cazden (Harvard, USA); Bill Cope (University of Technology Sydney, Australia); Norman Fairclough (Lancaster University, UK); Jim Gee (Clark University, USA); Mary Kalantzis (James Cook University of North Queensland, Australia); Gunther Kress (University of London, UK); Allan Luke (University of Queensland, Australia); Carmen Luke (University of Queensland, Australia); Sarah Michaels (Clark University, USA); Martin Nakata (James Cook University of North Queensland, Australia).

## References

Bernstein, B. (1971) *Class, Codes and Control, Vol. 1: Theoretical Studies Towards a Sociology of Language.* London: Routledge and Kegan Paul.

Bernstein, B. (1981) Code modalities and the process of reproduction: a model. *Language and Society*, 10: 327–63.

Bernstein, B. (1996) *Pedagogy, Symbolic Control and Identity.* London: Taylor and Francis.

Berry, Margaret (1987) 'Is teacher an unanalysed concept?'. In M. A. K. Halliday and R. P. Fawcett (eds), *New Developments in Systemic Linguistics*, vol. 1. London: Frances Pinter.

Bourdieu, P. (1974) The school as a conservative force. In J. Eggleton (ed.), *Contemporary Research in the Sociology of Education.* London: Methuen.

Bruner, J. (1986) *Actual Minds, Possible Worlds.* Cambridge, MA: Harvard University Press.

Carter, R. (1997) *Language, Literature and the Learner.* London: Longman.

Carter, R. and McCarthy, M. (1997) *Language as Discourse: Perspectives on Language Teaching.* Cambridge: Cambridge University Press.

Christie, F. (1985) *Language Education.* Geelong: Deakin University Press.

Christie, F. (1993) Curriculum genres: planning for effective teaching. In B. Cope, and M. Kalantzis (eds), *The Powers of Literacy: A Genre Approach to Teaching Writing.* London: Falmer.

Christie, F. (1994) Developing an educational linguistics for English language teaching: a systemic functional perspective. *Functions of Language*, 1(1): 95–127.

Christie, F. (1997) Curriculum genres as forms of initiation into a culture. In F. Christie and J. R. Martin (eds), *Genres and Institutions: Social Processes in the Workplace and School*. London: Cassell, 134–60.

Christie, F. (ed.) (1999) *Pedagogy and the Shaping of Consciousness: Linguistic and Social Processes*. London: Cassell.

Christie, F. (1998) Science and apprenticeship: the pedagogic discourse. In J. R. Martin and R. Veel (eds), *Reading Science: Critical and Functional Perspectives on Discourses of Science*. London: Routledge.

Clark, R. (1992) Principles and practices of CLA in the classroom. In N. Fairclough (ed.), *Critical Language Awareness*. London: Longman.

Cloran, C. (1989) Learning through language: the social construction of gender. In R. Hasan and J.R. Martin (eds), *Language Development: Learning Language, Learning Culture*. Norwood: Ablex.

Cloran, C. (1994) *Rhetorical Units and Decontextualization: An Enquiry Into Some Relations of Context, Meaning and Grammar*. Monographs in Systemic Linguistics Number Six. University of Nottingham: Department of English Studies.

Cloran, C., Butt, D. and Williams, G. (1996) *Ways of Saying: Ways of Meaning: Selected Papers of Ruqaiya Hasan*. London: Cassell.

Eggins, S. (1994) *An Introduction to Systemic Functional Linguistics*. London: Pinter.

Fairclough, N. (ed.) (1992) *Critical Language Awareness*. London: Longman.

Fairclough, N. (1995) *Critical Discourse Analysis: The Critical Study of Language*. London: Longman.

Fowler, R., Hodge, R., Kress, G. and Trew, T. (1979) *Language and Control*. London: Routledge.

Freebody, P. (1991) Inventing cultural-capitalist distinctions in the assessment of HSC papers: coping with inflation in an era of 'literacy crisis'. In F. Christie (ed.), *Literacy in Social Processes: Papers from the Inaugural Australian Systemic Linguistics Conference, Deakin University, January 1990*. Darwin: Centre for Studies of Language in Education, Northern Territory University, 96–108.

Galdone, P. (1968) *Henny Penny*. London: World's Work.

Goodman, S. and Graddol, D. (eds) (1996) *Redesigning English: New Texts, New Identities*. London: Routledge.

Halliday, M. A. K. (1973) *Explorations in the Functions of Language*. London: Arnold.

Halliday, M. A. K. (1975) *Learning How to Mean: Explorations in the Development of Language*. London: Arnold.

Halliday, M. A. K. (1978) *Language as Social Semiotic*. London: Arnold.

Halliday, M. A. K. (1979) One child's protolanguage. In M. Bullowa (ed.), *Before Speech*. Cambridge: Cambridge University Press.

Halliday, M. A. K. (1985) *An Introduction to Functional Grammar*. London: Edward Arnold.

Halliday, M.A.K. (1991) The notion of 'context' in language education. In T. Le and M. McCausland (eds), *Language Education: Interaction and Development*. Launceston: University of Tasmania.

Halliday, M. A. K. (1993a) Some grammatical problems in scientific English. In M. A. K. Halliday and J. R. Martin (eds), *Writing Science: Literacy and Discursive Power*. London: Falmer Press, 69–85.

Halliday, M. A. K. (1993b) *Language in a Changing World*. Occasional Paper 13.

Canberra: Applied Linguistics Association of Australia.

Halliday, M. A. K. (1994). *An Introduction to Functional Grammar* (2nd edn). London: Edward Arnold.

Halliday, M. A. K. (1996) Literacy and linguistics: a functional perspective. In R. Hasan and G. Williams (eds), *Literacy and society.* London: Longman.

Halliday, M. A. K. and Hasan, R. (1976) *Cohesion in English.* London: Longman.

Halliday, M. A. K. and Hasan, R. (1985) *Language, Context, and Text: Aspects of Language in a Social-Semiotic Perspective.* Geelong: Deakin University Press.

Halliday, M. A. K. and Martin, J. R. (1993b) The model. In M. A. K. Halliday and J. R. Martin (eds), *Writing Science: Literacy and Discursive Power.* London: Falmer.

Halliday, M. A. K. and Matthiessen, C.M.I.M. (forthcoming) *Construing Experience through Language: A Language-based Approach to Cognition.* Berlin: De Gruyter.

Hasan, R. (1990) Semantic variation and sociolinguistics. *Australian Journal of Linguistics* 9(2): 221–76.

Hasan, R. (1995) The conception of context in text. In P. Fries and M. Gregory (eds) *Discourse in Society: Systemic Functional Perspectives.* Norwood: Ablex (*Meaning and Choice in Language: Studies for Michael Halliday; Advances in Discourse Processes,* Vol. 50), pp.183–283.

Hasan, R. (1996) Literacy, everyday talk and society. In C. Cloran, D. Butt and G. Williams (eds), *Ways of Saying: Ways of Meaning: Selected Papers of Ruqaiya Hasan.* London: Cassell.

Hasan, R. (1996) The nursery tale as genre. In C. Cloran, D. Butt and G. Williams (eds) *Ways of Saying: Ways of Meaning.* London: Cassell.

Hasan, R. (in press) The disempowerment game: language in literacy. In C. Baker, J. Cook-Gumperz and A. Luke (eds) *Literacy and Power.* Oxford: Blackwell.

Hickman, M. (ed.) (1987) *Social and Functional Approaches to Language and Thought.* London: Academic Press.

Hodge, R. (1993) *Teaching as Communication.* London: Longman.

Iedema, R., Feez, S. and White, P. (1994) *Media Literacy* (Literacy in Industry Research Project: Stage 2). Sydney: Disadvantaged Schools Program.

Janks, H. and Ivanic, R. (1992) Critical language and emancipatory discourse. In N. Fairclough (ed.), *Critical Language Awareness.* London: Longman.

Keith, G. (1990) Language study at Key Stage 3. In R. Carter (ed.), *Knowledge About Language and the Curriculum.* Sevenoaks: Hodder and Stoughton.

Kress, G. and Hodge, R. (1979) *Language as Ideology.* London: Routledge.

Kress, G. and van Leeuwen, T. (1990) *Reading Images.* Geelong: Deakin University Press.

Kress, G. and van Leeuwen, T. (1996) *Reading Images: The Grammar of Visual Design.* London: Routledge.

Lee, A. (1996) *Gender, Literacy, Curriculum: Re-writing School Geography.* London: Taylor and Francis.

Lemke, J. (1990) *Talking Science: Language, Learning and Values.* Norwood: Ablex.

Lemke, J. (1995) *Textual Politics: Discourse and Social Dynamics.* London: Taylor and Francis.

Lemke, J. (1998) Multiplying meaning: visual and verbal semiotics in scientific text. In J. R. Martin and R. Veel (eds), *Reading Science: Critical and Functional Perspectives on Discourses of Science.* London and New York: Routledge.

Martin, J. R. (1984) Language, register and genre. In F. Christie, (ed.), *Children Writing: Reader.* Geelong: Deakin University Press.

Martin, J. R. (1991a) Intrinsic functionality: implications for contextual theory.

*Social Semiotics*, 1(1): 99–162.

Martin, J. R. (1991b) Critical literacy: the role of a functional model of language. *Australian Journal of Reading* 14(2): 117–32.

Martin, J. R. (1992a) *English Text: System and Structure.* Amsterdam: Benjamins.

Martin, J. R. (1992b) Types of grammar. Lecture to the Third Australian Systemics Summer School for Teachers, University of Sydney, 13 January.

Martin, J. R. (1993a) Genre and literacy: modelling context in educational linguistics. *Annual Review of Applied Linguistics* 13: 141–72.

Martin, J. R. (1993b) Life as a noun: arresting the universe in science and humanities. In M. A. K. Halliday and J. R. Martin (eds), *Writing Science: Literacy and Discursive Power* London: Falmer.

Martin, J. R. (1993c) Literacy in science: learning to handle text as technology. In M. A. K. Halliday and J. R. Martin (eds), *Writing Science: Literacy and Discursive Power* London: Falmer.

Martin, J. R. (1993d) Technicality and abstraction: language for the creation of specialised text. In M. A. K. Halliday and J. R. Martin (eds), *Writing Science: Literacy and Discursive Power* London: Falmer.

Martin, J. R. (1993e) Technology, bureaucracy and schooling: discourse resources and control. *Cultural Dynamics*, 6(1): 84–130.

Martin, J. R. (1994) Macro-genres: the ecology of the page. *Network*, 21: 29–52.

Martin, J. R. (1997) Analysing genre: functional parameters. In F. Christie and J.R. Martin (eds), *Genre and Institutions: Social Processes in the Workplace and School.* London: Cassell, 3–39.

Martin, J. R. (in press) A context for genre: modelling social processes in functional linguistics. In C. Stainton and J. Devilliers (eds), *Communication in Linguistics.* Toronto: GREF (Collection Theoria).

Matthiessen, C. (1995) *Lexicogrammatical Cartography: English Systems.* Tokyo: International Language Sciences.

New London Group (1996) A pedagogy of multiliteracies: designing social futures. *Harvard Educational Review* 66 (1): 60–91.

O'Toole, M. (1994) *The Language of Displayed Art.* London: Leicester University Press.

Poynton, C. (1985) *Language and Gender: Making the Difference.* Geelong: Deakin University Press.

Poynton, C. (1990) The marginalising of the interpersonal and the privileging of representation: a metaphor (and more) of contemporary gender relations. In T. Threadgold and A. Cranny-Francis (eds), *Feminine/Masculine and Representation.* Sydney: Allen and Unwin.

Poynton, C. (1993) Grammar, language and the social: poststructuralism and systemic functional linguistics. *Social Semiotics*, 3(1): 1–22.

Schirato, T. and Yell, S. (1996) *Communication and Cultural Literacy: An Introduction.* Sydney: Allen and Unwin.

Thibault, P. (1987) An interview with Michael Halliday. In R. Steele and T. Threadgold (eds) *Language Topics: Essays in Honour of Michael Halliday*, vol. 2. Amsterdam: Benjamins.

van Leeuwen, T. (1996) Moving English: the visual language of film. In S. Goodman, and D. Graddol (eds), *Redesigning English: New Texts, New Identities.* London: Routledge.

van Leeuwen, T. and Humphrey, S. (1996) On learning to look through a geographer's eyes. In R. Hasan and G. Williams (eds), *Literacy and Society.* London: Longman.

Vygotsky, L. (1986) *Thought and Language* (trans. and ed. A. Kouzlin). Cambridge, MA.: MIT Press.

Wallace, C. (1992) Critical literacy awareness in the EFL classroom. In N. Fairclough (ed.), *Critical Language Awareness*. London: Longman.

Wells, G. (1994) The complementary contributions of Halliday and Vygotsky to a 'Language-based Theory of Learning'. *Linguistics and Education*, 6(1): 41–90.

Wertsch, J.V. (1985) *Vygotsky and the Social Formation of Mind*. Cambridge, MA.: Harvard University Press.

Williams, G. (1993) Using systemic grammar in teaching young learners. In L. Unsworth (ed.), *Literacy Learning and Teaching: Language as Social Practice in the Primary School*. Melbourne: Macmillan.

Williams, G. (1995) Joint book-reading and literacy pedagogy: a sociosemantic examination. Unpublished doctoral dissertation, School of English, Linguistics and Media, Macquarie University, Sydney.

Wright, J. (1991) The contribution of teacher talk to the production and re-production of gendered subjectivity in physical education. Unpublished PhD thesis, University of Wollongong.

Wright, J. (1993) Regulation and resistance: the physical education lesson as speech genre. *Social Semiotics*, 3 (1): 23–56.

# 2  Getting started with functional analysis of texts

*Louise Ravelli*

## 2.1  Purposes of this chapter

One of the most exciting features of systemic functional linguistics (SFL), is the extent to which one can actually *say* relevant and useful things about what is happening in language, that is, the extent to which you can do something with analysis. Chapter 1 outlined the overall framework of the model particularly in terms of text–context relations, and how an analysis of language can be revealing in terms of social factors. Now we turn our attention to actually using this framework in the analysis of texts. The purpose of this chapter is to provide a very preliminary 'map' of analysis in SFL to help you understand the following chapters and get started with functional analysis.

SFL is a complex theory. Rather than trying to condense all this complexity into a single brief account, we provide the relevant reference points necessary for undertaking analysis, and illustrate how this works in relation to some actual texts.

The first thing to do when beginning analysis, is to *locate* yourself in relation to the overall map of possibilities. Analysis can proceed in terms of a number of variables: there are a number of different types of *unit*, which you may be working with. This is the first point at which to orientate yourself (see Section 2.2). Each unit may be approached from the perspective of *class* or *function* – another point at which to orientate yourself, also described in 2.2. Function itself can be approached in at least three different ways, three types of *metafunction*; these are described in Sections 2.3, 2.4 and 2.5. If at any stage – here or in other chapters – you feel overwhelmed by the terminology, or confused as to what you're doing, come back to these reference points: the unit of grammar, the class or function, and the metafunction.

The grammar is illustrated in relation to two texts, both of which appeared in the *Sydney Morning Herald* (7 March 1992). Both concern the proposed conversion of a building society (St. George Building Society) to a bank. St. George required the permission of its members to make this conversion and the texts are interesting in terms of their different roles in relation to the process. We will use these texts to illustrate functional analysis and to build up an understanding of the two texts as the analyses are carried out. Occasionally, in order to illustrate a particular point of analysis, it will be necessary to draw on fabricated examples (these are marked with an asterix *), but on the whole, examples will be taken from the St. George texts as they appeared in the newspaper. The texts are reproduced in Appendix 1. They are referred to as Text 2.1. (T2.1) and Text 2.2 (T2.2). Before reading Section 2.2 read the texts and form your own impressions.

This chapter is not intended as a substitute for any of the excellent introductions to SFL; the most recent are listed below, and I will refer to sections of some of them as we go along.

## Comprehensive introductions to the model

Bloor, T. and Bloor, M. (1995) *The Functional Analysis of English: A Hallidayan Approach.* London: Arnold.

Eggins, S. (1994) *An Introduction to Systemic-Functional Linguistics.* London: Pinter.

Halliday, M.A.K. (1994) *An Introduction to Functional Grammar* (2nd edn). London: Edward Arnold. The foundational reference in the field.

Martin, J.R., Matthiessen, C.M.I.M. and Painter, C. (1997) *Working with Functional Grammar.* London: Arnold. A workbook intended to complement Halliday's introduction.

Thompson, G. (1996) *Introducing Functional Grammar.* London: Arnold.

## Introductions written for undergraduates

Butt, D., Fahey, R., Spinks, S. and Yallop, C. (1995) *Using Functional Grammar: An Explorer's Guide.* Macquarie University: National Centre for English Language Teaching and Research.

Gerot, L. (1995) *Making Sense of Text.* Sydney: Gerd Stabler Antipodean Educational Enterprises.

Gerot, L. and Wignell, P. (1994) *Making Sense of Functional Grammar.* Sydney: Gerd Stabler Antipodean Educational Enterprises.

## Introductions written for primary teachers

Collerson, J. (1994) *English Grammar: A Functional Approach.* Sydney: Primary English Teaching Association.

Derewianka, B. (1990) *Exploring How Texts Work.* Sydney: Primary English Teaching Association.

Williams, G. (1994) *Using Systemic Grammar in Teaching Young Learners: An Introduction.* Melbourne: MacMillan. Also published in L. Unsworth (ed.), *Literacy, Learning and Teaching: Language as Social Practice in the Primary School.* Melbourne: MacMillan, 1993, pp. 197–254

## Introduction written for ESL teachers

Lock, G. (1996) *Functional English Grammar: An Introduction for Second Language Teachers.* Cambridge: Cambridge University Press.

**Conventions used in this chapter**
T2.1 = Text 2.1
T2.1:1 = Text 2.1, Clause 1
* = fabricated example

## 2.2 Where to start? units and functions

The first step in analysis is being able to identify the unit at stake: what is it that you are looking at? Language is more than a sequence of letters on a page, more than a stream of sounds. Language expresses meanings, and these meanings are carried by structures, in turn made up of component parts.

What we need is a notion of 'building blocks' – what parts does language have, in order to be able to construct meaning? This simple notion of a building block – also called a *constituent* – will be made more complex in two ways. Firstly, a distinction will be made between the class of a constituent, and its function; and secondly, function itself will be analysed in different ways, according to the metafunction which is at stake in the analysis. These complexities will be expanded upon below, and will explain the apparent proliferation of labels in SFL: they are there to suit different purposes.

It is important to remember that there is nothing intrinsically valuable in being able to identify a constituent for its own sake; the exercise only becomes significant when the constituents are examined in context, that is, within the framework of a larger body of text examined in relation to its socio-cultural context.

The definition of a text is not simple, but one version from Halliday and Hasan (1976: 1–2) argues that a text is 'any passage, spoken or written, of whatever length, that does form a unified whole . . . A text is a unit of language in use . . . A text is best regarded as a *semantic* unit' (original emphasis). A text is a meaningful stretch of language. (This definition, following Kress and van Leeuwen (1996), can be extended to include related semiotics, such as visual images, though such aspects will not be dealt with in detail here.)

The key to beginning a grammatical analysis is to identify a clause; this is the hub of the grammar. The clause is similar in concept to a sentence, except that a sentence pertains to written language, whereas a clause applies to spoken language as well. More specifically, a clause represents an event, that is, something happening or taking place, or a state of affairs. For example:

We've paid the postage . . . (T2.1:7)
And it always will be. (T2.1:12)
Your vote must be received before 30 March '92. (T2.1:21)

Clauses combine into clause complexes: two messages are combined to form a larger unit, as in:

We've paid the postage          and addressed the envelope. (T2.1:7–8)

| clause complex | |
|---|---|
| clause | clause |

If you are eligible to vote,          you will receive your ballot papers this week. (T2.1:19–20)

| clause complex | |
|---|---|
| clause | clause |

The clause itself is not a single undifferentiated unit; it has component parts, called groups or phrases, as illustrated below. (Don't worry too much at this stage about the reasoning behind these groupings or their labels; we're just illustrating a general point.)

We                      've paid                    the postage . . .

| clause | | |
|---|---|---|
| group | group | group |

And                it                  always              will be.

| clause | | | |
|---|---|---|---|
| group | group | group | group |

Your vote                  must be received          before 30 March, '92.

| clause | | |
|---|---|---|
| group | group | group |

And these units in turn are made up of other units, namely words. That is,

| clause | | | | |
|---|---|---|---|---|
| group | group | | group | |
| word | word | word | word | word |

We              've              paid              the              postage . . .

| And | it | always | will | be. |
|-----|-----|-----|-----|-----|

| clause | | | | |
|-----|-----|-----|-----|-----|
| group | group | group | group | |
| word | word | word | word | word |

Your    vote    must    be    received    before    30    March,    '92.

| clause | | | | | | | | |
|-----|-----|-----|-----|-----|-----|-----|-----|-----|
| group | | group | | | group | | | |
| word | word | word | word | word | word | word | word | word |

These units form the core of what is called the *rank scale*, the hierarchical arrangement of grammatical constituents. Clauses are made up of groups and phrases, which are made up of words. The arrangement can also be explained in the opposite direction – words make up groups and phrases, which make up clauses.

Every word contains at least one morpheme. These are the word forms, suffixes and prefixes which provide grammatical information, such as '-s' indicating the plural form of a noun, '-ing' indicating the present continuous tense of a verb. 'Dogs' consists of two morphemes: the lexical root, 'dog', plus the plural indicator. 'Running', as in 'she is running', has two morphemes, the lexical root, 'to run', plus the present continuous indicator. Generally we will not be concerned with morphemes; information can be found in introductory general linguistic text books, such as Emmitt and Pollock (1991).

This is the basis of the rank scale for English, and it can be represented as follows:

clause
|
group/phrase
|
word

When doing analysis, it is essential to locate the analysis in terms of its rank: does the analysis you are working with tell you about a clause, a group or a word?

Rank scale on its own is not enough to start analysis; it doesn't mean much to say 'Here is a group'. The grammatical units must be identified and this is done in two ways: by class and by function. Class refers to the formal characteristics of the unit and can, in principle, be identified out of context. Class can be recognized, and usually does not need to be interpreted. Major word classes include:

> *verb*: is, receive, make, do, delcare, pop
> *noun*: week, customers, invitation, St. George, envelope, box
> *adjective*: eligible, genuine, special, best, friendly
> *adverb*: simply, always, importantly, possibly, really
> *determiner*: a, the, this
> *numeral*: one, two, first, second
> *pronoun*: we, it, you, us, your, our
> *preposition*: in, at, of, as, for, before
> *conjunction*: because, and, or

Some words belong to more than one class: 'lodge' can be a verb ('We've made it easy for you to lodge it') or a noun ('The lodge is quite expensive'). In such cases the context is needed in order to determine class.

Many word classes have equivalent group and phrase classes.

> *verbal group*: have made; will receive; must be received
> *nominal (noun) group*: your vote; all eligible St. George customers; the postage; St. George's genuine interest in the wishes of its customers
> *prepositional phrase*: in the post; at any St. George branch; into the ballot box

There are also classes of clause, but we will not go into this level of detail here.

One complication in the notion of rank is that of *rankshift*, also called *embedding*. Perhaps you have noticed that some of the 'units' in the St. George texts look rather complicated. Sometimes this is because two units have been combined together into a *complex*, as described above for clause complexes. Where complexing occurs, the two (or more) units have essentially the same status, and work together to build up a larger structure. However, complexity in units sometimes occurs because of rankshift, or embedding. Rankshift occurs when a unit of one rank is itself made up of a unit from the same rank or from the rank above. That is, one unit operates 'inside' another, so to speak, complicating the unit internally, but not making the structure itself any 'bigger'.

Consider the nominal group, 'St. George's genuine interest in the wishes of customers' (T2.1:11). According to the rank scale (p. 31), this group should be divided into words. Doing so, however, would miss some of the internal patterning, the fact that 'in the wishes of customers' seems to 'belong together'. Here is a prepositional phrase acting *inside* a nominal group. The prepositional phrase has been *rankshifted* to take up a role in another group. That is,

St. George's　genuine　interest　　in the wishes of customers

| nominal group | | | |
|---|---|---|---|
| word | word | word | [prepositional phrase] |

The prepositional phrase itself has its own internal complexity, a preposition, 'in', with a nominal group, 'the wishes of customers'. This nominal group has further internal complexity:

St. George's genuine interest　in　　the　　wishes　of　　customers

| nominal group | | | | | | | |
|---|---|---|---|---|---|---|---|
| word | word | word | [ | prepositional phrase | | | ] |
| | | | prep'n | nominal group | | | |
| | | | | word | word | [prep'n phrase] | |
| | | | | | | prep'n | nominal group |

Confused? Think of it as Chinese boxes: boxes inside boxes; the largest box is no bigger just because it has others inside it, but its interior is more structurally complex than an empty box. Rankshifting enables interesting structures to occur. Clauses can be rankshifted as well as groups. Consider the following:

an invitation to vote to help St. George take the step forward to obtaining a banking licence. (T2.1:3)

This is in fact one nominal group: it's all to do with an 'invitation'. Clauses ('to vote') are used to modify the noun in order to specify exactly what kind of invitation is at stake.

The following notations are used to mark clause and group boundaries:

|| 　　　　clause boundary
| 　　　　group boundary
[[ ]] 　　embedded clause
[ ] 　　　embedded group

Angled brackets are used to signal included elements, for example, when one clause interrupts another, but is not an intrinsic part of its structure.

<<　　>> 　included clause
<　　> 　　included group

Conventionally, each clause is written on a new line:

Because St. George is St. George,
we do want
your vote returned. (T2.1:4–6)

Being able to divide a running text into its basic units is essential for beginning analysis. The identification of word and group classes is one of the key contributions of traditional grammar and you must be familiar with them; see, for example, Butt *et al.* (1995: 28–30) and Halliday (1994: 214), for further details. On rankshift see, for example, Halliday (1994: 242–50) and Martin *et al.* (1997: 16–18).

On its own, however, class information enables us to say very little about meaning. Compare the following examples, which have been identified in terms of their group classes:

*The customers | voted | enthusiastically.

| nominal group | verbal group | adverbial group |
| --- | --- | --- |

*St. George | notified | the customers.

| nominal group | verbal group | nominal group |
| --- | --- | --- |

In both examples, 'the customers' is a nominal group, but each plays a different role. In the first example, 'the customers' is the responsible element, the one actually doing the action; in the second, it is the object of the action. The label 'nominal group' does not on its own allow us to draw the distinction; additional labelling is necessary to represent the *function* of the constituent. Functional labels are an interpretation of meaning, and so can only be analysed in context. Without the context, it is impossible to say what the function of 'the customers' is (although it's possible to suggest a range of alternatives). Traditional grammar certainly entails some functional labelling (such as subject and object), but this labelling needs to be expanded.

In SFL, function is interpreted three ways, with respect to each of the metafunctions, as described in Chapter 1. Thus, along with class information, there can be up to three sets of functional labels, in order to draw out the full meaning potential of a clause. This results in a complex model, but the complexity is well worth the effort; it enables powerful analyses of language, and a rich account of meaning.

## 2.3 What's going on? Ideational meaning

Analysis needs to be focused on the questions being asked. Consider first of all, what aspect of meaning is at stake. *Ideational* meaning refers to what is going on in the world, what is being represented. We then need to ask, how does language represent what's going on in the world? It is in terms of events: whole goings-on, with different elements involved in those goings-on. If I'm talking to friends and want to tell them about the weekend, I don't do so by saying 'film'. I say 'We saw a great film this weekend' or 'Have you seen it yet?'. At the core of this representation is some activity or way of being, a going-on – what is called in SFL the *Process*. The process is brought about by elements involved in the event in some way; these are the *Participants* that bring the event about, or that are affected by it in some way. The event can also be represented in relation to further information, *Circumstances* which give further details. These choices – Process, Participant, Circumstance – together are referred to as the TRANSITIVITY system. Here are some examples analysed in terms of their transitivity structure:

| drop | it | in the post | (T2.1:9) |
|---|---|---|---|
| Process | Participant | Circumstance | |

| you | will receive | your ballot papers | this week | (T2.1:20) |
|---|---|---|---|---|
| Participant | Process | Participant | Circumstance | |

| the date for determining members' eligibility to vote in the postal ballot | is | 21 February 1992. (T2.2:22) |
|---|---|---|
| Participant | Process | Participant |

The Process is the action around which the clause is structured. It includes the main verb, any auxiliaries (e.g. 'will') and any markers of polarity (e.g. 'not'). The Process is always realized by a verb, and there is only one Process in a clause, although there may be other verbs in a clause that do not play the role of Process. They belong within other elements, as with 'determining' and 'to vote' in the example above.

In order for this Process to come about, some element must be involved in, must participate in, the Process. These are the Participants; an understood 'you' in T2.1:9, as well as 'it' (the ballot paper); this is what is to be dropped. In T2.2:22, the Participants are more abstract; a 'date', specified as the '21 February'. Participants are typically realized by nominal groups, as in the examples above, but may also be realized by other elements, such as embedded clauses. For example:

| * [[Voting for St. George]] | | is | a great idea. |
|---|---|---|---|
| Participant | | Process | Participant |

So, 'Participant' does not necessarily mean 'human' or 'concrete', but refers to the element/s involved in the Process in some way. Around the core of the Process-Participant structure, it is also possible to have additional information about the Circumstances of the event: where it happened, when, why, and so on. In T2.1:9, 'in the post' specifies a location for the action of 'dropping'; in T2.2:22, a time for the receipt of ballot papers is specified. Note that there is no Circumstance in T2.2:22; while '21 February' gives information about time, this information is not *additional* to the structure of the event; it is an intrinsic part of the event in this clause ('the date is . . . *what?*'). Circumstances are usually realized by prepositional phrases ('in the post'), nominal groups ('this week') or adverbs (e.g. 'carefully', in *'read the proposal carefully').

Being able to identify Participants, Processes and Circumstances is a useful start to analysis. Without going any further, it is possible to look at these elements in a text, and see if any patterns emerge. For example, you could look at all the Participants in a text and note general characteristics, such as whether they are concrete or abstract; if human, whether female or male, and so on. While T2.1 and T2.2 share a certain number of Participants (such as 'St. George' and 'the proposal'), there are important differences. T2.1 includes Participants such as 'we' (St. George) and 'you' (the customer). This highlights in T2.1 a more human representation of the voting situation, in contrast to the institutional 'any eligible voting member' of T2.2. Importantly, T2.1 speaks of 'the step forward to obtaining a banking licence', pointing at the less-than-detached stance taken in this text, whereas T2.2 refers only to a legally defined proposal.

Note that this very basic analysis is already an act of interpretation: as an analyst, you are reasoning about what the clause *means*. Look at the following example, from a child's scientific report, and compare the analyses:

| Snails | live | on plants. |
|---|---|---|
| Participant | Process | Circumstance |

| Snails | live on | plants. |
|---|---|---|
| Participant | Process | Participant |

The first analysis suggests that the action the snails are involved in is 'living', and they do this in a particular place, 'on plants'. The second analysis suggests that the action is 'live on' (a phrasal verb, something akin to 'eat'), and that 'plants' is what they eat. The surrounding text may suggest which analysis is appropriate, but the point is that the analysis involves grammatical reasoning (see Martin *et al.* 1997: 127–8 for reasoning about phrasal verbs). A functional analysis is not simply a question of labelling; the labels reflect a semantic and grammatical interpretation of a text.

A key feature of SFL is that all the analyses can be undertaken at different degrees of 'delicacy'. The degree of delicacy refers to the level of detail of the analysis, providing further distinctions within a broader category according to sub-types. For example, there are various types of Processes, each of which gives a different sense of action or happening and each Process type has a particular set of related Participants (described below). Again, this is not just a proliferation of labelling for the sake of having labels; the distinctions are based on both semantic and grammatical grounds. (The suggested readings give more information about this.) We will mention each of the key types of Process, and their key associated Participants; this will not be a full description, and in particular, some of the less central Participants will be omitted.

*Material* Processes give a sense of physical action; they refer to a strong sense of 'doing'. The main related Participants are those of *Actor*, the Participant responsible for 'doing' the action, and the *Goal*, the object of the action (but if these strike you as just new names for the familiar 'Subject' and 'Object', note that the latter are used in relation to a different analysis (Section 2.4), and would not on their own be enough to distinguish the different participant roles across the various Process types.) There are two other relevant Participants, the *Range*, the domain over which the action takes place, and the *Beneficiary*, a Participant which benefits from the Process in some way. Both T2.1 and T2.2 include material Processes, for example:

> we**'ve sent** all eligible votes a ballot paper and a pre-paid self addressed envelope (T2.1:16)
> just **drop** it in the post . . . or in the special ballot box at any St. George branch. (T2.1:9)
> Ballot papers **should be returned** to the returning officer . . . (T2.2:27)
> Ballot papers for the postal ballot **will be sent** to eligible voting members of St. George on or before 9 March 1992. (T2.2:20)

Just noting the presence of material Processes is an important step towards understanding that each text is concerned with concrete, physical actions. But another step needs to be taken and that is to look at the processes *in conjunction with* their associated Participants. Let's look at the above examples again, this time with the Participants identified. Note that not every element of the clause contributes to its ideational structure; 'just' is excluded from the transitivity analysis.

| we | 've sent | all eligible voters | a ballot paper and a pre-paid self addressed envelope |
|---|---|---|---|
| Actor | Pro: material | Beneficiary | Goal |

| (just) | drop | it | in the post |
|---|---|---|---|
| --- | Pro: material | Goal | Circumstance |

| Ballot papers | should be returned | to the returning officer . . . |
|---|---|---|
| Goal | Pro: material | Circumstance |

| Ballot papers for the postal ballot | will be sent | to eligible voting members of St. George | on or before 9 March 1992. |
|---|---|---|---|
| Goal | Pro: material | Circumstance | Circumstance |

It is the co-patterning of process type with participant roles which identifies the content. In T2.1, for instance, St. George constructs itself ('we')
as an Actor in relation to completed actions ('we've sent all eligible voters
a ballot paper and a pre-paid self addressed envelope'). In other words,
they have been, or are, an active organization: they've done their bit in
terms of this proposal. In T2.1:8 ('and addressed the envelope'), the
Actor has been ellipsed, but can still be understood as 'we', that is, 'St.
George'. The customer also takes on the role of an Actor, but in terms of
actions yet to be completed: the customers must now do their part
('[you] just drop it in the post').

In contrast, in T2.2, St. George is an Actor in relation to legal Goals
('that St. George apply for . . . an authority to carry on banking business'
T2.2:7); the 'eligible voting member' is an Actor in relation to practical
issues of obtaining/completing voting forms ('Eligible voting members in
these categories may contact the returning officer' T2.2:24). Sometimes,
the 'Actor' is the ineffable legal process/legal institution, but in these
cases it is omitted from the actual clause structure (T2.2:20 'Ballot papers
for the postal ballot will be sent to eligible voting members . . .' – but who
sends the ballot papers? T2.2:2 'Notice is given . . .' – but who by?). This
highlights the fact that it is not particularly important to know who determines such actions. Observing the presence of (in this case) material
processes is a useful step, because it reveals important actions in the text;
but observing the co-patterning with particular participants adds further
depth to the analysis, showing that, in these texts, different
groups/people undertake different activities.

*Mental* Processes are about aspects of thinking, feeling and seeing. The related Participants are those of *Senser* and *Phenomenon*. There are very few mental Processes in these texts. At the conclusion of T2.1, St. George asserts their 'personal' attachment to the outcome of the vote, as a persuasive tactic:

> At St. George, we **do believe** that every vote really counts. (T2.2:37–8)

*Phenomenon*

A feature of mental Processes is that they often *project*, that is, relate to a whole other clause. Thus, what St. George 'believes', in the above example, is a whole proposition, which would need to be analysed as a separate clause. If the clause was 'we believe you', then 'you' would be the Phenomenon.

In T2.2, the only mental processes occur in relation to the 'eligible members' deciding which way they will vote. These processes are highlighted below; because of the complex clause structure the box analysis is not included.

> ... for eligible members of St. George **to consider** and, if **thought** fit, approve the proposal that ... (T2.2:4–6)

*behavioural process*

In T2.2, then, the 'eligible voting member' has a key role to play in relation to the critical processes at stake: to 'consider and, if thought fit, approve the proposal that . . .' The mental processes make it clear that the voter does indeed have a choice; there is the possibility of rejecting this application, an option not highlighted in T2.1.

Note that 'approve' in the example above is not a mental process; it seems to have a sense of 'material' action. It cannot report (i.e. occur with a reported clause in a projecting clause complex), hence it is more appropriate to call this a *Behavioural* process. As described in Eggins (1994: 249–51), and Halliday (1994: 138–40), behavioural processes share some of the characteristics of material, and some of mental. They tend to be associated with physiological processes. The related Participant is the *Behaver*. An example:

| *St. George | cares | for its customers. |
|---|---|---|
| Behaver | Pro: behavioural | Circumstance |

*Relational* processes relate Participants to each other, showing that they are connected, without there necessarily being a strong sense of 'action' involved. Relational Processes are either forms of the verb 'to be' or 'to have', or related synonyms, such as 'seems' or 'represents' (see Halliday 1994: 120–3, Eggins 1994: 257–9). Both texts have relational processes. (The related Participants will be further described below.)

*to be, have, seem, represents*

Because St. George **is** St. George (T2.1:4)

Our reputation in home lending **is** second to none. (T2.1:28)

St. George's genuine interest in the wishes of its customers **is** part of the tradition that has always been St. George. (T2.1:11)

The proposal **consists of** the following separate resolutions (T2.2:10)

A vote in this postal ballot by an eligible voting member of St. George in favour of, or against, the proposal, **shall be taken as** a vote by that member in favour of, or against, as the case may be, each of these resolutions. (T2.2:18)

The date for determining members' eligibility to vote in the postal ballot **is** 21 February 1992. (T2.2:22)

Note that 'to be' and 'to have' occur frequently as auxiliaries in relation to other verbs (e.g. 'St. George *is dedicated to* . . .'); it is only when they occur as the main verb, that they are considered to be a relational process.

There are important sub-types of relational processes. This is an extremely subtle and complex part of the grammar, and you will need to refer to other sources to get a full description (for example, Halliday 1994: 119–38, Eggins 1994: 255–66, Thompson 1996: 86–96). In brief, the key distinctions centre around whether the role of the relational process is to ascribe some descriptive attributes to an entity, or to give the entity in question a definite identity; these are called the 'attributive' mode and 'identifying' mode. Both the 'to be' and the 'to have' relationals can occur as attributive or as identifying. It is a characteristic which cuts across all relational processes (including one other type, the Circumstantial, not described here). T2.1 has both attributive and identifying relational processes. For the attributive, the relevant Participants are the *Carrier* and the *Attribute*, as exemplified below:

St. George's genuine interest in the wishes of its customers     is     part of the tradition that has always been St. George. (T2.1:11)

| Carrier | Process: relational | Attribute |
|---|---|---|

Here, the attribute 'part of the tradition that has always been St. George', gives us an important detail about St. George, specifically about 'St. George's genuine interest in the wishes of its customers'. However, this is only one detail and it is not used to uniquely define the company.

For the identifying type, the relevant Participants are the Token and the Value: that which is being identified, and that which gives the 'Value' or identification:

(because)   St. George            is         St. George  (T2.1:4)

| --- | Token | Process: relational | Value |
|---|---|---|---|

Here, the Value, 'St. George', identifies the Token, 'St. George'. This circularity is a wonderfully ineffable example: the quality of St. George 'speaks for itself'. Both the attributive and the identifying types of relationals are used to define and describe St. George as an institution in terms of its positive qualities. No such description of St. George occurs in T2.2, emphasizing that T2.1 has a more overtly persuasive role, and that it is, indeed, a form of advertising. Both the attributive and the identifying relational processes occur in T.2, and they certainly have a crucial role to play in the text. But rather than describing the institution, their job is to define and describe key elements of the legal process in legal terms:

The proposal    consists of    the following separate resolutions (T2.2:10)

| Carrier | Process: relational | Attribute |
| --- | --- | --- |

A vote in this postal ballot by an eligible voting member of St. George in favour of, or against, the proposal,

| Token |
| --- |

shall be taken as

| Process: relational |
| --- |

a vote by that member in favour of, or against, . . . each of these resolutions. (T2.2:18)

| Value |
| --- |

*Existential* processes appear to be quite similar to relationals, involving a form of the verb 'to be', but there is only one 'real' Participant, the *Existent*.

*There           will be            a vote            next week

| --- | Process: existential | Existent | Circumstance |
| --- | --- | --- | --- |

In this example, 'there' is not actually referring to a location; it is an 'empty' Participant, and this is the only construction in which existential Processes occur.

   *Verbal* processes are to do with forms of saying and its related synonyms. The related Participants are the *Sayer* and the *Verbiage*, as well as the *Receiver*.

| * Tell | us | your answer. |
|---|---|---|
| Process: verbal | Receiver | Verbiage |

Note that as for mental processes, verbals can project, that is, relate to an entire other clause, and not just a Participant:

*The customer **said** ‖ that she would vote

As well as process and participant types, Circumstances can also be further distinguished. Think of Circumstances as answering a question, for example, '*when* did the action take place?' (at 3 p.m.); '*where* did the action take place?' (in the bank), and so on. Table 2.1, adapted from Martin *et al.* (1997: 104), summarizes some of the main circumstance types. Martin *et al.* (1994) and the other suggested readings give further details.

**Table 2.1** Circumstances (adapted from Martin *et al.* 1997: 104)

| Circumstance type | Probe question | Example |
|---|---|---|
| Extent | how long? | for three weeks |
| Location: time | when? | on or before March 30 |
|       : place | where? | in the special ballot box |
| Manner | how? | simply |
|  |  | with a pen |
| Cause | why? | for our future |
| Accompaniment | together with? | with other voters |

Circumstances are not particularly frequent in either text, but they do add important information. Time is crucial:

> *This week*, all eligible St. George customers will receive . . . (T2.1:3)
> Your vote must be received *before 30 March, '92.* (T2.1:21)
> Ballot papers for the postal ballot will be sent to eligible voting members of St. George *on or before 9 March 1992.* (T2.2:20)
> The postal ballot closes *on 30 March 1992.* (T2.2:26)

In T2.1, Circumstances of place are also important, specifying exactly what the customer should do with the voting form: (drop it) *in the post*; (post it) *in the envelope provided*; (pop it) *into the ballot box at any St. George branch*. In T2.2, Circumstances of manner (describing 'how') add crucial legal details: *in accordance with . . .* ; *pursuant to . . .* It is also a Circumstance of manner, *in favour of,* or *against . . .* which emphasizes that 'voting' can be either 'yes' or 'no'.

In terms of describing what's going on, the content of these texts might be said to be similar, but only at the most superficial level. Each text is concerned with the St. George banking proposal, but each approaches this broad domain in different ways, as is revealed by an examination of the predominant patterns of Processes, Participants and Circumstances. T2.1 is concerned with establishing the merit, value and strength of St. George as an institution, generating a positive orientation towards the vote (including one quite extreme, albeit subtle, measure, as discussed below), and facilitating the return of the members' voting forms. T2.2 is concerned with the vote in its legal terms: outlining the legal details and conditions, making it clear that voting may be for or against the proposal, and describing how legal voting may take place. It is not concerned with describing the institution in any way, nor with any arguments for or against the proposal. The 'content' of these two texts, while not unrelated, is significantly different.

As well as identifying the key process types and the major participant roles associated with each Process, it can also be useful to look 'inside' the Participants, so to speak, and see how they are structured. This requires moving down a rank, from the clause to the group (that is, Participant is a role played at clause rank; now we are looking 'inside' this element, to see what it is made up of). Participants are often realized by nominal groups, but may also be realized by clauses. There is not space here to go into the details of the nominal group (see, for example, Halliday 1994: 180–96; Thompson 1996: 179–84) but we can make some general observations. We've already noted that, in T2.1, St. George is referred to sometimes by its name (particularly when it is being described as an institution) and sometimes as 'we' (particularly when it is being presented in terms of its actions). One crucial participant in T2.1 is in the first clause of the body of the text: This week, all eligible St. George customers will receive *an invitation to vote to help St. George take the step forward to obtaining a banking licence* (T2.1:3). As noted in Section 2.2, this is a very complex participant, with much internal structuring and embedding, but it is clearly one participant in the clause: this is what the customers will receive. The core of this participant is 'the invitation', but it is not just any invitation: the invitation is modified by other (embedded) clauses: it is an invitation *to vote to help St. George take the step forward to obtaining a banking license.* In this way, the vote is cleverly defined as 'voting yes'. No other option is given. By defining the vote in this way, and then encouraging voters to send their (yes) vote in, the intention and expectation is that only those who vote 'yes' will indeed send their votes in. Those who don't approve, won't vote, won't even return the voting form – or at least, that is the hope. This strategy is reiterated in the penultimate paragraph, *Be part of this important step forward and make sure your vote is returned well before Monday, 30 March 1992* (T2.1:35–6). As already observed, T2.2 does allow for the possibility of voting no: voters need to 'consider *and, if thought fit,* approve . . .' and it is brought to readers' attention that they may vote 'in favour of, or against' the proposal.

This, then, is one way to approach analysis – from the point of view of ideational meaning. Beginning at clause rank, we look to see how the clause is structured to represent events, in terms of the TRANSITIVITY system of Processes, Participants and Circumstances. What sorts of actions or happenings are represented? In what way are Participants involved in these events? Under what Circumstances do these events take place? It is possible also to move down the rank scale to group rank and see if there are any relevant patterns at this level, for example, interesting choices in nominal groups.

### 2.4 Roles, relationships and attitudes: interpersonal meaning

Language does, of course, do far more than just represent content. Every act of communication is always an *interaction*. Communication happens between people (whether real or imagined). At the same time as conveying some kind of content, language also constructs and conveys some kind of interpersonal relationship: it has interpersonal as well as ideational meaning. As explained in Chapter 1, the relevant contextual variable here is that of Tenor – the roles and relationships relevant to the situation of the text. The Tenor of the situation is reflected in and constructed by the interpersonal meanings of the text: what kind of personal relationship is constructed between the interactants in the situation, the attitudes and opinions expressed, the degree of formality or familiarity, and so on.

Several grammatical resources carry interpersonal meanings in a text. Once again, we'll take a preliminary look at these resources and apply them to the St. George texts. Halliday (1994: 69) suggests that of all the things we do with language, there are four key distinctions which explain interpersonal communication. As speakers/writers, we can be either *giving* or *demanding*. What we give/demand is either *goods and services* (actual actions) or *information*. These four distinctions give rise to the speech functions identified in Table 2.2.

**Table 2.2** Speech functions (adapted from Halliday 1994: 69)

| Role in exchange | Commodity exchanged: goods and services | Information |
|---|---|---|
| Giving | 'offer': *Would you like an interest-free loan? | 'statement': *St. George is an excellent bank. |
| Demanding | 'command': *Vote soon. | 'question': *Are you eligible to vote? |

The speech functions are realized in grammar by the grammatical MOOD of the clause. MOOD is a technical grammatical term and bears no relationship to the everyday sense of 'mood.' The grammatical MOODS, matched with their speech functions, are illustrated in Table 2.3.

**Table 2.3** Speech function and grammatical MOOD (adapted from Eggins 1994: 153)

| Speech function | Grammatical MOOD | Example |
| --- | --- | --- |
| offer | modulated interrogative | *Would you like an interest-free loan? |
| statement | declarative | *St. George is an excellent bank. |
| command | imperative | *Vote soon. |
| question | interrogative | *Are you eligible to vote? |

The speech function labels identify the semantic import of the clause: what is it *contributing* to the exchange? The grammatical MOOD identifies the relevant grammatical structure, and we'll see below that these don't always align quite as neatly as illustrated.

While the MOOD of the clause may seem a fairly basic thing to identify, it can, in practice, be quite difficult. What, then, are the criteria for identifying the MOOD? The MOOD of the clause is dependent on the relative order of particular clause constituents, the Subject and Finite of the clause. The Subject of the clause is that element which agrees with the main verb in person and number, and which is also picked up in a *Mood Tag*. For example,

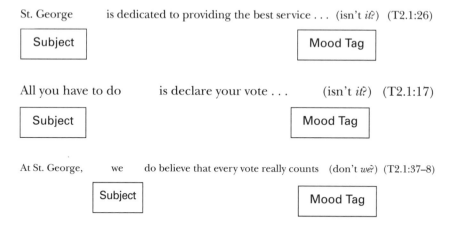

St. George        is dedicated to providing the best service ... (isn't *it?*)  (T2.1:26)

Subject                                                  Mood Tag

All you have to do        is declare your vote ...        (isn't *it?*)  (T2.1:17)

Subject                                          Mood Tag

At St. George,        we        do believe that every vote really counts   (don't *we?*) (T2.1:37–8)

Subject                                                  Mood Tag

The Finite is the part of the verbal group which indicates tense or MODALITY. The Finite '. . . tie(s) down the verb to its Subject so that the proposition in the clause is debateable or arguable' (Butt *et al.*, 1995: 80). A *non-Finite* clause is one which 'hangs in the air', so to speak, such as 'waiting for the results'. Who was waiting? When were (they) waiting? A Finite clause, including a Subject, specifies this information: 'The customers were waiting for the results', or 'The bank will be waiting for the results'. So, the Finite is a crucial element in 'tying the clause down'. For example:

St. George        is        dedicated to providing the best service.    (T2.1:26)

| Subject | Fin |
|---------|-----|

At St. George,    we        do        believe that every vote really counts. (T2.1:37–8)

| Subject | Fin |
|---------|-----|

When the verbal group includes multiple auxiliaries (as in 'they *may have been* voting'), the first auxiliary will be the Finite element. In the case of the simple present and the simple past tense, the Finite-ness of the verbal group is 'fused' with the form of the verb itself: so 'runs' indicates present tense; 'ran' indicates past. In such cases, and by convention, the Finite is written as being 'about half' of the main verb. For example

*Ballot papers    are available from . . .

| Subject | F |
|---------|---|

*St. George    in    vites everyone to vote

| Subject | Fin |
|---------|-----|

Thus, the role of Finite can be played either by a separate auxiliary, or by an indication of tense 'within' the main verb itself. In turn, the auxiliaries may be either forms of the verb 'to be' and 'to have', or modal auxiliaries: 'can', 'may', 'might', 'should', 'must', and so on.

Identifying the presence (or absence) of the Subject and Finite elements, and their respective order, is the basis for identifying the grammatical MOOD of a clause. When the Subject occurs before the Finite, the MOOD is *declarative*, as illustrated in the examples above.

When the Finite occurs before the Subject, the MOOD is *interrogative*.

*Are        you        going to vote?

| Fin | Sub |
|-----|-----|

When either or both of the Subject and Finite are ellipsed, the MOOD is *imperative.*

Just    drop it in the post (T2.1:9) (Subject 'you' ellipsed)

When the basic interrogative form begins with a modal auxiliary functioning as the Finite, this is called a *modulated* interrogative, and is a separate MOOD type.

*Would    you          like an interest-free loan?

Mood = Subject + Finite / Residue

The Subject and Finite together define the MOOD of the clause. The remainder of the clause is called the *Residue.* It, too, has a particular constituent structure, that is, special component elements. These are the *Predicator,* the remainder of the verbal group, after accounting for the Finite; the *Complement,* other participant elements in the clause which are not Subject; and the *Adjunct,* elements which provide other additional information. There is not space here to explain and illustrate these points; the suggested readings provide relevant details. For our purposes, the essential part of the analysis is identifying the grammatical MOOD.

While the speech functions and grammatical MOOD co-occur, this applies to congruent or typical cases only. It is often the case that a particular speech function is realized by a non-congruent MOOD, for example, using a declarative, *It's very noisy in here,* to achieve the function of a command, *Be quiet!* This is a most interesting part of the grammar, but it will not be elaborated here. For good discussions of this topic, see Halliday (1994: 354–67) and Eggins (1994: 149–54).

How would we expect the St. George texts to be functioning interpersonally? By now, we should be able to make some predictions. We would certainly expect both of them to be presenting large amounts of information, so to be predominantly declarative. T2.1 might also make use of commands and interrogatives, as it seems to be taking a generally more intimate and direct approach, and these MOODS involve more interpersonal engagement. T2.2, on the other hand, is rather distant, and we would be unlikely to find other MOODS occurring very frequently, if at all.

T2.1 does, indeed, primarily use declaratives, functioning to give information. It also makes use of imperatives to realize commands at selected points in the text, including, 'just drop it in the post' (T2.1:9); 'simply pop it into the ballot box' (T2.1:17); 'simply call us on our special information line' (T2.1:23). Note that these relate only to the practical aspects of the voting procedure; there is no imperative which actually says 'vote yes'.

There are some notable examples of incongruent MOOD realizations, for example, the declarative:

Your vote must be received before 30 March '92. (T2.1:21)

realizing the command, 'Send your vote in to get here before 30 March'.

Interestingly, no use is made of interrogatives. It could, for example, have been expressed as 'Are you eligible to vote?' or 'Have you sent your vote in?' Such strategies are often used to engage readers' attention – the direct request for information encourages readers' direct engagement with the text, as if it were a conversation. Perhaps the slight distancing effect created by the less direct strategies (that is, by *not* using interrogatives) enables the text to retain an air of impartiality and credibility, one that is reasonably friendly but still authoritative.

T2.2 is, as predicted, almost entirely declarative. The only exceptions are at the end, with the imperatives, 'call the returning officer...' (T2.2:28); 'call St. George Direct on...' (T2.2:29). Note that the 'tone' of the text changes markedly here, and the change in grammatical MOOD and speech function explains why.

An analysis of MOOD is a useful start for an examination of interpersonal meaning, but we need to go much further. The MOOD analysis helps capture the *inter* side of interpersonal meaning; that is, it explains how the text is functioning, in terms of creating a relationship between the interactants (producer/receiver) of the text. But what about the *personal* side? How are feelings and attitudes incorporated into a text?

There is a range of devices which indicate other aspects of interpersonal meaning. Firstly, writers/speakers can indicate the strength (or detachment) of their opinions, through the use of *modality*. MODALITY refers to a small range of devices – modal auxiliaries such as *can, should, must, may, ought,* and so on – which indicate whether the writer is presenting a straight fact or something which is opinionated; whether a straightforward act is intended, or whether the act is attached to obligation, and so on. MODALITY in relation to facts (giving/demanding information) is referred to as *modalization.* MODALITY in relation to acts (giving/demanding goods and services) is referred to as *modulation.* For example:

No MODALITY:      The proposal consists of the following separate resolu-
                  tions... (T2.2:10)
+MODALITY:        *The proposal *might* consist of the following separate
(modalization)   resolutions...

The addition of the modal Finite, 'might', turns the clause from a categorical statement of fact, into one which may or may not occur.

No MODALITY:    *Ballot papers are to be returned to the returning
                officer . . .
+MODALITY:      Ballot papers *should* be returned to the returning
(modulation)    officer . . . (T2.1:27)

The inclusion of 'should' here adds an air of (moderate) obligation on
the part of the customer.

Further descriptions of MODALITY and their effect can be found in the
readings. MODALITY tends to fall into groups – ranging from very strong or
'high' MODALITY (e.g. must, should) through to low/soft MODALITY (e.g.
may, could). High MODALITY indicates strength/urgency on the part of the
producer; low MODALITY indicates tentativeness or indirectness. T2.1 has
few examples of high MODALITY. As noted above, since St. George is not in
a position to be highly directive of its customers, high MODALITY occurs in
the declarative – 'Your vote must be received before 30 March '92'
(T2.1:21) – rather than the imperative. The imperatives do not have high
MODALITY, so that St. George appears to be only *encouraging* its customers –
'and make sure your vote is returned well before Monday, 30 March 1992'
(T2.1:36).

In T2.2 there is one very significant use of high MODALITY: 'The proposal consists of the following separate resolutions, each of which *must* be
passed as separate special resolutions of St. George for the proposal to be
approved' (T2.2:10–12). This high-MODALITY element emphasizes that
there is no room for indeterminacy in the vote: the resolutions *must* be
passed in order for the banking proposal to take effect.

Additionally in T2.2, there are two instances of MODALITY worth commenting on. Firstly, 'may' in 'Eligible voting members in these categories
*may* contact the returning officer to obtain ballot papers' (T2.2:24) indicates that this is an option, not an instruction; it is up to the readers' discretion as to whether they take up this possibility. Secondly, 'should' in
'Ballot papers *should* be returned to the returning officer . . .' (T2.2:27)
indicates a moderate degree of obligation being placed on the reader, but
note that this is not as strong as a direct command (such as 'Return the
ballot papers to the returning officer!'). It's interesting to consider why
the direct command might have been avoided in this text: is it because
the writers are being polite, by not foregrounding the legal authority of
the text, or is it because they are being obfuscatory, trying to hide this
legal authority? There is not necessarily a definite or correct answer to
such a question, but the incongruence of the MOOD choice in this example suggests that the question is worth posing.

Perhaps you are thinking that an analysis of MOOD and MODALITY does
not, indeed, seem to explain the whole story as far as interpersonal meanings go. And you would be right. There are, of course, a range of other
interpersonal devices which contribute to the 'personal' side of the meanings being established in the text. These tend to occur more prosodically
in the text, that is, scattered throughout it, without necessarily being

attached to a particular grammatical structure. Some of the devices include the use of vocatives: how are people named/addressed in the text? Look also at the use of politeness formulae, such as 'please' and 'thankyou', as well as – at the other end of the spectrum – the use of taboo or swear words. The use of 'softeners' or 'emphasizers' (such as 'just', 'very') is also relevant. Look at the two texts for yourself and see if any general contrasts emerge. One point to note is that T2.1 uses a lot of softeners: 'just' drop it in the box; 'all you have to do'; 'simply' pop it in the ballot box, and so on. This deflects any sense of instruction being encoded by making it sound as if the task is an easy and pleasant one to comply with. A simple glance at such features can, in fact, be the best way to begin the exploration of interpersonal meaning, by looking for the 'obvious' indicators of the general nature of the relationship being established.

Another significant aspect of interpersonal meaning is the 'attitude' that is encoded in the text. This refers to the encoding of feelings, attitudes and judgements through the lexical choices, for example, describing a person as 'clever' versus 'devious', a document as 'clear' versus 'simple', and so on. This domain is generally called 'attitudinal lexis'; more recently, Martin has described this as 'APPRAISAL', encompassing systems of Affect (to do with emotions); Judgements (to do with assessments of people) and Appreciation (to do with assessment of things/objects). It's not possible to explain these systems in detail (see Eggins and Slade 1997: 124–43, Martin in press), but it's worth noting that appraisal can turn up in verbs, nouns, adjectives and adverbs, that it can carry positive or negative loading, and that as well as being directly inscribed (that is, carried by a word that is *obviously* attitudinal), it can be 'evoked' (that is, something which is neutral on the surface can be read as having an attitudinal meaning). One of the most important aspects to remember about appraisal analysis is that the analysis must be contextualized in relation to actual textual instances. That is, the same word might have positive or negative loadings, depending on the context. So, while 'happy' might generally be assumed to be positive, it is not difficult to imagine a context where this could be used as a criticism of a person, for example, where someone is resentful of another's seemingly unproblematic life, suggesting with a sarcastic use of the term that they are, perhaps, too simple.

Not surprisingly, Affect is entirely absent from the second text. T2.2 has nothing to do with any emotion, judgement, or evaluation; its role is not to persuade in any way, but to be the impersonal voice of an institutional and impartial authority. T2.1, of course, shares no such impartiality. The text is not by any means saturated with APPRAISAL, but there are key clusters, beginning with the evaluation of the proposal as 'important': something the customer needs to take seriously. Most of the significant appraisal occurs around the description of St. George as genuine, having a strong tradition, as dedicated, providing best service, as friendly. This gives St. George the attributes we would ascribe to a person, as having positive ethics, being reliable, trustworthy. In addition, other features, such as the visual image of the familiar Julie Anthony, and the inclusion of the St George 'Dragon' logo, encode a positive Affect: St. George is a happy, friendly place. (See Kress and van Leeuwen 1996 for further details on the analysis of visual images.)

An examination of interpersonal meaning is, then, something quite different from a referential notion of 'content'. By looking at the choices made from the systems of MOOD, MODALITY, and from other interpersonal systems such as APPRAISAL, much can be learnt about how the text is pitched, how the writer is projected, how the reader is positioned, and what attitudes are conveyed. While we tend to call some texts (of which T2.2 might be an example) 'impersonal', this does not mean that they are without interpersonal meaning; on the contrary, every text has interpersonal meaning as an intrinsic part of its structure. Those texts which tend to be called 'impersonal' just have a particular type of interpersonal positioning within the range of possible positionings used in our culture. The so-called 'impersonal' text still creates a relationship, takes up a stance, and conveys an attitude.

## 2.5 What is prioritized in the message? Textual meaning

The third domain of meaning, textual meaning, relates to the *organization* of the message: how is language used to carry the message? This is not a 'post-production' choice (Matthiessen 1995), but refers to the fact that, *as we speak*, there are choices available in terms of how to organize our language: which part of the message to foreground, which to background, which part to signal as being of most interest, what connections to create between different parts of the message, and so on. A text lacking organization lacks meaning; someone who is 'incoherent' might be uttering intelligible words or sentences, but their message makes no sense as a whole. Often, messages which are ostensibly 'the same' can be given quite different meanings, according to how they are organized.

Thus, textual meaning is a very important part of language. As explained in Chapter 1, it is most closely connected with the register variable of *Mode* in the context of situation. That is, organization varies according to the role that language is playing in the situation: directly accompanying action, as in very 'spoken' texts, or reflecting upon it, as in 'written' texts.

What is it, then, that carries these organizational choices? In English, it is word order, or more correctly, the order of elements of the clause, which carries organizational meanings. For most clauses, the order of the clause elements can be changed without necessarily changing the ideational or interpersonal meanings. For example:

a. This week, all eligible St. George customers will receive an invitation to vote . . . (T2.1:3)

  b. *All eligible St. George customers will receive an invitation to vote
     this week

  a. We've paid the postage (T2.1:7)
  b. *The postage has been paid by us.

  a. Eligible voting members in these categories may contact the return-
     ing officer to obtain ballot papers. (T2.2:24)
  b. *The returning officer may be contacted by eligible voting mem-
     bers in these categories to obtain ballot papers.

  a. The postal ballot closes on 30 March 1992. (T2.2:26)
  b. *On 30 March 1992, the postal ballot closes.

Out of context, these choices don't seem particularly significant, other
than that some expressions perhaps seem a little more awkward. But, in
text, the choice of first position is highly significant. Texts typically have
predominant patterns as to what goes in first position, either for the text
as a whole, or for sections of the text, and this affects the meanings being
made. We will come back to the choices made in the St. George texts
later; first, let's look at how this analysis works.

The analysis at stake is that of *Theme*. The THEME of a clause *functions* as
its point of departure (Halliday 1994: 37–9); it is the position from which
the clause starts, from which a message is developed. THEME is *recognized* in
English (but not in all languages) by first position in the clause. So, in
order to begin to analyse the organizational meanings of text, you need to
identify first position in the clause.

The THEME of a clause will usually be carried by the first Participant,
Process or Circumstance of that clause. This element is labelled THEME;
the remainder of the clause is labelled *Rheme*.

We                        've paid the postage (T2.1:7)

| Participant | . . . |
|-------------|-------|
| Theme       | Rheme |

St. George's genuine interest in the wishes of customers  is part of the tradition . . .  (T2.1:11)

| Participant | . . . |
|-------------|-------|
| Theme       | Rheme |

All you have to do        is declare your vote  (T2.1:17)

| Participant | . . . |
|-------------|-------|
| Theme       | Rheme |

This week          all eligible St. George customers will receive . . . (T2.1:3)

| Circumstance | . . . |
| --- | --- |
| Theme | Rheme |

. . . post          it in the envelope provided (T2.1:17)

| Process | . . . |
| --- | --- |
| Theme | Rheme |

When the THEME is realized by a Participant, Process, or Circumstance, it is called a *topical Theme*. Most clauses have a topical THEME, but there is only *one* topical THEME per clause. So, whichever comes first, the Participant, Process or Circumstance, has thematic status.

Ballot papers for the postal ballot     will be sent to eligible voting members on or before 9 March 1992. (T2.2:20)

| topical Theme | Rheme |
| --- | --- |

*On or before 9 March 1992,     ballot papers for the postal ballot will be sent to eligible voting members.

| topical Theme | Rheme |
| --- | --- |

It is possible to have other elements occurring *before* the topical THEME, which are also labelled as thematic. These elements may be *interpersonal* and/or *textual.* Interpersonal THEMES include vocatives, intensifiers, and adjuncts. Remember, these elements only count as thematic if they occur *before* the topical THEME:

Just          drop          it in the post  (T2.1:9)

| interpersonal | topical | |
| --- | --- | --- |
| Theme | | Rheme |

*please          vote          before March 30.

| interpersonal | topical | |
| --- | --- | --- |
| Theme | | Rheme |

*Fortunately,          the proposal    is easy to follow.

| interpersonal | topical | |
|---|---|---|
| Theme | | Rheme |

A clause may or may not have an interpersonal THEME, and there may be more than one interpersonal THEME.

Textual THEMES include conjunctive elements, linking clauses to each other. Again, these elements are only thematic if they occur before the topical THEME.

   And                it         always will be.  (T2.1:12)

| textual | topical | |
|---|---|---|
| Theme | | Rheme |

    If              you        are eligible to vote . . .  (T2.1:13)

| textual | topical | |
|---|---|---|
| Theme | | Rheme |

    So        please,        don't      just leave it to others to vote.  (T2.1:34)

| textual | interpersonal | topical | |
|---|---|---|---|
| Theme | | | Rheme |

There may or may not be textual THEMES in a clause, and there may be more than one. You will need further information in order to be able to analyse the THEME of clauses with other grammatical MOODS (interrogatives, imperatives, modulated interrogatives); see Eggins (1994: 284–94) for this.

One other important category of THEME is that of *unmarked* or *marked* THEME. Unmarked THEME is the 'most typical' choice, and is identified in conjunction with a MOOD analysis. The THEME is unmarked when the roles of topical THEME and Subject are played by the same element, as in the following examples:

    We            've paid the postage  (T2.1:7)

| topical Theme | Rheme |
|---|---|
| Subject | |

| And | it | always will be.  (T2.1:12) | |
|---|---|---|

| textual | topical | |
|---|---|---|
| THEME | | Rheme |
| | Subject | |

In contrast, *marked* THEMES are those where the topical THEME and Subject are realized by *different* elements, as in the following example:

This week          all eligible St. George customers will receive . . .  (T2.1:3)

| topical Theme | Rheme |
|---|---|
| | Subject |

The marked THEME signals 'that something in the context requires an atypical meaning to be made' (Eggins 1994: 296). The clause above occurs in the opening of the body of T2.1, and the marked THEME draws attention to the special status of this clause.

What, then, are the sorts of THEME choices being made in the St. George texts? T2.1 makes use of quite a lot of textual THEMES ('because', 'or', 'and', 'if' . . .), typically located at the beginning of sentences ('*And* it always will be' T2.1:12). This kind of linking mimics the dynamic organization of spoken language, suggesting an easy and casual flow between ideas. T2.2 also uses some textual THEMES, but has fewer, and they tend to occur between clauses, within a clause complex ('. . . for eligible voting members of St. George to consider *and, if* thought fit, approve the proposal that . . .' – T2.2:4–6). This recreates the complexity of legalistic texts, with their long and complex clauses. The relative absence of textual THEMES at the beginning of sentences is also typical of highly 'written' language.

Not surprisingly, given what we have seen of the texts so far, T2.1 makes greater use of interpersonal THEMES. These tend to be used to emphasize a point ('*simply* pop it into the ballot box' – T2.1:17; '*importantly* [St. George is dedicated] to helping Australians own their own homes' – T2.1:27). Interestingly, much of the highly personalized nature of this text comes not from interpersonal THEMES as such, but from the *nature* of the topical THEMES. T2.1 tends to be about 'we', 'St. George', 'you', that is actual people, or the institution presented in its most personal light. That is, what the text is *about*, in terms of topical THEME, is something which is by nature personal and human. In contrast, T2.2 is 'about' impersonal things: institutions ('St. George Building Society Ltd'), and institutional processes and products ('the proposal'; 'a vote in this postal ballot by an eligible voting member of St. George in favour of, or against, the proposal . . .'; 'ballot papers').

It is useful to pull out the THEMES of each text and write them down in separate columns. Table 2.4 shows some selected THEMES from the two texts; this is neither complete nor systematic, but highlights some key contrasts (and avoids some difficult examples!). All the THEMES in Table 2.4 are topical, unless noted as being textual (tex) or interpersonal (intp). The only marked THEME is 'this week', from T2.1; the others are all unmarked.

**Table 2.4** Comparison of THEMES

| T2.1 | T2.2 |
|---|---|
| we | Notice |
| this week | that a postal ballot |
| because (tex)\| St. George | the proposal |
| Just (intp)\| drop | each of which |
| St. George's genuine interest in the wishes of customers | (that) St. George Building Society |
| if (tex)\| you | A vote in this postal ballot by an eligible voting member of St. George in favour of, or against, the proposal |
| all you have to do | Ballot papers for the postal ballot |
| or (tex)\| simply (intp)\| pop | Eligible voting members in these categories |

The lists of THEMES in Table 2.4 will quickly reveal the main contrasts between the texts. The list for T2.1 suggests a spoken, reasonably informal text, with some hints of more 'written' contrasts. T2.2 is evidently much more 'written' and formal. Your analyses of your own texts might also be primarily concerned with contrast, a simple but useful technique for clarifying differences between text types in terms of their thematic choices.

It is important to also look at the THEME choices *within* the given text itself; that is, given the information that is within a text, what has been selected as the point of departure? What significance does that carry? T2.2 begins with the highly impersonal 'Notice is given . . .' (T2.2:2). There is no mention of who is responsible for that action (given by . . .?), and there is certainly no foregrounding of a responsible agent (*We* give notice that . . .?) Presumably, so long as this text fulfils its legal requirements, it is not so important to specify who is giving the notice (We? The returning officer? St. George?) What is important is that the notice has been given. T2.2 serves a very important legal function, laying out the rules and conditions of voting, the nature of the vote, and so on. But in T2.1, an important feature of the thematic patterning is that St. George *is* frequently foregrounded as the responsible agent ('*we*'ve made voting as easy for you as we possibly can' – T2.1:33; '*we*'ve paid the postage' – T2.1:7; '*we*'ve sent all eligible voters a ballot paper' – T2.1:16). St. George is also foregrounded as the resting point of positive evaluation ('*St. George's genuine interest in the wishes of customers* is part of the tradition that has always been St. George' – T2.1:11; '*St. George* is dedicated to providing the best service to our customers' – T2.1:26; '*our reputation in home lending is second to none*' – T2.1:28), including the ineffable 'Because *St. George* is St. George' (T2.1:4). This is a very important part of the orientation of this text, emphasizing the positive, active, responsible aspects of St. George.

Interestingly, while 'you' (the customer) is frequent in T2.1, this is only foregrounded thematically in relation to relatively 'dry' and technical points ('if *you* are eligible to vote' – T2.1:13; 'if *you* have any questions' – T2.1:22); it is the *action* of the customer which is more likely to be foregrounded ('*Vote* this week' – T2.1:18; 'just *drop* it in the post' – T2.1:9). 'You' is more likely to occur in Rheme position, at the end of the clause ('we do want *your* vote returned' – T2.1:5–6; 'to make it as easy as possible for *you*' – T2.1:15; 'we've made voting as easy for *you* as we possibly can' – T2.1:33). The end of the clause is where the *point* of the information, what is called 'New' information, occurs. While the clause typically starts with 'Given' information, in THEME position, the message is structured so that New information comes at the end. In this case, the inclusion of the customer in the 'news' position highlights their special role; all that activity of St. George is focused on their very special customers. See Halliday (1994: Ch. 8), or Bloor and Bloor (1995: Ch. 4), for further discussion of 'Given' and 'New'.

No doubt it is already clear that an analysis of THEME requires an examination of the text as a whole. It is the consistency of thematic choices, or disruptions to an established pattern, that creates textual significance. The THEMES of individual clauses contribute to the textual meaning of the text. However, an understanding of THEME in text requires more than just understanding the cumulative effect of THEMES in individual clauses. It is important to also look at how the THEMES flow from one to the other. We need to consider *thematic development,* the way in which the THEME patterns unfold in the text. Does the text develop by repeating the same THEME, and adding new Rhemes to it? Or by picking up something from the Rheme, and using this to start a following clause? Or does the text develop by having multiple points in a Rheme picked up by successive THEMES? See Eggins (1994: 302–5) for exemplification of these possibilities.

In addition, the structure of the whole text, not just an individual clause, needs to be considered. Is there an opening to the text which signals the point of departure for that text as a whole? Or is there an opening to a section which signals the point of departure for that section? T2.2 uses the following: 'The proposal consists of the following separate resolutions . . .' (T2.2:10) to signal that resolutions 1 to 4 are related, albeit distinct. Otherwise, the text makes little use of overt signalling devices, suggesting that the organization of the text *as text* is not particularly important; it is the presence of the individual legal points that is relevant. T2.1 tends to make use of typographical layout to give structure to the overall text. The heading, with the highly exaggerated 'Because your vote counts', and the slightly less prominent 'we've made it easy for you to lodge it' would seem to sum up the whole text: the process of voting (defined ideationally as voting 'yes') has been facilitated as much as possible by St. George, because they value their customers so much. The overall structure is further supported by the highlighted subheadings, signalling the different stages of the text. Martin (1992) refers to these higher levels of textual organization as hyper- and macro-THEMES.

Textual meaning, then, is realized by organization; the choices may be relevant at the clause level, section/stage level, or text level, and textual meaning may be facilitated by layout. It is not ancillary to other meanings in a text, but is an intrinsic part, contributing to the text's very nature and identity. By isolating or highlighting the THEMES of a text, one can quickly see the orientation or point of departure for that text. The successive choice of THEMES across a sequence of clauses and the higher-level organizational features contribute to the organization of the text as a whole.

You will have noticed in this section that the THEME analysis intersects and interacts with both the TRANSITIVITY and MOOD analyses. The three metafunctions, or types of meaning, unfold simultaneously in a text; while each contributes different structures to the text, they are always co-present. Sometimes, what is said from the perspective of one analysis will seem to overlap with or reiterate a finding from another analysis. Thus, for example, the 'impersonality' of T2.2 is revealed in a number of ways: the role of Actor is frequently backgrounded; there is little overt attitudinal lexis; the topical THEMES, usually also the Participants in the text, are by nature institutional, rather than personal. It is not always the case that the analyses reinforce each other in this way; you may find in other texts a tension created through the different systems. However, it is the case that even if the metafunctions are approached one at a time in analysis, they co-occur in text; meaning is always a complex of these three perspectives – THEME, TRANSITIVITY, MOOD.

## 2.6 Conclusion

While these analyses have all been presented with a view to understanding what is going on in the texts, there remains an additional layer of analysis relevant to the text itself. This is an analysis of the discourse patterns, those patterns which hold *across* grammatical units and which tie the text together, giving it cohesion and coherence. The relevant patterns are those of *lexical cohesion, reference, conjunction,* and *ellipsis and substitution.* Unfortunately, there is not space here to explore them, but see the suggested readings (p. 28), especially Halliday (1994: Chapter 9), Eggins (1994: Chapter 4), and Thompson (1996: Chapter 7). Important background references include Halliday and Hasan (1976) and Martin (1992).

This chapter is about making a start on a functional analysis and the sorts of observations which you might be able to make about a text. We have not demonstrated a comprehensive analysis of the texts, nor discussed many of the analytical difficulties which arise the instant one deals with real examples (where to draw boundaries, how to recognize embedded clauses, 'grey' categories, and so on), but the examples selected should demonstrate what can begin to be seen with just a little analysis. As will have been clear from the constant references to other sources, this chapter is only a basic introduction to SFL. But it should be sufficient to enable those new to SFL to follow the remaining chapters and to begin functional analysis.

## Additional references

Eggins, S. and Slade, D. (1997) *Analysing Casual Conversation*. London: Cassell.

Emmitt, M. and Pollock, J. (1991) *Language and Learning*. Oxford: Oxford University Press.

Halliday, M.A.K. and Hasan, R. (1976) *Cohesion in English*. London: Longman.

Kress, G. and van Leeuwen, T. (1996) *Reading Images: the Grammar of Visual Design*. London: Routledge.

Martin, J.R. (1992) *English Text: System and Structure*. Amsterdam: Benjamins.

Martin, J.R. (in press) Beyond Exchange: appraisal systems in English'. In S. Hunston and G. Thompson (eds), *Evaluation in Text*. Oxford: Oxford University Press.

Matthiessen, C.M.I.M. (1995) Theme as an enabling resource in ideational 'knowledge' construction. In M. Ghadessy (ed.), *Thematic Development in English Texts*. London: Pinter.

## Appendix 1: Original format of texts

Dimensions of the original texts:

Text 2.1    approximately 56 cm x 40 cm
Text 2.2    approximately 27 cm x 14.5cm

# ST. GEORGE

# Because your vote counts

## ...we've made it easy for you to lodge it.

This week, all eligible St.George customers will receive an invitation to vote to help St.George take the step forward to obtaining a banking licence. Because St.George is St.George, we do want your vote returned.

We've paid the postage and addressed the envelope. Just drop it in the post...or in the special ballot box at any St.George branch.

### A GENUINE INTEREST IN YOUR WISHES...

St.George's genuine interest in the wishes of customers is part of the tradition that has always been St.George.

And it always will be.

If you are eligible to vote, please take advantage of this opportunity to have your say on this important step forward for all St.George customers.

To make it as easy as possible for you, we've sent all eligible voters a ballot paper and a pre-paid self addressed envelope.

All you have to do is declare your vote, post it in the envelope provided...or simply pop it into the ballot box at any St.George branch.

### VOTE THIS WEEK

If you are eligible to vote, you will receive your ballot papers this week. Your vote must be received before 30 March, '92.

If you have any questions, simply call us on our special information line. 008 801 132 (that's a free call too).

### ST.GEORGE DEDICATION

St.George is dedicated to providing the best service to our customers, and importantly, to helping Australians own their own homes. Our reputation in home lending is second to none, as is our friendly staff service.

The proposal for St.George to obtain a banking licence has been covered in the information book, "Creating a Level Playing Field", available from any branch and in the "Explanatory Statement" mailed to eligible voters.

### DON'T FORGET TO VOTE

We've made voting as easy for you as we possibly can. So please don't just leave it to others to vote. Be part of this important step forward and make sure your vote is returned well before Monday, 30 March 1992.

At St.George, we do believe that every vote really counts.

What a great idea
St.George

PATTS C2606

# N O T I C E

Notice is given that a postal ballot will be conducted by St.George Building Society Ltd. ("St.George") in accordance with orders made by the Minister for Cooperatives on 24 February 1992, pursuant to Section 46F of the Permanent Building Societies Act 1967 (NSW) for eligible voting members of St.George to consider and, if thought fit, approve the proposal that:

*St.George apply for, and take all steps necessary to obtain, an authority to carry on banking business and, in that process, St.George convert its status from a permanent building society to a company.*

The proposal consists of the following separate resolutions, each of which must be passed as separate special resolutions of St.George for the proposal to be approved.

1. *THAT St.George Building Society Ltd. apply for, and take all steps necessary to obtain, an authority under Section 9 of the Banking Act 1959 of the Commonwealth of Australia (as amended) to carry on banking business.*
2. *THAT St.George Building Society Ltd. apply to be registered as a company under the Corporations Law.*
3. *THAT the name under which St.George Building Society Ltd. applies to be registered as a company be St.George Bank Limited.*
4. *THAT St.George Building Society Ltd. adopt a memorandum and articles of association on its registration as a company in the form signed for identification by the chairman of St.George Building Society Ltd.*

A vote in this postal ballot by an eligible voting member of St.George in favour of, or against, the proposal, shall be taken as a vote by that member in favour of, or against, as the case may be, each of these resolutions.

Ballot papers for the postal ballot will be sent to eligible voting members of St.George on or before 9 March 1992. Eligibility of a member to vote in this postal ballot is determined in accordance with Rule 90 of the Rules of St.George. The date for determining members' eligibility to vote in the postal ballot is 21 February 1992.

Ballot papers will not be sent to any eligible voting member:

- who has given a 'no mail' direction to St.George; or
- who has not advised St.George of his or her current correct address.

Eligible voting members in these categories may contact the returning officer to obtain ballot papers.

The postal ballot closes on 30 March 1992.

Ballot papers should be returned to the returning officer at the address below:

P F Wales (Partner, BDO Binder)
Returning Officer
GPO Box 2712
SYDNEY NSW 2001

For enquiries concerning voting in the postal ballot, call the returning officer on: (02) 286 5791 during the hours of 9.00 am to 5.00 pm weekdays.

For all other enquiries concerning the proposal, call St.George Direct on: (008) 801 132 during the hours of 9.00 am to 5.00 pm weekdays.

## Appendix 2: Texts 2.1 and 2.2 analysed for clause boundaries

### Text 2.1

The original text has been divided into clauses; each new line represents a new clause; rankshifted clauses have been indicated with double square brackets, i.e. [[ ]]; included clauses (i.e., interrupting another clause but otherwise independent) have been indicated with double angled brackets, i.e. << >>. Where a rankshifted clause includes a clause complex within it, the clause boundary is indicated by double vertical lines, i.e. ||.

1 Because your vote counts
2 . . . we've made it easy [[for you to lodge it]].
3 This week, all eligible St. George customers will receive an invitation [[to vote || to help St. George take the step forward to [[obtaining a banking licence]] ]].
4 Because St. George is St. George
5 we do want
6 your vote returned.
7 We've paid the postage
8 and addressed the envelope.
9 Just drop it in the post . . . or in the special ballot box at any St. George branch.
10 A genuine interest in your wishes . . .
11 St. George's genuine interest in the wishes of customers is part of the tradition [[that has always been St. George]].
12 And it always will be.
13 If you are eligible to vote,
14 please take advantage of this opportunity [[to have your say on this important step forward for all St. George customers]].
15 To make it as easy as possible for you,
16 we've sent all eligible voters a ballot paper and a pre-paid self addressed envelope.
17 [[All you have to do]] is [[declare your vote, || post it in the envelope provided . . . || or simply pop it into the ballot box at any St. George branch.]]
18 Vote this week.
19 If you are eligible to vote,
20 you will receive your ballot papers this week.
21 Your vote must be received before 30 March, '92.
22 If you have any questions,
23 simply call us on our special information line 008 801 132
24 (that's a free call too).
25 St. George Dedication
26 St. George is dedicated to [[providing the best service to our customers,]]
27 and importantly, to [[helping Australians own their own homes.]]
28 Our reputation in home lending is second to none,
29 as is our friendly staff service.
30 The proposal for St. George [[to obtain a banking licence]] has been covered in the information book, 'Creating a Level Playing Field', << 31 >>, and in the 'Explanatory Statement' [[mailed to eligible voters.]]
31 <<available from any branch>>

32  Don't forget to vote
33  We've made voting as easy for you [[as we possibly can]].
34  So please, don't just leave it to others to vote.
35  Be part of this important step forward
36  and make sure [[your vote is returned well before Monday, 30 March 1992.]]
37  At St. George, we do believe
38  that every vote really counts.

**Text 2.2**

1  NOTICE
2  Notice is given
3  that a postal ballot will be conducted by St. George Building Society Ltd. ('St. George') in accordance with orders [[made by the Minister for Co-operatives on 24 February 1992]], pursuant to Section 46F of the Permanent Building Societies Act 1967 (NSW)
4  for eligible voting members of St. George to consider
5  and, if thought fit,
6  approve the proposal that:
7  St. George apply for, << 8 >> an authority [[to carry on banking business]]
8  <<and take all the necessary steps to obtain>>,
9  and, in that process, St. George convert its status from a permanent building society to a company.
10  The proposal consists of the following separate resolutions,
11  each of which must be passed as separate special resolutions of St. George
12  for the proposal to be approved.
13  1. That St. George Building Society Ltd. apply for, << 14 >>, an authority under Section 9 of the Banking Act 1959 of the Commonwealth of Australia [[(as amended)]] [[to carry on banking business]].
14  <<and take all steps necessary to obtain>>
15  2. That St. George Building Society Ltd. apply to be registered as a company under the Corporations Law.
16  3. That the name [[under which St. George Building Society Ltd. applies to be registered as a company]] be St. George Bank Limited.
17  4. That St. George Building Society Ltd. adopt a memorandum and articles of association on its registration as a company in the form [[signed for identification by the chairman of St. George Building Society Ltd.]].
18  A vote in this postal ballot by an eligible voting member of St. George in favour of, or against, the proposal, shall be taken as a vote by that member in favour of, or against, << 19 >>, each of these resolutions.
19  <<as the case may be>>
20  Ballot papers for the postal ballot will be sent to eligible voting members of St. George on or before 9 March 1992.
21  Eligibility of a member to vote in this postal ballot is determined in accordance with Rule 90 of the Rules of St. George.
22  The date [[for determining members' eligibility to vote in the postal ballot]] is 21 February 1992.

23 Ballot papers will not be sent to any eligible voting member: [[who has given a 'no mail' direction to St. George || or who has not advised St. George of his or her current correct address]].

24 Eligible voting members in these categories may contact the returning officer

25 to obtain ballot papers.

26 The postal ballot closes on 30 March 1992.

27 Ballot papers should be returned to the returning officer at the address below:

> PF Wales (Partner, BDO Binder)
> Returning Officer
> GPO Box 2712
> SYDNEY NSW 2001

28 For enquiries [[concerning voting in the postal ballot]], call the returning officer on: (02) 286 5791 during the hours of 9.00 am to 5.00 pm weekdays.

29 For all other enquiries [[concerning the proposal]], call St. George Direct on: (008) 801 132 during the hours of 9.00 am to 5.00 pm weekdays.

# 3. Researching first language development in children

*Clare Painter*

## 3.1 The domain of child language research

We are born with neither the power of speech nor of understanding language yet it is our capacity for language that perhaps discriminates us most from other species; and it is our engagement in language behaviour that most surely defines who we are. It is not surprising, then, that understanding how an individual makes the transition to becoming a talker has long been a matter of great interest to scholars pursuing a variety of concerns and questions. While the linguist addresses language development in order to ask and answer questions about the nature of language itself – its forms, organization, functions and role in human life – other scholars focus on matters other than language which can be illuminated by a study of children's linguistic development. Such inquiries may involve questions about different forms of socialization, about the child's developing mind, imagination or moral sensibility, or questions about processes of learning in early childhood. However, where these issues are explored through the collection and analysis of 'child language' data, research must draw not only on psychological, sociological or educational theories but on insights from linguistics about the structure and functions of language itself, its relation to the contexts of its use and its potential for change. Child language is thus a multi-disciplinary domain crucially informed by understandings drawn from linguistics.

## 3.2 Aspects of SFL theory relevant to child language research

SFL theory is a linguistic model that has the advantage for interdisciplinary studies that its conception of language necessarily implicates issues of social and cognitive development in any consideration of first language development. As explained in Chapter 1, the theory argues that the adult language system is 'metafunctionally' organized, that is it comprises sets of options that relate to meanings of three different kinds. There are interpersonal options that allow us to interact with others to express feelings and points of view; there are ideational options that allow us to represent experience; and there are textual options that allow us to create coherent text while we do this. Each of these sets of choices is sensitive to different aspects of the local situational context, which in turn has a place in realizing broader cultural meanings.

In this model, then, the process of language development from birth is necessarily one of building up social and cultural understandings as well as linguistic ones. This allows us to study language development as a way of exploring the child's development as a social subject. In addition, a study of language development from an SFL perspective is a study of conceptual development. If language itself is theorized as a system for meaning, including an ideational component which functions in the interpretation of reality, then in exploring its development we are exploring the individual's growing capacity to make sense of experience. This means that as we map children's changing linguistic 'meaning potential' we simultaneously build a picture of their knowledge and capacity to think using symbols. And since children's knowledge is created interactively in talk with others, an exploration of language development can also be an exploration of the processes of teaching and learning.

An important aspect of the theory is the fact that although we may think of language as a generalized system 'inside' the head of the speaker, it is actualized as speech – as specific and fragmented instances of behaviour on specific occasions of use. There is no sharp dichotomy set up in SFL between the system and the use of language; they are seen as two perspectives on the same phenomenon. This means that we can look to speech for evidence of the 'underlying' system. It also allows us to explain the possibility of change in the system. To explore change we must remember that meaning is something actualized between two minds in the process of dialogue. Young children and their dialogue partners obviously do not share exactly the same meaning potential, but together the two parties must, in any conversation, negotiate an actual text which is meaningful and relevant to both. In the process, the child may be able to make sense of a particular linguistic form for the first time or may come to attempt a new meaning. In other words, the contingencies of the spontaneous interaction may lead to a new understanding or may lead the child to produce an utterance that is in some way 'beyond' what has gone before. Such a text will then minutely 'perturb' the child's current system. Then, if new cases of the same kind subsequently occur, the child's system may adjust to accommodate new meaning choices. By tracking changes over time in the nature of the speech uttered we can infer changes to the child's linguistic system – the meaning-making potential.

### 3.3 Collecting developmental data

I have argued that children's changing speech patterns provide the essential data for exploring their changing meaning systems, but collecting suitable samples requires considerable thought. Partly reflecting the different research strategies of different disciplines, child language studies have typically used one or more of three broad kinds of methodologies: the experimental, what might loosely be called the 'semi-structured' observational approach and the unstructured longitudinal case study. Each of these approaches has its own advantages and pitfalls but for those researching within the SFL framework, the most suitable data are samples of naturally occurring speech in context. The longitudinal case study has therefore had the most appeal.

### 3.3.1 Experimental studies

Experimental work in language development often involves designing a task to elicit a particular kind of language form from the child or to provide evidence of its comprehension. The great advantage of a well-designed experiment is that it is a speedy and economical way to collect data. However, quite apart from the fact that infants and very young children may not be very cooperative subjects and may 'tune out' to a task or attempt to subvert it, the very nature of the experimental paradigm can be problematic in language studies. The experimental method is premised upon the notion that all variables can be controlled apart from the specific one being isolated for attention. But linguistic phenomena are intrinsically relational rather than discrete. A child's ability with regard to a single grammatical choice, such as the passive voice or the quantifier 'more', cannot be cleanly isolated from any textual context relevant to the use of that option. And of course the influence of the experiment as itself a semiotic context impinging upon the speech produced needs always to be borne in mind.

Such issues come to the fore even more strikingly when interactional patterns are under investigation. One research question that has been pursued for the past twenty-five years is the issue of whether and how an adult's contribution to conversation with children might constitute an implicit 'language lesson' (e.g. Snow and Ferguson 1979, Gallaway and Richards 1994). The issue is to identify exactly which of the distinguishing features of 'caregiver' speech (also called 'motherese' or 'child-directed speech') facilitate language learning. For example, we know that adults frequently 'expand' or 'recast' a child's utterance, as in the following example:

C: Bird; eat
M: Yes, the bird's eating

Several well-known studies have attempted to demonstrate the efficacy of recasting as a teaching strategy by comparing groups of conversationalists, in one of which the mothers are directed to recast all or certain types of the children's utterances in particular ways (Cazden 1965, Nelson *et al.* 1973, Nelson 1977). The children's speech is then examined at a later date to see whether the experimental group has made faster progress. The problem arises in extrapolating from an experimental result to a generalization about styles of caregiver speech in everyday life, since asking parents to monitor their speech and to respond in a prescribed way obviously disturbs much that would have been characteristic of any actual mother/child interaction where the adult would be quite unconscious of her speech patterns, including when and why she recasts the child's speech.

In sum, while there has certainly been valuable experimental work done in child language, this methodology has also been responsible for a general tendency to underestimate young children's abilities. It has also proved difficult to design worthwhile experiments from which generalizations can be drawn about the interactive processes of language learning as they occur in the contexts of everyday life.

### 3.3.2 'Semi-structured' observations

For the reasons I have outlined, developmental researchers frequently attempt to gain more 'natural' data by substituting observation for experiment. I will use the term 'semi-structured' for any method which abandons the attempt to constrain the context so as to elicit or produce a specific range of desired responses or grammatical forms, but which is designed to gain stretches of speech that are in some way comparable and pertinent to the particular issues being explored. In effect this means constructing a context of situation within which language can occur and then sampling the speech of different children within such a context. For example, Katherine Nelson and her colleagues proposed that children gradually develop mental 'scripts' of repeated events involving a recognizable sequence of actions and a 'cast' of 'players'. To explore this they asked young children of different ages '*What happens when . . .?*' questions about familiar events like going to McDonald's or having lunch at the childcare centre (Nelson and Gruendel 1981). While this is still 'experimental' research in that the interaction between the child and researcher exists solely for the purpose of eliciting speech in order to explore a hypothesis or theoretical point, the interaction is analogous to one that might occur elsewhere, in that an interested adult poses a question about the child's experience and does not attempt to shape or intervene in the discourse in any particular way.

Even less structured are some of the many studies which bring a parent and child into an environment (such as an audio-visual recording studio) where they can be recorded as they interact together. Sometimes parent and child are simply left alone to play and chat. Alternatively the context may be more constrained, with the mother instructed to incorporate particular kinds of props, toys, games or situations, such as a book-reading session. Such episodes provide an opportunity for observing any number of things, whether focusing on the caregiver (e.g. examining the mother's intonational patterns as done by Garnica 1977, Fernald and Mazzie 1991), or on the linguistic interactional style of the mother-child pair (e.g. Howe 1981) or on the language of the children (e.g. strategies for enacting imaginative play, as explored in Bretherton 1989).

### 3.3.3 Observations of the child in the contexts of everyday life

A final option is to study children in their own environment without intervening to set up special activities or tasks. Sometimes speech recording is done 'by proxy', asking parents to keep records (e.g. of new vocabulary). However, the details a parent can be expected to keep track of are limited and so this would be most useful as a supplementary source of data in a semi-structured study (as in Bloom 1993). Parents could be asked to audio-record conversations, as has been done for semantic variation studies (see Chapter 7). This might be feasible for a simulated longitudinal study (see Section 3.4), but it is unwise to expect parents to undertake long-term responsibility for the chore of collecting regular samples of conversation.

Because of this, a more frequent option is for the researcher to pay regular visits to a family (or families), to observe and record the child/children in whatever interactions occur (e.g. Scollon 1976, Miller 1982, Dunn and Dale 1984). Where the researcher is an observer only, and not an insider, there is of course greater risk of failing to capture the most natural data. And, as in other contexts of collecting spoken language, one has to balance the value of having a visual as well as audio record against the greater constraints on the language and activity produced by intrusive recording apparatus. In order to understand the context in which speech is occurring, it is advisable to keep field notes of as many relevant details of the situational and cultural context as possible. This 'ethnographic' approach recognizes the relation between context and text and has been used by researchers exploring the development of language in other cultures (see in particular Ochs and Schieffelin 1984).

Now that so many children attend pre-school or other forms of child-care from a very early age, this more institutional environment may also be of especial interest since it is a major part of the child's daily life. Researchers can make visits over a period of time to observe the children in their everyday routines within this setting. This may be particularly appropriate where the development of strategies for verbal conflict or collaboration between peers is of interest (as in Sheldon 1990). It is also crucial for addressing questions of comparisons between the home and the childcare/preschool institution as learning environments for children (e.g. Tizard and Hughes 1986). The main drawback is the practical one of collecting spoken language data in a noisy setting with active and mobile subjects. Pilot studies and trial runs of equipment are certainly advisable.

### 3.3.3.1 Participant/observer case studies

Finally, if you are lucky enough to have an infant or young child within your own family or household, you will be in an ideal position to undertake a case study of that child's language development over a particular period. Here you will be adopting the role of a 'participant-observer'. Parental 'diary' studies in particular have provided a rich source of data over the years (e.g. Leopold 1949, Bloom 1973, Kuczaj and Maratsos 1975, Fletcher 1985 for non SFL studies). This is also the method that has been employed by most of the research done so far within the SFL framework (e.g. Halliday 1975, Painter 1984, 1987, 1990, 1999, Torr 1998), where a single child has been the focus of a development case study.

Of course a case study by its very nature provides a limited set of data in that it tells us about only one child's development. That child is situated socially in terms of gender, position in the family, family's social-class positioning and so on, quite apart from specific traits of personality among family members and attitudes towards parenting, which make every individual's development in some sense a unique story. Yet despite the uncertainty of how generalizable case study findings may be, the longitudinal case study of a single child's language by a family member has a number of particular advantages:

- It provides the best opportunity to collect data naturalistically and to observe learning in the contexts in which it is actually taking place.
- It allows the researcher the best access to the intertextual history of any text; that is, to previous relevant conversations the child has participated in.
- It allows for the most reliable recording of new developmental moves.
- It allows for language to be observed and recorded in a variety of contexts, which is advantageous for an exploratory study.

### 3.3.4 Dealing with the time dimension in data collection

Obviously if we are interested in studying development, we need data which can display changes in the child's language over time. Longitudinal case studies are ideal for this. However, not every researcher has the luxury of actually collecting longitudinal data over a period of months or years. One way round this is to simulate a longitudinal study by collecting data at one point in time from groups of children of different ages. Even though age is only a rough guide to stage of linguistic development, it may be possible to infer patterns of development from the differences observed in the speech of children of different ages. While it may be less easy to address issues of how changes evolve, this approach can certainly provide a workable compromise when time is limited.

The other possibility, where time is not available for longitudinal research, is to make use of data already collected by other researchers, who may have been looking at different questions. The most useful source currently available is the expanding CHILDES data base (Child Language Data Exchange System) which includes data from a number of naturalistic longitudinal studies of English-speaking children. This is a much larger data set than any one research project would be likely to accumulate (though it contains no Australian data) and is available on CD-ROM. Another feature is that the data are stored in a form which allows for mechanical searching of the set for particular language items, although not in terms of the kind of rich functional description of English grammar provided by Halliday (1994). Nonetheless, CHILDES provides researchers with the kind of access to data on children's speech which cannot be obtained from the published literature. MacWhinney and Snow (1990) and MacWhinney (1995) should be consulted for details of this resource and how to make use of it.

### 3.4 Transcribing naturalistic data

The first step towards analysis is to obtain a transcription of all or part of the audio or audio-visual record. Many issues and procedures are essentially the same as for the analysis of any conversational material (see Chapter 6), but there are additional points to consider in a developmental study, some of which are usefully addressed by Ochs (1979), and Bloom (1993, 1993a). One issue that arises when using data from very young children concerns the importance of including information on non-verbal behaviours, which may carry a considerable weight of meaning, but for which transcription procedures are not standardized. Another issue is the problem of transcribing pre-linguistic vocalizing, which requires the use of phonetic notation and some system for recording intonation contours, even if the phonology is not the particular focus of the study.

### 3.5 Linguistic coding of developmental data

Much applied language research which is based on text data involves analysing discourse in terms of one or more of the systems of meanings which have been described for English in such sources as Halliday (1994), Halliday and Hasan (1984), Martin (1992). Having analysed the text, or 'coded' the particular linguistic features being focused on, it is possible to count instances, compare speakers, compare the same speaker in different contexts or at different points in time, make interpretations about the meanings being built up, and so on. However, in a developmental study using data from infants and young children who do not yet control the adult choices, our concern is with the range of options we can justifiably infer that the child controls rather than simply with the options taken up on a particular occasion on the assumption that all are available. In other words, we are not necessarily taking any description of English as a template to be superimposed on the text.

The following brief excerpt of family conversation is an example of some of the issues. (Note that this text has been transcribed at a very general level of detail with lexical renderings of the child's pronunciation and simple 'stage directions' on intonation and non-verbal action.)

**Text 3.1**

Child 18 months, 10 days. C=child, M=mother, F=father
(C runs into parents' bedroom, holding stuffed koala toy. M and F are having coffee in bed)

| | | |
|---|---|---|
| 1. | C: | Teddy, teddy [falling tone] |
| 2. | M: | Yeah |
| 3. | C: | Up, up, up, up [level tone] (C is lifted onto bed) |
| 4. | F: | (indecipherable) |
| 5. | C: | (lies on stomach on bed) More; more [high pitch, level tone] |
| 6. | M: | More what? We haven't done anything yet. |
| 7. | | Oh, the tickly game. (Tickles C's neck with furry koala toy) |
| 8. | C: | (Giggles) |
| 9. | M: | (Tickling) Tickly tickly teddy |
| 10. | C: | More [high level tone] (other indecipherable speech) |
| 11. | | Teddy, teddy, teddy (dangling it over side of bed) |
| 12. | | Down; up [falling tone] (laughs as lifts teddy and climbs onto F) |
| 13. | F: | Hello! You're a cheerful little soul this morning aren't you? (turns to M and chats about this and that) |
| 14 | C: | (looking up) Kooky, koohing [falling tone] |
| 15 | M: | Cooking? |
| 16 | C: | Kochy [falling tone]; allgone [sing song tone] |
| 17. | M: | Coffee |
| 18. | F: | Coffee! All gone. |
| 19. | C: | Coffee [falling tone] |
| 20. | F: | Get your finger out of your nose (to M) He's always poking his finger up his nose |
| 21. | C: | Nose (pointing) nyose; chin [falling tone] (points at cheek) |
| 22. | M: | That's the cheek (pointing carefully) cheek (points) chin (points) cheek (points) |
| 23. | C: | (giggles and romps with F) Teddy! (picking it up) |
| 24. | | Cuddle! [rise-falling tone] (turning to M) |
| 25. | M: | Cuddle? Going to cuddle with Mummy? (opening arms) |
| 26. | C: | Cuddle [falling tone] (clambering on M) |

Let us assume that we are interested in undertaking an analysis of interpersonal meaning here. As far as an adult's speech is concerned, it would be relevant to consider the mood structure of each clause, which would in turn require decisions about whether a verbless utterance like 'Yeah' (2) or 'Oh the tickly game' (7) should be regarded as a 'minor' clause, lacking any grammatical clause structure or as an abbreviated 'elliptical' structure (e.g. an elliptical declarative). In principle, an elliptical structure allows the hearer to 'fill in' some wording that has just previously been uttered. But there may be cases where there is no preceding wording, but some part of the grammatical structure can still be 'filled in' from the immediate context of situation. This applies for example when a speaker omits the second person Subject, and the associated Finite, when asking a question, or making an offer, as in line 25, when M says '[Are you]Going to cuddle with Mummy?' (see Halliday 1994: 94). The point is that adult speech will contain 'reduced' structures of both kinds (minor and elliptical) and while there may be uncertainty about a particular case, we can be confident that any adult native speaker's system allows for either of these options.

With the child the situation is different. This text exemplifies how children's first mother-tongue utterances are likely to be single-word and then two-word structures. These may look similar or identical to elliptical adult forms; indeed the adult partner may make an interpretation in terms of her own system and treat them as if elliptical. But if we are trying to map the options available to the child, then a child who has not yet produced a full grammatical structure can hardly be making use of the option of ellipting it. Nor can the child be said to be consistently choosing the option of 'minor' clause since there is no contrasting option within the child's system. Ultimately grammatical choices realize meanings and our interpretations of a text depend on our 'reading' of those meanings. If we code the text for choices that are not part of the system, the interpretations we make on the basis of that coding will be questionable.

How then can one approach a text of this kind? First, of course, one would need rather more evidence than a single tiny example to make inferences about the child's linguistic abilities. But assuming that other data from this period were entirely comparable, two principles for analysis can be suggested. The first is that meaning rather than form should be the 'way in' to the text. For interpersonal analysis this means exploring the (proto) speech functions or conversational moves that the child makes, rather than trying to use grammatical mood choices as the starting point. In the above text, we could argue for the child's ability to initiate an exchange (e.g. lines 1, 3, 5, 14, 24) and to respond at least to 'clarification' moves by the adult (e.g. lines 16, 19). (See Eggins and Slade 1997 for description of move types.)

The second principle is to consider both the meaning choices and the realizations in terms of 'oppositions' or contrasts that are evident from the child's speech rather than the complete adult system. In Text 3.1, this would mean taking account of the child's intonation choices and how these relate to speech function. The excerpt illustrates how this child made a distinction between moves which demanded action from the adult and were coded with a high level tone (e.g. lines 3, 5, 10) and other moves which had a falling (or rise-falling tone). These latter seem to function to provide a commentary on his own actions (e.g. lines 11, 12, 23, 24, 26) or to label or comment on things around him (e.g. lines 1, 14, 16, 19, 21). There is no evidence here for the child's ability to ask questions or indeed to answer them, apart from giving confirming responses to clarification requests, so we cannot say that the child simply has different realizations for the English speech function system. The case is rather that the child has a different and simpler speech function system – one allowing for demanding and commenting moves, as initiations or responses to requests for clarification. This system is realized through a simple intonation choice overlaid on ideational meanings realized as single words.

The ideational meanings in turn cannot be described in terms of the TRANSITIVITY choices of adult clause grammar. They are better seen in terms of contrasts between a linguistic representation of actions (realized by adult verbs and prepositions: *cuddle, down, up*) things (realized by nouns: *coffee, teddy, nose, cheek*) and an attribute (realized by *allgone* with its own special intonation).

Let us now consider an analogous situation with an older child, one who *has* developed grammatical choices at clause rank and who uses both full and elliptical clauses:

**Text 3.2**
(C is 2 years, 5 months)
M:       Did you like Jimmy's ditch digger truck?
C:       Yes; *I* might get one of those trucks.

Here, the clause *I might get one of those trucks* is a perfectly viable utterance in terms of the adult grammar of English. In terms of that grammar, *might* would be coded as realizing the MODALITY features of [modalization: probability] and [low value] (see Chapter 2). Now suppose that for the child, *might* appears to realize the modal meaning of probability but this is the child's *only* modalization option. We can adopt one of two stances towards the analysis. We can begin with a model of the adult system (see Halliday 1994), whereby [modalization] allows for options of both [probability] and [usuality] and can be realized as a verb (*might*) or an adverb (*possibly*), depending on whether the 'ORIENTATION' is implicitly [subjective] or [objective]. The adult system also includes choices for different degrees of 'MODAL VALUE' (i.e. [high] (*must, certainly*), [median] (*will, probably*) or [low] (*might, possibly*)). When we analyse the child's structure we can choose to analyse the structure just as we would an adult one (i.e. as realizing the options [probability], [median value] and [subjective orientation]). Strictly speaking, however, the child's system does not have such fine-grained choices, so we are overinterpreting if we do this, just as we overinterpret the one-word-at-a-time speaker if we imply grammatical choices not yet available.

The particular goals and orientation of any study may, however, make this question of placing an 'adult' interpretation on the child's speech more or less of an issue. If we are trying to work out the contrasts that constitute the options of the child's language at this time – in other words, if we are interested in mapping the *system* underlying these structures – then we will certainly want to avoid suggesting that this child has a system of MODAL VALUE or of [subjective]/[objective] ORIENTATION. (Within the child's system there is simply the choice of modalizing or not.) If, on the other hand, we wish to explore this particular text in the light of the 'target' adult language and in the light of its ongoing interpretation by interactants controlling that language, then we could be less worried about the 'distortion' of seeing it as an instantiation of the adult system. In other words, depending on the research questions being addressed, our focus may be on mapping the contrasts of the child's system in its own terms or on analysing the child's text as manifesting a limited range of the options of the adult system. The important thing is to be clear that analysing child speech in terms of the full adult system is taking a particular perspective on the data, one very much oriented to the end goal of development and to adult interpretations, rather than to the current potential in its own terms.

Ideally, if you maintain a consciousness that the child's language system is not the same as the adult's, you are more likely to be sensitive to both the absences and the presences in the text, a requisite in fact for a functional linguistic analysis of any text. Absences – options not taken up – define and delimit the meaning of the choices that *are* instantiated. In a text involving an immature speaker, the meanings not realized (e.g. differing modal values) need to be considered not just in the light of what the adult might have chosen (but didn't) but in the light of what possibilities were open to the child in terms of his/her system. Presences – the lexico-grammatical (and phonological) forms in the text – must be interpreted not just in terms of what they realize from the adult meaning potential, but what meaning they appear to instantiate for the child, which is not always the same thing.[1]

### 3.6  Framing research

*3.6.1  The SFL account of initial language development*

One theoretically possible goal for a developmental study is to map the emergence/growth of the entire language system from its origins. An undertaking as ambitious as this obviously requires the most broad-ranging data collection possible, so that all available forms arising in any context of use are captured. Clearly, the smaller the system, the more feasible this is. Such a goal is realistic only for the very earliest phase of language development. A famous study of this kind is Halliday's (1975) landmark study of his son, Nigel, up to the age of two, which has been supplemented by my own study of Hal (Painter 1984, 1990) and Torr's (1998) case study of Anna. (Note that even these single child studies do not explore the whole language, they ignore the evolution of the phonological stratum.)

Briefly, these studies have provided the basis for proposing three phases in the development of language. Phase one begins at about nine months of age and continues for about six months. This is the period of what Halliday calls the 'protolanguage', a set of baby vocalizations and/or gestures whose forms are idiosyncratic to the infant and do not constitute words of the adult language. They carry meanings like 'I want that', 'I like that' or 'you do that' and fulfil four to six different functions in the baby's life. Phase two is a transitional period, again lasting about six months, when the child begins to use words of the mother tongue and later grammatical structures. During this period the child's utterances meet one of two quite general functions: either that of acting on other people (pragmatic function) or that of learning about the world (mathetic function); these two functions may be discriminated by a distinction in intonation (see Text 3.1). During this period, however, there is no true information-giving by the child, no telling of an experience genuinely unknown to the other, since the child does not conceive of language as a means of creating an unshared reality. Phase three begins once the function of information exchange is understood and the parallel grammatical choices of MOOD and TRANSITIVITY are used to render every utterance both interpersonal and representational (ideational) in status.

### 3.6.1.1 Questions arising from SFL studies of initial language development

The three case studies mentioned earlier provide a fascinating picture of similarities and differences among the children in their protolanguages and their routes into the adult grammar. At the same time, the current data base is small, even when considered together with non-systemic studies, such as those of Bates (1976), Dore (1975), Carter (1978) and others, which have explored the earliest phases of language development. Further research would therefore be valuable and welcome and you can refer to the studies cited for 'how to' issues of data collection and analysis. Some of the questions which remain to be answered on the basis of SFL research so far include:

1.  Do symbols arise initially as a set of choices at around nine months or is there earlier experimentation by the baby in the creation of vocal/gestural symbols? (See Halliday 1978.)
2.  What is the minimum/maximum range of protolanguage functions?
3.  Do all children distinguish phonologically between mathetic and pragmatic speech in the early transition phase?
4.  Which function – mathetic or pragmatic – provides the major impetus for new grammatical developments?
5.  What are the typical contexts for initial information-giving by the child?

6. What are the possible routes into a metafunctional grammar?
7. When and how does the textual metafunction emerge? (See Halliday 1979.)

As well as telling us more about infants and their capacities, answers to these questions would address fundamental theoretical issues in linguistics: questions about the nature of symbols, the universality or specificity of the communicative intents of human infants, the different semiotic possibilities of different kinds of symbol systems (protolanguage, language), the relation between the organization of the grammar and its functions in human life, and so on.

### 3.6.2 Framing new research questions informed by SFL

Understanding the emergence of language is of enormous theoretical importance within both linguistics and psychology, but directly adopting Halliday's own research goals and methods is by no means the only way to use SFL theory to inform developmental research. The model outlined in Chapter 1 can be used to find principled ways to focus attention more narrowly than on 'the developing language' and to allow for the exploration of more specific and/or applied issues. In general terms, the model suggests the possibility of focusing on any of genre, register or language, and within these, on any particular genre, any of the three register variables (field, tenor, mode) or on any level, metafunction or system of the language itself. In what follows I will elaborate on this a little and refer you to relevant child language studies for further exploration of the field.

### 3.6.2.1 Development of a generic text type

According to SFL, an important aspect of becoming a member of the culture is learning to participate in the generic forms that are recognizable to its members. A key issue concerns the spoken genres young children participate in, and at what age and in what manner they learn to do so. These questions are of interest from a number of different perspectives, including that of educators who have become increasingly engaged in children's development of written genres in school, such as recount, narrative and exposition (Cope and Kalantzis 1993).

Since no genre will emerge fully fledged, it may be important to focus here on the key features of the text type in question and its most basic linguistic realizations, so that over time it is possible to observe how additional stages or features of the genre are incorporated. (See Eggins and Slade 1997 for details of conversational genres.) So for example, with any of the storying genres, the temporal sequencing of events is fundamental; with argument, it is the contradicting of another position.

With this in mind, it will be possible to extract relevant segments from an unstructured longitudinal study.[2] Alternatively, a context can be set up or monitored within which the genre or proto-genre under attention is likely to be engaged in. For example American children's argument texts have been studied in peer group play by Goodwin and Goodwin (1987) and Sheldon (1990), while Beals and Snow (1994) look at family dinner table talk as a context for proto-narrating and explaining. For a consideration of children's knowledge of (rather than performance of) a 'language as action' genre (eating out), there is also Nelson and Gruendel's (1981) work on 'scripts'. All of this research gives us some insight into children's abilities, though since much of it is not focused on developmental change, there is still plenty to find out about how children learn to participate in or produce generic forms.

### 3.6.2.2 Focusing on a particular context for speech

While genres realize culturally recognizable ways of achieving culturally recognizable goals and their development relates very obviously to the child's becoming a member of the socio-cultural group, the relation of language use to the immediate situational context is also a fruitful one to explore developmentally. SFL theory suggests that language is systematically linked to the immediate situational context in that ideational meanings realize field, interpersonal meanings realize tenor and textual meanings realize mode. At the same time, our developmental studies also suggest that many of the first instantiations of ideational meanings arise in contexts which focus on 'goods and service' exchange or which are charged with affect (see Halliday 1993, Painter 1996, 1999), so it is not always obvious what kind of context will provide optimum opportunities for deploying *new* meanings. For anyone with responsibility for organizing the contexts of a child's life to maximize opportunities for language development, explorations of the effect of variation in situational variables must therefore be of interest.

One kind of exploration would be to monitor the child's development and use of language within two or more contexts (identified as combinations of field, tenor and mode), such as reading a book with a parent, eating meals with the family, playing board games with a sibling, playing imaginative games with age-peers, and so on. You could then use SFL to focus your analysis and interpret any differences you found. For example, if the main difference in the contexts related to field (e.g. playing different kinds of games with peers) then you would be guided to analyse the data in terms of systems such as TRANSITIVITY (i.e. verbalization of who does what, who is what, what is the case, how things are done, etc.) and LOGICAL RELATIONS (e.g. verbalization of giving explanations). However, because one register variable may impinge upon another and one linguistic metafunction may impinge upon another, you must always be sensitive to the possibility that a shift in the field entails some overlooked or unpredicted shift in tenor or in mode (perhaps the role of non-verbally realized meanings in the latter case). Becoming alert to this is a matter of noticing differences in the text at an intuitive level and determining which metafunction and which register variable seems to be involved. This can then guide you as to what further linguistic analysis might be useful. A general observation of difference in turn-taking patterns would suggest that tenor and the interpersonal metafunction are at stake. You would explore this further by looking in more detail at interpersonal linguistic systems. Similarly a difference noted in the degree of dependence on the non-verbal meanings would imply that mode varies across the contexts studied, suggesting that aspects of the textual metafunction should be examined, such as ELLIPSIS (leaving part of the message understood), REFERENCE (e.g. use of words like *this, that, it, there*) or given and new INFORMATION (placement of 'stress' within the clause).

An example of a small study framed in terms of register is one conducted by Irene Higgins (1990), in which a major research question was whether playing a 'problem-solving' computer game with a partner is a context which promotes the language development of school-aged children. She analysed the texts in terms of PROCESS TYPE and LOGICAL RELATIONS, being particularly interested in how the field was realized and whether mental processes were used by the children to reflect on their problem-solving in utterances like *We know it can't be Peking because they speak Chinese* or *We know where that is cause it's Aborigines.*

Interestingly, Higgins found that language of this type occurred only between the two boys partnered and that different, more interpersonal, areas of the language were foregrounded in speech between two girl partners. A change in tenor had resulted from the girls' less competitive, less goal-oriented interpretation of the task, and this affected not only the interpersonal choices but ideational ones. Comparison with a different game also revealed a marked difference in the extent to which different games actually depended on verbalization between the partners for their successful completion, making it clear that the mode, as well as field, varied between one game and another.

To keep a research study more constrained and tightly focused, you would limit the register variation as much as possible to a single variable. For example, the same kind of activity (field) could be involved, making the same general demands on language (mode) but involving different interactant roles and relations (tenor), as would be the case between parent and child, child and peer, child and preschool carer. To explore the effect of this variation on the child's potential for linguistic expression, the data on the same activity, such as eating a meal, reading books or playing games, could be collected at home and at preschool, or at home with mother and at home with sibling or friend.

The data could then be explored for the use, and changes over time in the use, of the kinds of interpersonal meanings one would expect to be affected by variation in tenor: SPEECH FUNCTION, MOOD, MODALITY, ATTITUDE, and so on. In this way a contribution would be made to understanding whether any one of these contexts was a potentially richer one for fostering development. By working with a model of context/text relations, you can reflect in a systematic way about contexts for learning and languaging and you will have a rationale for determining what aspects of the language system will most fruitfully be addressed. Conversely, if your research is addressed to some aspect of the language system, the use of which is to be explored (e.g. questions), the model is useful for setting up comparable or contrasting contexts of situation likely to produce relevant data.

### 3.6.2.3 Exploring a semantic domain

For those interested in cognitive development, children's changing use of language can provide access to their developing understandings. Your concern may be with a particular area of meaning like time, causality, number, the 'mental world', or with particular strategies of meaning like hypothesizing, making evaluations, making comparisons, and so on. Any particular domain or strategy of meaning may be realized across different areas of the grammar and may serve to construct a variety of types of text. For example, the area of 'hypothetical meaning' may be realized as a relation between clauses, constructing clause complexes linked with *if*, or initiated with *suppose* . . . or could be realized within the clause as a modal Adjunct (*possibly*) or a Finite (*might, could*). It may turn up in contexts where control, instruction, exploration or imaginative purposes are foregrounded in the situation. Similarly, meanings related to time may be realized through many grammatical systems (tense within the verbal group), circumstantial elements of the clause (such as *in the morning*), nominals (such as *time, ten years*), dependent clauses (such as *before we get home*), and so on.

For addressing questions of social formation, interpersonal semantics would be particularly relevant. For example, meanings related to 'point of view' could be documented over time to give us some insight into the child's changing angle on experience. Such meanings gain expression through PROJECTION as a form of clause combining (e.g. direct and indirect speech), comment Adjuncts (e.g. *unfortunately*), MODALITY within the clause, modifications of verbal groups (e.g. *seems to, tends to*), and so on.

Working with a semantically oriented functional grammar suggests, then, another way of angling the lens in a developmental study so as to focus on a particular domain of meaning to find out which areas of the grammar develop before others and in what kinds of situational and cultural contexts. The approach to analysis would be to focus on the semantic territory of interest and to use a resource like Halliday's (1994) functional grammar of English to work out all the possible lexico-grammatical realizations to be coded. With longitudinal or simulated longitudinal data we could begin to map a developmental trail, or a multiplicity of trails (perhaps related to gender, position in the family or other social factors), for the development in everyday use of key areas of meaning.

### 3.6.2.4 Monitoring the development of a lexico-grammatical system

Since the various systems of the lexico-grammar serve to actualize meaning, it is still possible to reflect on the child's cognitive growth and learning potential even if we narrow our focus considerably by tracing the development of a single grammatical system. This would obviously also provide insights into aspects of the linguistic system itself. In this case, rather than beginning with a semantic domain and following multiple realizations across the grammar, we would have the more manageable task of coding realizations of a single grammatical system, allowing us to examine how it changes and grows and what expansion of meaning accompanies that growth.

As an exemplification, I will take 'conditional' conjunctive links as a linguistic system of interest, which has been explored in at least a few studies. For example, McCabe *et al.* (1983) looked at the language of siblings at play; French and Nelson (1985) asked children to explain what happens in various routine situations; and Painter (1999) looked at data on this topic from a single child recorded in conversations within the family.

The first step in any analysis of this kind is to understand the possible options of the adult system, then to identify all instantiations of the system (or rather the child's developing version of the system) in the data set being explored. In my own study, I used the SFL framework to code the data according to interpersonal and ideational criteria:

1. Each clause complex was coded according to what kind of conversational move (speech function) was involved. At the broadest level this meant distinguishing between instances where the exchange was negotiating goods and services (*if you take it, I'll scream*) and instances where the exchange was negotiating information (*if you put it there it will get wet*). It also meant noting dialogically achieved examples (*I don't want the fish – Have some chips then*).
2. To maintain a focus on meaning, grammatically parallel examples were discriminated according to the kind of ideational meaning being linked, such as a generalization based on familiar experience (*if you hit cats they scratch you*), a purely hypothetical case (*if a dragon bites you, your bones will go crunch*), and a logical syllogism (*if all cats eat meat then our cat eats meat*).
3. Focusing then on the logical structure, as another aspect of ideational meaning, each instance was coded according to its logical grammatical realization: whether hypotactic (*if you put it there it will get wet*) or paratactic (*I'll take my socks off, then it won't get wet*), whether external (linking ideational meanings) or internal (linking speech acts, e.g. *we must be early if Frank's not here*).

Using analytical tools such as these I was able to observe a developmental pattern in which the earliest use of the relation was interpersonally focused. It was used to support negotiation of action and to link across turns in a dialogue. Following this the relation was deployed to generalize relations between processes (*if you hit them, they scratch you*), then to explore alternative and purely hypothetical experience. Internal links developed next but were used rarely, while the final development was the use of the relation to explore logical inconsistency (*if X is the case, how come Y does not follow?*).

Findings such as these are clearly open to interpretations about the child's developing ability to use language as a tool for thinking, which was the principal focus of this study. Equally, such data allow for observations about the course of language change. For a linguist, it is relevant to observe how the architecture of a system can change as the system grows. It is equally relevant of course to focus on the role of text here, in other words the extent to which adult models were understood and taken up verbatim or adapted for new situations, which will be of more obvious relevance for conclusions about processes of learning or socialization.

Using the tools of a functional grammar, many other grammatical systems could be fruitfully examined. Where interpersonal systems such as modality are under focus, naturalistic data would be particularly valuable since such systems are so susceptible to distortion from highly structured data collection methods.

### 3.6.2.5 Examining the role of caregiver speech

While the focus of discussion in this chapter has been on the child's language, any approach such as SFL which is oriented to the development of meaning is necessarily an interactive approach. This suggests the need to analyse not only the child's changing language but the speech addressed to the child and the relations between the two. It is well known that, in many cultures, children are addressed in distinctive ways and the influence of adult dialogue partners on the course of development has been hotly debated for many years (see Gallaway and Richards 1994). Ideas from Vygotskyan learning theory concerning children's 'zone of proximal development' (1978) and the notion of adult speech as a form of 'scaffolding' for the child's development (Bruner 1978) can fruitfully be explored within any of the forms of framing suggested in this section as long as the speech of the child's dialogue partners is analysed as closely as that of the child. Ninio and Bruner's (1978) is a classic paper to refer to here, providing exemplification of adult support within the picture book reading situation. Painter (1986) also illustrates different aspects of the adult's scaffolding role, while Snow's (1983) exploration of 'deferred imitations' provides examples of a child's later incorporation of adult models into his own speech.

## 3.7 Conclusion

The development of a child's first language can be an intellectual site for exploring fascinating questions about language and about human development. However, it is neither a simple nor a speedy matter to collect useful data which display developmental patterns or bear on learning processes. Analysis of the data is complicated by the fact that descriptions of adult language cannot necessarily be imposed on the data, especially data from the very earliest phases, when the child's language system is furthest from the adult system. Nonetheless, as long as the focus is kept on the language as a system of meaning, the idiosyncratic nature of any of the child's forms can be dealt with in a systematic way. As well, a theoretical orientation to the language system as developing through its instantiation in speech in situational and cultural contexts provides the possibility of framing research to address a varied range of issues arising from a number of disciplinary perspectives.

## Notes

1. Some researchers, notably Greenfield and Smith (1976), have argued that as long as an ideational meaning was being analysed, 'missing' elements of the clause could be 'filled out' from the situation, but such an approach ignores the interpretive role of language and assumes that the child's task is simply to match words to elements of a pre-given 'situational structure'. A second problem is that if we are too oriented to the adult language we may fail to be sensitive to the possibility of the child adapting an adult form for a slightly different function or meaning. (See Halliday 1975: 31 for a fascinating example of this.)
2. See Painter 1986, 1989: 55–7 for some points on how an adult may 'scaffold' the child's production of simple recounts and anecdotes.

## References

Bates, E. (1976) *Language and Context: The Acquisition of Pragmatics.* New York: Academic.

Beals, D. E. and Snow, C.E. (1994) 'Thunder is when the angels are upstairs bowling': narratives and explanations at the dinner table.' *Journal of Narrative and Life History*, 4: 331–52.

Bloom, L. (1973) *One Word at a Time.* The Hague: Mouton.

Bloom, L. (1993) *The Transition from Infancy to Language: Acquiring the Power of Expression.* New York: Cambridge University Press.

Bloom, L. (1993a) Transcription and coding for child language research: the parts are more than the whole. In J.A. Edwards, M.D. Lampert (eds), *Talking Data: Transcription and Coding in Discourse Research.* Hillsdale: Erlbaum.

Bretherton, I. (ed.) (1984) *Symbolic Play: The Development of Social Understanding.* Orlando: Academic.

Carter, A. L. (1978) The development of systematic vocalizations prior to words. In N. Waterson and C. Snow (eds), *The Development of Communication*. New York: Wiley, 127–38.

Cazden, C. (1965) Environmental Assistance to the Child's Acquisition of Grammar. Unpublished doctoral dissertation, Harvard University.

Cope, W. and Kalantzis, M. (eds) (1993) *The Powers of Literacy: A Genre Approach to Teaching Literacy*. London: Falmer.

Dore, J. (1975) Holophrases, speech acts and language universals. *Journal of Child Language*, 2: 21–40.

Dunn, J. and Dale, N. (1984) I a Daddy: 2-year-olds collaboration in joint pretend with sibling and with mother. In I. Bretherton (ed.), *Symbolic Play: The Development of Social Understanding*. New York: Academic: 131–58.

Eggins, S. and Slade, D. (1979) *Analysing Casual Conversation*. London, Cassell.

Fernald, A. and Mazzie, C. (1991) Prosody and focus in speech to infants and adults. *Development Psychology*, 27(2): 209–21.

Fletcher, P. (1985) *A Child's Learning of English*. Oxford: Blackwell.

French, L. A. and Nelson, K. (1985) *Young Children's Knowledge of Relational Terms: Some Ifs, Ors, and Buts*. New York: Springer.

Gallaway, C. and Richards, B. J. (1994) *Input and Interaction in Language Acquisition*. Cambridge: Cambridge University Press.

Garnica, O. K. (1977) Some prosodic and paralinguistic features of speech to young children. In C. E. Snow and C. Ferguson, (eds), *Talking to Children: Language Input and Acquisition*. Cambridge: Cambridge University Press, 63–8.

Goodwin, M. H. and Goodwin, C. (1987) Children's arguing. In S.U Philips, S. Steele and C. Tanz (eds), *Language, Gender and Sex in Comparative Perspective*. Cambridge: Cambridge University Press, 200–49.

Greenfield, P. M. and Smith, J. H. (1976) *The Structure of Communication in Early Language Development*. New York: Academic.

Halliday, M. A. K. (1975) *Learning How to Mean*. London: Arnold.

Halliday, M. A. K. (1978) Meaning and the construction of reality in early childhood. In H. L. Pick and E. Saltzman (eds), *Modes of Perceiving and Processing of Information*. Hillsdale; Erlbaum, 67–96.

Halliday, M. A. K. (1979) The development of texture in child language. In T. Myers (ed.), *The Development of Conversation and Discourse*. Edinburgh: Edinburgh University Press, 72–87.

Halliday, M. A. K. (1993) Towards a language-based theory of learning. *Linguistics and Education* 5: 93–116.

Halliday, M. A. K. (1994) *Introduction to Functional Grammar* (2nd edn). London: Arnold.

Halliday, M. A. K. and Hasan, R. (1985) *Cohesion in English*. London: Cambridge University Press.

Higgins, I. (1990) Computers and language in a NSW primary school. Unpublished MATESOL Research Project Report, University of Technology, Sydney.

Howe, C. (1981) *Learning Language in a Conversational Context*. New York: Academic.

Kuczaj, S. and Maratsos, M. (1975) What children *can* say before they *will*. *Merrill-Palmer Quarterly*, 21: 87–111.

Leopold, W. F. (1949) *Speech Development of a Bilingual Child: A Linguist's Record.* Evanston: Northwestern University Press.

McCabe, A., Evely, D., Abramovitch, R., Corter, C. and Pepler, D. (1983) Conditional statements in young children's spontaneous speech. *Journal of Child Language,* 10: 253–8.

MacWhinney, B. (1995) Computational analysis of interactions. In P. Fletcher, and B. MacWhinney, *The Handbook of Child Language.* Oxford: Blackwell, 152–78.

MacWhinney, B. and Snow, C. (1990) The Child Language Data Exchange System: an update. *Journal of Child Language,* 17: 457–72.

Martin, J. R. (1992) *English Text: System and Structure.* Amsterdam: Benjamins.

Miller, P. J. (1982) *Amy, Wendy, and Beth: Learning Language in South Baltimore.* Austin: University of Texas Press.

Nelson, K. and Gruendel, J. (1981) Generalised event representations: basic building blocks of cognitive development. In A. Brown and M. Lamb (eds), *Advances in Developmental Psychology, vol. 1.* Hillsdale: Erlbaum, 131–58.

Nelson, K. E. (1977) Facilitating children's syntax acquisition. *Developmental Psychology,* 13: 101–7.

Nelson, K. E, Carskaddon, G. and Bonvillian, J.D. (1973) Syntax acquisition: impact of experimental variation in adult verbal interaction with the child. *Child Development,* 44: 497–504.

Ninio, A. and Bruner, J. (1978) The achievement and antecedents of labeling. *Journal of Child Language,* 5: 1–16.

Ochs, E. (1979) Transcription as theory. In E. Ochs and B.B. Schieffelin, *Developmental Pragmatics.* New York: Academic, 43–72.

Ochs, E. and Schieffelin, B. B. (1984) Language acquisition and socialization: three developmental stories and their implications. In R.A. Shweder and R.A. LeVine (eds), *Essays on Mind, Self, and Emotion.* Cambridge: Cambridge University Press, 276–320.

Painter, C. (1984) *Into the Mother Tongue.* London: Pinter.

Painter, C. (1986) The role of interaction in learning to speak and learning to write. In C. Painter and J.R. Martin (eds), *Writing to Mean: Teaching Genres Across the Curriculum.* Applied Linguistics Association of Australia (Occasional paper no. 9): 62–97.

Painter, C. (1989) Learning language: a functional view of language development. In R. Hasan and J.R. Martin (eds), *Language Development: Learning Language, Learning Culture: Meaning and Choice in Language: Studies in Honour of Michael Halliday.* Norwood: Ablex, 18–65.

Painter, C. (1990) *Learning the Mother Tongue* (2nd edn). Geelong: Deakin University Press.

Painter, C. (1996) The development of language as a resource for thinking: a linguistic view of learning. In R. Hasan and G. Williams (eds), *Literacy in Society.* London: Longmans, 50–85.

Painter, C. (in press) *Learning Through Language in Early Childhood.* London: Cassell.

Scollon, R. (1976) *Conversations With a One Year Old.* Honolulu: University of Hawaii Press.

Sheldon, A. (1990) Pickle fights: gendered talk in preschool disputes. *Discourse Processes,* 13: 5–31.

Snow, C.E. and Ferguson, C. (eds) (1979) *Talking to Children: Language Input and Acquisition*. Cambridge: Cambridge University Press.

Tizard, B. and Hughes, M. (1986) *Young Children Learning at Home and at School*. London: Fontana.

Torr, J. (1998) *From Child Tongue to Mother Tongue: A Case Study of Language Development in the First Two and a Half Years*. Nottingham: Nottingham University (Monographs in Systemic Linguistics).

Vygotsky, L. (1978) *Mind in Society: The Development of Higher Psychological Processes*, ed. M. Cole, V. John-Steiner, S.Scribner and E. Souberman. Cambridge, MA: Harvard University Press.

# 4 Researching second and foreign language development

*Gillian Perrett*

## 4.1 Introduction

Every human learns a first language, many also learn a second. The old monolingual perception that knowing only one language is the norm is challenged both by the fact that in many parts of the world a minority of people are monolingual and by the experience of living in communities which are becoming increasingly multicultural and in a world that is rapidly globalizing. While children learn their first language from their primary caregivers beginning from the first months of life, the circumstances in which subsequent languages develop vary enormously. Second language learners may be children, adolescents or adults. They may have access to their target language all of the time, some of the time, or for very short periods. They may take lessons, study alone, or 'pick it up' with varying degrees of awareness of what they are doing. Some learners will become fluent and accurate language users, others will achieve lower levels of fluency and accuracy, or perhaps be proficient users in only a limited range of situations.

In today's world the most frequently learnt second language is English, but there are many others. Those which enjoy a global status are taught both as school subjects and in adult foreign language classes. Languages such as English, German and Chinese are taught formally for both educational and leisure purposes, and they are also developed through contact situations by travellers and migrants. Some learners, for example migrant workers, go through a hybrid process of natural development mixed with various periods of formal teaching. Others may have a rather 'pure' experience of just one type of language development.

Teachers know that different language teaching methods suit different situations. The social circumstances and aspirations of adult migrants learning English as a Second Language (ESL) and the approaches most appropriate to teaching adult ESL are considerably different from those associated with teaching a 'foreign' language to students who need to pass college exams. School ESL classes are often so different from the foreign language classes being conducted down the corridor that the ESL staff and the French foreign language staff feel they have little in common. English is the most frequently taught foreign and second language in the world at the moment. ESL is taught to newcomers to once-monolingual English-speaking countries and in other countries where it fulfils a range of possible roles complementary to other official and unofficial languages (Hasan and Perrett 1994). Teachers of English in countries where English is not used at all teach the same target language as ESL teachers, but the range of factors associated with infrequent exposure to the target language make their classes much closer to Japanese or Spanish foreign language classes in 'anglo' secondary schools and colleges. For this reason the type of teaching they engage in is better described as teaching English as a foreign language (EFL).

Although the study of different teaching situations and methods is important the particular aim of this chapter is to suggest how SFL can contribute to the study of second language development (SLD). It will begin by showing that different schools of linguistics approach SLD from widely different points of view and asking why SFL has seldom been used as a basis for SLD research. The literature review which follows provides an outline of different approaches to SLD and positions SFL in relation to these, suggesting that, because of its meaning-based approach to language and the interest it takes in pedagogy, it has the potential to make a valuable contribution to SLD. The rest of the chapter is concerned with undertaking SFL/SLD research: it suggests a methodology, provides an example of this methodology, discusses related issues and suggests areas for further research.

## 4.2  Background

This chapter accepts the assumption that, for an approach to pedagogy to be effective, its practice and development need to be tied both to an understanding of what actually happens while learners are learning and to an understanding of how the target language functions, is structured and is used. Although language teachers around the world operate in dissimilar settings there is no reason why the same methods of studying how learners learn may not be utilized.

In most schools of linguistics, apart from SFL, research into SLD is commonly known as second language acquisition (SLA) research. Within SFL the term SLD is preferred because a distinction in meaning between *acquisition* and *development* has emerged. The choice of term indicates the assumptions about language learning a researcher holds. 'Acquisition' connotes the involvement of independent forces within an individual's mind. 'Development' is preferred by SFL linguists since it connotes the social nature of language learning. In this chapter the term SLA will be used only for research that falls within the SLA paradigm.

This chapter introduces a type of linguistic analysis unfamiliar within SLA research. SFL has contributed a coherent functional view of first language development (Chapter 3) and of literacies at home and at school (Chapters 5, 8 and 11); this view has been influential in the development of curriculum materials and approaches (Section 4.3.2). A similar contribution to the study of SLD remains to be made. If we wish to ask why SFL lags comparatively in SLD compared to these other areas we could point to several factors:

1. In almost every school of linguistics the study of SLD tends to follow in the wake of the study of mother tongue development. SFL is no exception.
2. The techniques used in SFL for mother tongue research are difficult to apply to learners who cannot be observed continuously.
3. SFL contributions to language pedagogy have focused on providing descriptions of how language is actually used and suggesting ways of helping students understand these uses, in other words it has tended to focus on the intended products of learning rather than the process of learning.

To understand the nature of SLD a full range of investigations is required; we need studies of learners in the process of actually using language, engaged in learning to use language, and of how their language use changes over time as their learning progresses. SLD research is interested in learner language rather than in target language description. The theoretical framework of SFL and some of its practical procedures can provide particular advantages for the study of SLD, especially with regard to how language use changes over time. Here I suggest bringing these together with more widely known social science research methods. Before this approach is described in detail, the next section briefly reviews the positions held within SLA/SLD, and also SFL, to matters connected with second language learning.

## 4.3  Review of research

### 4.3.1  Second language acquisition research

SLA research, which dates back only to the early 1970s, is not a discipline with a single coherent theory and a homogeneous set of research procedures. Rather, it constitutes an area of inquiry with a common interest in the question, 'How do people learn languages subsequent to their mother tongue?' It has been driven both by the belief of teachers that knowing more about the language learning process can lead eventually to improvements in language pedagogy and by the belief of certain linguists that the study of SLA can shed light on the nature and properties of language in general.

So many approaches to SLA have been suggested that the beginning researcher can expect to feel bewildered. My intention in this section is to do little more than indicate the range that exists and to suggest starting points for further reading. (The three most accessible introductory surveys of SLA research are Lightbown and Spada (1993), Gass and Selinker (1994) and Ellis (1997).) Early approaches were surface-level linguistic ones in which the target language was compared with the mother tongue and likely areas of difficulty were identified (Contrastive Analysis); the learner's interlanguage was compared with the target language (Error Analysis); or the learner's interlanguage was examined as a developing system in its own right (Performance Analysis). Subsequently two branches of linguistic study have focused on universal grammar and markedness theory (White 1989), whilst another which is different in basic theoretical orientation has developed out of research in discourse analysis (Ellis 1986). Psycholinguistic approaches include the monitor model (Krashen 1981, 1982), Information Processing Model (McLaughlin 1987), and processing constraints (Clahsen 1990, Pienemann and Johnston 1988). Sociolinguistic approaches have developed out of pidgin and Creole studies (Schumann's Pidgeonisation Hypothesis, Schumann 1978), variation studies (Tarone's Variable Performance Model, Tarone 1983) and Giles' Accommodation Theory (Beebe and Giles 1984). Functional approaches (Bates and MacWhinney 1987, Gass and Selinker 1994, Givón 1984, Lightbown and Spada 1993) have developed within American schools of functional linguistics.

Each of the approaches mentioned above insists on the use of language data to build its theory; this is a second unifying aspect of SLA research. In this respect SLA researchers can, as a group, be contrasted with earlier theorists, such as Skinner (1957) and Chomsky (1959), who did not rely on 'real data'. Rod Ellis, a leading researcher and surveyor in SLA, explains why language data is basic to SLA research:

> A better approach might be to find out what learners actually do, as opposed to what they think they do, when they try to learn an L2. One way of doing this is by collecting samples of **learner language** – the language that learners produce when they are called on to use an L2 in speech or writing – and analyse them carefully. These samples provide evidence of what the learners know about the language they are trying to learn (the **target language**). If samples are collected at different points in time it may also be possible to find out how learners' knowledge gradually develops ... One of the goals of SLA, then, is the description of L2 acquisition. Another is explanation; identifying the external and internal factors that account for why learners acquire an L2 in the way they do. (Ellis 1997: 4)

The nature of the language data that is considered useful varies enormously. Research along the psychological/grammar nexus is interested in language only as a self-contained system of rules and not in the social context of communication or the role of possible interlocutors. Interest is centred on morphology and sentence structure. However, within SLA studies there are some social and functional proposals which do admit that those other considerations play a role. This is Tomlin's (1990: 157) summing-up:

> A general premise of functional approaches [to SLA] is that the acquisition of a language arises from general circumstances of use and communicative interaction.

This expresses a view which is held in SFL; however, readers should take care, as the word *functional* can be used with very different meanings in language studies. As a starting point on the discussion on functionalism within SLA research readers are referred to Ellis (1994: 142). If you pursue the issue you will note that, while *functional* in SLA studies may be used to refer to language use (context or speech function in SFL) or to textual organization (theme in SFL), there is no coherent model that allows these uses to be related to each other. Furthermore, the SFL proposal that the clause is organized on metafunctional lines is never considered in SLA studies.

## 4.3.2 Second language pedagogy

Hallidayan linguistics and TESOL have enjoyed a long association, dating from his early influence in the UK on the development of communicative language teaching and language for specific purposes (Halliday *et al.* 1964). The development of SFL in Australia first resulted in genre-based pedagogy being developed in the Disadvantaged Schools Program (Christie 1993, Christie and Martin 1997). Other NSW teaching institutions such as the Adult Migrant Education Service (Hagan *et al.* 1993, Feeze *et al.* 1993) and the Language Assistance Centre at the University of Sydney have adapted the model to the teaching of adults (Jones *et al.* 1989). It is achieving increased recognition beyond NSW as is evidenced by the discussions in the leading American journal, *TESOL Quarterly* (Hyon 1996).

Two fully developed proposals for putting SFL insights into a communicative language course have been published. Melrose (1991) suggests an SFL-based, 'topical-interactional course', and in so doing claims he is promoting a process-based syllabus. The course he suggests uses teaching dialogues to show how social processes of interaction relate to their settings. His conclusion is, 'Thus the interactional exercises . . . highlight the process of using a language rather than the process of learning a language' (p. 166). Readers should be aware that Melrose's use of the term process-based syllabus is different from the use made by other TESOL educators. The process-based syllabus as proposed by Prabhu (1987) and expounded by Nunan (1989), Willis (1996) and others focuses on the process of language learning and the provision of tasks in which learners can be active and productive. A more recent proposal is that of Feez (1998). Developed from the assumption that language learning involves learning how to interact with texts in different situations, it claims that a text-based syllabus can be aligned with most syllabus approaches used in ELT other than the process syllabus. It shows how the SFL genre-based approach to language teaching and the needs analysis popular in ELT (Nunan 1988) can be combined to plan and implement coherent courses. Such courses consist of teaching/learning cycles which provide opportunity both for skill development and an understanding of text as social product.

### 4.3.3 SFL and second and foreign language learning

SFL has always been more interested in the target language than in the processes by which it is learnt. It has delivered hardly any research findings on the process of second language learning, although there are some unpublished descriptions of learner language by honours and graduate students. This may seem surprising in view of the richness of the material on child language, which is reviewed in Chapter 3 of this volume.

In fact, it is not surprising. The method most appropriate to the on-going close observation of small changes in verbal behaviour – the continuous diary study – is most easily employed by a researcher-caregiver. To track an adult learner in the way that a parent can track a child would not only be impractical, it would be a gross infringement of personal privacy. Again, planning a child language study has some certainty: all young children learn language easily and rapidly, so it is easy to record lots of talk and we can be confident that we will find evidence of development over months or even weeks. Planning an adult language learning study is full of uncertainty: Will the learners drop out? Will they fossilize? How long will those who succeed in learning take to progress? Given that the rate of learning by older learners is unpredictable, how often should data be collected? There is a risk that insufficiently frequent data collection will miss crucial developments.

According to Halliday and Painter (Chapter 3), in first language development there is a move from the infant protolanguage system where babies use individual sounds to make individual meanings to the 'adult' system where young children learn how to make two sets of meanings at once: the ideational and the interpersonal, reflection and action (Halliday 1987: 8). This is the case whatever the first language. Because different languages construct reality and classify phenomena in slightly different ways, learners still have to find out exactly what ideational and interpersonal meanings are possible in a second language, but they do not have to rediscover these two basic metafunctions (Halliday 1986: 14).

They must also discover how these ideational and interpersonal meanings are expressed (Halliday 1987: 14). It is grammar which allows people to express both of these meanings simultaneously (Halliday 1983: 210). Learners have to find the particular resources the new language has for realizing its ideational and interpersonal meanings, and they have to develop sufficient fluency to be able 'to think with it and to act with it in one and the same operation' (Halliday 1986: 4). For some learners thinking will develop more rapidly than acting. They may develop their ideational repertoire more fully than their interpersonal grammar; others may advance their interpersonal repertoire more rapidly. The type of learning environment and teaching methodology applied (Section 4.1) may be influential, as may individual learner characteristics (Ellis 1997).

But whatever the learning situation it is the case, as Halliday (1987: 14) claims, that:

> we must be able to represent the system [of learner language] as variable in extent and in elaboration, in order to show how its power increases as the learner makes progress. We have been able to do this with the language development of small children as they learn their mother tongue. We still need to find out how to do it with learners of a second language. The systemic concept of 'delicacy', the progressive differentiation within a semantic space, is highly relevant here.

The very fact that there is little SFL research into SLD makes it an exciting enterprise to undertake. Doing so will entail ways of utilizing three aspects of SFL:

1. The power of the concept of systemic 'delicacy' (this will be explained further below).
2. The clear differentiation/association of the metafunctions: ideational, interpersonal and textual.
3. The power to account for text in context through the concepts of register and genre.

### 4.4  A methodology for researching SLD

There is no claim that this chapter meets Halliday's challenge '. . . to do it with learners of a second language' adequately, but this section does contain one proposal for a general methodology for researching SLD. The proposal involves marrying some assumptions based on the SFL model of language with assumptions made generally within the field of SLA. It is based on a number of premises, all of which have been touched upon in this chapter:

1. To describe language development, comparisons have to be made between different points in time.
2. We can find out what learners actually do by collecting samples of learner language.
3. These samples need to be complete texts, complete instances of language-in-social-use.
4. Language development arises from general circumstances of use and communicative interaction.

5. Because the SFL model of language includes genre, register, and grammar it provides researchers with the opportunity to find out how features in the context of use may influence what grammatical features are learnt.

6. This suggests a top-down analysis of language use in contexts of culture and situation, and of how developing language features respond to the functional demands of the situation.

7. The aim is not to extrapolate systems of rules (as in SLA) but systems of choices of meanings and ways of expressing them. (For examples of system networks see Figures 4.3, 4.5, 4.7; for an explanation of how to read them see Section 4.5.4.1.)

8. These systems can be developed into more extensive networks at different levels of language, for example of speech function or mood.

9. Systems networks from different points in time can be compared to determine the language development paths of individual learners.

10. Networks of the choices made by learners at different stages of development can be compared in order to establish generalities.

These ten points can be instantiated in the steps which are sketched in the flow chart in Figure 4.1. The first three steps are often interactive. They may be undertaken in any order and the researcher may need to move backwards and forwards between them. The steps are to select texts for analysis (a) at the same time as choosing the focus (b) and developing a preliminary description (c). A whole-text, top-down approach is employed.

At this preliminary stage researchers need to bear in mind that although the study includes description, it will also go beyond description to comparison, because without comparison we cannot draw conclusions about change or development. Therefore it is important when selecting texts for analysis to plan which ones will be compared. When texts are collected from the same learner a decision about the time intervals of collection will have to be made. When texts are collected from different learners at the same time a clear decision about what characteristics differentiate the learners must be made. Learners can be differentiated according to various criteria: mother tongue, grade in school, length of time learning English, or English proficiency according to some acceptable measure.[1]

The fourth step is to select and analyse the features which we wish to focus on. Figure 4.2 reminds us that it is possible to choose different features at the levels of genre, register, semantics, lexico-grammar or phonology. Of course, the stratum at which we decide to work and the analysis we will do at that level depends on what characteristics of learner language we wish to study.

Step five involves comparison and for the purpose of observing language development this can be done in two ways. One is to construct system networks (Figures 4.3, 4.5, 4.7) to display the choices which have

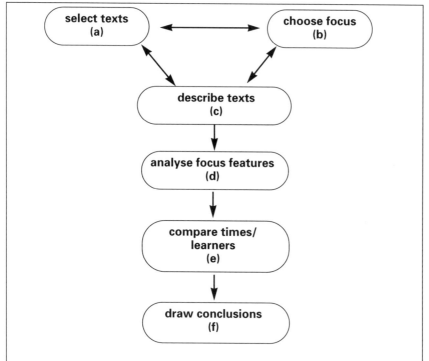

**Interpreting the first three steps starting from texts which are to hand:**
1. Identify the generic features of the texts
2. Identify the register and participants
3. Decide which texts are to be compared with which
4. Decide the parameters upon which they will be analysed
5. Analyse focus features

**Interpreting the first three steps starting from an interest in the development of a particular aspect of language:**
1. Identify the stratum at which this aspect lies
2. Decide what genre of texts to collect (choose a genre where it will occur frequently)
3. Decide in what ways the texts are to be compared
4. Deal with practical issues in identifying where and how the texts should be collected
5. When the texts have been collected (and if necessary transcribed) identify the features of the superordinate strata to check that these have been held common
6. Analyse focus features

**Figure 4.1** Researching second language development

been made in any one text (or group of texts from the same time or the same group of learners) and to compare the systems which are identified. Language development is a continual process. We can use system networks to show what choices a learner has available at a particular time and

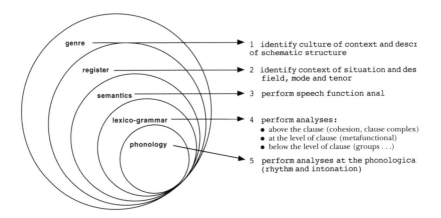

**Figure 4.2** Focus features at the different language strata

by drawing a network of the choices available at another time we provide a basis for comparison. The changes that we see between time 1 and time 2 represent some of the developmental changes that have taken place. We can observe increases in delicacy, as learners make finer distinctions in meaning and the networks proliferate with branches to the right; we can observe the restructuring of systems when the shape of the networks changes as learners reorganize the distinctions they are making. A second way is to compare the texts in terms of the proportions of different choices made. To do this the choices are counted and their relative incidence is compared statistically.

Different conclusions can be drawn depending on how the comparisons have been made. It may then be possible to extrapolate generalizations and to form hypotheses about the nature of language development in general. This must be done with care and conclusions must respect the nature of the study design. If a series of texts have been collected from one learner over time, differences observed *may* be attributable to language development (as long as the texts are all of the same genre). If texts have been collected from different learners care must be exercised in drawing conclusions about what the differences mean. If we hope to make conclusions about the nature of language development, we must be able to convince other people that differences between the learners are actually due to differences in development and are not due to some other factor, such as, for instance, genre or mother tongue.

## 4.5 Investigating the language development of adult migrants

I will now present as an example one analysis and some findings from a research project called 'How do Learners Answer Questions?'. This study (Perrett 1990b) investigated the 'oral interview' often used to test adult learners of English. It aimed to discover how proficient native speakers

(NS) assist non-native speakers (NNS) to keep talking within this particular context, and to identify the ways in which this happens for learners who are at different proficiency levels. The initial impetus for the study was interest in work done in SLA research on the negotiation of meaning (Gass and Varonis 1985, Long 1983). I felt that studies which had been conducted in this paradigm up to that time (1992) had two major drawbacks. They did not take account of the contextual features of different situations of use, preferring to generalize about the conversation of learners in any situation as if they were certain to be the same in others: that is, they ignored genre. Also they were not based on a clear model of speech function; clarity is necessary in order to distinguish functions from each other and to show how speech function and mood grammar relate to each other.

### 4.5.1 Establishing the focus and selecting the texts

The project did not commence with an interest in oral language test interviews. My initial interest was with scaffolding and interaction between NSs and NNSs, and it was some time before I realized that oral interviews could be an ideal source of data. It was necessary to have data of the same genre and it was desirable to examine a genre in which the interactional patterns between NSs and NNSs would be relatively easy to establish. So, in terms of Figure 4.1, the movement was initially from step (b) – choose focus, to step (a) – select texts, to step (c) – describe texts, back to step (a). However, it is quite possible that similar projects could have their inception in a direct interest in language testing interviews. Some researchers, particularly teachers who have been working with a particular genre in lessons, will prefer this approach. In such cases the movement would be through steps (a) to (b) to (c).

I had access to a body of language testing interviews which had been conducted a few years previously with adult migrants for a different research project in SLA (Johnston 1985). The interviews in this data set seemed appropriate, and a preliminary description of the texts (step c) confirmed this. Thus a choice was made to do a *cross-sectional* study rather than a *longitudinal* study such as is the norm in SFL mother tongue studies. As noted in Section 4.3.3, longitudinal studies which track individuals closely for longish periods of time provide very firm information about the learner's development of a language, but involve certain risks in studying SLD. In contrast, a cross-sectional study involves collecting texts from a number of learners at a single point in time (Brown 1988: 3) and comparing them in order to make general conclusions about the nature of language development. If this method is chosen it is extremely important to use data from learners who are at different proficiency levels and to exercise the greatest care to ensure that the differences found between the texts are due only to differences in proficiency and not to some other difference among the learners. As the 48 interviews had already been

graded according to the Australian Second Language Proficiency Rating
(ASLPR) scale (Ingram 1984) it was possible to select from four distinct
levels on the scale.[2] As the interviews had been collected from 12 Polish
speakers and 12 Vietnamese speakers it was also possible to make sure
there was one Polish and one Vietnamese speaker in each pair.

### 4.5.2 Describing the texts

The next step was to establish the generic structure potential of the interviews through analysis of the data and through comparison with two other
unpublished studies of language testing interviews (Neeson 1985, Curtin
1987). This is described in Perrett (1997). The relevant findings about
the genre of the interviews were that they all had one major stage, that
this stage took up more than 96 per cent of the interview text, and that
this was the only long stage to occur in every interview examined. This is
the stage that we would intuitively judge to be the main business of the
interview: the NS interviewer asks questions and the NNS learner answers
them.[3] This was the stage that was examined in detail.

### 4.5.3 Analysing focus features

The next step was to choose and analyse the focus features (Figure
4.1(d)), which in this case meant analysing the utterances of both NSs
and NNSs in terms of speech function since Halliday's work on first language acquisition indicates that, when language is learned through use,
the development of the speech function systems and the mood grammar
are closely related (Halliday 1984). The first step in the procedure was to
divide each utterance in the major stage into one or more moves. Moves
were often the same as a clause, but sometimes contained only fragments
of clauses and sometimes consisted of more than one.[4] (Consult Chapter
2 for an introduction to the concepts of clause and mood and for further
reading. Chapter 2 also introduces the idea of speech function and cites
Halliday (1994) in claiming that 'there are four key distinctions which
explain interpersonal communication . . . giving . . . demanding . . . goods
and services . . . information'. Elsewhere (1984) Halliday includes initiating and responding because of the importance of the way in which personal communication is organized in time.)

   In the interview data each move was coded as giving or demanding, initiating or responding, and also for the type of commodity being exchanged.
In trying to decide whether this commodity was goods-and-services or information, it became apparent that some moves contributed neither goods-
and-services nor information. They seemed rather to be attempts to
terminate the interaction or to help it along in some way if it was in trouble.
Martin (1992: 66–76) calls this type of move dynamic in comparison with the
synoptic moves which realize the speech functions identified in Chapter 2.
Unlike Martin, I decided to model synoptic and dynamic moves within

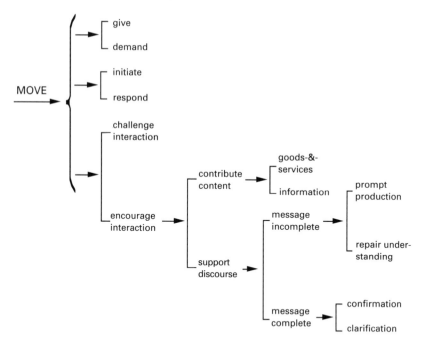

**Figure 4.3** Network of possible speech function choices

the same system network (Figure 4.3). A system network is read by following the arrows from left to right and choosing one term from each of the
square brackets until all the choices have been exhausted. A description
of a move in terms of the features of the Figure 4.3 system network will
consist of three features. In Section 2.4 (p. 44) the statement has the features give-initiate-information; the question has the features demand-
initiate-information; an answer to a question would have the features
give-respond-information. This speech function network generates 28 different speech functions. Rather than give each of them a name
(cf. Martin 1992: 70) I will just describe them in terms of their three categories of features: the features of give or demand; the features of initiate
or respond; and the features of information, challenge, prompt, repair,
confirmation or clarification. Figure 4.4 provides some examples from
the interview texts of moves coded in sequence. It will be seen from the
instances in this figure that dynamic moves usually lack mood structure.
They are most likely to be expressed with a discourse strategy of repeating
or paraphrasing; in Figure 4.4 this is the case with the confirmation sub-
exchanges. Challenges are either mounted through complete silence or a
comment on the undesirability of continuing. Other typical strategies
include supplying a missing element (as in the first prompt production
sequence), correcting, using a non-verbal strategy (as in the repair understanding move), or translation.

**INFORMATION EXCHANGE**

| Examples: | NS | Did Thuy study French as well? | **i & d** |
|---|---|---|---|
| | NNS | No. | **r to d** |
| | NS | We came here together. | **i & g** |
| | NNS | I see. | **r to g** |

**CHALLENGE**

| Example: | NNS | No understand. (very flat tone) | **i & g\*** |
|---|---|---|---|
| | NS | Yeah. (changes topic) | **r to g** |

[*Informal gloss: *'I am not willing to continue this exchange.'*]

**PROMPT PRODUCTION SUB-EXCHANGE**

| Examples: | NNS | Now is good, but in the summer maybe . . . | **information** |
|---|---|---|---|
| | NS | . . . gets very hot? | **i & g\*** |
| | NNS | Yes, very hot. | **r to g** |

[*Informal gloss: *'This is probably what you want to say.'*]

| | NNS | Mountains . . . in pen . . . in pension . . I don't know . . . word. | **information** **i & d\*** |
|---|---|---|---|
| | NS | In a boarding house or something. | **r to d** |

[*Informal gloss: *'I need some help expressing this.'*]

**REPAIR UNDERSTANDING SUB-EXCHANGE**

| Example: | NS | Do you have work in Australia? | **information** |
|---|---|---|---|
| | NNS | Er? | **i & d\*** |
| | NS | Job, do you have a job? | **r to d** |

[*Informal gloss: *'I didn't hear/understand part/all of what you said.'*]

**CONFIRMATION SUB-EXCHANGE**

| Examples: | NS | How long can you stay in the hostel? | **information** |
|---|---|---|---|
| | NNS | How long? | **i & d\*** |
| | NS | Mmm. | **r to d** |

[*Informal gloss: *'Did you say/mean X?'*]

| | NNS | My home er live two families in, my husband and two people, er, Argentina, three rooms. | **information** |
|---|---|---|---|
| | NS | Three rooms. | **i & g\*** |
| | NNS | Three rooms. | **r to g** |

[*Informal gloss: *'I receive you as having said/meant X.'*]

**CLARIFICATION SUB-EXCHANGE**

| Example: | NNS | We studied English at high school, but not much I think. | **information** |
|---|---|---|---|
| | NS | Not much, what a couple of hours a week or...? | **i & d\*** |
| | NS | Yes, I think so. | **r to d** |

[*Informal gloss: *'I know what you said, but I need additional information.'*]

**[i = initiate, r = respond, d = demand, g = give]**

**Figure 4.4** Examples of speech functions

### 4.5.4 Comparing learners

Once all the moves had been coded for the three features contributing to their speech function the codings were analysed in different ways. Two approaches were taken: to construct system networks for each speaker and to compute numerical totals. The two methods provide complementary information: the first shows the full range of choices made, the second the frequency with which each choice is made.

#### 4.5.4.1 Speech function compared systemically

To make systemic comparisons, systems of features chosen for a particular text, or group of texts, are drawn up and examined for similarities and differences. Figures 4.5 and 4.6 show the systems for the two lowest-level speakers. In the system CONTRIBUTE CONTENT the options used are the same. Both speakers can make only one type of initiation, and they can respond in only two ways. However, when we examine the system SUPPORT DISCOURSE we see that learner Y has used a greater variety of choices than learner X. It is also possible to compare the learners at level A, the lowest level, with those at the higher proficiency levels. Figure 4.7 shows how the learners at the higher levels have both the give and demand options available for initiations as well as for responses in the CONTRIBUTE CONTENT system. However, if we compare Figure 4.7 with the CONTRIBUTE CONTENT option in the network which represents the target system (Figure 4.3) we can see that for all the learners there is one option missing: negotiating goods-and-services rather than information. Should we conclude that all these learners are only capable of negotiating the exchange of information? Here we find the importance of the genre analysis (step (c) of the research procedure). It is the business of interviews to exchange information: if we want to investigate the learners' facility in negotiating the exchange of goods and services we need to collect data from a different genre. As researchers we must take care not to overgeneralize the conclusions we draw.

#### 4.5.4.2 Speech function compared numerically

Numerical comparison will be illustrated through two classifications: synoptic and dynamic moves, and types of dynamic move. In the research project the numbers of each speech function type employed by each of eight speakers were counted. These were then combined into totals for the learners at each level and computed as proportions.

The results of the first classification are presented in Figure 4.8. Here we can see, just as we should be able to work out from the table of raw data[5] that the less proficient NNSs have a greater proportion of dynamic moves in their interaction with NSs than the more proficient NNSs. The proportion of dynamic moves is greatest at the lower proficiency levels,

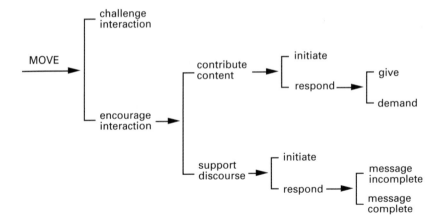

**Figure 4.5** Speech function system for learner X

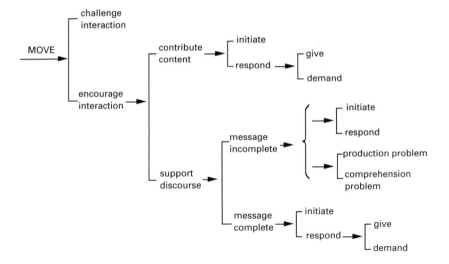

**Figure 4.6** Speech function system for learner Y

becomes progressively smaller, and is smallest at the highest level. Conversely, the proportion of synoptic moves increases as proficiency level increases.

The results of the comparison made on the basis of the second classification are shown in Figure 4.9. This shows the proportion of dynamic moves of different types used by the pairs at the four proficiency levels. We can observe that the proportion of prompts and clarifications increases with increased proficiency. We can also observe that, if we combine them, the proportion of the other types of dynamic move (i.e. confirmations, repairs

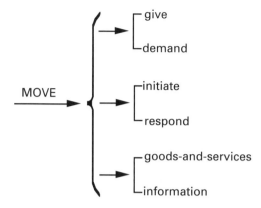

**Figure 4.7** Fully developed synoptic speech function network

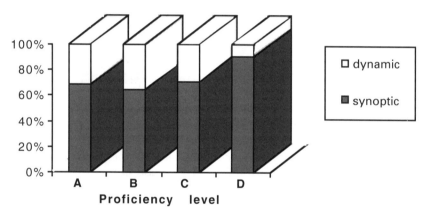

**Figure 4.8** Proportions of synoptic and dynamic moves in the major stage of the interview

and challenges) decreases with the increase in proficiency.

The method of comparison illustrated in this section involves counting and simple descriptive statistics. Depending on the size of the project and the amount and nature of the data being coded, it may be appropriate to use more complex descriptive statistics or even some inferential statistics (as is frequently done in SLA research) to establish the solidity of the findings.[6] This analysis complements the systemic one: it can show which choices are made most frequently.

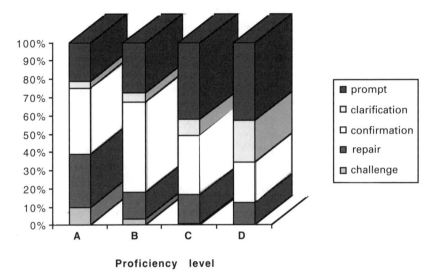

Proficiency   level

**Figure 4.9** Proportions of dynamic move types in the major stage of the interview by proficiency level

### 4.5.5 Drawing conclusions

In Section 4.5.3 we reported the results of the speech function analysis; this completed step (d) in Figure 4.1. In Section 4.5.4 (step e) we reported summary results of the coding process and made factual comparisons based on these. The final step, step (f), which we move to now, is the most interesting because here interpretation should occur. This must be done judiciously because readers will inspect the factual reports in order to judge whether conclusions are reasonably drawn.

The comparisons we have already reported can be summarized as:

1. There are no differences in generic structure between the interviews, even those at different proficiency levels.
2. The CONTRIBUTE CONTENT system is less developed for speakers at the lowest proficiency level (level A) than it is for speakers at the other levels (B, C, D), where it is still not complete.
3. The SUPPORT DISCOURSE systems are most complex at levels B and C, with the lowest and highest levels showing simpler systems with fewer choices made.
4. The proportion of dynamic speech functions used in the main stage of the interview decreases continuously as proficiency level rises; conversely the proportion of synoptic speech functions increases.
5. The types of dynamic speech function most favoured change with changes in proficiency level.

In interpreting the results we address the questions which originally engaged our interest:

1. What sort of interaction between NSs and NNSs helps NNSs to talk?
2. Does the pattern of this interaction change as proficiency level increases?

The oral interview is a very rigidly structured genre in that the stages of generic structure are clearly signalled and the types of interaction which take place within each stage are very constrained. Whilst it is possible to conclude, as in Perrett (1990a), that this shows the amount of power and control exercised by the interviewer, it is also possible to conclude that the firmness of the generic structure creates a predictable environment in which NSs can scaffold and support NNSs' utterances, and in which NNSs can understand what contribution is required and can therefore express themselves with confidence.

The overt purpose of the oral interview is to exchange information. This is done through the use of synoptic speech functions. This accounts for the lack of exchange of goods-and-services in the data set, but it does not account for the more limited set of speech functions in the level A interviews. Here we can feel confident in attributing the difficulty with initiation to being at a beginning proficiency level.

We have noted a clear shift in proportions between synoptic and dynamic speech functions among the four proficiency levels:[7] here again there seems to be evidence of developmental change in patterns of conversation worthy of further consideration. The more fluent the NNSs are, the less evident the dynamic speech functions. From this we can conclude that dynamic speech functions must have some role in interaction with less-fluent NNSs. At the lower levels we find on the one side challenge moves which seek to terminate the interaction and on the other confirming and repair moves which have the opposite function. While confirmations do occur in fluent conversation, they are much more prevalent in the less fluent. Faltering speakers receive confirmation more often, both in the gaps between propositions and also in the gaps which occur whilst individual propositions are being developed. The function of the dynamic moves is to negotiate whether the conversation should proceed and, if so, to keep it going at all costs.

With the more fluent speakers we see not only a reduction in the occurrence of dynamic speech functions, but a shift in the type of dynamic function used. Two other types, prompts and clarifications, occur more frequently. These function to keep the conversation going in a slightly different way. They both provide opportunities for extending what is said. (We might say they have a forward rather than a backward orientation, a promoting rather than a rescuing function.) Prompts assist in the building of propositions by providing the opportunity for negotiating appropriate language to fill an empty space, while clarifications create a bit more space around the proposition which can be filled.

From the speech function analysis reported we are able to conclude that:

1. The oral interview provides a stable context which makes it easier for non-fluent speakers to engage in the exchange of information.
2. Less fluent speakers do not initiate as freely as more fluent speakers.
3. The use of dynamic speech functions by NSs and NNSs helps to keep the conversation going.
4. Confirmations and repairs, the most common dynamic functions at the lower levels, have a more restricted function than the prompts and clarifications which occur at the higher levels; these open up new space within the proposition being negotiated.

In reporting these conclusions can be supported with evidence from the texts. The quantitative analysis will enable us to select typical rather than atypical examples and to substantiate the claim that they are typical.

Having drawn conclusions from this analysis, we can consider further questions which we might ask while working with the same data set.

1. Are the strategies used to realize each type of move the same across all the proficiency levels?
2. How are sequences of related moves organized?
3. Does this organization change across proficiency levels?
4. How do the learners begin to map features of the mood grammar onto the different types of speech function?

The original study, 'How do Learners Answer Questions?', attempted to answer all these questions. Working through them we can begin to build up a fuller picture of NSs and NNSs interaction in order to help learners of different proficiency levels learn to talk in English.

## 4.6 Suggestions for further research

These questions cannot be answered solely by reference to one data set. We need to explore the same questions both with similar data sets and with other sets drawn from a wide range of genres. We need to be able to sort out differences due to language development from differences due to genre. There is also a need to explore different parts of the language system (Figure 4.2), and different types of learning environment. In exploring language learning in the classroom, the speech function model will be useful in interactive, 'learner-centred' settings; but in others where there is little interaction, more appropriate questions would concern the development of the ideational metafunction (Chapter 2).

There is also almost unlimited scope to explore the development of the noun and verb phrase below the level of the clause, the development of the clause complex, and the development of discourse grammar above the level of the clause, not to mention the development of grammatical metaphor in the language of advanced learners (Halliday 1994). A more delicate analysis of synoptic speech functions is also needed and could be accomplished through the use and adaptation of Hasan's semantic networks which are introduced, in a different context, in Chapter 7.

There is not, as yet, an SFL account of how second language development occurs. Studies of the areas suggested in the previous paragraph will help to paint the picture in fuller detail. The field is wide open to enthusiastic researchers who are willing to accept the challenge of working in an area full of great complexities and great rewards.

## Notes

For more information about these approaches readers are referred to Long and Larsen-Freeman (1991) and Ellis (1994).

1. This can be done early and built into the research design, as suggested here, or it can be done later based on the results of analysis. If it is done after analysis it will involve seeking common characteristics for those learners who have shown similarities in their outputs or modes of language development.

2. No special claim is being made for the status of the ASLPR here (it is one of a number of commonly and successfully used measures), and for that reason precise ASLPR levels are not used in this chapter. Individual researchers will use their own desired proficiency measure or some other distinguishing criteria.

3. The whole purpose is to facilitate display by the NNS. Brindley (1979) makes this explicit when he states in his notes for AMES interviewers, 'the main purpose of the interview is to encourage the students to speak so the interviewer should resist the temptation to talk at length'.

4. For a more complete discussion of move see Ventola (1987: 93) and Martin (1992: 59).

5.

|                  | A   | B    | C    | D    |
|------------------|-----|------|------|------|
| synoptic moves   | 12  | 729  | 875  | 948  |
| dynamic moves:   |     |      |      |      |
| challenge        | 10  | 13   | 3    | 0    |
| prompt           | 21  | 112  | 151  | 45   |
| repair           | 29  | 59   | 57   | 13   |
| confirmation     | 36  | 202  | 116  | 23   |
| clarification    | 4   | 19   | 32   | 24   |
| **totals**       | 112 | 1134 | 1234 | 1053 |

6. Interested readers are referred to books on SLA research methodology which have an introduction to statistical methods such as Brown (1988), who has a long section (chapters 5–12) and in chapter 12 (182–98) includes information about comparing frequencies, which is what we would do in this case.

7. In fact appropriate analysis would show it to be statistically significant.

## References

Bates, E. and MacWhinney, B. (1987) Competition, variation and language learning. In B. F. MacWhinney (ed.), *Mechanisms of Language Acquisition*. Hillsdale: Erlbaum.

Beebe, L. and Giles, H. (1984) Accommodation theory: a discussion in terms of second language acquisition. *International Journal of the Sociology of Language*, 46: 5–32.

Brindley, G. (1979) *Evaluation of ESL Speaking Proficiency Through the Oral Interview*. Sydney: AMES.

Brown, J. D. (1988) *Understanding Research in Second Language Learning: A Teacher's Guide to Statistics and Research Design*. Cambridge: Cambridge University Press.

Christie, F. (1992) Literacy in Australia. *Annual Review of Applied Linguistics*, 12: 142–55.

Christie, F. (1993) Text as curriculum and as technology: a systemic functional linguistic perspective. In Bill Green (ed.), *Curriculum, Technology and Textual Practice*. Geelong: Deakin University Press.

Christie, F. and Martin, J. R. (1997) (eds) *Genre and Institutions: Social Processes in the Workplace and School*. London: Cassell.

Chomsky, N. (1959) Review of *Verbal Behaviour*. *Language*, 35: 26–58.

Clahsen, H. (1990) The comparative study of first and second language development. *Studies in Second Language Acquisition*, 12: 135–54.

Curtin, P. (1987) Considerations in measuring speaking proficiency in the second language learner: another look at the interview. Unpublished MA thesis, University of Sydney.

Ellis, R. (1986) *Understanding Second Language Acquisition*. Oxford: Oxford University Press.

Ellis, R. (1994) *The Study of Second Language Acquisition*. Oxford: Oxford University Press.

Ellis, R. (1997) *Second Language Acquisition*. Oxford: Oxford University Press.

Feeze, S. (1998) *Text-based Syllabus Design*. Sydney: NCELTR.

Feeze, S., Hagan, P. and Joyce, H. (1993) *Advanced Certificate in Spoken and Written English: Employment Focus*. Sydney: Adult Migrant Education Service.

Gass, S. and Selinker, L. (1994) *Second Language Acquisition: An Introductory Course*. Hillsdale: Erlbaum.

Gass, S. and Varonis, E.M. (1985) Variation in native speaker speech modification to non-native speakers. *Studies in Second Language Acquisition*, 7: 37–58.

Givón, T. (1984) Universals of discourse structure and second language acquisition. In W. Rutherford (ed.), *Typological Universals and Second Language Acquisition*. Amsterdam: Benjamin.

Hagan, P., Hood, S., Jackson, E., Jones, M., Joyce, H. and Manidis, M. (1993) *Certificate in Spoken and Written English* (2nd edn). Sydney NSW: Adult Migrant Education Service and National Centre for English Language and Teaching Research.

Halliday, M. A. K. (1983) On the transition from child tongue to mother tongue. *Australian Journal of Linguistics*, 3: 201–15.

Halliday, M. A. K. (1984) Language as code and language as behaviour: a systemic-functional interpretation of the nature and ontogenesis of dialogue. In R. Fawcett, M. A. K. Halliday, S. M. Lamb and A. Makkai (eds), *The Semiotics of Culture and Language* vol. 1. London: Pinter, 3–35.

Halliday, M. A. K. (1986) *Learning Asian Languages*. Sydney: University of Sydney

Centre for Asian Studies.

Halliday, M. A. K. (1987) Some basic concepts of educational linguistics. In V. Bickley (ed.), *Proceedings of the ILE International Seminar on Languages in Education in a Bilingual or Multilingual Setting.* Hong Kong: Institute of Language in Education.

Halliday, M. A. K. (1994) *An Introduction to Functional Grammar* (2nd edn). London: Edward Arnold.

Halliday, M. A. K., McIntosh, A. and Strevens, P. (1964) *The Linguistic Science and Language Teaching.* London: Longman.

Hasan, R. and Perrett, G. (1994) Learning to function with the other tongue: a systemic functional perspective on second language teaching. In T. Odlin (ed.), *Perspectives on Pedagogical Grammar.* Cambridge: Cambridge University Press.

Hyon, S. (1996) Genre in three traditions: implications for ESL. *TESOL Quarterly,* 30: 693–722.

Ingram, D. (1984) *Report on the Formal Trialing of the Australian Second Language Proficiency Ratings.* Canberra: Government Publishing Service.

Johnston, M. (1985) *Syntactic and Morphological Progressions in Learner English.* Canberra: Department of Immigration and Ethnic Affairs.

Jones, J., Gollin, S., Drury, H. and Economou, D. (1989) Systemic Functional Linguistics and its application to the TESOL curriculum. In R. Hasan and J. R. Martin (eds.), *Language Development: Learning Language, Learning Culture* (vol. 27). Norwood: Ablex.

Krashen, S. (1981) *Second Language Acquisition and Second Language Learning.* Oxford: Pergamon.

Krashen, S. (1982) *Principles and Practice in Second Language Acquisition.* Oxford: Pergamon.

Lightbown, P. and Spada, N. (1993) *How Languages Are Learned.* Oxford: Oxford University Press.

Long, M.H. (1983) Native speaker/non-native speaker conversation and the negotiation of comprehensible input. *Applied Linguistics,* 4: 126–41

Long, M. H. and Larsen-Freeman, D. (1991) *An Introduction to Second Language Acquisition Research.* London: Longman.

Martin, J. R. (1992) *English Text: System and Structure.* Amsterdam: Benjamin.

McLaughlin, B. (1987) *Theories of Second Language Learning.* London: Edward Arnold.

Melrose, R. (1991) *A Systemic-Functional Approach to Language Teaching.* London: Pinter.

Neeson, S. (1985) An exploratory study of the discourse structure of the Australian Second Language Proficiency Ratings Test of Oral Proficiency. Unpublished MA thesis, University of Birmingham.

Nunan, D. (1988) *The Learner-Centred Curriculum.* Cambridge: Cambridge University Press.

Nunan, D. (1989) *Designing Tasks for the Communicative Classroom.* Cambridge: Cambridge University Press.

Perrett, G. (1990a) The language testing interview: a reappraisal. In J. H. A. L. de Jong and D. S. Stevenson (eds), *Individualising the Assessment of Language Abilities.* Clevedon: Multilingual Matters.

Perrett, G. (1990b) How do learners answer questions? discourse and the development of interlanguage. Unpublished PhD thesis, University of Sydney.

Perrett, G. (1997) Discourse and rank: the unit transaction in the oral interview (or what is the purpose of this conversation anyway?). *Australian Review of Applied Linguistics*, 20: 1–20.

Pienemann, M. and Johnston, M. (1988) Processing constraints and learnability. Mimeo. Sydney: University of Sydney.

Prabhu, N. (1987) *Second Language Pedagogy: A Perspective*. Oxford: Oxford University Press.

Schumann, J. (1978) *The Pidginization Process: A Model for Second Language Acquisition*. Rowley, MA: Newbury House.

Skinner, B. (1957) *Verbal Behaviour*. New York: Appleton-Century-Crofts.

Tarone, E. (1983) On the variability of interlanguage systems. *Applied Linguistics*, 4: 143–63.

Tomlin, B. (1990) Functionalism in second language acquisition. *Studies in Second Language Acquisition*, 12: 155–77.

Ventola, E. (1987) *The Structure of Social Interaction: A Systemic Approach to the Semiotics of Service Encounters*. London: Pinter.

White, L. (1989) *Universal Grammar and Second Language Acquisition*. Amsterdam: Benjamin.

Willis, J. (1996) *A Framework for Task-Based Learning*. London: Longman.

# 5. Children's literature, children and uses of language description

*Geoffrey Williams*

## 5.1 Introduction

Research in the field of children's literature is a diverse phenomenon, ranging across a wide span of disciplines and investigating a rich diversity of questions. Some scholars study intricate historical problems of relations between editions of major works, others are preoccupied with the immediate problems of mediation of texts as part of literacy education in schools. Some survey patterns of reading in various cultural groups, others explore relations between avant garde forms of writing in a culture and the mediation of these forms to young readers. There is an impressive range in a field which has struggled for so long to achieve academic recognition.

Looking back over research in this field during the twentieth century it is clear that language itself has been an important focus of study for many scholars. Chukovsky's argument for 'the sense of nonsense verse' draws attention not only to a particular category of verse play, but also to literary language in social use – that is, the functionality of nonsense verse in children's development of sense. The Opies' work on the lore and language of school children is particularly interesting because it describes how verse texts as instances of language play participate simultaneously in the maintenance of a long oral tradition, the definition of childhood competence in language use and the simultaneous subversion of adult culture. The Macquarie Dictionary points out that 'lore' signifies both 'the body of knowledge, especially of a traditional, anecdotal, or popular' kind and also 'learning, knowledge, or erudition'. So the language of playground play is both a linguistically constructed body of knowledge about how the world is constituted, and also a marker of children's linguistic competence to participate in socially defining activities with their peers.

Focusing more specifically on children's literature in literacy learning, Margaret Meek claims that 'texts teach what readers learn', thus drawing attention to the often overlooked fact that children's literacy development depends on their understanding of the significance of variation in semantic patterning in texts. Learning to be literate does not mean learning just about relations between print and spoken language, but about differences between written language in registers to which children have access in the first years of life.

Problems of language use, children's fiction and ideology have been prominent in discussions in the last decade or so, in works such as Hollindale's *Ideology and the Children's Book* (1988), Stephens' *Language and Ideology in Children's Fiction* (1992) and Knowles and Malmkjær's *Language and Control in Children's Literature* (1996), a work which also uses elements of systemic functional linguistics (SFL) as an analytic frame. As a final set of examples, there are important theoretical discussions of the structures of narrative and their effects in children's literature such as in Chambers' 'The reader in the book' (Chambers 1985, 1993), Wall's *The Narrator's Voice* (1991) and Nikolajeva's *Children's Literature Comes of Age* (1996). Obviously these are just a few examples of work on language in the field of children's literature. When compared with the huge volume of general, evaluative literary criticism and historical scholarship in the field of children's literature it is a small fraction, but nonetheless an important one.

However, so far as I am aware there is almost no research specifically on the language children use in reflection on the language of literature written for them, in contrast with their reflection on character, setting and plot. There appears to be very little exploration of children's fiction as a site where children themselves develop awareness of how language means in a literary text. An important exception is Aidan Chambers' work with teachers using a strategy to encourage children to search for significant patterns in literary texts. This work was first introduced in his thought-provoking article 'Tell me: are children critics?' (Chambers 1985).

The discussion here is, in part, in dialogue with this work, though it clearly differs in some key respects. Its purpose is to open up a new aspect of research for readers interested both in children's literature itself and children's development of competences to read that literature appreciatively and critically. The discussion is directly related to Chambers' question in that it explores children's capacities for reflective, critical work but it differs by asking what might be achieved in literary education and in children's critical understanding of language use if they were introduced to descriptive resources such as elements of a functional grammar. In the context of this chapter I am making a double move: to consider some uses of SFL analyses in the children's literature field and, simultaneously, to consider possibilities for children to explore the construction and patterning of literary meanings using SFL.

In writing about children's literature the terms 'story', 'children' and 'grammar' are not often found in proximity. The thought that children might learn to use a grammar in the context of shared reading of fiction is not something many teachers would accept, especially with the spectre of Mr Gradgrind lurking in the deadening proposals of politicians to return children to drill in traditional school grammar. However, I argue that we are unnecessarily and unproductively constrained in work on literary texts by the hegemony of traditional school grammar and all that it entails pedagogically. In particular, it limits the kind of textual work which can be achieved under its aegis by constraining the investigation of grammatical patterning through which meaning effects are achieved. A different, meaning-oriented, multifunctional grammar offers opportunities to ask different questions about the nature of language study in schools and different possible effects of this study, as Martin argues in Chapter 12 (see also Hasan 1996 for a detailed argument for reflection literacy).

In passing, it is notable just how little research has actually investigated ways of developing children's abilities to describe language at the semantic and grammatical strata. Though debates rage about the utility of explicit knowledge of language structure, only very rarely has this aspect of children's linguistic development been the focus of close research analysis. In fact, one could reasonably claim that debate over the utility of grammatical knowledge is a pseudo-debate and a paradigmatic case of an educational issue in need of some grounded research, some evidence from actual examples of socially located subjects engaged in real institutional practice.

It is sometimes argued that children develop informal ways of reflecting on language through their play, and that in the primary years this knowledge is sufficient for the scope of current curricula. Obviously children do informally develop knowledge about language at the same time as they learn to use language in social interaction. Children's jokes about language attest to this, as the Opies' ethnographic work on children's playground rhymes showed years ago. (Sometimes this play even included reference to grammar itself. 'What,' some of their informants asked, 'is the difference between a cat and a comma?' And the reply: 'A cat has its claws at the end of its paws and a comma has its pause at the end of a clause' (Opie and Opie 1959: 79). And children do naturally attend to language itself, if by natural it is meant that talk about language is a common enough feature of the everyday discourse of young children. But informal, discursively local ways of reflecting on language are limited. There remains the important question of children's access to more powerful, abstract metalinguistic tools. Is providing such access both possible and productive in primary schooling? Facing a very similar problem in children's mathematics education, mathematicians have responded by helping children attend to significant patterning through enjoyable play with meaningful structures in recognizable, everyday contexts of use. Language curricula have been slow to even take up the issue, typically being trapped in a reaction to banal educational practices associated with traditional school grammar and the intense political pressure which supports it.

My colleagues and I have wondered, in the research to be discussed later in this chapter, if children might learn some primary features of systemic functional grammar as conceptual tools through which to explore how grammatical patterning affects meaning, perhaps in a way similar to advanced practice in mathematics education.

## 5.2 A brief theoretical excursus: Vygotsky, children's development of voluntary attention and learning about language

To ask about the possibility of using grammatical metalanguage as a 'tool' suggests the relevance of Vygotsky's theory of the ontogenesis of higher mental functions. Since his work is now widely known in the field of child literacy development I shall assume familiarity with his general proposals and focus specifically on his discussion of the development of voluntary attention in order to be able to explicate possible differential effects of *initially* learning different grammars.

By voluntary attention Vygotsky meant sign-mediated attention, in contrast with forms of attention to phenomena which result directly from features of objects themselves. For our work there are two key problems:

1. To what aspects of language is attention directed by the nature of the metalinguistic signs to which children are introduced?
2. How do these aspects relate to practical activities in which children engage and which they can perceive to be meaningful?

Vygotsky himself accorded his work on voluntary attention primary status in his account of the development of higher mental functions. In *Thought and Language* (1986: 166), for example, he commented:

> The central issue of development during school age is the transition from primitive remembering and involuntary attention to the higher mental processes of voluntary attention and logical memory.

To begin this account, it is useful to notice that Vygotsky was completely opposed to the formal presentation of grammatical features and drill through decontextualized exercises. He comments about Tolstoy's approach to education that

> with his profound understanding of the nature of word and meaning, [Tolstoy] realized more clearly than most other educators the impossibility of simply relaying a concept from teacher to pupil . . . he found that one could not teach children literary language by artificial explanations, compulsive memorizing, and repetition. (150)

He goes on to quote Tolstoy

> 'We have to admit that we attempted several times to do this, and always met with an invincible distaste on the part of the children, which shows that we were on the wrong track.' (152)

Further, he agreed with Tolstoy's view that

> the path from the first encounter with a new concept to the point where the concept and the corresponding word are fully appropriated by the child is long and complex. (152)

However, what Vygotsky did not accept was Tolstoy's call for 'natural unhindered development' and the abandonment of any attempt to direct the acquisition of concepts. In a comment which has been central to our work in the project I will shortly describe, Vygotsky asserts,

> it is not only possible to teach children [explicitly: GW] to use concepts, but . . . such 'interference' may influence favourably the development of concepts that have been formed by the student himself . . . to introduce a concept means just to start the process of its appropriation. Deliberate introduction of new concepts does not preclude spontaneous development, but rather charts the new paths for it. (152)

The beginnings of these processes Vygotsky saw to be in directing children's attention to features of some phenomenon through what he called 'the indicative function' of the sign. He and his colleagues carried out a number of intriguing experiments with children to demonstrate how signs initially direct attention and then subsequently enable children to sustain attention voluntarily to phenomena which otherwise they find it difficult to manage. For example, with Leontiev he conducted a series of studies of the very beginnings of sign-mediated attention for specific phenomena, and of the difficulties experienced by children in resolving puzzles without the advantage of some initial direction of attention through a sign. (See, for example, studies of children's play in the 'forbidden colours' game (Kozulin 1990).)

Abstracting from his work for the purposes of this discussion, we might hypothesize that a primary function of a grammatical term in ontogenesis is to direct attention to some linguistic feature. So, the implied question is: which grammatical terms in relation to which linguistic features? This is, I think, the nub of the issue. It is a multi-faceted problem, but the primary issue must necessarily be what the child 'notices' in some elementary way about the linguistic features through the metasemiotic resource. If the metalinguistic term mediates attention initially to some grammatical features which are accessible through specific semantic features of a text because the grammatical description is pushed close to the semantic stratum, for example to Actor and Goal or to contrasting types of Processes, then it is plausible that children will be able to *use* their new knowledge for interpretation in ways which are not possible with traditional descriptions.

We can illustrate the point through Vygotsky's contrast between the learning of a first language and a foreign one.

The acquisition of a foreign language differs from the acquisition of the native one precisely because it uses the semantics of the native language as its foundation. (1986: 159–60)

Analogically, it might be argued: for children, the acquisition of a meta-language differs from the acquisition of language precisely because it uses the semantics of the language as its foundation.

This way of thinking suggests a different starting point for developing children's knowledge of grammar and, quite crucially, a different way of thinking about what grammatical knowledge might be for. Instead of conceiving of grammar in primary school as 'basic' descriptive work on parts of speech in isolated sentences, an alternative is to make exploring *how texts mean* the orientation, and to develop thinking about effects of language patterns through a meaning-oriented, functional grammar. Children's literature is a rich site for exploring these issues, not least because of the way in which literary texts mean through the patterning of language and, even more significantly, a necessary further patterning of those patterns to articulate abstract themes (Hasan, 1985: chs. 3 and 4).

In the remainder of the chapter I will explore some of these ideas by introducing evidence of children talking about a text they enjoyed reading, Anthony Browne's *Piggybook* (1986) with the benefit of some SFL tools. *Piggybook* is an intriguing picture book, in which both linguistic and visual semiosis plays an important role. Here the research focus was on children's development of abilities to consider *meaning effects* of linguistic patterning based on their observations about the grammar of experience in different phases of the narrative.

## 5.3  Primary school children considering some meaning effects of linguistic patterning in *Piggybook*

### 5.3.1  Background to the study

The children who participated in this work were in their seventh year of schooling (Year 6 in the New South Wales primary school system). They came from a wide range of language backgrounds, including Mandarin, Tamil, Portuguese, Tagalog, Italian and Spanish. Their class was one of three in the year group. The classes had been arranged in the previous year to distribute the children by ability and academic achievement to form three parallel learning groups. Family social positioning was varied: many parents worked in manual occupations, though there were a few in professions such as teaching and medicine, and several families owned small suburban businesses. The teacher, Ruth French, collaborated closely with the university researchers (Joan Rothery and Geoff Williams) in developing the research techniques and the pedagogic strategies.[1]

Certain general features of Ruth French's teaching approaches are important background to the research. First, the children read a wide range of literary texts, both with Ruth and independently, as part of ordinary classroom work. Ruth herself read a lot of new children's books, both for her own professional development and in order to be able to encourage children to read new, more complex texts through her enthusiastic recommendations. Similarly, poetry had a prominent role in the classroom, sometimes simply for play and general enjoyment, sometimes for intensive discussion.

Second, Ruth paid a lot of attention to visual representation of the children's work. The classroom walls were filled with work samples and the children's records of their understanding of concepts. These samples involved colour and shape coding of mathematical principles and, as the grammatical work built up, they soon included representations of grammatical principles. Figure 5.1 is a photograph two elements of a set of charts the children developed in collaboration with Ruth, illustrated here in black and white. The selection of colours and shapes to signify grammatical features was the children's work, and often involved careful discussion of which shapes and colours might be most effective. The value of children's development of multimodal representation in easing the immediate burden of abstract learning and in assisting learners to attend to relevant linguistic features is itself an issue much in need of research.

**Figure 5.1** A detail from the children's working record of the grammatical concepts they learned in Ruth French's classroom

Third, the work we are to consider was introduced after the children were already familiar with some key concepts in functional grammar. The features Theme and Rheme, clause, Participant and Process had been introduced earlier in the year to help children to extend their writing abilities. Again, it was practical work with texts which formed the general environment into which these grammatical descriptions had been introduced. We hypothesized that the features would be useful tools for solving some practical writing problems. (For a discussion of this early work and some of the results from it, see Williams 1995.) The children began the discussion of *Piggybook* with some experience of a functional grammar, but at this stage there had been no discussion of specific Participant roles in relation to different types of Processes.

In this phase of the work the specific research question was whether or not the introduction of a description of Actor and Goal would help the children to describe patterns of relations between Participants, and the significance of changes in those patterns, as the text evolved. We sought evidence about the following statements:

- **The *initial* language features to which the children spontaneously attended as aspects of patterning in first discussions of *Piggybook* demonstrated no observable meta-awareness of the grammatical features Actor and Goal, however informal.**
  This evidence is crucial for a claim that the introduction of the specific Participant roles directed children's attention to new metalinguistic features, following Vygotsky's arguments outlined above.

- **The children were independently able to distinguish Processes and Participants, and to identify process types before being introduced to the grammatical features Actor and Goal.**
  This evidence was important for determining how meaningful the introduction of the more delicate features Actor and Goal might be.

- **The children learned to distinguish the specific transitivity participant roles in effective material clauses: active voice independently.**
  If the children were not able to do so there would be no basis for assuming the concepts could be utilized in the description of linguistic patterns and interpretation of the text.

- **Attending to the grammatical roles Actor and Goal enabled the children to think about the construction of literary figures in *Piggybook* in newly abstract ways.**
  We needed to be able to contrast what the children could say at the beginning of the unit, prior to the new knowledge being introduced, with what they could say as a group without prompting from Ruth at the conclusion, as evidence about the relative abstractness of their reading of the text.

- **(At least some of) the children could represent the new, more abstract level of interpretation independently at a later time.**
  Evidence about this issue forms the basis for any claim for relative stability of the new concepts concerning the functions of grammatical patterning in building meaning.

To address this question we gathered a wide range of data, attempting to describe the children's work from a range of perspectives. We were also very interested in data on the evolution of the children's ideas rather than just the levels of learning they might achieve at the end of the unit. For example, we wanted as much information as possible about what pedagogic strategies assisted or impeded their evolving ideas, whether or not they experienced frustration as they moved into more abstract ways of thinking about language through texts (rather than through single sentences), and whether the introduction of the grammar diminished or increased their enthusiasm for the literary text and other reading and writing they were engaged in. These were some of the many questions about learning processes. The major data-gathering strategies were: close classroom observation by Ruth, Joan and Geoff; audio and video recordings of the children's discussions; transcripts of key discussions; interviews with individual children; Ruth's teaching journal notes; the children's reflections in their learning journals; and the children's drawings about the patterns and relations they observed. (In other phases of the project we made comparisons between writing by children in the focal class and one of the parallel classes, written tests of grammatical knowledge and substantial interviews with children about changes to draft writing in the focal class and one of the parallel classes.)

### 5.3.2 Observations about patterns in Piggybook prior to the discussion of Actor/Goal

After their first reading of *Piggybook* the children engaged in vigorous searches for visual patterns, delighting in the pictures showing the light switches transforming into pigs' faces, the wallpaper decorations into pigs' feet and the kitchen into a pigs' sty. However, when Ruth initially focused the group's attention on the question of patterns in the language the comments were rather uncertain. The children engaged in the task very willingly and enjoyed talking with each other, but they seemed to be searching for a means to think about the language and its patterns. The talk in Text 5.1 exemplifies the kind of search obvious during a long class discussion.

**Text 5.1  The children's initial search for language patterns**

| | |
|---|---|
| Ruth: | Any comments about 'nice house', 'nice garage'? |
| Cd: | I just thought that um you know it just sounded a bit like 'Mr Piggott lived with his two sons, Simon and Patrick' [HEAVILY SARCASTIC TONE] . . . nice house, nice carpet, and nice car and nice garage . . . and I guess like over and over and over again it gets like really boring, everything is so nice, nothing wrong happens in this house, everything is so *perfect*. It gives you that effect. |
| Ruth: | And what happens when you read a bit further into the book? |

| Cd: | Um well what happens when the mother moves, the opposite of that . . . had to make their own meals, had to make their own meals and stuff. |
| Ruth: | So it's a big contrast. So when she leaves them |
| Cd: | like it was horrible, it was horrible and it took hours, it took hours and all that kind of stuff and they learned they weren't as good as they had pretended. |

Clearly the children do understand the change in the family environment, but they were thus far unable to articulate the linguistic basis for interpreting the change. In this same discussion Ruth encouraged the children to search further for patterning associated with the human Participants. They were able to make some quite interesting observations about differentiating lexis but that is the most abstract level they reached prior to the introduction of the more detailed grammatical tools.

### Text 5.2  Further searches for language patterns

| Ruth: | OK, so you noticed there were quite a few human Participants but can you say anything more about them? Did you notice a pattern with them? |
| Cd: | Yes, the pattern was that most of them were (?the males) and there were only a few that were only Mrs Piglet. The rest were mostly Mr Piglet or they were sort of like describing the people, the narrator. |
| Ruth: | The narrator describing the people. What sort of words were used for Mrs Piggott? Did you notice that? |
| Cd: | Yeh, um, she just had 'Mrs Piggott' and she she didn't like have any other one. |
| Cd: | She had like . . . |
| Ruth: | What did you say, Carolina? |
| Cd: | Um, 'old girl'. |
| Ruth: | Yeh, that's a name for Mrs Piggott. |
| Cd: | But they just like said anything to her, 'Do this, do that!' |
| Cd: | The words that, like when the Participants when it came to Mrs Piggott weren't very like as glamorous as Mr Piggott's sort of words. |
| Ruth: | Give me an example. |
| Cd: | Like here with Mrs Piggott's got 'Old girl' and then with Mr Piggott it's always got 'Mr Piggott, Mr Piggott'. |

The first comment suggests there is a difference simply in the frequency with which the males and female are present in the narrative. The comment '. . . and there were only a few that were only Mrs Piglet' refers to the relative frequency with which Mrs Piggott occurred as a Participant, in contrast with the greater presence of the males. This was a particularly interesting theoretical moment because, for all their sophistication in detecting the gender attitudes constructed by the lexis, the children did not comment on any linguistic patterning through which differences in the distribution of work is brought about, nor anything about changes in that distribution during the narrative. In summary, to this point in the children's discussions we could find no evidence at all, despite Ruth's repeated attempts to provide relevant opportunities, that the children were attending spontaneously to different roles for Participants, nor any effects of role differentiations.

### 5.3.3 Introduction of the grammatical features Actor and Goal

At this stage Ruth gave the children a copy of the text of *Piggybook*, divided into clauses.[2] (It would have been possible for the children to achieve this analysis themselves in small group discussion, given the facility of their previous analyses of clauses, but it was a rather tedious and time-consuming task when there were now more exciting language issues to discuss.) One immediate finding surprised us. Some of the children didn't at first recognize the reproduced language as the same language of *Piggybook* they had read many times with Ruth. Apparently even this small step to making the language visible and available as an object of study, in this case quite literally, was important for some children.

Through reading the typescript the children were able to notice rather more patterns than previously, perhaps simply through the linear presentation of the text on two A4 pages, in contrast with the complexity of the interweaving of text and illustrations in the book itself. One particularly visible pattern was 'all the', as in 'all the breakfast things'. In turn, noticing this repetition gave a basis for the children to observe that the pattern was preceded by an element indicating 'what they'd done' to the Thing in the pattern. In Text 5.3, drawn from a whole class discussion, it can be seen how Ruth uses their observations to begin to build a more abstract understanding of the nature of the Process type through which 'what they'd done' is encoded.

### Text 5.3  Drawing children's attention to a pattern of Processes

Ruth:   Today's date is the 3rd August[3] and this is the children continuing to explain the patterns they found in *Piggybook* when they were first given a copy of the written text. I think I was asking about the 'all the' patterns that you found. You notice there was a repetition first of all of the 'all the'. Didn't you? [LAUGHS] And then what else did you notice?

Cd:   It would go . . . 'all the' . . . and then it would go like 'breakfast things', or 'beds' or 'carpets' and lead onto that.

Cd:   And then on the front of it it would have like the things that they, what they'd done to the thing that was, like what they'd done to the bed or what they'd done to the carpet.

Cd:   'washed'

Cd:   'all the breakfast'

Cd:   'washed all the breakfast things, they *made* all the beds, they *vacuumed* all the carpets and then she went to work'.

| Ruth: | So there was a pattern not just of 'all the' being repeated but the word before 'all the'. What did you say the word was doing or what was it? |
|---|---|
| Cd: | The word that was in front of 'all the' was um the word that was describing she was *doing* to the breakfast things or the beds or the carpets, like she was |
| Cd: | She *made* the bed, or she *vacuumed* the carpet. |
| Ruth: | Just out of interest do you know what type of word that is? |
| Cd: | Like how . . . would you dec . . . |
| Cd: | Process. |
| Ruth: | It is a Process, Emily, that's right. Eleanor, you haven't been here for most of this work and it's pretty new to you. Isn't it? Yep. Do you know what type of Process? Are they all the same type? |
| Cd: | Um well |
| Ruth: | Have a look at the types of Processes that are over there. Has anybody else been able to work it out? You should be able to watch on the stencil where they are up to. A lot of people noticed that this was the section that talked about the jobs Mrs Piggott did. |
| Cd: | P . . . |
| Cd: | It's a pa . . . a Participant is a person or a thing . . . |
| Ruth: | Yes involved in the Process. That's right. Just pause for a minute whilst I listen to this message. [BREAK IN TAPE] What were we thinking about? |
| Cd: | It was a Participant like um a thing, beds, carpets, breakfast . . . |
| Ruth: | Oh yeh, the beds, well done. The beds and carpets and what else? |
| Cd: | Breakfast things. |
| Ruth: | Breakfast things are Participants because they are involved in the Process. OK. Um we said that 'washed' and 'cleaned' and what is it? 'Washed' and 'vacuumed' and stuff were Processes and we were trying to work out what type. |
| Cd: | (WHISPERS) Yes, what type? |
| Ruth: | What do you think, Emily? |
| Cd: | Material . . . Material Processes. |
| Ruth: | Yeh, well done. So you've noticed a pattern and there's actually some grammatical names for that pattern. So instead of saying these words are kind of the same you can actually explain they are the same. They are all Material Processes. Yeh. Fantastic girls. |

The children were then in a position to begin describing the different Process types in the text so Ruth set a task for them to work through the typescript making this analysis.

### Text 5.4    Analysis of Process types

| Ruth: | I would like you to find the Processes in all the clauses on that first page, but not just find the Processes. I want you to decide whether that they are Relational, Existential, Verbal, Material, Mental. |
|---|---|

The obvious question is: were the children able to manage such an abstract task? To exemplify their facility, here is an excerpt from a small group discussion in which three children reviewed their analyses.

**Text 5.5  The children's facility in identifying Process types: 1**

\* indicates simultaneous talk

| | |
|---|---|
| Cd: | Cathy's going to join in our group just to mark the first page. OK, what did you get for the first, well we've already marked that. Well, what did you get for number 6? |
| Cd: | We got, 'hurry up' mat . . . mat, 'hurry up'. |
| Cd: | Yep, that's right. |
| Cd: | Then we got mat. where are we . . . verbal 'called'. |
| Cd: | Oh, yes, we got it wrong. |
| Cd: | Oh yeh. |
| Cd: | Then we got mat 'went'. |
| Cdn: | Yep. |
| Cd: | mat 'left' |
| Cd: | mat 'washed' |
| Cd: | mat 'made' |
| Cd: | mat 'vacuumed' |
| Cd: | mat 'went' |
| Cd: | mat 'hurry up' |
| Cd: | No, no. |
| Cd: | Yeh, yeh, mat. 'hurry up'. |
| Cd: | Oh I've got . . . I've got Relational |
| Cd: | mat. |
| Cd: | Verbal 'called' |
| Cdn: | mat. 'came' |
| Cdn: | mat. 'hurry up' |
| Cd: | \*mat. 'called' |
| Cd: | \*verbal 'called' |
| Cdn: | mat. 'came' |
| Cdn: | verbal 'called' |
| Cdn: | mat. 'came' |
| Cdn: | mat. 'eaten' |
| Cdn: | mat. 'washed' |
| Cdn: | mat. 'washed' |
| Cdn: | mat. 'did' |
| Cd: | mat. 'cooked' |
| Cd: | OK. |

This discourse was spoken very fast, conveying a sense of the pleasure, almost cockiness, the children felt as they confirmed their answers and enjoyed their success.

The following extract is of even greater significance for the question of children's facility in making such analyses.

**Text 5.6  The children's facility in identifying Process types: 2**

| | |
|---|---|
| Cd: | OK, 'hurry'. |
| Cd: | Another Material Process. |
| Cd: | \*'Was' |

| Cd: | *'Was' |
|---|---|

Cd:      *'Was'
Cd:      'was'.
Cd:      I'm not really sure about that, I think it might be . . .
Cd:      Yes, I think it's another Material Process.
Cd:      No, it's either a Relational, it could be a Relational
Cd:      OK.
Cd:      'Inside' Hold it. 'Inside the house was' means I think it is . . . I can't think it . . . Existential Process. That could be that. I'll write that down because 'was' means that his wife was there, it exists.

It was at this point that Ruth introduced the more specific concepts of Actor and Goal to the group. She did so through some constructed examples, and diagrams which represented relations between the general concept Participant and the specific roles in Material Processes. The children worked with a table of examples, experiencing little difficulty in deciding which grammatical element was Actor and which Goal, or which of the two occurred in clause examples with a single Participant such as in 'They waited' or 'The dinner was burned'.

When the children felt reasonably secure with this new knowledge they explored how the element which was Goal affected a reader's sense of the character of the figure in the Actor role. To illustrate, the sense of 'Janet' as a character is rather different in the following clauses:

1. Janet organized the flowers.
2. Janet organized the agenda.
3. Janet organized his demise.

The children played with these ideas by constructing a character and then reconstructing her by varying the range of Material Processes and Goals. They found that what Janet might build or sew or cook or destroy helped them to construct very different kinds of people. (One child dramatically demonstrated his understanding by contrasting 'Janet made a doll's house' with 'Janet made a bomb'!) Some effects of this understanding for their readings of *Piggybook* are evident in the following segment of discussion.

**Text 5.7  Observing linguistic patterns during classroom discussion (abstraction of the significance of Goals)**

Ruth:    I think Ian would like . . . Maybe Ian would like to have a turn.
Cd:      OK. Um . . . You can see from the front title that Mother is carrying Mr Piggott and two sons, so . . .
Ruth:    And why are they . . .?
Cd:      Miss Piggott is doing all the work and they are, like, just going for holidays, or something like that.
Ruth:    So there's a bit of a hint in the picture, isn't there? The illustrations are probably very important. And how does the grammar as well, I mean look at the writing. How does the grammar help to make the

character?

Cd: Um . . . well, like with the activity before, like, we had to make our own character, or before that, we did one with Janet and we put um . . . Goals and things. Well, if you write, sort of 'build a city' and 'build a town' and everything, you'd know that um . . . it's an older person, it's an adult, who's an architect or something. If we say 'she plays with a Barbie' and . . . um . . . 'she disturbs his older brother' and everything, then you would think that it's just a little girl, so . . . um . . . and the Process and the Goals usually give it away, or not always the Process but the Goals, what she's doing.

Joan: Material Process and Goals can build up a picture of the character.

Cd: Yeah.

From this point it was a relatively small step for the children to map (in technicolour, for display around the classroom!) the patterning of Actor, Process and Goal in different phases of the text. From charting the distributions (and again we hypothesize that the multimodal representation is crucial to the development of their meta-awareness) the children were able to articulate new understandings of the significance of patterning. Here is a further illustration from the classroom discussions:

**Text 5.8  Types of Goals in different phases of *Piggybook***

Ruth: [ASKING THE CHILDREN TO REPORT THEIR FINDINGS TO JOAN] What did you notice that you pointed out to the class?

Cd: The Mrs Piggott pattern . . . all the job she does . . . the Goals.

Ruth: And what about them?

Cd: They're all work, like, and all the . . . Mr Piggott and the boys are, like, they don't do any work. That's all.

Ruth: Good. Would you like to get someone to add something? Jarad.

Cd: Um . . . well, we noticed that everyone was doing something, but . . . um . . . Mrs Piggott was doing something *to* something and the other . . . um . . . the rest of the family, like Mrs . . . um . . . oh, Mr Piggott and the boys, they were just doing things but they weren't doing things to anything. They didn't have any Goals, they only had . . . um . . . Actors and Processes, whereas Mrs Piggott had Actor, Process and Goal and . . . yeah.

Ruth: Yeah, OK. That's what you pointed out this afternoon, wasn't it? Would you like to pick someone to add something? I think there seems to be people who think we haven't covered everything we noticed yet. Tamilselvan.

Cd: Um . . . that's what every clause in *Piggybook*? No, they're the clauses . . . um . . . which have Material Process in them.

Ruth: And just from the first page of the text that we have copied out, wasn't it?

Cd: Yeah.

Ruth: Catherine?

Cd: Last week when I was doing a working on the sheet, trying to find a pattern, I was telling Dr Rothery that all . . . um . . . Mrs Piggott's

|         | Goals were to do with housework. |
|---------|----------------------------------|
| Ruth:   | So there was a pattern inside the Goals. It wasn't just that she had lots of Goals, things that she was doing things to. |

Catherine's remark serves to illustrate the kind of understanding almost all of the children had achieved at the conclusion of the unit.

There is, however, the further important question of the relative permanence of the children's understanding. Anyone who has worked closely with children is all too aware of how learning which appears to be clear may, within a few months, be not very clear at all. As a further step for this phase of the project we therefore sought evidence of the children's thinking about the linguistic patterning and its significance. We used a variety of research techniques, including children's development of charts to report their findings to another class group, and written comments and interviews. Information about one of the summary charts, developed by the whole class, is presented by Martin (Chapter 12). Additionally, here is an excerpt from an interview between Joan (the research associate) and Gary (one of the children) that illustrates the confidence with which a large number of the children could talk about their experience.

**Text 5.9 Final interview: the research associate discussing Gary's understanding of the work on *Piggybook* two months after it had ended**

| Joan: | So what was it about the grammar that made the characters the way they were? You've said a little bit about that. What was it about the grammar? |
|-------|--------|
| Gary: | The mother had the Goals, she did everything and the father and the two sons didn't have Goals, they just had (INAUDIBLE) talked to the mother in not a very nice way. |
| Joan: | OK, so what was often Goal in the first part of the book? |
| Gary: | Work. |
| Joan: | Work, what kind of work? |
| Gary: | Making beds. |
| Joan: | What's one word for that kind of work? |
| Gary: | Housework. |
| Joan: | So that was the Goal for the first part of the book. So was there any difference between the clauses where Mr Piggott or the two sons were Actor, you've answered this in a way, or where Mrs Piggott was Actor? |
| Gary: | (INAUDIBLE) |
| Joan: | The clauses where Mr Piggott and the two sons were Actor or where Mrs Piggott was Actor? |
| Gary: | Well . . . um . . . the two boys and the father, they usually talked and they didn't do much and so that's different because she usually just did work and they talked, she didn't talk at all. |
| Joan: | Uh huh, OK. Did the Actor and Goals change during the story? |
| Gary: | Yep, because um, first of all the mother had the Goals and at the |

|        | end the two sons and the father and the mother all had Goals. |
|--------|---------------------------------------------------------------|
| Joan:  | So um, what did that show about the book? |
| Gary:  | That in the beginning that only one person was doing the work and in the end the whole family was helping out. |
| Joan:  | And did Mrs Piggott's work change at all? |
| Gary:  | Yep, she mended the car. |
| Joan:  | So, how is that a different Goal? |
| Gary:  | It's a different Goal because she is doing something that she wouldn't usually do. She usually did the work in the house. |

## 5.4 In summary

There is obviously no road which leads to QED in educational linguistics. The significance of the findings introduced here is not that they 'prove' children's ability to learn and use a functional grammar. Rather, the account serves as a critique of common assumptions about the limitations to what children can do in reasoning abstractly about language. The findings are also a signpost to much needed further research into children's development of metalinguistic critical awareness through a meaning-oriented grammar.

The strong impression we have gained from this work, and also another phase of the project with a group of six-year-olds who have also been able to learn to use the concepts Actor and Goal descriptively, is that children's ability to reason abstractly and enthusiastically about language has been grossly underestimated by curricula from the mid-1970s to the present. (See Williams (1998) for a discussion of the work with the six-year-old children.)

Language curricula have remained relatively under-theorized and static while other features of school work have made some, if sometimes faltering, progress towards developing children's meta-awareness about learning and interpretive strategies. In fact, we have been able to benefit greatly by demonstrating to children some analogies between mathematical patterning, with which they are quite familiar, and linguistic patterning, which has been quite new to them. In language education two restrictions are particularly evident. One is a kind of 'stratal' trap through which teachers of young children have been obliged to spend large amounts of time on relations between phonology and graphology, as though this stratum were more basic for basic ideas about language than the stratum of meaning. The other restriction results from an unhinging of meaning and grammar in education, dating back at least to the beginnings of compulsory universal schooling. It is important that other possibilities for developing meta-awareness through literacy pedagogy are imagined and researched vigorously, to expand a sense of how children might think about meaning-making in literary texts and, of course, other registers equally.

Finally, an end-note about a critique of critical awareness itself in the field of children's literature. It has sometimes been suggested that work towards critical discourse awareness in literature leads to another form of authoritarian teaching. This is argued to be so when learners are given no clear access to descriptive principles which they are able to use independently of the particular interpretive text, the pedagogic occasion and the specific teacher.

Is such an outcome also produced through learning to use a functional grammar for critical interpretation of literary texts? Clearly this is itself an issue in need of further research, but there are at least some relevant fragments of evidence from our data. These suggest that through engaging in this work the children felt more confident about making independent criticism than was evident earlier in the year. They were, for example, vigorously critical of the limits of the text's representation of the work Mr and Mrs Piggott did outside the house. This was not expressed as a criticism of the text per se, but rather as an important issue in thinking about why Mrs Piggott was so particularly exploited by the unequal distribution of work. The children were equally vigorous in indicating what this selection of grammatical analysis had not netted in. They considered that there were other, equally important changes in meaning. For example, they pointed out that we had not explored Mrs Piggott's silence, nor the way in which she was addressed by the males in the first phase of the text. These were phenomena they regarded as of equal semantic significance as the patterning of Actor and Goal.

Though the grammatical features were introduced explicitly and very carefully, and though the children practised distinguishing these features extensively, in this data there is no evidence at all that a loss of critical ability or impetus resulted. Reviewing the evidence, we conclude the opposite to be the case. The teaching of grammar is often associated with authoritarian practices and negative outcomes. The crucial point is that this is not a necessary relation between all grammars and outcomes for children's learning. A functional grammar, and a pedagogy which orients learners to thinking about effects of grammatical patterning for ways texts mean, may produce some important positive effects for critical discourse analysis.

In attempting to represent the nature of such work as this to ourselves we have found it helpful to think of it as serious play about language, rather than as primarily a means for learning grammar palatably. It is serious play in the way Gregory Bateson (1972: 14) thought about it in one of his famous metalogues:

| Daughter: | Daddy, are these conversations serious? |
| Father: | Certainly they are. |
| D: | They're not a sort of game that you play with me? |
| F: | God forbid . . . but they are a sort of game that we play together. |
| D: | Then they're *not* serious! |

# Notes

1. The three co-workers gratefully acknowledge the sensitive assistance of Kelly Stephens with this phase of the project.
2. For an analysis of the language into clauses see Martin's chapter, this volume.
3. This date is early in the Third Term of a four term school year in New South Wales. The children were aware of the presence of an audiorecorder for research purposes, and of Ruth's routine identification of the date of the discussions.

# References

Bateson, G. (1972) *Steps Towards an Ecology of Mind*. New York: Ballantine Books.

Browne, A. (1986) *Piggybook*. London: Julia MacRae Books.

Chambers, A. (1985) *Booktalk: Occasional Writing on Literature and Children*. London: Bodley Head.

Chambers, A. (1993) *TELL ME: Children, Reading and Talk*. Stroud: Thimble Press.

Chatman, S. (1978) *Story and Discourse: Narrative Structure in Fiction and Film*. Ithaca: Cornell University Press.

Hamley, D. (1996) Thoughts on narrative, tradition, originality, children, writing, reading. *Signal*, 79: 5–16

Hasan, R. (1985) *Linguistics, Language and Verbal Art*. Geelong: Deakin University Press.

Hasan, R. (1996) Literacy, everyday talk and society. In R. Hasan and G. Williams (eds), *Literacy in Society*. London: Longman.

Halliday, M.A.K. (1994) *An Introduction to Functional Grammar* (2nd edn). London: Edward Arnold.

Hollindale, P. (1988) *Ideology and the Children's Book*. Stroud: Thimble Press.

Knowles, M. and Malmkjær, K. (1996) *Language and Control in Children's Literature*. London: Routledge.

Kozulin, A. (1990) *Vygotsky's Psychology: A Biography of Ideas*. New York: Harvester Wheatsheaf.

Meek, M. (1988) *How Texts Teach What Readers Learn*. Stroud: Thimble Press.

Nikolajeva, M. (1996) *Children's Literature Comes of Age: Toward a New Aesthetic*. New York: Garland.

Stephens, J. (1992) *Language and Ideology in Children's Fiction*. London: Longman.

Toolan, M.J. (1988) *Narrative: A Critical Linguistic Introduction*. London: Routledge.

Wall, B. (1991) *The Narrator's Voice: The Dilemma of Children's Fiction*. New York: St. Martin's Press.

Vygotsky, L.V. (1986) *Thought and Language*. Ed. and trans. A.Kozulin. Cambridge, MA: MIT Press.

Williams, G. (1995) Learning systemic functional grammar in primary schools. In P.H. Peters (ed.), *Australian English in a Pluralist Australia*. Proceedings of Style Council 95. Dictionary Research Centre, Macquarie University.

Williams, G. (1998) Children entering literate worlds: perspectives from the study of textual practices. In F. Christie and R. Missan (eds), *Literacy in Schooling*. London: Routledge.

# 6 Researching everyday talk

*Suzanne Eggins*

## 6.1 Why study everyday talk?

In information cultures of the late twentieth century, literacy is a vital social skill. Yet for most people, at most ranks of the social hierarchy, talk time far outweighs reading and writing time.

But just what are we doing when we talk? For the earliest researchers of everyday talk, the Conversation Analysts, the answer was almost mechanical: talking is about managing the turn-taking machinery which drives interaction (Sacks *et al.* 1974). Conversation Analysts approached talk from an ethnomethodological perspective, asking what everyday talk shows us about how people 'do' social life (Sacks 1972). For example, how social members use laughter to elicit and display affiliations with each other, how they manage to get their topics talked about, how they start and end their interactions, and how they manage 'troubles' in interaction (Sacks 1992a, 1992b, Schegloff and Sacks 1974, Jefferson 1984, Jefferson and Lee 1992). Through detailed analyses of the micro-interactional and topic features of talk, the Conversation Analysts came to view everyday talk as a dynamically negotiated 'interactional achievement' (Schegloff 1981).

For functional linguists, the approach to everyday talk is slightly different. We recognize that talking is a *semantic* activity, a process of making meanings. As we take turns in any interaction we negotiate meanings about what we think is going on in the world (ideational meanings), how we feel about it and how we feel about the people we interact with (interpersonal meanings). By analysing ordinary, spontaneous interactions we can better understand how language is structured to enable us to make meanings with each other. We view language as a resource for doing social life and ask just how that resource gets used in everyday talk.

Because functional linguistics theorizes a realizational relationship between context and language, researching everyday talk allows us to uncover how we jointly construct the social reality within which we live. Thus, by exploring the meanings we make with each other in what Halliday (1978: 40) describes as 'the microsemiotic encounters of daily life', functional linguists can offer critical explanations of how we both enact and confirm the social world. This critical functional investigation leads us directly to the paradox of everyday interactions: that the very encounters we think of as the most trivial and unimportant turn out to be instrumental in constructing and maintaining the social identities and interpersonal relations that define our social lives.

In this chapter I present examples of two very different kinds of everyday talk to highlight some research questions you could explore from this critical functional linguistic perspective.[1]

## 6.2 Talking to get things done: pragmatic interactions

Sometimes when we talk, we take part in interactions very similar to Text 6.1: Information Dialogue. This text is the transcription of a telephone conversation between a caller and an operator. (The column on the right will be explained later and can be ignored for the moment.)

**Text 6.1 Information Dialogue**

| Turn | Speaker | Transcribed talk | Schematic Structure Stage |
|---|---|---|---|
| 1 | Operator | Good afternoon. Information Service | **CONTACT** |
| 2 | Caller | Yes. Um I'd like um information on some panel beaters. | **SERVICE REQUEST** |
| 3 | Operator | On some panel beaters. Um, where you live locally? | **LOCATION NOMINATION** |
| 4 | Caller | Um Chippendale, yeah. | |
| 5 | Operator | In Chippendale? | |
| 6 | Caller | Yeah. | |
| 7 | Operator | Just a moment | **SERVICE COMPLIANCE** |
| [operator types something into a computer] | | | |
| 8 | Operator | Not sure that we have anything for Chippendale, um but I'll check for you. | **SERVICE PREDICTION** |
| | | While we're waiting for the computer to come up with that information, do you have an account code for me? | **ACCOUNT CODE SPECIFICATION** |
| 9 | Caller | Mmm hm. It's nine four three | |
| 10 | Operator | Nine four three | |
| 11 | Caller | One nine five six | |
| 12 | Operator | One nine five six. Nine four three one nine five six? | |
| 13 | Caller | Correct. | |
| 14 | Operator | Right. Just a moment. | |
| [computer noise in the background] | | | |

| 15 | Operator | I think the nearest panel beaters are probably going to be in Newtown. | **PRE-OFFER** |
| 16 | Caller | Yeah? That's alright | |
| [pause; then computer displays information for the operator] | | | |
| 17 | Operator | Ah there's um . . . one in Chippendale. Would that be? | **OFFER** |
| 18 | Caller | Yep. Great. | |
| 19 | Operator | Uh it's Cleveland Motor Body Repairs | **INFORMATION PROVISION** |
| 20 | Caller | Mmm hm | |
| 21 | Operator | one five three Cleveland Street | |
| 22 | Caller | Right | |
| 23 | Operator | telephone number is six nine eight | |
| 24 | Caller | six nine eight | |
| 25 | Operator | two eight four one | |
| 26 | Caller | two eight four one. Was that Cleveland Motor? [deliberately unfinished] | **INFORMATION VERIFICATION** |
| 27 | Operator | Cleveland Motor Body Repairs | |
| 28 | Caller | Body repairs [falling intonation] | |
| 29 | Operator | Mmmm | |
| \30 | Caller | one five three Cleveland Street | |
| 31 | Operator | Yes | |
| 32 | Caller | Okay [rising tone] | **PRE-CLOSURE** |
| 33 | Operator | Okay [falling tone] | |
| 34 | Caller | Thanks very much | **CLOSURE** |
| 35 | Operator | Right, bye bye== | |
| 36 | Caller | ==Bye | |

This text shows us one very obvious dimension of everyday talk that differentiates it fundamentally from written text: talking involves turn-taking. Whereas a written text is always *implicitly* interactive, in spoken language two or more interactants must contribute actively by making meanings turn by turn if the interaction is to be successful.

But Text 6.1 also shows us that interaction is functionally motivated: we interact with each other in order to achieve some social purpose. Very often we talk to others to achieve quite specific, pragmatic goals: to exchange information (as in Text 6.1), to buy and sell, to pass on knowledge, to make appointments, to get jobs, or to jointly accomplish practical tasks.

A number of characteristics typical of the language of such pragmatic interactions are illustrated by Text 6.1.

### 6.2.1 Spontaneity phenomena

Text 6.1 contains various spontaneity phenomena: hesitations (*um*), incompletions (*would that be. . .?*) etc. One of the challenges of researching everyday talk is to adopt a transcription system which allows you to capture systematically in written form at least some of these features of the spoken-ness of interaction (see Section 6.5).

### 6.2.2 Everyday vocabulary and colloquial expressions

The vocabulary items and idiomatic expressions in Text 6.1 are very ordinary, rather than technical or elevated. Spoken language typically draws on a simpler, more widely shared vocabulary than does written text.

### 6.2.3 Brief, elliptical clauses

The grammatical structures in Text 6.1 are frequently short, either because they are brief, ritualized expressions (e.g. *Good morning; Just a moment*), or because they involve the ellipsis that is a major resource exploited in interaction (e.g. *Yes; on some panel beaters; correct*).

### 6.2.4 Congruent language

Everyday spoken language generally lacks the density and abstraction that characterize formal written language. The congruent language of interactions like Text 6.1 is part of what makes spoken texts more accessible, easier to process.

### 6.2.5 Role differentiation: patterns in mood and exchange

Pragmatic interactions usually occur between interactants where the Tenor involves a low frequency of contact and a low affective involvement. In other words, the interactants are not close, and may even be strangers, as is the case in Text 6.1.

When relative strangers meet and talk in order to achieve a specific, shared goal they are usually taking on social roles. Rather than interacting as Jane Doe and Mary Smith, our two interactants are interacting as 'a caller who wants information' and 'an operator whose job it is to provide it'. Pragmatic interactions typically involve such role differentiation. The differentiated roles (inquirer/informer, client/provider, teacher/student, buyer/seller, doctor/patient, etc.) are often not only functionally distinct but also hierarchically or status distinct. In other words, one role carries a higher status or is hierarchically superior to the other role.

Functional differentiation of roles generally involves role stability and complementarity. Typically the interactants will stay 'in' their social roles throughout an interaction (so, the caller does not suddenly slip into the role of 'best friend', nor does the operator suddenly decide she is no longer an operator). And the roles complement each other: each person does different things in the interaction (one participant requests the information, the other provides it), and together they achieve a successful negotiation.

Functional differentiation is enacted through the interpersonal patterns in the participants' linguistic behaviours. Two main areas of language use show these patterns: mood choice, and speech function and exchange structure. These patterns will be illustrated here by tabulating mood and speech function choices in Text 6.1.

### 6.2.5.1 Mood choices

Mood is one of the grammatical resources English has for expressing interpersonal meanings. Mood is the system that differentiates declarative clauses (*I'd like information on some panel beaters*) from interrogatives (*Do you live in Chippendale?*) or imperatives (*Give me the information*). It also differentiates full clauses (*You want information on some panel beaters*) from elliptical clauses (*On panel beaters*), and major clauses (all the examples so far) from minor clauses, such as greetings and feedback expressions (e.g. *Good afternoon; Yeah; Mmm hm*). For details of how to analyse mood in spoken language see Eggins and Slade (1997: ch. 3) and Halliday (1994: ch. 4).

When we're behaving in a particular social role, we generally make mood choices which the culture 'expects' for that role. Or, to put this the other way round, certain social roles carry expectations about the mood choices that will be appropriate. For example, the social role of 'teacher' carries the expectation that full interrogative, declarative and imperative clause structures can be produced, whereas the social role of 'student' is most often expressed through a more restricted range of mood classes (no imperatives, for example, but a high use of elliptical interrogatives). These mood choices enact the different social rights and obligations of each role, and suggest that in our culture at least teachers have greater social power (expressed as greater grammatical potential) than students. Table 6.1 summarizes the mood choices in Text 6.1.[2]

As Table 6.1 shows, the speakers each take an almost equal number of turns, thus indicating the reciprocal work they are doing to sustain the interaction. However, the Operator works harder in her turns, producing 28 clauses to the caller's 22. More of her clauses are full, rather than elliptical, suggesting that she does more work to initiate exchanges, while the Caller plays a more responsive role. The Operator also does more work finding out things – she asks many more interrogatives of all types than the Caller, suggesting that her role demands that she check and query information. Both speakers achieve much of the interaction through minor clauses, suggesting the high level of ritualization of the interaction (not every clause has to be created afresh). The Operator makes the

Caller Subject, alone and inclusively with the Operator, while the Caller never makes the Operator Subject but does make herself as Subject. This again indicates that the Operator is working 'for' the Caller and not vice versa. The Operator produces almost all the Adjunct elements in the interaction, most of them circumstantial, suggesting that it is her job to deliver 'content', or information. The Operator uses one modulation to check the Caller's inclination, and the Caller uses one to state her inclination. The Operator also expresses deference through her use of modalizations. Thus the mood analysis shows that, although both speakers contribute to the turn-taking, the Operator works hard throughout to meet the Caller's needs.

**Table 6.1** Mood choices in Text 6.1: Information Dialogue

| Mood (clause type) | Operator | Caller |
|---|---|---|
| number of turns | 19 | 17 |
| number of clauses | 28 | 22 |
| declarative | | |
| full | 5 | 3 |
| elliptical | 8 | 6 |
| polar interrogative | | |
| full | 1 | – |
| elliptical | 3 | 1 |
| wh-interrogative | | |
| full | – | – |
| elliptical | 1 | – |
| minor | 10 | 12 |
| most frequent Subject | you (=Caller): 2 | I |
| choice (non-ellipsed) | we (Information Service) | account code: 1 |
| | we (caller & operator) | the information: 3 |
| | panel beaters (& details | |
| | of ) 3 | |
| negation | 1 | – |
| Adjuncts | | |
| circumstantial | 8 | 1 |
| interpersonal | 1 | – |
| textual | 1 | –˙ |
| Modalization | | |
| probability | 3 | – |
| Modulation | | |
| (i) obligation | – | – |
| (ii) inclination | 1 | 1 |
| (iii) capacity | – | – |
| total number of | 4 | 1 |
| modalities | | |

### 6.2.5.2 Speech function choices and exchange structure

Role differentiation is also enacted through patterns 'above' the grammar, specifically those of speech function and exchange structure. A speech function is a functional label for what a speaker 'achieves' in a particular move in dialogue.[3] For example, when the Caller in Text 6.1 says *Um I'd like um information on some panel beaters*, she is making a demand that the operator provide her with a service (by providing some linguistic 'goods', i.e. information). Using a shorthand label, we can say that the speech function of her move is 'command'. Once the Caller has voiced her command, the Operator is faced with various options: she can agree to comply with the Caller's request (expressed through various 'supporting' speech functions); she can refuse the demand (expressed through various 'confronting' speech functions); or she can temporize, perhaps asking for further information before she commits herself either way. The social context carries the strong expectation that the Operator *will* comply, that speech function choice is the discourse obligation of her social role. And indeed she does, although she also goes on to get more information (about location in turns 3 to 5, and about the Caller's account code, in turns 8 to 14) before she delivers, in turns 19 to 31, the details the Caller had demanded. Thus the speech function choices in the text provide further understanding of how the social roles of 'Operator' and 'Caller' are typically unproblematically enacted in our culture.

The relationship between the speech function choices and their expression in mood types is also revealing. Given the Caller's need, to demand some linguistic 'goods', there are many different grammatical forms she could have used to express it. For example:

- Can I have the name of a service centre in my area please? *(modulated interrogative)*
- Where's the nearest car service centre to my area? *(wh-interrogative)*
- Tell me where I can get my car serviced in my area, please. *(imperative)*
- I want the name and number of a service centre in my area. *(declarative)*
- What I'd do for the name and number of a place to get my car serviced! *(exclamative)*

Her choice of the modulated declarative form identifies her (to the Operator) as a reasonably polite Caller, not one likely to be difficult or rude.

But although the Caller may seem to control the interaction, since it is her command speech function that the Operator must comply with, analysis of the exchange structure of the talk reveals that the Operator 'drives' the interaction at almost every stage. An exchange is a sequence of speech functions concerned with negotiating the same parcel of information (e.g. the account code is negotiated through the exchange in turns 8 to 14). Exchange analysis shows that the Operator initiates all but the 'command' exchange: she establishes contact by greeting the Caller;

she elicits the account code exchange; she initiates polite talk by predicting the search results (perhaps also foreshadowing complications); she
makes an offer of the information, before she initiates the exchange in
which it is provided; and finally she gives permission for the interaction to
end – notice how the Caller checks that it's okay to sign off, with her
'Okay?' in turn 32.

### 6.2.6 Relative brevity of the interaction

A further characteristic of everyday pragmatic interactions is their brevity.
In just 36 turns in Text 6.1, for example, the caller's request has been sat-
isfied and the interaction is terminated to the mutual satisfaction of both
interactants. While not all pragmatic interactions are as short and sweet as
this one, it is a characteristic of pragmatic talk that there is an end point
being talked towards.

### 6.2.7 Discernible generic structure

This brevity relates to a further characteristic of everyday pragmatic talk:
texts like Text 6.1 have a discernible staging or generic structure. The
stages through which the interactants talk in order to achieve their goals
are marked down the right-hand column on the text. These same stages,
in much the same order, are found in most of the other 150-odd successful phone calls made to the Information Service (Eggins *et al.* 1991). This
suggests that participants have ritualized, or habitualized, the interaction,
analogizing from other similar interactions in the culture. Following the
schematic structure enables interactants to achieve their purposes co-
operatively in a stress-free, economic way.[4]

### 6.2.8 Stability of Field, Mode and Tenor

From the perspective of context of situation, we can note that there is an
overall stability to the Field, Mode and Tenor. The topic at the beginning
of the talk (information about getting a car repaired) is the same topic
being negotiated at the end of the talk. The distance (experiential and
interpersonal) between the interactants and the process they are engaged
in does not change from beginning to end (they do not suddenly shift
from talk that takes account of the phone as medium to talk that would
only be comprehensible face-to-face). And, as we've already seen, the
interactants remain in their social roles throughout the talk.

### 6.2.9 Research questions relevant to pragmatic interactions

Pragmatic interactions feature large in everyday social life and they provide functional linguistic researchers with many interesting research questions, including:

- What discourse roles do certain social roles seem to obligate?
- What grammatical patterns are typical for different social roles?
- How can the stability of the interaction be challenged, and what are the linguistic and social consequences? i.e. what happens when something goes wrong?
- What kind of variation on the generic structure is possible before interactants begin to find the interaction problematic?
- How are particular kinds of pragmatic interactions performed differently in different cultures?
- How do ways of talking become ritualized (i.e. develop as genres)?
- How do genres adapt as social needs evolve?
- What can we teach about language and culture based on the analysis of common pragmatic interactions?

## 6.3 Casual conversation: talking to affirm interpersonal reality

Although pragmatic interactions are common, we need also to recognize that a great deal of the time we talk to each other not so much to achieve material goals, but (apparently) simply for the sake of talking itself. It is this kind of talk that we usually call casual conversation. Text 6.2: Lifting Weights, presented below, is the transcription of an interaction involving a couple in their early thirties (Tom and Lisa), who have invited Tom's workmate, Pete, over for dinner. As you read this text, you will no doubt be struck by the many differences between it and Text 6.1.

### Text 6.2 'Lifting Weights'[5]

Participants: Tom: Australian; Lisa's de-facto (common law husband); 34; architect
Pete: Irish; 23; student of architecture; colleague of Tom
Lisa: Australian; 32; student
Setting: Dinner at Tom and Lisa's
Additional information: Sally (mentioned from turn 14) is Tom's work colleague

#### Transcription conventions

| | |
|---|---|
| = | indicates overlap/run on, as follows: |
| | = at end of S1's turn and beginning of S2's turn indicates no appreciable break, i.e. latching or contiguity occurred. |
| | = during S1's turn and at the beginning of S2's turn indicates that S2 started taking her turn at this point, i.e. overlap occurred |
| . . . | short hesitation |
| – | false start, re-start |
| + ++ | expresses the intensity of laughter |
| **words in bold** | emphatic stress |
| , | slight break within a turn (a breath group) |
| . | finality, falling intonation |

| ? | question and/or rising intonation |
| no final punctuation | implies speaker did not indicate finality |
| [ ] | encloses non-verbal and/or paralinguistic information |
| ( ) | untranscribable speech |

| Turn | Speaker | Transcribed talk |
|---|---|---|
| 1 | Lisa | =I've intro- I've introduced Tom to people and the first night they've met him they've ended up punching him . . . I mean all in friendliness, but I mean = |
| 2 | Pete | =Yeah but he's got that kind of= |
| 3 | Lisa | =No. But it – it's quite =interesting |
| 4 | Tom | =Oh punch the fuck out of me **please** = |
| 5 | Pete | =[while laughing] Yea, you do. You've got that . . . [making a gesture to demonstrate people meeting Tom] 'How ya Tom?' |
| 6 | Lisa | It's just as well you do the weights, isn't it? [while laughing] To develop enough resistance= |
| 7 | Tom | =Oh **yeah** [laughter ++] |
| 8 | Lisa | for all the thumps you get. =But I? |
| 9 | Pete | =[while laughing] They've been getting a right **hiding** those weights, haven't they? |
| NV1 | Tom & Lisa | [laughter ++] |
| 10 | Tom | At least I brushed the dust off 'em before you came over. |
| 11 | Pete | [while laughing] Yeah. [makes blowing noise to imitate blowing the dust off the weights] |
| NV2 | Lisa & Pete | =[laughter ++] |
| 12 | Pete | =You threw |
| 13 | Lisa | =Is that what you were doing?= |
| 14 | Pete | You threw= |
| 15 | Lisa | =You were dusting, were you? |
| 16 | Pete | You threw a tea towel over the weights to make it look like they've just been used . . . and you put a bit of water on the ground [while laughing] to make it seem like you'd just been sweating |
| 17 | Lisa | He does use them. But I can never understand the order in which he uses it. He has a shower? and then comes out of the shower and= |
| NV3 | Pete | =[laughter+] |
| 18 | Lisa | then does weights. Wouldn't that be better if you= . . . had a shower after you did the weights, Tom? |
| NV4 | Pete | =[laughter+] |
| [pause – 2 secs] | | |
| 19 | Pete | The theory is mate right . . . that you work up a sweat and then you have your shower to clean yourself so that when you go out you're actually clean and you're not smelling = |
| 20 | Tom | =Ah. That's like= |
| 21 | Pete | =instead of going in feeling a little bit grotty, havin' a shower 'I'm clean now. I'll – I'll go an' ' – It's like walking into the toilet= |

| 22 | Tom | **=Well=** |
| 23 | Pete | =and washing your hands then= |
| 24 | Tom | **=that's exactly what I was goin' to say=** |
| 25 | Pete | =( ) and taking your flute out and= |
| 26 | Tom | =Yeah |
| 27 | Pete | having a piss putting it back up an' going. [laughter] You don't do that. [laughter ++] |
| NV5 | Tom | [bashes table in recognition/amusement] |
| 28 | Tom | [while laughing] Bloke that I used to work with used to do that and I used to say 'What?' He said 'I have great respect for my dick, don't I?' |
| NV6 | Pete | [laughter ++, lasting 6 secs] |
| 29 | Lisa | Who was that? |
| 30 | Tom | Carlos, the Spanish bloke. |
| 31 | Lisa | He used to wash his hands before?= |
| 32 | Tom | =Wash his hands, pull his bloody flute out and play it. |
| 33 | Pete | [while laughing] Play it |

[pause – 4 secs]

| 34 | Tom | Flute |
| 35 | Lisa | And did he wash his hands afterwards? |
| 36 | Tom | **Nuh**, just picked his bum and walked off. |

[Tom leaves the room at this point.]

| NV7 | Pete | [laughter] |
| 37 | Lisa | Well how many men **do** wash their hands afterwards, though? |
| 38 | Pete | **See** I thought working in an architect's office, **right** . . .with like educated people, who've . . . got some sense of etiquette – like you're not working with – with brick layers . . . that – that they have their hands mucky and soiled hands all day =everyday |
| 39 | Lisa | =Mhmm |
| 40 | Pete | that you know, you – you're talking with people – like I mean I've got softer hands than my mother, you know? **Not** from trying to have soft hands, I never use =**skin care** or anything |
| 41 | Lisa | =It's just that she's washed more dishes than you have. |
| 42 | Pete | She'd washed more dishes and she'd, you know? She'd do different things and . . . maybe being in the garden or something, d'you know what I mean? She'd have slightly stronger hands or **harder** and am . . . Yea, you'd think that more men **would** in an office situation, but you **walk** in and consistently – Or a **worse** thing **is**, you're sitting on the toilet in the office and you're sitting there, you know, kind of contemplating life's . . . throes and whatever and . . . an' ah you hear the f-door of the toilets open 'Alright then. Hope he doesn't got for a shit 'cause if he does then I'm going to have to listen to him have a shit and he's goin' to have to listen to me have one.' |
| 43 | Lisa | Eh |
| 44 | Pete | And, and then . . . then – then they've done it and they're goin' for a piss and you think right – right I should hear a tap now and the next thing you hear is [imitates the squeaking sound of an opening/closing door] the door= |

| 45 | Lisa | =Straight out. |
|----|------|----------------|
| 46 | Pete | And you go 'Oh dear. Hope he's not – hope it wasn't somebody I know.' |
| 47 | Lisa | It's not just men though. I – I've noticed a lot of women . . . that do **that**? and= |
| 48 | Pete | =Mhmm |
| 49 | Lisa | it always . . . surprises me because I kind of – it's probably a bad thing to say but I expect it of men maybe= |
| 50 | Pete | =Mmm |
| 51 | Lisa | to be a bit slack in that department, but . . . I see women and they'll go up to the mirror, and they'll look at themselves, and then they'll just walk straight out and you'd think even if they weren't into hand washing that they'd **think** because somebody was standing right there washing =**their hands** |
| 52 | Pete | =**Yeah**. They'd be more or less **shamed** into it. |
| 53 | Lisa | Yep. **Nothing** happ'ning. Straight out the door. [noise of disgust] |

Unlike Text 6.1, this talk does not seem to be motivated by any specific pragmatic purpose: Tom, Lisa and Pete are not talking 'to get something done'. However, some analysts have gone so far as to claim that everyday talk such as this is – despite its apparent triviality – is concerned with no less than the social construction of reality (e.g. Berger and Luckmann 1966). We can best understand this claim by examining the features of the talk.

### 6.3.1 Colloquial language

Text 6.2: Lifting Weights differs noticeably from Text 6.1: Information Dialogue in its degree of informality. While, as we saw above, Text 6.1 does exhibit characteristics of the spoken grammar of English such as colloquial lexis, minor and elliptical clauses, and congruent language, Text 6.2 is far more informal and colloquial. Part of this informality involves the contraction of words and the assimilation of sounds that happen in fast speech. For example, Tom said 'off 'em' instead of 'off them', and Pete says 'havin'' rather than 'having'.

### 6.3.2 Multilogue: the pressure to get a turn

Text 6.2 is typical of many casual conversations in that it is a multiparty conversation, or multilogue. Talk becomes significantly more complex once you have three rather than two people if simply because alliances become possible. For example, in Text 6.2 we see Lisa and Pete together 'ganging up' in teasing Tom. In multilogue there is also increased competition for turns, and some speakers may speak loudly or at a rapid pace to cut other participants out. With two or more participants not speaking, it becomes possible for the speaker to direct his/her comments to only one of the other participants. Thus multilogue provides interactants with opportunities not present in dialogue for asserting control, dividing the audience and re-calibrating interpersonal relations.

### 6.3.3 Functional identity of roles: more open interpersonal choices

Text 6.2 also differs significantly from Text 6.1 in the social roles and role relationships being enacted. In Text 6.1 we had role differentiation: each interactant took on a different but complementary role, and each remained in that role throughout the interaction. In Text 6.2, we are eavesdropping on three people who relate to each other as 'friends', i.e. they are all playing more or less the same social role though not, as we'll see in a minute, in exactly the same way. This difference in role relations can be described by noting that the Tenor in casual conversations very often involves high frequency of contact (we have these kinds of conversations with people we see a lot of) and high affective involvement (these are interactions with people who matter to us interpersonally).

In addition, when people are acting towards each other in the same social role (friend to friend), differences of power or status appear to be suspended by tacit consent. This is generally considered to be a defining characteristic of casual conversation: that in casual conversation we interact on the basis of social equality. And this is how we would like to think it actually happens.

When you read the Lifting Weights text, you might get the feeling that the roles are not set into differences in the way they were in the Information Dialogue. There is a sense in which the role of speaker is open more or less to any of the interactants present to make of it what they will.

This apparent role similarity impacts on casual talk through four aspects of interpersonal meanings: mood choice, the expression of attitude, 'involvement' resources (slang, naming, etc.), and humour. Patterns exemplified by Text 6.2 will be discussed briefly; for more details about analytical techniques and interpretation, see Eggins and Slade (1997).

### 6.3.3.1 Mood choices

Although role similarity makes for a freer role structure, analysis would also suggest that some speakers seem to be more equal than others! Consider Table 6.2 which summarizes the speakers' mood choices for the text. Table 6.2 shows that Pete dominates the talk, producing many more clauses in his 20 turns than Lisa does in hers. He thus gets more value for his talk time than either of the other speakers. It is also striking that he produces mainly full declarative clauses, suggesting that he initiates and prolongs more exchanges. Tom's contribution is limited, as he is seeing to the food, and when he does contribute it is often to respond (elliptically). Both Tom and Lisa produce proportionally more minor clauses; Lisa produces the most interrogatives. This suggests she is other-oriented in her talk – asking questions is one way of giving up the turn.

**Table 6.2** Mood choices in Text 6.2: Lifting Weights

| mood (clause type) | Tom | Pete | Lisa |
|---|---|---|---|
| number of clauses | 18 | 73 | 44 |
| (incomplete or | 2 | 6 | 4 |
| abandoned clauses) | | | |
| no. of turns | 12 | 20 | 20 |
| declarative | | | |
| full | 5 | 42 | 24 |
| elliptical | 5 | 7 | 4 |
| tagged | 1 | 1 | 2 |
| polar interrogative | | | |
| full | – | 1 | 3 |
| elliptical | – | – | – |
| wh-interrogative | | | |
| full | – | – | 2 |
| elliptical | – | – | – |
| imperative | 1 | – | – |
| non finite | – | 16 | 3 |
| minor | 5 | 7 | 5 |
| most frequent Subject | Carlos (most frequent) | Tom | Tom (++) |
| choice | various: I, you | the weights | who/Carlos |
| | (generic), that | the theory | men |
| | | you – generic | women |
| | | I | |
| | | his mother | |
| | | they – work colleagues | |
| negation | – | 8 | 2 |
| Adjuncts | | | |
| circumstantial | 1 | 19 | 5 |
| interpersonal | 2 | 14 | 6 |
| textual | 4 | 32 | 22 |
| Modalization | | | |
| probability | – | 3 | 5 |
| usuality | 2 | 1 | 3 |
| Modulation | | | |
| (i) obligation | – | 3 | – |
| (ii) inclination | – | – | – |
| (iii) capability | – | – | 1 |

Pete's contribution covers a range of grammatical Subjects, including Tom, himself and his work colleagues. Tom talks mainly about a third person, Carlos, and Lisa talks mainly about Tom or other people (rarely about herself), again suggesting her other-orientation. Lisa also leads in the use of modality.

Overall, these findings are consistent with general trends identified in mixed-sex interactions: women ask more questions, talk less about themselves than about others and respond rather than initiate.[6] Thus, although the three interactants may meet as equals, as three 'friends', both their social roles (host vs guests) and their sociocultural conditioning (male vs female) are reflected by and on-goingly maintained in their talk.

### 6.3.3.2 Expressions of personal attitude: appraisal choices

In pragmatic interactions, where we are usually interacting with strangers or at least with people we do not know well, we tend to limit the amount of personal attitude we express. We act 'institutionally', which generally means we act in a restrained, non-attitudinal way. However, in casual contexts, with people we are affectively involved with, we really let our hair down. Much of the talk in Text 6.2 is concerned with the swapping of opinions, the sharing and disputing of attitudes. We can see this through the frequent use of what we call appraisal items, words and phrases which are attitudinally loaded (see Eggins and Slade 1997: ch. 4). For example, participants in Text 6.2 argue moral obligations (people *should* wash their hands after going to the toilet), and reinforce speakers' gender-differentiated judgements of appropriate social behaviour – men can be *a bit slack in that department* but women should be *shamed into it.*

### 6.3.3.3 Expressions of involvement: swearing, slang, name-calling

In casual interactions participants also express interpersonal meanings through the use of what we call the involvement resources of language (see Eggins and Slade 1997: ch. 4). The main kinds of involvement lexis of interest in everyday talk are:

1. Vocatives: the terms of address people use to each other give insights into the social identity the interactants discursively construct for themselves, and the degrees of solidarity, intimacy, affective involvement they wish to display; e.g. compare Lisa's use of the diminutive form *Tom* with Pete's use of male solidarity vocative *mate.*
2. Slang: the use of words and expressions which have restricted circulation and/or special meanings within sub-cultural groups enables interactants to display their affiliations. Note that the men's use of slang (*to take your flute out and play it; have a shit; going for a piss; bloke; dick*) are not matched by any slang from the female participant.
3. Swearing: more significant than the frequency of swearing is the reciprocity of it (do all the participants swear or just some of them?) and the level of explicitness of the swearing (from highly taboo sexually explicit words to very mild exclamations of shock/surprise). Tom's swearing (*punch the fuck out of me please; pull his bloody flute out*) aligns him with traditional models of macho Australian male behaviour and differentiates him from his female partner.

### 6.3.3.4 Humour

One of the most striking differences between Text 6.1 and Text 6.2 is that the casual conversation text has a lot of laughs in it. The relative infrequency of humour in formal, pragmatic interactions relates to the fact that in such interactions there is generally a high consensus about the rights and responsibilities of the different social roles. Humour tends to appear where agreement about roles is less assured, where there may be problems or conflicts in the interpersonal context, or where the generic structure cannot be followed unproblematically. In these situations, humour provides an alternative to aggressive or confrontational responses, enabling people to 'lighten up' in order to deal with an interactional (and therefore social) problem (see Mulkay 1988).

When chatting with friends, we often draw on a range of humorous strategies, including: telling jokes (dirty or just funny), teasing, telling funny stories of various types, bantering, sending each other up, etc. Several of these strategies are used in Text 6.2, with Tom the focus of some teasing and sending up by Pete and Lisa. Tom relates a humorous anecdote about Carlos (sending up his ethnically identified friend), and Pete shares his humorous work experiences with Lisa.

At one level, the humour functions to entertain, but some theorists have suggested there may be a more critical, or strategic, dimension to conversational humour, where interactants use it to censor each other's behaviour (from behind the safety screen of 'I was only joking!'), test out affiliations ('if you laugh at this, you must be OK'), and where issues of concern in the culture at large (e.g. race, gender, ethnicity, class difference, sexual orientation) can be opened up and 'managed' in private interactions (see Eggins and Slade 1997: 155–67).

### 6.3.4 The sustained nature of casual conversation

A further marked contrast between Text 6.1 and Text 6.2 is that the casual conversation is much longer (and it is only a brief excerpt from a long conversation).

This difference in length relates to the motivating purpose of each interaction, and it explains the very different ways in which the texts are structured. If you have a specific pragmatic purpose to achieve through talk, it generally follows that you talk your way to it as quickly as possible, and then get out of the interaction once your goal has been met. With interpersonally motivated interactions, however, the goal is to keep the talk going, because it is only *in the process of talking* that we can be exploring and extending our social relations. This points leads to the question of overall structure in casual interactions.

### 6.3.5 Limited generic structure: alternating 'chat' and 'chunks'

We saw that in the Information Dialogue interactants talked their way through a sequenced set of stages, where each stage made part of the meanings necessary to bring the interaction to its successful end. The stages also had generic identity because other interactants would handle same interaction in a very similar way. However, with casual conversation we frequently cannot identify any overall schematic structure. Like every interaction, a conversation has a beginning, a middle and an end, but unlike our pragmatic interactions, it is very difficult to give more specific functional glosses to what gets done in the beginning, middle or end phases of a casual conversation. Casual talk seems to lack overall generic structure.

This does not mean, however, that casual talk is unstructured, but that the talk is often structured locally (i.e. on a turn-by-turn basis) rather than more globally. This local structure means that predictability is limited: one move sets up expectations for the immediately following move, but after that we can't be sure where the talk will go. It depends on what's done in that next move. We sometimes speak of the structure of casual conversation as being more dynamic and open-ended.

However, even in Text 6.2 there *are* moments of talk where generic structure is more clearly discernible. For example, when Pete begins to tell his story about 'working in the architects' office' we do have an expectation that he has something else to say. And it has been recognized that genres can occur in casual conversation, mostly when interactants tell a story, or when an argument develops. So it may be truer to say, as Eggins and Slade (1997) suggest, that casual conversation involves an alternation between 'chat' (the highly interactive, rapid turn-taking bits) and 'chunks' (the more stable, often more monologic segments). For a full discussion of some of the most common genres that occur in casual conversation, see Eggins and Slade (1997: ch. 6).

### 6.3.6 Ranging topic choice

Because casual conversations last much longer and are not focused on achieving a set task, they are also characterized by topic shift. In any one casual conversation (which may last up to a few hours), many different topics may be talked about. However, as the CA researcher Harvey Sacks pointed out, topic shift is rarely achieved discreetly or abruptly. Instead, Sacks noticed that topic shift is usually achieved through a process he called Stepwise Topic Transition (Schegloff and Sacks 1974). In this process, interactants who may have topics they want to move on to find ways of connecting up their topics to topics currently being discussed. This creates an impression of topic continuity. Common stepwise transition techniques include:

- keeping the participant the same but moving the topic to another aspect of that participant's behaviour (e.g. in Text 6.2 conversation shifts from talking about Tom's first night behaviour to talking about Tom's behaviour with the weights);
- keeping the activity being discussed the same or similar, but changing the participants (e.g. in Text 6.2 the talk shifts from talk about Carlos's toilet behaviour to the toilet behaviour at Pete's workplace);

- constructing generalizations, i.e. representing the current topic as an example of some general situation. This then allows interactants to choose another member of the generalization as the next topic. For example, in Text 6.2 Pete shifts the topic from a discussion of Tom's treatment of the weights to a discussion of people's toilet behaviour by making the generalization that the issue is one of cleanliness (turn 19), which can then be related by analogy to toilet behaviour.

All these techniques ensure that textual cohesion is never completely disrupted between topics. Continuity is maintained.

### 6.3.7 *Research questions relevant to studying casual conversation*

As interactants chat, exchanging interpersonal and ideational meanings, they are both enacting and constructing their sociocultural identities and their interpersonal relationships. This means that analysing casual conversation can help us understand just how we do social life, and how the personal/private connects with the public/institutional. Research questions of interest include:

- In what ways, and to what extent, do interactants *not* behave 'as equals'?
- What kinds of roles do interactants take on in the exchanges they participate in? Do certain people regularly initiate? Or confront? Or give feedback?
- How is topic shift achieved? By whom? Whose topics get talked about?
- What kinds of attitudes are expressed? By whom? About what?
- What kinds of slang are used? By whom? With what effects?
- How are terms of address used? What does their use tell us about power and intimacy in the relationships?
- Do interactants tell stories? Of what kinds? What 'cultural work' gets done through stories?
- Is there humour in the talk? If so, of what kind (e.g. teasing, dirty jokes, funny stories, sarcastic remarks, etc.)? Is the humour strategic in any sense? How does it relate to dimensions of difference in the culture?
- How do casual conversations differ among different groups, for example same-sex groups vs single-sex groups? Anglo-Australians vs ethnically diverse groups?
- To what extent can all these differences be related to dimensions of stratification in the culture at large, such as gender, socio-economic class, ethnicity, age? How does the micro social context connect with the macro social context?

### 6.4 Collecting spoken data

In order to analyse everyday talk, you need access to data in the form of audio or video recordings. Two main methods of data collection can be contrasted:

1. Naturally occurring methods of data collection: the researcher collects data from everyday contexts, public or private, without intervening to control the context or the participants' behaviour in any way. Variables relevant in these methods include: whether the researcher is not present, is present as an observer, or is present as a participant; whether the participants are aware that taping is taking place (disclosed recording) or not (surreptitious recording).
2. Experimental methods of data collection: the researcher controls various aspects of the context, including participants' behaviour. The most common experimental methods are varieties of role plays (e.g. simulations, prompting techniques),[7] and various modifications of the sociolinguistic interview.

It is preferable to collect data during naturally occurring situations of everyday life, since this is the only way you can be sure that you are researching what people actually do in their real, everyday lives.[8]

You could begin by collecting data in situations which are naturally occurring in your own life, with the consent of participants who will be members of your own social network. This method was used to collect Text 6.2, and much of the data presented in Eggins and Slade (1997) and Tannen (1984). This method gives you access to large quantities of private talk, but it does mean that your corpus will be limited by your own social world, or the social world of students and colleagues who may make their data available to you. It may therefore be difficult for you to observe variation for social class or age.

However, a great many of the basic issues of everyday talk can be explored through data collected in the course of your daily life. Choose situations such as dinner parties, mealtimes, tea breaks, games playing, where the demands of the social occasion (and substances consumed while it is going on) are likely to limit any inhibitory effects the taping may have on you and the participants.

## 6.5 Transcribing spoken data

Transcription of your data is essential, as it makes it possible for you to make your data and analysis public, and to benefit from other researchers examining your data. However, even the most detailed transcription is no more than an imperfect record of taped speech (itself an imperfect record of the original event). Working only from a transcription prepared early in the analytical process will almost certainly lead to mis-analysis, and may cause you to find ambiguities and difficulties which could be resolved instantly if you listened to the talk frequently when analysing.

The process of transcribing involves making two types of decisions which can have important theoretical consequences for subsequent analysis: *what* to transcribe and *in how much detail.*

## 6.5.1 What to transcribe

In the transcription of informal spoken interaction, there are five main aspects to consider:

1. The relationship between the orthographic and phonological representation of speech: whether you represent the talk in normal English orthography, thereby missing out on dialect and idiolect features, or whether you do a more phonemic transcription. For example, will you transcribe 'What did you do?' or 'Whaddya do?'?
2. Prosodic features: whether and how to capture aspects such as rhythm, intonation, stress. Will you show them systematically, or only when particularly salient (e.g. emphatic stress, high rising intonation, sudden change in rhythm)?
3. Interactional phenomena: whether to show pauses and overlap, and if so with how much detail. Will you time all pauses and hesitations, or only those over three seconds long? Will you show points at which overlaps finish, or only the points at which they start?
4. Spontaneity phenomena: whether to show 'performance errors' such as repetitions, hesitations, false starts, stumblings, fillers, stallings. Will you allow any 'normalizing' of the transcript? Or will you try to capture whatever you hear, for example if a particularly incoherent participant says, 'ah um, ah, like I reckon right, right ah sh- will we, ah'?
5. Paralinguistic information: what aspects of non-linguistic behaviour to include and in how much detail to note them. For example, how many different degrees of laughter will you recognize? How will you capture shifts in voice quality?

## 6.5.2 How much detail? Alternative transcription systems

For each aspect of spontaneous talk the analyst is forced to decide what degree of delicacy (or detail) is necessary given her analytic purpose. It is possible for a transcription to be very delicate in the way it represents some aspects (e.g. showing exact points of overlap, or length of all pauses), and less delicate in others (e.g. using normal orthography, or not capturing rhythm/intonation unless contrastive).

Every transcription system must be accompanied by a key which explains what the transcript shows and how to interpret any unusual conventions used. There is a range of transcription systems in regular use, and you should study a number of them carefully. Schiffrin (1994) presents the keys from three leading discourse analysts: Jefferson, Schiffrin and Tannen. Halliday (1985: 271–86 and 1994: ch. 8) uses a very different system in which rhythm and intonation are shown systematically. One more recent suggestion has been the 'score' method of transcription (see, for example, Eckert 1993), while the system used by Eggins and Slade (1997), exemplified in the transcriptions in this chapter, is yet another alternative, designed to be easy for non-specialists to read and usable for both grammatical and interactional analysis.

### 6.6 Conclusion: potential outcomes of researching everyday talk

We live in a discursive reality: most of the time we cannot escape language and the world that language gives us. In no genres are the effects of this more significant than in everyday talk where, though we might feel we're not doing anything important, the chat we engage is in fact both reflecting our social world to us, and simultaneously constructing us as participants with social identities, roles and relationships within that social world.

We do ourselves and the discourse community a great service if we can raise our level of awareness of just how we are using language – and how language is using us – to achieve these reflections and constructions.

### Notes

1. This chapter concentrates on a functional linguistic approach to everyday talk. For critical introductions to other theoretical approaches to spoken language, see Taylor and Cameron 1987, Schiffrin 1994, Eggins and Slade (1997: ch. 2).
2. Mood types for which there are no instances in Text 6.1 (e.g. tagged declarative) are not shown.
3. Speech function patterns are covered in detail in Eggins and Slade (1997: ch. 6).
4. See Berger and Luckmann (1966) for a discussion of the social benefits of developing institutionalized (i.e. generic) modes of interacting.
5. Text collected and initially transcribed by AS, whose permission to use the text is gratefully acknowledged.
6. For a good overview of research in language and gender, see the *International Journal of the Sociology of Language* 94 (special issue on language and gender). For a functional linguistic account of language and gender, see Poynton 1985. See also Tannen 1993, Cameron 1990.
7. Text 6.1: Information Dialogue was collected using a prompting method – see Eggins *et al.* 1991.
8. Although there are occasions when you may wish to control some aspect of your corpus and may therefore need to use an experimental method of data collection, space does not permit a review of such methods here. See Schiffrin 1994: 160–80 for a discussion of the sociolinguistic interview.

### References

Berger, P. and Luckmann, T. (1966) *The Social Construction of Reality: A Treatise in the Sociology of Knowledge*. New York: Doubleday.

Cameron, D. (ed.) (1990) *The Feminist Critique of Language: A Reader*. London: Routledge.

Eckert, P. (1993) Cooperative competition in adolescent 'girl talk'. In D. Tannen (ed.), *Gender and Conversational Interaction*. New York: Oxford University Press.

Eggins, S. and Slade, D. (1997) *Analysing Casual Conversation.* London: Cassell.

Eggins, S., King, R., Matthiessen, C., Sefton, P. and Vonwiller, J. (1991) Research and development of a linguistic model of human dialogues: systemic-functional interpretation of dialogues. Report of the Dialogue Project. Departments of Linguistics and Electrical Engineering, University of Sydney.

Halliday, M. A. K. (1978) *Language as Social Semiotic.* London: Edward Arnold.

Halliday, M. A. K. (1985) *Spoken and Written Language.* Geelong: Deakin University Press.

Halliday, M. A. K. (1994) *An Introduction to Functional Grammar* (2nd edn). London: Edward Arnold.

Jefferson, G. (1984) On stepwise transition from talk about a trouble to inappropriately next-positioned matters. In J. Atkinson and J. Heritage (eds), *Structures of Social Action: Studies in Conversation Analysis.* Cambridge: Cambridge University Press, 191–222.

Jefferson, G. and Lee, J. (1992) The rejection of advice: managing the problematic convergence of a 'troubles-telling' and a 'service encounter'. In P. Drew and J. Heritage (eds), *Talk at Work: Interaction in Institutional Settings.* Cambridge: Cambridge University Press, 470–521.

Mulkay, M. (1988) *On Humour.* London: Polity Press.

Poynton, C. (1985) *Language and Gender: Making the Difference.* Geelong: Deakin University Press.

Sacks, H. (1972) An initial investigation of the usability of conversational data for doing sociology. In D. Sudnow (ed.), *Studies in Social Interaction.* New York: Free Press, 325–45.

Sacks, H. (1992a, b) *Lectures on Conversation* (2 vols). Oxford: Blackwell.

Sacks, H., Schegloff, E. and Jefferson, G. (1974) A simplest systematics for the organization of turn-taking for conversation. *Language,* 50(4): 696–735.

Schegloff, E. (1981) Discourse as an interactional achievement: some uses of 'Uh huh' and other things that come between sentences. In D. Tannen (ed.), *Analyzing Discourse: Text and Talk.* Washington: Georgetown University Press, 71–93.

Schegloff, E. and Sacks, H. (1974) Opening up closings. In R. Turner (ed.), *Ethnomethodology.* Harmondsworth: Penguin, 233–64.

Schiffrin, D. (1994) *Approaches to Discourse.* Oxford: Blackwell.

Tannen, D. (1984) *Conversational Style: Analyzing Talk Among Friends.* Norwood: Ablex.

Tannen, D. (ed.) (1993) *Gender and Conversational Interaction.* Oxford: Oxford University Press.

Taylor, T. and Cameron, D. (1987) *Analysing Conversation: Rules and Units in the Structure of Talk.* Oxford: Pergamon Press.

# 7 Socio-semantic variation: different wordings, different meanings

*Carmel Cloran*

## 7.1 Introduction

Certain meanings get meant by just about everyone at certain ages and stages of their lives. Consider Texts 7.1 and 7.2:[1]

**Text 7.1**[2]

| 160 | Mother | Are you enjoying it? |
|-----|--------|----------------------|
| 161 | Linda | Yes Mama |
| 162 | Mother | Good darling |
| 163 | | Don't talk with food in your mouth alright? |
| 164 | | You can talk |
| 165 | | when you've finished . . . |

**Text 7.2**

| 251 | Stephen | [?                          ] |
|-----|---------|-------------------------------|
| 252 | Mother | I can't hear what you said |
| 253 | | because you filled your mouth full of peanut butter sand-wich . . . |
| 254 | | It's hard talking to you <255> isn't it |
| 255 | | when you've got your mouth full |
| 256 | | It's a bit rough I think |

No doubt most readers will be familiar with the scenario construed in these two extracts by virtue of the fact that these or similar lines were probably spoken by each one of us in at least one of the roles – adult or child. So, if pressed, we would probably agree that the same purpose is being achieved by the adult speaker in each extract, i.e. the mother is regulating her child's behaviour with respect to 'table manners'. From the perspective of the research reported in this chapter, the question is: Despite differences in wordings used, does each text represent different ways of saying the same thing? Or do the different wordings construe differences in meanings? This question implies the possibility that 'different ways of saying are different ways of meaning' (Hasan 1984/96). And underlying this possibility is a view of the nature of language that makes such a possibility feasible – that language is itself a system that is crucially involved in creating, maintaining and (potentially) changing social reality (Berger and Luckmann 1966). This is, in fact, the basis of its functionality. Meanings do not exist independently of those who mean; and even within the same language group, e.g. speakers of Australian English, the social realities in which language users live may vary. If we accept this view then we must also admit the possibility that different social realities may be expressed in and maintained by different ways of meaning. It is this possibility of socio-semantic variation with which this chapter is concerned.

Socio-semantic variation may be defined as a specific kind of socio-linguistic variation; it is variation in orientation to meaning which, as with all socio-linguistic variation, is conditional upon some identifiable social factor(s). However, studies in socio-semantic variation differ from other kinds of socio-linguistic variation studies in that the latter have generally been concerned with variation in form (phonological and lexicogrammatical) among speakers possessing particular social attributes – gender, social class, ethnicity (e.g. Labov 1966, Trudgill 1974, Horvath 1985). Such social variation has tended to be explained without reference to any coherent social theory.

The conceptualization and study of socio-semantic variation was pioneered by Hasan (e.g. 1989, 1991, 1992, 1993). Hasan's work departs from previous socio-linguistic studies not only in her concern with variation in orientation to meaning; in addition, she explains her findings by locating them within the framework of a sociological theory which recognizes the importance of language in the construction of reality; that is Bernstein's (e.g. 1971) socio-linguistic hypothesis. The concept of socio-semantic variation, its underlying conception of language and its explanation by reference to Bernstein's theory will be briefly outlined in Section 7.2.

Hasan's investigation focused on the discursive practices of mothers interacting in everyday situations with their preschool children. Among other things, she found that mothers systematically differ with respect to what meanings they consider relevant when they regulate their child's behaviour (Hasan 1992, Cloran 1989); and how adequately and expansively they answer their children's questions (Hasan 1989, 1992, Hasan and Cloran 1990). The methodology and some of the findings of Hasan's research will be briefly reviewed in Section 7.3.

Hasan's approach (and her data) was adopted in a study which sought to add a further dimension to her findings regarding the discursive practices of mothers in interaction with their preschool children by characterizing the interactions as being concerned with 'contextualized' or 'decontextualized' meanings. This investigation will be reviewed in Section 7.4.

## 7.2 Language, meaning and society: some theoretical assumptions

The possibility of the existence of socio-semantic variation depends on one's view of the relation between language, society and reality and, as a corollary of this, how one conceptualizes meaning in language. In order to entertain the possibility that socio-semantic variation exists, we need a theory of language in which the social is central, where meaning-making is viewed as a task that is undertaken by people interacting in some context; in short, 'where social organisation, social context and language are related to each other in a non-ad hoc manner' (Hasan 1989: 271). The required theory needs to view language as a means of establishing and maintaining the social reality of speakers so that, where social realities vary, such variation is seen to be intimately associated with linguistic variation. In other words, the tendency to use particular varieties of language is predictable on the grounds that varieties of language are functional. From this perspective, variation in language use is seen as a way of accommodating to the various situations of interaction (contexts of situation) that constitute one's life situation (context of culture). This description of the requirements of a linguistic model matches the attributes of the systemic functional model of language.

### 7.2.1 The 'naming' model

The above description contrasts with a conception of meaning as mirroring or naming a pre-existing invariant reality and this latter conception logically disallows the possibility of the existence of variation in orientation to meaning. It is this 'naming' conception of meaning that is held by many eminent scholars of linguistic variation. For Labov, for example, linguistic variation is meaning-preserving. Variants of linguistic forms (such as active versus passive) are simply variable ways of saying the same thing. Meaning, in this view, is a matter of the social significance of the use of formal variants, or a matter of the extent of the match between a non-linguistic state of affairs and its linguistic representation, i.e. truth functional semantics (for a critical review of this position see Hasan 1989).

### 7.2.2 The systemic functional model

Proponents of the 'naming' view of language do not consider that there is any systematic relationship between form and meaning such that the one – form – construes the other – meaning. From the perspective of the systemic functional model, however, variation in form implies variation in meaning. This is because the model views language as multi-functional, expressing three different kinds of meaning. Speakers construe (interpret) experiential meaning and construct interpersonal meaning simultaneously and cohesively by means of the facilitative textual resources. Variation in form, that is in wording, is motivated according to this model; the active and passive are not only different ways of saying, they are also, in one sense at least, different ways of meaning. Though experiential meaning may remain constant (and presuming interpersonal meaning does as well), there is variation in textual meaning between the two: *If you chase him (he'll just keep flying away)* versus *If he's chased (he'll just keep flying away)*. In order to be totally faithful to the experiential meaning the agent omitted in the passive version can be inserted: *If he's chased by you (he'll just keep flying away)* though it seems counter-intuitive to do so since one of the functions of passivization is to 'hide' agency. Either way, the variation in textual meaning as indicated by the variation in the selection of topical Theme (*you* versus *he*) is clear.

As noted in Chapter 1, these three kinds of meaning – ideational, interpersonal and textual – construe the context of situation. Indeed, it was by considering what it is that language has to do (in terms of these three metafunctions) in the lives of speakers that Halliday postulated the linguistically relevant contextual parameters – field, tenor and mode. The multi-stratal model of language thus conceives of linguistic meaning as an interface looking 'inward' to linguistic form and 'outward' to the non-linguistic goings-on of people in various social and linguistic roles using language to get the goings-on done.

Different groups of speakers may hold different views concerning, for example, how to get the linguistic or non-linguistic things done, or to enact particular social roles. As sociologists might say, underlying the social structure are principles of coherence which guide a community's selection and organization of relevant meanings. These principles of coherence are linguistically expressed via patterns of language use. Where these principles vary across communities there will be different linguistic patterns. The patterns expressing the principles of a particular group are inter-generationally transmitted in the contexts of primary socialization of the child in the family.

### 7.2.3 Bernstein's tri-stratal model

This is basically the sociolinguistic thesis of the British sociologist Basil Bernstein who locates the origin of the selection and organization of relevant meanings within social structure, specifically in the social division of labour. Thus, depending on one's location – whether one occupies a dominating or a dominated position – the meanings considered relevant, the forms realizing the meanings and the contexts which evoke them will vary (Bernstein 1990).

Bernstein's thesis implies a tri-stratal model of language – context, meaning and wording. Indeed, because of the realizational relationship postulated in the systemic functional model between context, meaning and wording, one may investigate Bernstein's thesis by focusing on any one of these. Hasan's focus is on the semantic. She examines variation in the kinds of meanings that speakers choose in order to construe contexts.

This focus, however, does not in any way exclude wording; it is centrally implicated since it is via wordings that meanings are construed. The precise way in which this is conceptualized will be elaborated in Section 7.3. The discussion will necessarily become somewhat technical but I will define and give examples of the technical terms as they occur. Sections 7.3 and 7.4 are designed to give you some appreciation of the theoretical and methodological underpinnings of the work and to enable you to use them as a point of departure in your own investigations.

## 7.3 Investigating semantic variation: Hasan's methodology

### 7.3.1 Semantic and lexicogrammatical structures

Why focus on the semantic (meaning) stratum since semantic variation may be revealed via variation in lexicogrammatical (wording) structures? The answer to this question leads to important issues concerning the nature of the realizational relationship between the strata of language. For example: Is the relationship one of correspondence so that the facts of one stratum (say, lexicogrammar) are simply recoded as semantic facts? Or is the matter more complex? Hasan (e.g. 1995) makes two points in discussing this issue. The first concerns the relationship between the strata. In any multi-stratal model, the strata must be *non-conformal* (they cannot enter into a one-to-one correspondence relation), otherwise the postulate of multiple strata is meaningless. The second point takes into account the concept of *grammatical metaphor* (the non-congruent realizations of meanings). Halliday (e.g. 1994: 342–4) refers to congruent forms expressing ideational meanings as 'the typical way in which experience is construed' and the 'typical patterns of wording'. These typical forms may be replaced by a non-typical or metaphorical representation of the same event or state of affairs: *Mary saw something wonderful* versus *A wonderful sight met Mary's eyes*. He makes the point that these variants 'are definitely not synonymous; the different encodings all contribute something different to the total meaning. But they are potentially co-representational' (Halliday 1994: 344). Similarly, there are variant expressions of modality (Halliday 1994: 354ff) and mood (Halliday 1994: 363ff) which permit the expression of such speech acts as asking questions by using declarative (rather than interrogative) mood structures and issuing commands using the full range of mood structures. Despite this wide potential, Hasan (1992) has shown that it is possible to specify at least a fragment of the range of semantic options and their lexicogrammatical realizations, though she makes no claim to have exhaustively identified the possibilities. Similarly, she has provided the semantic features and lexicogrammatical realizations for a fragment of the various ways of asking questions (e.g. Hasan 1989). The methodology is briefly reviewed in Section 7.3.2. (For a more comprehensive theoretical account and discussion see Hasan 1996.)

In summary, then, the relation between the strata of language (semantics and lexicogrammar) is non-conformal and may, in any instance, be metaphorical. This means that lexicogrammatical facts cannot simply be translated into the more abstract semantic facts. The relation between the strata of semantics and context is similarly non-conformal and one of increasing abstraction. It is hypothesized that it may on occasion be considered to be metaphorical, mimicking this characteristic of the relation between the lexicogrammatical and semantic strata. Such a possibility will be considered in Section 7.5.

### 7.3.2 *Semantic networks*

#### 7.3.2.1 System and structure at the lexicogrammatical stratum

According to Hasan (1989: 237)

> [the SFL] conception of the place of meaning in human language opens a genuine possibility for the study of semantic variation. If some feature in the context of situation is treated as the content, we can ask what are the semantic options available for expressing that feature. The system of semantic options available for expressing that content can be thought of as the semantic variable.

Note the term *semantic options*. In the systemic functional model language is viewed as a resource modelled as a system of interlocking options. This system network modelling is most familiar at the lexicogrammatical stratum (e.g. Halliday 1976, Matthiessen 1995). The following discussion describes the conventions used in representing language as system. In order to explain the system network representation we will focus first on a lexicogrammatical system network and then move on to semantic networks.

To represent language as a system and to move from system to structure, three basic concepts are necessary:

- systemic option
- selection expression
- realization statements.

Figure 7.1 is a simplified fragment of the lexicogrammatical system of Mood. It shows that in the clause systems in English the basic distinction is between [major] and [minor] clauses. In other words, technically speaking, clause is the environment for the selection of the systemic options [major] or [minor]. It is only when the feature [major] is selected that selections can be made in the Mood system. The following conventions as designated by Hasan (1989) are used: systemic options are enclosed within square brackets; options other than those at the stratum of lexicogrammar are given in bold type; lexicogrammatical options are in plain roman type. There are no examples of this in Figure 7.1.

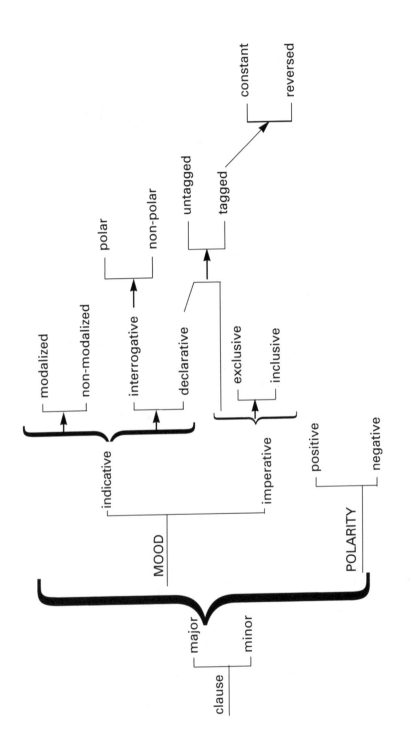

**Figure 7.1** A simplified fragment of the system of mood in the English clause (adapted from Hasan 1991)

Figure 7.1 contains a number of simple conventions. The shape of a bracket is significant:

a square bracket [ ] signifies the 'or' relation
a brace { } bracket signifies the 'and' relation.

Thus, in Figure 7.1, the left-facing brace embracing the systems MOOD and POLARITY indicates that an option from **both** of these systems must be selected. The square bracket separating the options within Mood and within Polarity indicate that **one** of these options must be selected – **either** indicative **or** imperative mood, and **either** positive **or** negative polarity. Figure 7.1 also shows that some options in systems themselves become the environment for choice in another system. The feature [indicative], for example, permits entry to the system whose terms are [interrogative] versus [declarative]; and the option [interrogative] is itself the point of entry for the choice between [non-polar] and [polar]. This movement through the system is known as movement towards a greater degree of delicacy in description.

### 7.3.2.2 Selection expressions

Simultaneous selection within the systems of mood, modalization and polarity, and variation in delicacy means that a number of pathways through the network are systemically permitted when an option is selected. Such pathways or configurations of systemic options are termed **selection expressions** and are represented by a conventional shorthand.

[indicative:interrogative:non-polar; modalized;positive]

Punctuation is significant.
a colon (:) indicates that each term is dependent upon the choice previously made. In the selection expression

[indicative:interrogative:polar]

colons indicate that the term [polar] depends on the prior selection of the term [interrogative] which itself is dependent on the prior selection of the term [indicative].

a semi-colon indicates that the term which follows it is one in a system which operates simultaneously with another system or systems. In the selection expression

[indicative: interrogative:non-polar;modalized;positive]

the semi-colons indicate that options from the polarity and modalization systems are selected simultaneously with selections from the mood system. A sample of the selection expressions permitted by the network in Figure 7.1 when the primary choice is [indicative] is shown in Table 7.1:

**Table 7.1** Some selection expressions arising from Figure 7.1

| | |
|---|---|
| i) | [indicative:interrogative:non-polar; modalized;positive] |
| ii) | [indicative:interrogative:non-polar; non-modalized;negative] |
| iii) | [indicative:interrogative:polar; modalized;negative] |
| iv) | [indicative:interrogative:polar; non-modalized;positive] |
| v) | [indicative:declarative:untagged; modalized;positive] |
| vi) | [indicative:declarative:untagged; non-modalized;negative] |
| vii) | [indicative:declarative:tagged:constant; modalized;positive] |
| viii) | [indicative:declarative:tagged:constant; non-modalized;negative] |
| ix) | [indicative:declarative:tagged:reversed; modalized;positive] |
| x) | [indicative:declarative:tagged:reversed; non-modalized;positive] |

### 7.3.2.3 Realization statements

The network in Figure 7.1 of systems of the clause and the selection expressions arising from it (Table 7.1) may leave you wondering how the familiar Mood structure – Subject Finite Predicator Complement Adjunct – fits into the picture. In fact, the options in the system have no structural shape; structure must be derived via **realization statements** that are associated with the options in the system. In a selection expression, each of the options has attached to it three types of realization statements. These are basically sets of instructions which specify:

1. how it is that each of the options is expressed by the lexicogrammatical structures – clause, group, word and morpheme;
2. what the constituents are which realize the functions within a specified structure, e.g. Subject, Finite.

Structures are thus formed by the process of realization. (As an aid in conceptualizing the relation between systemic options and realization statements it might be useful to visualize each option in a network as a peg upon which to hang sets of instructions about how to form particular structures.)

Hasan (1992: 39) classifies realization statements in terms of three categories: structure, layering and preselection.

*Structure* statements specify and order structural elements,
*Layering* statements specify which elements of the structures of different metafunctions are to be mapped onto the same constituent,
*Preselection* statements specify which formal item from a particular subclass of formal items is to be selected to manifest a structural element.

It is through the application of realization statements that every selection expression is realized as a structure – a configuration of functions (or elements) which in turn is actualized as a syntagm or ordered string. Realization statements translate system into structure because they specify the structure(s) realizing the choices in a selection expression. Additionally, they specify the constituents which realize the specified structural functions. To illustrate, some of the realization statements associated with the systemic option [indicative] from the network in Figure 7.1 are given in Table 7.2.

**Table 7.2** Realization statements associated with the systemic option [indicative]

| option | realization |
|---|---|
| [major] | insert element Predicator |
| [indicative] | insert element Mood and Residue; expand Mood into S F |
| [declarative] | order S and F = S ^ F |
| [interrogative:polar] | order S and F = F ^ S |
| [interrogative:non-polar] | insert WH-; order WH- ^ F |
| [tagged] | insert Mood Tag after Residue; expand Mood Tag S F; |
| | order S F= F ^ S; |
| | preselect at Tag-F modal or tense as at Mood-F |
| | preselect at Tag-S pronoun co-referential with Mood-S |
| [untagged] | no function inserted after Residue |
| [constant] | Tag-F polarity identical with Mood-F polarity |
| [reversed] | Tag-F polarity contrasting with Mood-F polarity |
| [positive] | preselect positive polarity at Mood-F |
| [negative] | preselect negative polarity at Mood-F |
| [modalized] | preselect from modal operator class at F |
| [non-modalized] | preselect from primary tense class at F |

## 7.3.2.4 Semantic system and environment

A system network operates in an environment. The network of Mood in Figure 7.1 is the unit clause. What is the unit which acts as the environment for the semantic networks devised by Hasan? The answer to this question is 'the *message*' but it is far from the simple matter that it seems for it forms the basis of a theory of units at the semantic stratum, a theory of text. Hasan (e.g. 1989, 1991, 1996) has theorized the unit message as the smallest unit that is capable of realizing an obligatory element of the generic structure of a text. This perspective considers the message from the point of view of the text type of which it is a part. However, a unit at the semantic stratum must also be rec-ognizable in terms of its linguistic form (its wording), so from this perspective a message is said to be realized by a clause which is ranking (non-embedded) and non-projected (Hasan 1989, Cloran 1994, 1995). 'Non-projected' means that wherever a clause complex is related by projection, such a clause complex construes a single message, e.g. *Did you know that they're going to leave?*

Figure 7.2 presents a simplified fragment of Hasan's network of seman-tic options in expressing questions.

The primary distinction in the lexicogrammatical system of Mood, that is between [indicative] and [imperative] clauses (Figure 7.1), is that it construes the semantic distinction between messages about exchanging

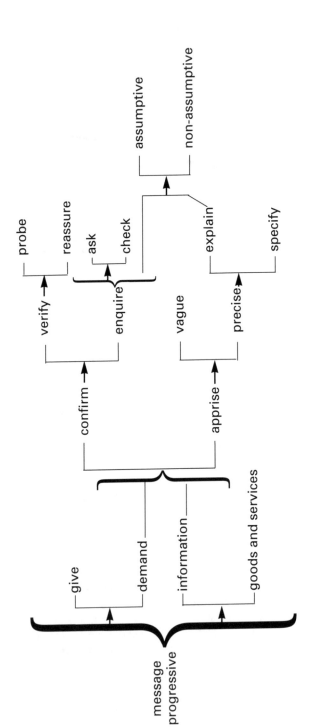

**Figure 7.2** Some semantic options in expressing questions (Hasan 1989: 246)

information and those about exchanging goods or services. However, as every native speaker of English knows, this default condition may be over-turned and the various structures put to different uses: we can issue a command using an interrogative structure (*Could you open the window?*) or a declarative form (*I want you to open the window*). Similarly, we can ask a question using a declarative form (*You don't like the ice cream?*).

In making use of the full range of available structures, a speaker is making a choice in meaning at a further degree of delicacy. This is shown in the network in Figure 7.2. Given the conjunct (i.e. combined) entry conditions ([**demand;information**]), the primary choice is [**confirm**] or [**apprise**]. A speaker selects the option [**confirm**] in order to elicit a yes/no response (*Have they come yet?*); but in order to elicit some specific item of information (*When are they coming?*) the option [**apprise**] is selected.

### 7.3.2.5 Semantic options

Realization statements apply at the semantic stratum also. Their function here is to translate the content of one stratum – semantics – into the form of their realization at the stratum below – lexicogrammar (Hasan 1992: 91). The semantic features must be translated into lexicogrammatical ones. We may therefore define a semantic option as some content whose expression in lexicogrammatical form is specified in terms of some choices in the relevant lexicogrammatical system(s). As shown in the pre-vious section, the realization statement attached to the relevant lexi-cogrammatical system choice specifies the lexicogrammatical structure which is derived from the system and the constituent manifesting the structural functions. So, for semantic networks, structure specifications which are part of the lexicogrammatical level are repeated in order to make realization statements at the semantic level. Let's turn now to how this is done in practice using the network in Figure 7.2, and referring to Figure 7.1.

The realization statement for the semantic feature [**confirm**] is: Pre-select [indicative Mood];

for the semantic option [**apprise**] the realization statement is: Preselect [interrogative:non-polar]. The realization statements relevant to the lexi-cogrammatical feature [indicative] and [interrogative:non-polar] are then applied in order to derive the particular lexicogrammatical struc-tures.

As Figure 7.2 indicates, the option [**confirm**] permits a choice between [**verify**] and [**enquire**]. A message selecting the feature [**enquire**] may either [**ask**] or [**check**]. [**ask**] is realized in the lexicogrammar by pre-selecting (Figure 7.1) the options [interrogative:polar] from the system of Mood (note that the feature [**confirm**] has already preselected the lexi-cogrammatical systemic option [indicative]). [**check**] is realized by a declarative clause said on a rising tone. Its realization statement is therefore: Preselect [declarative:untagged; tone 2].

A question selecting the option [**verify**] may seek to either [**probe**] or [**reassure**]. [**probe**] occurs where a speaker wants to probe the veracity of a proposition and is realized by preselecting the lexicogrammatical selection expression [tagged:constant] (*It's raining is it?*) [**reassure**], realized by the lexicogrammatical selection expression [tagged:reversed] (*It isn't raining is it?/ It's raining isn't it?*) is used when a speaker seeks to be reassured about the veracity of a proposition.

The option [**apprise**] permits a systemic choice between [**vague**] and [**precise**]. The option [**vague**] occurs where the question is realized by a clause with Mood and Predicator ellipsis and in which the Theme is *How/What about*. In these vague questions there is no way of establishing, without reference to a following message, what precisely is sought (*What about Daddy?(Is he coming too?)*).

This kind of question contrasts with questions having the feature [**precise**], where the item of information sought is precisely specified. [**precise**] is itself the environment for a more delicate choice between [**explain**] and [**specify**]. The option [**specify**] is realized by clauses whose Theme may be a Wh– participant (*who, what*) or a Wh– circumstance (*where, when, how*). In other words, what is sought may be the identity of a participant or the specification of some circumstance. The option [**explain**] is expressed by a clause whose Theme is *Why* (or *What for* or *How come*).

The feature [**assumptive**] is realized by negative polarity in the clause realizing the message and is a choice that is open to questions having the feature [**apprise:explain**] or [**confirm:enquire**]. Some selection expressions and examples of this feature are shown in Table 7.3 (see Hasan 1996: 121–23 for a discussion of the significance of the feature [**assumptive**]).

**Table 7.3** Some selection expressions and examples of assumptiveness

| Selection expression | Example |
|---|---|
| [**confirm:enquire:ask:non-assumptive**] | *Did you get too big to call me Mummy?* |
| [**confirm:enquire:check:assumptive**] | *You wasn't so hungry then?* |
| [**explain:non-assumptive**] | *How come you're breaking that?* |
| [**explain:assumptive**] | *Why didn't you have something to eat earlier?* |

## 7.4 Hasan's mother–child research

Each of the options in the network is identified as a semantic variant, a particular way of asking a question. In her investigation of the discursive practices of mothers in interaction with their preschool children, Hasan prepared networks such as this for the description of interpersonal aspects of messages – commands and offers for unsolicited information-giving as well as information that came in response to questions. She also described the semantic options available to messages from the point of view of experiential, logical and textual meanings. In all, 22,000 messages formed the data set of everyday conversation. This consisted of approximately 1000 messages from each of 24 mother–child dyads. Each of these messages was described in terms of up to approximately 50 semantic features.

### 7.4.1 The subjects

The 24 mothers and their children were drawn from two social groups (middle and lower class) and the children were evenly represented by sex. Hasan (1989) defined social class in terms of the degree of autonomy that the occupation of the family breadwinner permitted. High autonomy professionals (HAP) were those in which the breadwinner's occupation permitted a high degree of autonomy in decision-making, affecting not only his/her own working life and practices but also that of others; bank and business managers, doctors, teachers, etc. represented the HAP families in Hasan's study. Lower autonomy professionals (LAP) work in occupations in which they have little control over their work practices and none over that of others in the workplace. Such LAP families in Hasan's study included a council truck driver and a paint mixer, as well as single mothers.

The 24 mothers participated in the study on a voluntary basis and in response to advertising in Sydney preschools in suburbs which were mainly middle class or mainly working class. Volunteering mothers were given an audiotape recorder and tapes and asked to switch on the recorder whenever their preschooler was present and to simply let the tape run as long as the talk continued. Impressionistically, the resulting six hours (on average) of talk recorded by each of the mothers was quite natural. That this is indeed so is almost guaranteed by the fact that if a mother tried to act in other than her usual way, her atypical behaviour was detected and queried by the child who was too young to be at all inhibited by the presence of the recorder. The recording situation itself guaranteed the naturalness of the data. Mothers were reassured that they could erase or record over anything that they did not want overheard by strangers though it is extremely doubtful that this offer was ever taken up.

### 7.4.2 Statistical processing of the data

The analysed messages were statistically processed using a multivariate technique known as principal components analysis (PCA). This technique had two advantages: it identified patternings or clusters among the variables, assigning scores to speakers on the basis of the identified variable clusters or principal components rather than on individual variables in isolation; and it distributed speakers on the basis of the linguistic patterns they used. The distribution could then be examined to ascertain any consistency in terms of speakers' social attributes, such as social class or sex of the child. (For a more detailed explanation of PCA see Cloran 1989.)

The results of the statistical processing clearly showed that variation in the use of semantic features of messages does exist. Patterns identified include mothers' control styles (Hasan 1992) and mothers' (and children's) questioning and answering behaviours (Hasan 1989, 1991, Hasan and Cloran 1990). Variation was found to be principally a function of the social class of speakers, though the sex of the child was also a factor in some of the analyses (Cloran 1989). Hasan identified these patternings as complex socio-linguistic variables which were interpretable in terms of some higher order principle. One such analysis (reproduced from Hasan 1989) and its interpretation is presented in Table 7.4.

**Table 7.4** Principal components analysis of features of mother's questions and answers (MQMA) (adapted from Hasan 1989: 262)

| semantic features | PC1 MQMA |
|---|---|
| A [responsive] | 0.67 |
| Q [assumptive] | -0.52 |
| Q [prefaced] | 0.69 |
| Q [confirm] | 0.37 |
| A [adequate] | 0.56 |
| Q [related] | 0.65 |
| Q [explain] | -0.32 |
| Q [ask] | 0.21 |
| Eigenvalue | 2.72 |
| % variance | 30.20 |

The pattern of asking and answering behaviour delineated here characterizes HAP mothers rather than LAP ($p < .0003$). Hasan (1989) points out that it is not the kind of information that is sought which differentiates the two groups of mothers since the features [**ask**], [**explain**] and [**confirm**] do not load criterially on the component, i.e. a feature must have a loading on (i.e. an association with) the principal component of .50 or above in order to contribute towards the definition of the component. Rather, what differentiates the speakers, argues Hasan (1989: 266), is 'a regard for individuality, a belief in the uniqueness of persons, and a readiness to grant that states of affairs can be viewed from different angles'.

Hasan interprets the complex sociolinguistic variable identified in Table 7.4 in terms of the higher order principle of 'individuated informativeness' because the criterial features (i.e. those loading at 0.50 or higher) are **Q[related]**, **Q[prefaced]**, **Q[non-assumptive]**, **A[adequate]**, **A[responsive]** and **A[related]**. In other words, speakers who score high on PC1 tend to frame a question in such a way that it is presented as someone else's idea or locution (**Q[prefaced]**, e.g. *When did Daddy say he's coming back?*) but it does not assume some unvoiced thesis (**Q[non-**

**assumptive**]), and further information is presented that makes the question more precise (**Q[related]**). Answers also have this latter feature and are, furthermore, adequate in terms of what is demanded (**A[adequate]**) in addressing the point of the question (**A[responsive]**). Text 7.3 exemplifies these features of answering behaviour:

**Text 7.3**

| 336 | Mother | D'you think <337> a mandarin tree would grow |
| 337 | | if we planted a pip |
| 338 | Stephen | It might |
| 339 | | so I better plant two mandarin pips |
| 340 | Mother | The trouble is it might not have very good mandarins |
| 341 | Stephen | Why? |
| 342 | Mother | Well with fruit trees the top part of the tree is often different to the bottom part of the tree |
| 343 | | With the last lemon tree that we bought the bottom half was the kind of tree that has very good roots |
| 344 | | and then the top half of the tree was the kind of tree that had very good fruit |
| 345 | | and so they took the tree that has good roots |
| 346 | | and they chopped the top off it |
| 347 | | and they took the tree that has good fruit |
| 348 | | and chopped the top off it |
| 349 | | and they stuck the nice-fruiting top on the good-rooting bottom |
| 350 | Stephen | Mummy, I want to plant this one |
| 351 | Mother | But you might not get mandarins from it |
| 352 | Stephen | Why? |
| 353 | Mother | Because when you plant seeds from mandarins or oranges |
| 354 | | sometimes you get very strange fruit |
| 355 | | or sometimes you don't get much fruit at all |
| 356 | | so you have to plant a tree that's been grafted – that's been stuck on |
| 357 | | They're special trees that they make by sticking one tree to another tree |
| 358 | Stephen | How do they stick it? |
| 359 | Mother | Well I think they cut it in a special way |
| 360 | | They cut them in a special way |
| 361 | | and they put them together |
| 362 | | and then they bind stuff around the outside |
| 363 | | to hold them together |
| 364 | | 'til they grow together . . . |

Stephen's mother is among the high scorers on PC1 (Table 7.4); she is given to a high degree of 'individuated informativeness'. Her answers to Stephen's questions in this extract demonstrate the meaning of the features **A[adequate]**, **A[responsive]** and **A[related]**.[3]

### 7.4.3 Listening to the audiotapes

Repeated listening to the audiotapes leaves the listener with two overwhelming impressions: there is very little difference between the children
at this age (3.5 years on average) in terms of cognitive and language
development, interests, etc.; and some mothers (those high in 'individuated informativeness') swamp their preschool child with information
almost to the extent of seeming to control the child by this means. From
these impressions, the following considerations arose. Despite the impression that there is little developmental difference in the children, it is
highly likely that they will vary greatly in terms of their academic success
as they proceed through the education system. Why? Is there any association between this and mothers who apparently overwhelm their children
with information?

The type of information exchange identified as 'individuated informativeness' is the habitual tendency of HAP rather than LAP speakers, and it
is the members of the LAP group who are more likely to be at risk in the
education system. Text 7.3 shows that, particularly in the elaborated
giving of information, the discourse in which HAP children participate is
very similar to the kind of instructional discourse that is typical of schools.
Text 7.4 provides an illustration from a kindergarten classroom:

**Text 7.4**

| 128 | Teacher | Do you think it'd be very sensible to have a red whale? |
|---|---|---|
| 129 | Children | No . . . ! (SINGING) |
| 130 | Teacher | Why wouldn't it be sensible? |
| 131 | Teacher | Cameron, you tell me |
| 132 | | Wait a minute (TO CHILDREN BREAKING IN) |
| 133 | | Cameron you tell me |
| 134 | Cameron | 'Cause they couldn't hide from danger |
| 135 | Teacher | No, that's right |
| 136 | | Think it'd be sensible Elizabeth, to have a blue crocodile? |
| 137 | Elizabeth | No |
| 138 | Teacher | Why not? |
| 139 | Elizabeth | [?    ] |
| 140 | Teacher | Right |
| 141 | | When a crocodile is in the water, in the muddy kind of water |
| 142 | | he looks grey, greyie green |
| 143 | | he looks like a log floating in the water |
| 144 | | and so he can sneak up on his dinner |
| 145 | | and eat it |
| 146 | | but if he were bright blue |
| 147 | | everyone'd see him coming |
| 148 | | and get out of the way |
| 149 | | and he'd starve to death |

If habitual patterns of language use – orientations to meaning – have a role in educational success then the possibility of further characterizing the instructional discourse exemplified here seemed relevant. A further semantic characterization would permit an investigation of the extent to which such discourse is already established in the habitual ways of saying of children before they enter school. This was the rationale behind the development of the analytic framework for an investigation into 'decontextualized' language use.

## 7.5  Decontextualized language use

Bernstein (e.g. 1990) has characterized the instructional discourse of the school as 'decontextualized' language use. According to educationists (e.g. Olson 1977, Wells 1981) and psychologists (e.g. Bruner 1970, Vygotsky 1978, Donaldson 1987, Snow 1983) such language use is a necessary precondition for the development of cognition and literacy. However, this variety of language has tended to be defined descriptively in terms that are a-theoretical (see Cloran in press for a review of the literature). Nowhere has the notion of decontextualized (text-dependent, autonomous, disembedded) language been operationalized in a systematic way in terms of its linguistic correlates nor has it been related to a central underlying concept, that of context. Instead, it has tended to be characterized in global terms. Indeed, the question of 'decontextualized' language use has been particularly problematic from the perspective of functional theories of language for such theories view all language use as activated by – i.e. construing of – context. In this sense, then, all language use is contextualized. Though educationists and psychologists have applied the notion of decontextualization to describe a kind of language use, it seems that in the process of this application the concept's lack of clarity has become invisible. The result has been a somewhat piecemeal and a-theoretical description of the phenomenon.

For purposes of the investigation outlined in the closing paragraph of Section 7.4.3, the concept of decontextualized language use was initially conceptualized non-technically as that kind of language use in which:

• the *entities* referred to are not co-present in the material environment of the occasion of language use; rather they are either absent from it or are incapable of being co-present as is the case with class-exhaustive (generalized) entities;
• the *events* spoken about are not happening concurrently with the moment of speaking or immediately after as a consequence of the act of speaking (as is the case when commands are given). (See Sections 7.5.1.1, for explanations of **entity** and **event** and 7.5.1.2).

By implication, 'contextualized' language use would seem to have the following features:

- The *entities* referred to are co-present in what Hasan (e.g. 1973) terms the material situational setting.
- The *events* spoken about are concurrent with the moment of speaking.

This conceptualization immediately suggests two important clarifications:

1. The phenomenon – contextualized and decontextualized language use – should, in fact, be represented as a continuum with the entity and event types described above at opposing ends.

$$\begin{array}{lcl} \text{co-present} & \longleftrightarrow & \text{not co-present} \\ \text{concurrent} & \longleftrightarrow & \text{not concurrent} \end{array}$$

2. The varieties thus identified appear to be relatable to an aspect of the contextual variable mode of discourse, specifically the role of language in the social process. So the phenomenon is able to be located within a theoretical framework – the SFL model – and its semantic (and lexicogrammatical) features motivated.

### 7.5.1 Semantico-formal features of (de)contextualized language use

#### 7.5.1.1 Relevant semantic features of *entity*

As suggested in the previous paragraph, the two concepts relevant to the identification of the varieties of (de)contextualized language are **entity** and **event orientation**. These concepts will be briefly explicated below (for a more detailed discussion, see Cloran 1994, 1995).

Entity is a semantic notion; it is a component of the semantic unit, message, and it is realized lexicogrammatically by a nominal group having a functional role in the clause. Messages can potentially contain more than one entity; however, only one entity is central to the identification of (de)contextualized varieties. The crucial or central entity is typically the one that functions as Subject in the clause realizing the message (see Cloran 1994, 1995 for more detailed discussions). The relevant semantic features of entity will be discussed presently after brief mention of the orientation of the message event.

Message event orientation is concerned with the temporal reference of an event as well as its frequency, possibility, necessity or hypotheticality. Generally speaking, the temporal orientation of the event is realized by the Finite element in the clause realizing the message. However, other lexicogrammatical phenomena may express an event's temporal orientation, e.g. adjuncts or conjoined dependent clauses. Indeed, the latter is the only means of explicitly expressing hypotheticality. Note that the variety of lexicogrammatical means for expressing time is an example of the non-conformal relation between the strata of lexicogrammar and semantics referred to in Section 7.3 (p. 156).

For the purposes of the investigation of (de)contextualized language use, entities need to be described in terms of whether or not they are identified by reference to the immediate situation as, for example, are the interactants. The description is represented as a semantic system network where the primary systemic contrast is, first of all, whether or not the entity in question is [**known**] or whether its identity is [**sought**]. The latter option is, predictably, realized by a WH– item typically in thematic position in the clause realizing the message *Who are my Mummy (when I was a little baby)*. When the identity of an entity is [**known**], the primary opposition is concerned with whether or not the entity in question refers to one or more messages of the text itself – [**expression**] – rather than to some thing – person or object – here described by the term [**content**]. The term [**expression**], then, is realized by the text referents *it, that*. This option is not further described. The primary terms in the system of entity component are shown in the network in Figure 7.3.

Space limitations preclude a discussion of each of the semantic features relevant to the description of entities (for a discussion of these features see Cloran 1994). Table 7.5 provides a summary of the lexicogrammatical features preselected to realize some of the semantic features in the entity network (Figure 7.3). Table 7.5 also gives actual or exemplificatory items deriving from the realization statements.

### 7.5.1.2 Relevant semantic features of event

The temporal orientation of events refers to the location-in-time of the event that is spoken (or written) about with respect to the moment of speaking (or writing): did the event occur **prior** to the moment of speaking? Is it occurring **concurrently** with the moment of speaking? Or is it **forecast** to occur at some time after the moment of speaking? These terms, then, are the primary semantic options in the system of time. Whether an event is habitual or occurs (or occurred or will occur) on a single occasion (non-habitually) is also important. The feature [**habitual**] construes generic or law-like statements which may, however, be restricted to a past or future time (Dahl 1985: 100). The system of habituality operates simultaneously with the system of time.

An event's occurrence may be estimated as a matter of probability or necessity. A speaker's (or writer's) estimate of the likelihood or necessity of an event's occurrence is realized by what Halliday (1994: 358–9) terms high, median and low value modals, in the form of auxiliaries, modal adjuncts or devices of verbal group complexing. These two dimensions – probability and necessity – may combine (*You might have to go soon*) and in terms of direction from the moment of speaking, both systems combine with temporal reference – *soon* ([**forecast**]).

Finally, consider the following example: *They would (might) go home if you asked them*. Should the first mentioned event (i.e. their going) occur, such

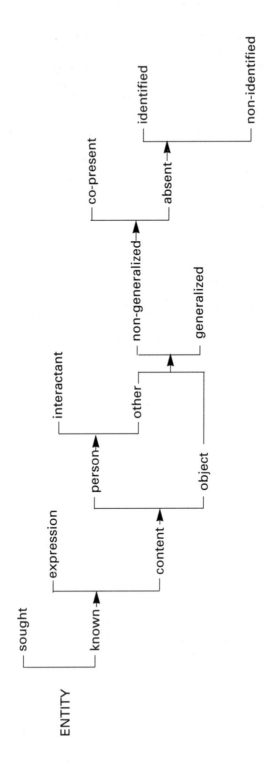

**Figure 7.3** Relevant semantic choices for entity component

**Table 7.5** Realizations of some semantic options in entity component network (Figure 7.3)

| semantic feature | lexicogrammatical realization |
|---|---|
| [expression] | NG = extended text referent *It, that* |
| [content:person:interactant] | NG = 1st or 2nd person singular/plural |
| [content:person:other: generalized] | *NG = a) [non-specific;plural], **or** <br> b) [non-specific; anaphoric; plural] with inter-pretative source = NG of the kind in a) **or** <br> c) [specific:homophoric; singular], **or** <br> d) [specific:anaphoric; singular] with interpre-tative source = NG of the kind in c). |
| [content:person:other: non-generalized:co-present] | i) a) NG = pre-modified by demonstrative <br> b) [specific;3rd person:human; anaphoric] with interpretative source = NG of the kind in a) <br> ii) NG with proper name as Head <br> iii) exophoric reference |
| [content:person:other: non-generalized:absent: identified] | i) a) NG pre-modified by *the* <br> b) NG with proper name as Thing <br> ii) anaphoric reference with interpretative source = NG of the kind in a) or b) |
| [content:person:other: non-generalized:absent: non-identified] | a) NG pre-modified by a non-specific deictic; <br> b) anaphoric reference with interpretative source = NG of the kind in a) |
| [content:object:generalized] | NG as in * above except for pronominal refer-ence, i.e. pronominal reference = [3rd person:non-human] ) |

occurrence is clearly in the future relative to the moment of speaking. However, the expectation of the event's occurrence in the future is both probabilistic and conditional upon the occurrence of another event (your asking). Here the relevant category is hypotheticality.

A hypothetical message is typically realized by a clause complex in which the logical relationship between the primary and secondary clause is one of condition, though as Leech (1971: 113) points out the condi-tional clause is often suppressed as Text 7.5 shows:

**Text 7.5**

| 252 | Mother | I may as well eat it skin and all |
| 253 | | It looks so delicious . . . |
| 254 | Cameron | Going to really eat the skin? |
| 255 | Mother | No |
| 256 | | **It would taste revolting, Cameron** |

In Text 7.5, the condition *If I were to eat it* is co-textually implied rather than stated explicitly as a condition of message 256.

The event orientation system is complex and involves a number of simultaneously operating systems. When a selection from the event system combines with a selection from the entity system a configuration emerges which can be considered the necessary condition for the construal of a unit of text, the rhetorical unit (RU).

### 7.5.2 Rhetorical units

The conjunction or combination of particular values of the two message components – entity and event – tends to be constant for a number of messages within a text, although the necessity for this is simply a matter of what a speaker or writer wants to do. When what is being done involves telling about some past event then such recounts tend to be constituted by a stretch of messages; where a speaker is trying to persuade a hearer to his/her point of view then often the conjunction of entity and event will change from message to message as the speaker switches rhetorical tack, as it were.

A number of configurations of central entity and event were identified. These configurations construe what are termed rhetorical units. The RUs identified for purposes of the investigation of (de)contextualized language use are shown in Table 7.6.

Table 7.6 is read as follows: messages in which the central entity and event orientation have specific semantic features construe the given RU, e.g. where the identity of the central entity is [**interactant**] and the event orientation is a goods/services exchange then the message constitutes the RU Action. The kind of activity in which a speaker simply comments on an event or state of affairs in which (at the time of speaking), s/he or a co-present and therefore perceptually identifiable entity is engaged, expresses the RU Commentary and is construed by the configuration:

> **Event orientation**: [concurrent;non-habitual] AND
> **Central entity**: [interactant/other person/object in MSS]

Note that, as Table 7.6 indicates, two RU types – Recount and Conjecture – are identified solely on the basis of the nature of the event orientation. This means that the RU Recount is defined by reference to the event feature [**prior**] and is not differentiated according to the nature of the central entity. Similarly, the event orientation by itself construes the RU Conjecture, though two features of event orientation must be co-selected, i.e. [**conditional**] and [**probable**]. (The fact that these two RUs are not further distinguished on the basis of the identity of the central entity does not mean that such a distinction cannot be made; rather, the distinction was not considered necessary in the study reported here.)

Finally, as the table suggests, the event orientation options [**non-habitual**] and [**forecast**] are not able to combine with the entity feature [**class**] (i.e. generalized entity).

As previously suggested, the RU types identified here construe that

**Table 7.6** Values of central entity and event orientation in the identification of classes of RU

| EVENT ORIENTATION / CENTRAL ENTITY | HABITUAL | REALIS — CONCURRENT | REALIS — PRIOR | GOODS/SERVICES EXCHANGE | IRREALIS — INFORMATION EXCHANGE — FORECAST | IRREALIS — INFORMATION EXCHANGE — HYPO-THETICAL |
|---|---|---|---|---|---|---|
| **Within material situational setting (MSS)** | | | | | | |
| interactant | Reflection | Commentary | Recount | Action | Plan/Prediction | Conjecture |
| other: person/object | Observation | | | | Prediction | |
| **Not within MSS** | | | | | | |
| person/object | Account | Report | | | Prediction | |
| class | Generalization | | | | | |

aspect of the contextual variable Mode of discourse known as the role of language in the social process, conceptualized as a continuum at one end of which language is ancillary to the task in hand and at the other, language constitutes the activity. The relationship between RU types and role of language is given in Figure 7.4.

Action-Commentary Observation-Reflection-Axiom Report Account Plan-Prediction Conjecture Recount Generalization

ancillary _____ constitutive

role of language

**Figure 7.4** Continuum of role of language in the social process

Text 7.3 is analysed in Table 7.7 in terms of the rhetorical configurations in each message. This extract begins with the mother conjecturing about a possible course of action. The child responds and announces a Plan which is, however, discouraged by a further Conjecture on the mother's part. In response to Stephen's query, the mother generalizes about the nature of fruit trees and then attempts to tie down this Generalization by recounting her own personal experience of the phenomenon under discussion. The child persists in his Plans, however, so the mother reformulates the earlier Conjecture and, in response to Stephen's query again generalizes about fruit trees. Let us compare this exposition with the teacher's, the RU analysis of which is given in Table 7.8.

There is a striking resemblance in terms of RU classes used by the adult speakers in Texts 7.3 and 7.4. The question is: are all children equally likely to participate in this kind of discourse prior to entering school? If this is not the case, then is there any systematic difference between those children who do and those who do not? These questions were investigated (see Cloran 1994, 1999). A subset of Hasan's data was used to examine the RU classes constituting the 400-odd message dialogues; only eight dyads were investigated so the study can only be considered suggestive. The results, however, indicated that indeed it was precisely frequency in the use of these RUs – Conjecture and Generalization – that distinguished the HAP and LAP dyads. The HAP group tended to use these more frequently than the LAP group who, however, tended to make more frequent use of the RU Action located at the most ancillary end of the continuum of the role of language in the social process (Figure 7.4).

## 7.6 Concluding remarks

It was suggested in Section 7.4.3 that mothers scoring high in 'individuated informativeness' seem almost to use information-giving as a means of controlling their children's behaviour. It is possible to investigate this suggestion using RU analysis and, in the process, to throw some light on the concept of (a)typical – therefore congruent versus metaphorical – construal of context, specifically the four critical socializing contexts

**Table 7.7** RU analysis of Text 7.3

| | | | |
|---|---|---|---|
| | | | Conjecture |
| 336 | M | D'you think <337> a mandarin tree would grow | |
| 337 | | if we planted a pip | |
| 338 | C | It might | |
| | | | .1 Plan |
| 339 | | so I better plant two mandarin pips | |
| 340 | M | The trouble is it might not have very good mandarins | Conjecture |
| 341 | C | Why? | |
| | | | .2 General-ization |
| 342 | M | Well with fruit trees the top part of the tree is often different to the bottom part of the tree | |
| | | | .2.1 Recount |
| 343 | | With the last lemon tree that we bought the bottom half was the kind of tree that has very good roots | |
| 344 | | And then the top half of the tree was the kind of tree that had very good fruit | |
| 345 | | And so they took the tree that has good roots | |
| 346 | | And they chopped the top off it | |
| 347 | | And they took the tree that has good fruit | |
| 348 | | And chopped the top off it | |
| 349 | | And they stuck the nice-fruiting top on the good-rooting bottom | |
| | | | .3 Plan |
| 350 | C | Mummy, I want to plant this one | |
| | | | .3.1 Conjec-ture |
| 351 | M | But you might not get mandarins from it | |
| 352 | C | Why? | |
| | | | 3.1.1 General-ization |
| 353 | M | Because when you plant seeds from mandarins or oranges | |
| 354 | | sometimes you get very strange fruit | |
| 355 | | or sometimes you don't get much fruit at all | |
| 356 | | So you have to plant a tree that's been grafted – that's been stuck on | |
| | | | 3.2 General-ization |
| 357 | | They're special trees that they make by sticking one tree to another tree | |
| 358 | C | How do they stick it? | |
| 359 | M | Well I think they cut it in a special way | |
| 360 | | They cut them in a special way | |
| 361 | | and they put them together | |
| 362 | | and then they bind stuff around the outside | |
| 363 | | to hold them together | |
| 364 | | 'til they grow together . . . | |

**Table 7.8** RU analysis of Text 7.4

| | | | |
|---|---|---|---|
| | | | Conjecture |
| 128 | Tr | Do you think it'd be very sensible to have a red whale? | |
| 129 | Chn | No . . . ! (SINGING) | |
| 130 | Tr | Why wouldn't it be sensible? | |
| | | | .1 Action |
| 131 | | Cameron, you tell me | |
| 132 | | Wait a minute (TO CHILDREN BREAKING IN) | |
| 133 | | Cameron you tell me | |
| 134 | C. | 'Cause they couldn't hide from danger | |
| | | | .2 Commentary |
| 135 | Tr | No, that's right | |
| 136 | | Think it'd be sensible Elizabeth, to have a blue crocodile? | |
| 137 | E. | No | |
| 138 | Tr | Why not? | |
| 139 | E. | [?          ] | |
| 140 | Tr | Right | |
| | | | .3 Generalization |
| 141 | | When a crocodile is in the water, in the muddy kind of water | |
| 142 | | he looks grey, greyie green | |
| 143 | | he looks like a log floating in the water | |
| 144 | | and so he can sneak up on his dinner | |
| 145 | | and eat it | |
| | | | .3.1 Conjecture |
| 146 | | but if he were bright blue | |
| 147 | | everyone'd see him coming | |
| 148 | | and get out of the way | |
| 149 | | and he'd starve to death | |

identified by Bernstein (e.g. 1971) – the regulative, the interpersonal, the instructional and the imaginative. According to Bernstein the regulative context is that which is construed by those specialized interactional practices which make the child aware of the rules of the moral order and their various supports through the enactment of authority relationships. The kind of language use construing this context is, then, logically expected to include messages such as a command prescribing or prohibiting certain behaviour(s), perhaps supported by an assertion expressing the rationale for the prescription or prohibition. On this basis, it might be expected that the regulative context is likely to be realized by the RU Action with/without, for example, a Prediction, Generalization or

Conjecture functioning in the text as a reason for the prescription or pro-hibition. The RU analysis of Text 7.1 indeed supports this expectation (see Table 7.9).

Text 7.2 was also held to construe the regulative context. Consider its constituent RUs (see Table 7.10).

In Text 7.2 Stephen's mother issues no command proscribing his behaviour; rather, she gives him information concerning the conse-quences and her evaluation of his attempt to speak whilst eating. He therefore must infer from this information that he is required not to act in this way. Linda, by contrast, has no need to draw inferences; her mother makes clear what kind of behaviour she expects. In other words, Text 7.1 may be said to congruently construe the regulative context while Text 7.2 may be thought of as a non-congruent or metaphorical con-strual. It may be that it is such metaphorical construals of the regulative context which contribute to the highly informative nature of the HAP mothers' discourse.

Is congruent versus metaphorical construal of context to be considered a sociolinguistic variable since there would seem to be a correlation between this and social class? Figueroa (1994: 100) in a review of critiques of Labovian sociolinguistics, has pointed out that sociolinguistic variation and the identification of sociolinguistic variables 'is founded on unexpli-cated notions' of social class. The sociolinguistic study of semantic varia-tion pioneered by Hasan has not suffered this fate since it is, by contrast, grounded in a sociological theory which has explicated the notion of social class, i.e. Bernstein's sociology. This theory shows how the division of labour generates principles of power and control which, depending on whether one occupies a dominating or a dominated position, result in dif-ferent coding orientations, orientations to meaning. These codes, sug-gests Bernstein, call forth interactional practices which support or relax the insulation between categories such as contexts. In the case of the HAP mother of Text 7.2, the regulative context is only weakly insulated from other types of context in which the giving of information is genuine in the sense that it does not require some non-verbal action on the part of the child. In a 'genuine' exchange of information, it is up to the hearer to act on information. When an information exchange realizes a regulative context, however, such discretion is only apparent; in fact, as a result of the information the hearer is required to act. The regulation is thus made 'invisible' (Bernstein 1975, Hasan 1992). The LAP mother's construal of the regulative context (Text 7.1), by contrast, clearly demarcates this con-text from any other context (in this instance, the preceding interpersonal context) thus supporting her tendency to insulate this from other con-texts and making regulation 'visible'.

In discussing the speech variants regulated by the underlying coding orientations, Bernstein (1990: 15) 'rewrites' evoking contexts as 'special-ized interactional practices', relevant meanings as 'orientations to mean-ing', and realizations as 'textual productions'. We may say, then, that the

**Table 7.9** RU analysis of Text 7.1

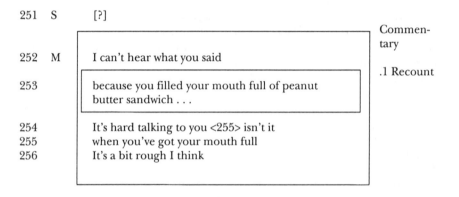

|     |   |                                              | Commentary |
|-----|---|----------------------------------------------|------------|
| 160 | M | Are you enjoying it?                         |            |
| 161 | L | Yes Mama                                     |            |
| 162 | M | Good darling                                 |            |
|     |   |                                              | .1 Action  |
| 163 |   | Don't talk with food in your mouth alright?  |            |
|     |   |                                              | .1.1 Prediction |
| 164 |   | You can talk                                 |            |
| 165 |   | when you've finished . . .                   |            |

**Table 7.10** RU analysis of Text 7.2

|     |   |                                              | Commentary |
|-----|---|----------------------------------------------|------------|
| 251 | S | [?]                                          |            |
| 252 | M | I can't hear what you said                   |            |
|     |   |                                              | .1 Recount |
| 253 |   | because you filled your mouth full of peanut butter sandwich . . . |            |
| 254 |   | It's hard talking to you <255> isn't it      |            |
| 255 |   | when you've got your mouth full              |            |
| 256 |   | It's a bit rough I think                     |            |

HAP and LAP mothers in Hasan's data have variant specialized interactional practices construed by variant orientations to meaning. This results in their variant textual productions. Bernstein's theory accounts for, indeed predicts, such variation. Hasan's semantic framework and its development in terms of RU analysis has permitted rigorous (and replicable) investigation, revealing how it is that in the process of primary socialization within the family the worded meanings speakers choose are activated by the social relations in which they are positioned.

## Notes

1. The dialogues presented as texts in this chapter are from Hasan's corpora of mother–child and teacher–child interaction. I am indebted to her not only for access to this data but also for her comments on the first draft of this chapter.
2. Transcription conventions:
   unintelligible item = [?]

2. Transcription conventions:
       unintelligible item = [?]
M = Mother
C = Child
Chn = Children
Tr = Teacher
[?] = unintelligible item
[? item] = uncertain transcription of item
. . . three dots = pause in conversation
. . . . . . . several dots = lengthier pause
CAPITALS = transcription commentary (LAUGHING)
indented line = overlapping speech
       157    M    What's that one got?
              158    C    Hurry up.

* = speaker does not allow time for hearer to answer question
       157    M    What's that one got?*
       158           Has that one got a seed?

3. The following point concerning the variants included in each of the principal
   components analyses is relevant. The technique requires that the ratio of subjects to variables be 3 to 1. This means that only a subset of the total number of
   semantic features characterizing each message can be included in any single
   analysis. The semantic features to be included were therefore selected on the
   basis of the logical possibilities associated with the realization of some contextual feature. This is how the feature set characterizing questioning and answering behaviour (Table 7.4) was derived.
      In relation to this restriction on the number of features, the linguistic framework
   itself, through the notion of delicacy of focus within the network, permits a principled reduction without too much loss of information. To illustrate: in the feature set
   in Table 7.4 there is clearly variation in the degree of delicacy; the most delicate features of questions included here are [**ask**], [**explain**] and [**assumptive**]; other delicate features such as [**probe**] have been excluded. Note that the association of an
   excluded feature ([**specify**] not included in the dataset of Table 7.4) may be
   deduced, given its systemic contrast – the feature that opposes it in the network, that
   is [**explain**] in Table 7.4. This ability to deduce the value of a feature compensated
   to some extent for the limitation imposed by the 3 to 1 subjects to variables ratio.
      The principled reduction in the number of features included in the PCA was
   particularly useful in the analysis characterizing mothers' control styles.
   Hasan's (1992) network pertaining to the description of (some of) the ways of
   getting people to do things (commands) is a particularly delicate description.
   Even with the large number of messages analysed, the most delicate features of
   commands applied to too few to make a statistically feasible category of variant.
   Therefore, commands were characterized for example as [**indirect**], subsuming all commands having the features [**non-exhortative**] or [**suggestive**], i.e.
   those that are non-congruently realized by interrogative or declarative mood
   structures or by [imperative:inclusive] preselecting first person plural at
   Subject (e.g. *let's get dressed now*).

## References

Berger, P. and Luckmann, T. (1966) *The Social Construction of Reality.* Harmondsworth: Penguin.

Bernstein, B. (1971) *Theoretical Studies: Towards a Sociology of Language, Class, Codes and Control, Vol.1.* London: Routledge.

Bernstein, B. (1990) *The Structuring of Pedagogic Discourse: Class, Codes and Control, Vol.4.* London: Routledge.

Bruner, J. (1970) *Poverty and Childhood.* Detroit: Merrill-Palmer Institute.

Cloran, C. (1989) Learning through language: the social construction of gender. In R. Hasan and J. Martin (eds), *Language Development: Learning Language, Learning Culture: Meaning and Choice in Language: Studies for Michael Halliday.* Norwood: Ablex.

Cloran, C. (1994) *Rhetorical Units and Decontextualisation: An Enquiry into Some Relations of Context, Meaning and Grammar.* Nottingham: Department of English Studies, University of Nottingham.

Cloran, C. (1995) Defining and relating text segments. In R. Hasan and P. Fries (eds) *On Subject and Theme: From a Discourse Functional Perspective.* Amsterdam: Benjamin.

Cloran, C. (1999) Contexts for learning. In F. Christie (ed.), *Pedagogy and the Shaping of Consciousness: Linguistic and Social Processes.* London: Cassell.

Dahl, O. (1985) *Tense and Aspect Systems.* Oxford: Basil Blackwell.

Donaldson, M. (1987) The origins of inference. In J. Bruner and H. Haste (eds), *Making Sense: The Child's Construction of the World.* London: Methuen.

Figueroa, E. (1994) *Sociolinguistic Metatheory.* Oxford: Pergamon.

Halliday, M. A. K. (1976) English System Networks. In G. Kress (ed.), *Halliday: System and Function in Language.* London: Oxford University Press.

Halliday, M. A. K. (1994) *Introduction to Functional Grammar* (2nd edn). London: Edward Arnold.

Hasan, R. (1973) Codes, register and social dialect. In B. Bernstein (ed.), *Class, Codes and Control, Vol.2.* London: Routledge.

Hasan, R. (1984) Ways of saying: ways of meaning. In R. Fawcett, M. A. K. Halliday, S. Lamb and A. Makkai (eds), *The Semiotics of Culture and Language, Vol. 1: Language as Social Semiotic.* London: Pinter, 105–62.

Hasan, R. (1989) Semantic variation and socio-linguistics. *Australian Journal of Linguistics,* 9: 221–75.

Hasan, R. (1991) Questions as a mode of learning in everyday talk. In T. Le and M. McCausland (eds), *Language Education: Interaction and Development.* Launceston: University of Tasmania, 70–119.

Hasan, R. (1992) Meaning in sociolinguistic theory. In K. Bolton and H. Kwok (eds), *Sociolinguistics Today: International Perspectives.* London: Routledge, 80–119.

Hasan, R. (1993) Contexts for Meaning. In James E. Slate (ed.), *Georgetown University Roundtable on Language and Linguistics 1993: Language, Communication and Social Meaning.* Washington, DC: Georgetown University Press.

Hasan, R. (1995) The conception of context in text. In P. Fries and M. Gregory (eds), *Discourse in Society.* Norwood: Ablex

Hasan, R. (1996) Semantic networks: a tool for the analysis of meaning. In C. Cloran, D. Butt and G. Williams (eds), *Ways of Saying: Ways of Meaning: Selected Papers of Ruqaiya Hasan.* London: Cassell.

Hasan, R. and Cloran, C. (1990) A sociolinguistic study of everyday talk between mothers and children. In M. A. K. Halliday, J. Gibbons and H. Nicholas (eds), *Learning, Keeping and Using Language, Vol.1. Selected Papers from the 8th World Congress of Applied Linguistics*, Sydney, August 1987. Amsterdam: Benjamin.

Horvath, B. (1985) *Variation in Australian English: The Sociolects of Sydney*. Cambridge: Cambridge University Press.

Labov, W. (1966) *The Social Stratification of English in New York City*. Washington: Center for Applied Linguistics.

Leech, G. (1971) *Meaning and the English Verb*. London: Longman.

Matthiessen, C. (1995) *Lexicogrammatical Cartography: English Systems*. Tokyo: International Language Sciences Publishers.

Olson, D. R. (1977) From utterance to text: the bias of language in speech and writing. *Harvard Educational Review*, 47 (3).

Snow, C. E. (1983) Literacy and language: relationships during the preschool years. *Harvard Educational Review*, 53 (2).

Trudgill, P. (1974) *Sociolinguistics: An Introduction*. Harmondsworth: Penguin.

Wells, G. (1981) Language, literacy and education. In C. G. Wells (ed.), *Learning Through Interaction*. Cambridge: Cambridge University Press, 240–76.

Vygotsky, L.S. (1978) *Mind in Society*. Cambridge, MA: Harvard University Press.

# 8 The language of classroom interaction and learning

*Frances Christie*

## 8.1 Introduction

Two important responsibilities for any conscientious teacher are first to clarify goals for teaching and second to ensure the goals are met. A good deal of careful thought must go into establishing what the actual purposes are for teaching the 'content', what kinds of knowledge and skills the students are ideally to develop, how best to teach for an understanding of these, and finally how to be sure the students have learned what they were intended to learn. The principal resource available to teachers and students with which to achieve educational goals is language. It is in the language of the classroom that a great deal of the work will go on towards negotiating understandings, clarifying tasks, exploring sources of difficulty and assessing students' progress. While language is the principal semiotic system in which so much teaching and learning activity is conducted, there are of course many other semiotic systems at work, including pictures, videos, charts and graphs. The uses of language need to be understood along with uses of the other semiotic systems. Nonetheless, there is an important sense in which language is primary, for it is central to the ways in which teachers and students work together. So central is it in fact, that language is often drawn upon to interpret and explain the other forms of semiosis that students are learning to use.

Given the central role of language in teaching and learning, teachers need to develop tools with which to judge the effectiveness of the language patterns they initiate and develop. This is essential to their capacity to plan and monitor their teaching, as well as to judge the success of their students' learning. In this chapter I shall outline a method for studying the patterns of language use in schools that teachers might use to research and monitor their own teaching practice. To do so, I shall focus on the role of spoken language in teaching and learning, and I shall make only some references to literate language. This is not because literate language doesn't merit attention, but rather because space doesn't permit that I do equal justice to speech and writing. Concerns with literate language are variously addressed in Chapters 5, 9, 10 and 11.

I shall refer to classroom talk as a form of 'pedagogic discourse' (Bernstein, e.g. 1990, 1996): a discourse, that is, in which persons are apprenticed into particular pedagogic subject positions, involving adoption of methods of working, and ways of addressing and defining issues of a kind characteristic of the discourse concerned.[1] I shall argue that a pedagogic discourse works in patterned and predictable ways for the achievement of educational goals. I shall also argue that it is possible to arrive at a principled account of the manner in which the pedagogic discourse of school learning occurs.

## 8.2  Regulative and instructional registers

Most teaching-learning activity takes place in a sequence or cycle of several lessons in which educational goals are realized. While some lessons are discrete 'one-off' affairs, the most common pattern is to commit several lessons in which a curriculum unit is taught and learned. Such a cycle constitutes a curriculum macrogenre. Each genre (sometimes lasting more than one lesson) is staged and goal-directed; it constitutes an element in the larger unity of the curriculum macrogenre. (See Christie 1995c, 1997, 1998, in press, for discussion of curriculum macrogenres. Also see Martin 1994, 1995 for some discussion of macrogenres.)

Essential to the unfolding of a curriculum macrogenre is the functioning of two registers, the regulative and the instructional. The notion of the two registers is adapted from the work of Bernstein on pedagogic discourse (e.g. 1996). According to Bernstein, a pedagogic discourse involves a regulative discourse to do with the overall goals of the pedagogic relationship, while the instructional discourse is to do with the particular 'content' being taught. The former, in his terms, 'embeds' the other. The instructional discourse will be taken from some location outside the school and relocated for the purposes of teaching and learning. The analysis adopted proposes that the regulative register 'projects' the instructional register. The metaphor used is drawn from Halliday's functional grammar (1994): where one clause projects another, it takes an idea or a verbal expression and reproduces the latter, as in for example 'He said, "what's the time?"' Projection in this sense involves taking something said earlier and giving it new significance by re-stating it. So too, a great deal of educational endeavour takes the discourses of history, science, the social sciences and so on, and reinstates them for teaching and learning.

Curriculum macrogenres vary, depending on the age group of the students, the subject itself, and the strengths and attitudes of the teacher. Nonetheless, I can generalize with some confidence about the organization of curriculum macrogenres in early childhood education (1989), the upper primary years (1994, 1995c, 1998) and the secondary years (Christie 1995a, 1995b, 1998). I find that the regulative register is dominant in the opening stages of the macrogenre, and henceforth at any points where it is necessary to clarify and define goals. Where the teaching is really successful there will be long sequences in which the two registers converge as students engage with learning about the 'content' (realized in the instructional register), while working towards clearly defined tasks (realized in the regulative register). Nonetheless, as the sequence of lessons proceeds, the instructional register is eventually foregrounded, while the regulative register remains operating only tacitly, predisposing students to behave in ways valued for pedagogic purposes. With the growth of the classroom text, there will be a process of *logogenesis*: an unfolding of the text in such a manner that a kind of momentum builds as the students move towards the capacity to use language to represent new understandings (Halliday and Martin 1993: 18).

## 8.3 A curriculum genre in early childhood education

We will first consider an early childhood education classroom genre. The text involves a teacher 'Mrs L.' and her class of Year 1 children learning about the life cycle of a chicken. The children were grouped in a semicircle on the floor around the teacher, who sat on a chair so that she could command eye contact with all the students. The  physical disposition of the participants symbolically underlined the relative size and authority of the teacher, and the corresponding smallness and lack of authority of the children. Mrs L. displayed a book about the life cycle of chickens, and the opening of the Task Orientation went as follows:

**Text 8.1**

> T: We're going to start off with a little story this morning. Firstly, I want to show you some of the pictures in this little book called 'Egg to Chick'. And we're just going to find out what you people know about this little book. I won't read it all to you. I'll show you some of the pictures and we'll have a little chat about them. Lesley, what sort of creature is this little creature here? Deborah? (Deborah is addressed because Lesley doesn't answer.)
> Deborah: A hen.
> T: It's a hen, and what do you think this is here?
> Deborah and several other children: Egg.

The regulative register is dominant in the opening clauses of teacher talk, though the instructional register also has some expression. With respect to the regulative register note the following:

Textually:

- the text starts in teacher monologue and student interruption or comment would not be welcome at this point;
- textual Theme choices in teacher talk (often more frequent than here) signal that the teacher is pointing directions and pushing the discourse

forward: *firstly*, I want to show you some of the pictures; *and* we're just going to find out; *and* we'll have a little chat about them.

Experientially:

- process types are to do with establishing student and/or teacher behaviours:
  *we're going to start off with a little story this morning.* (material)
  *Firstly, I want to show you some of the pictures in this little book called Egg to Chick.* (affect; material)
  *And we're just going to find out* (cognition)
  *what you people know about this little book.* (cognition)
  *I won't read it all to you.* (behavioural)
  *I'll show you some of the pictures* (material)
  *and we'll have a little chat about them.* (behavioural)

The Participants involved in the processes are notable. The roles of Actor, Senser and Behaver typically are realized in pronouns identifying class members: the first person plural pronoun 'we' (very commonly found in opening stages like this regardless of the ages of the students) is used to establish solidarity in the joint enterprise in which students and teacher are to engage. The first person singular pronoun identifies the teacher, and is used when she wants to indicate clearly what it is she wants to do.

Participants other than Actor, Senser and Behaver are all realized in fairly general items, while Circumstances often also contain nominal groups that are general in character:

> with *a little story* this morning
> *some of the pictures* in this little book [[called Egg to Chick]]
> *some of the pictures*

Such general referents typically occur in openings, when the object is to establish in general or broad terms what is to be done.

One of the general referents used by the teacher in her opening remarks pointed to some confusion in her planning of the language of her regulative register and, as we shall see later, it caused some confusion in the children's thinking. This was her reference to starting with a 'story'. The book she displayed was a science information book, offering a factual explanation of the phenomenon involved. The teacher probably chose the word 'story' because she wanted an accessible term to offer young children. However, given that the children were familiar with stories, the teacher could have exploited this by saying that the book was not a story book, and that instead it explained how a chicken grew. A term more accurately part of the regulative field being considered would help to develop in the children an appropriate language to deal with it. As we shall see, she was on the whole much better prepared to build with the

children a sense of the instructional field to do with chickens than she
was to build the regulative field to do with ways to handle that field.

Interpersonally:

The opening teacher talk is in the declarative mood, as of one who is
establishing some basic information for others whose role is to listen.
Vocatives have no place in this kind of teacher talk and they are normally
invoked, if at all, as a management measure.

There is a shift in register with the shift in mood and the asking of the
question: *Lesley, what sort of creature is this little creature here?* The question
marks the entry to dialogue and also the entry to the instructional field.
Pointing to a picture in the book, the teacher says:

**Text 8.2**

> T: Oh I wonder if someone can tell me what's happening in this picture?
> Child: It's a special place.
> T: Yes and what's happening in this special place? Joseph? (addressed because
>     he has raised his hand)
> Joseph: It's on a farm
> T: Have you ever seen great big long silver sheds?
> Several children: Yes.
> T: Where chickens are kept or hens are kept for laying eggs. They're
>     called batteries or battery chickens or battery hens
> Olivera: Battery cage.
> T: And when they lay their eggs, the eggs fall down into this little shute. (She
>     points to the illustration in the book.)
> Anthony: Mrs L. I know where they are. I know where they are.
> T: Where are they?
> Anthony: They're where you buy the chickens.
> T: That's right. And are these litttle eggs going to turn into chickens?
> Chorus: No.
> T: How do we know they're not going to? Diana?
> Diana: 'Cos the mother's not in a warm spot, and they're not keeping warm.
> T: That's right. She can't sit on them.
> Diana: 'Cos the steel is cold.

The discourse continued for another twenty minutes, as the teacher and
students engaged with the instructional register. Topical Theme choices
normally, but not universally, realize aspects of the instructional field:

> <u>It</u>'s on a farm
> <u>They</u>'re called batteries or battery chickens or battery hens
> 'Cos <u>the mother</u>'s not in a warm spot, and <u>they</u>'re not keeping warm.

Transitivity choices for the most part (but again not universally) realize
the instructional field:

*they're called* batteries or battery chickens or battery hens. (identifying process)
*they're not keeping warm.* (attributive process)

On occasion, the discourse involves some expression of the regulative register, as in: *Oh I wonder if someone can tell me what's happening in this picture?*, where the opening mental and verbal processes ( *wonder* and *can tell* ) are involved in guiding the children's talk. But in general, as noted, it is the instructional field that is at issue.

I shall cite a little more of the classroom text, to demonstrate how the teacher and students moved to building a sense of the development of the chick:

**Text 8.3**

T: Which part of the egg does the little chicken start to grow? Jodie which part of the eggs does the little chick start to grow?
Jodie: (A long pause) The middle?
T: Mm. What's the middle part of the egg called?
Several children: The yolk.
T: This is the inside of the egg and this little white spot here (points to illustration) is where the little chicken will start to grow. That's the yolk that it will feed on. It's got that little tube to his tummy.
Anthony: A cord.
T: Yes, a little cord. And that's, he feeds on all of that yolk. As he grows he feeds on that yolk and the yolk shrinks. It gets smaller and smaller.

A lot of work went into building the instructional field, and the technical language associated with it. Thus, an identifying process was used to introduce the technical term *yolk*: *What's the middle part of the egg called?* Even the more 'commonsense' examples of language used here in different Participant roles, including for example *that little tube to his tummy* or *a cord*, have very useful roles in building the instructional field.

Patterns of talk of the kind just cited – involving sequences of IRE (Initiation, Response, Evaluation) (Mehan 1979) or IRF (Initiation, Response, Followup) (Sinclair and Coulthard 1975) – are sometimes criticized on the grounds that the students are locked into making only one-word responses in a stretch in which the teacher dominates. Yet it can be argued that such a pattern is very defensible (see Christie 1995c; also Wells 1993), when we can show that it either leads to useful joint construction of a shared language for dealing with the field, or leads to capacity on the part of the students to participate independently as the discourse proceeds. In either case there will be a growth in logogenesis, but we can only know if such growth occurs by studying often very long passages of classroom text to trace the changes. In the classroom text here, the children increasingly contributed to the collective shared understanding of the instructional field, as in the following passage, occurring some minutes after the last extract:

**Text 8.4**

T:  (turns a page in the book and reads) Two weeks or thirteen days.
Several children: Oh.
T:  Two weeks or thirteen days - nearly two weeks. And you can start to see again he's really starting to get like a real chicken.
A boy: And he's sleepy too.
Another child: He's turning yellow.
T:  Yes he's turning yellow because he's got feathers. Sixteen days.
Olivera:  There's not too much of the yolk left.
T:  No there's not too much of the yolk left. It's getting pushed right away, and there's even less now.
Olivera:  Nineteen days.
T:  Nineteen days, and there he's starting to look like he looked when he first hatched out. (A reference to an illustration earlier examined in the start of the book) You've got the air space there, (points to the features in the diagrams and pictures) you've got his claws and the leathery part of his foot, very little of the egg sac left, of the yolk left, his beak, and his head tucked up under his wing.
Olivera:  He's squashing.
T:  He's squashing. He's filling up nearly the whole of that shell. Yes, Susy?
Susy:  Well when I went to the Melbourne market we were walking and I saw this lady and she had this part of her head black and the rest all red like uh, like uh a cock
T:  Like the top of the comb of a hen or rooster.
Susy:  Yeah it looked funny.
T:  Hens and roosters have got a comb at the top, right? And then they've got-
Susy:  It was all red.
T:  It looked a bit like that, did it? (pointing to a picture in the book)
Susy:  Yeah.
Jeffrey:  A cone.
T:  No, comb, not a cone. A cone is what you eat an ice cream in, but a comb is that. Right, twenty-one days, or three weeks, and there you see the egg starting to hatch out. The little hole and then it starts  to peck a little line around. It says 'The twenty-one days inside the egg are over. The chick pecks at the shell. It pecks thousands of times. At last the shell cracks.' It's a very very very hard job for that little chick to get out.
Mirko:  It would take a long long time.

Several of the children's contributions in constructing the instructional field are noteworthy, demonstrating how successfully they participated in the ongoing development of the text. Such capacity has to be fostered with a great deal of teacher guidance and intervention. Note the way the children literally build upon what the teacher says in several ways. Thus, when the teacher remarks that the chicken has reached the thirteenth day of development in the shell, she observes *And you can start to see again he's really starting to get like a real chicken.* This provokes from two children two useful responses in terms of building the field: *And he's sleepy too,* and *He's turning yellow.* Here the children use two attributive processes in order to build relevant instructional field information. The teacher in turn builds upon the child's last contribution, adding to it by giving a reason in her second clause: *Yes he's turning yellow because he's got feathers.* Another child, Olivera, then offers another contribution to the field-building, using an existential process, *There's not too much of the yolk left.* Again the teacher builds with this latter contribution to the discourse, repeating the existential process, and now elaborating upon its meaning with two other clauses that build a little more field information: *No there's not too much of the yolk left. It's getting pushed right away, and there's even less now.* Thus a process of genuine joint construction continues.

A few minutes later, after the teacher had drawn attention to the nature of the chicken after nineteen days, Olivera again contributed, using a material process to observe of the now almost fully developed chicken: *He's squashing,* and the teacher, accepting this, and again elaborating, says: *He's squashing. He's filling up nearly the whole of that shell.* A subsequent contribution offered by Susie (at first sight not wholly relevant) to do with a lady whose headpiece looked like a comb, led to a useful exchange about the differences between *a cone* and *a comb.* Finally, the teacher's observation of the chicken using an attributive process: *It's a very very very hard job for that little chick to get out,* led to the thoughtful response from Mirko, also using an attributive process: *It would take a long long time.*

The grammar in the sequences of classroom talk we have been considering  is very different from that of the opening sequence of talk. Textually, we have already commented on the dialogic nature of the talk, as teacher and students construct shared understandings. Topical Theme choices mostly realize aspects of the instructional field, especially the chicken:

> <u>this</u> is the inside of the egg
> <u>he</u>'s starting to look
> <u>he</u>'s turning yellow

There are some textual Theme choices, mainly realized in structurals that have a role in carrying forward the discourse about the chicken:

> It's getting pushed right away, <u>and</u> there's even less now.
> Nineteen days, <u>and</u> there he's starting to look like he looked

Interpersonal Themes are sometimes realized in a WH-, as in:

> Which part of the egg does the little chicken start to grow?

but interpersonal Themes are very few overall. The discourse flows freely with no particular recourse to interpersonal Themes.

Interpersonally more generally, the Mood choices, while involving some teacher interrogatives, are declarative as students and teacher exchange information. Experientially, as noted, the talk overwhelmingly realizes the instructional field.

Gone are the grammatical choices that featured in the start. For the most part, the regulative register has no expression in the sequences of text just reviewed. Yet it was the operation of the regulative register which made possible the entry to the instructional register and which gave it purpose, order and direction. Following Bernstein's observations (Bernstein 1996: 182–90), I would argue that the regulative register determines the pacing, sequencing and ordering of the operation of the instructional register. The pacing, sequencing and ordering all have consequences for the ideal pedagogic subject position in construction.

What can we say of the pedagogic subject position involved? This needs to be explained partly in terms of the spatial relations of the participants in the discourse construction: as noted earlier, the children are grouped on the floor about the teacher, their status affirmed as obedient, attentive young learners looking up at the teacher as she directs the activity. But the pedagogic subject position has other aspects, realized in the oral text and in the uses made of the written text and illustrations in the textbook. It involves willingness and capacity to participate in joint construction of shared understandings, in this case about the life cycle of chickens. It involves capacity to pursue a sequential explanation, built with use of good illustrations, in the manner of a great deal of scientific learning. It involves observation of details about the chicken's growth at the different stages and it involves use of relevant technical language to handle the instructional register. Some of the knowledge gained is particular to the instructional field of chickens and their development, but some has more general application, having relevance for the other kinds of explanations the children will no doubt need to consider and construct in other areas of learning.

The early childhood curriculum genre led to a Task Specification phase where the students were given a series of six pictures depicting a simplified series of stages in chick development. They were asked to cut these out and paste them into their books in the right order and then to write about chickens. The adoption of such a strategy was in principle a good one, predisposing the students to think sequentially through the stages of chick development and predisposing them to see the task in knowledge construction as something facilitated by a combination of written text and illustrations. While uses of image and written text are not peculiar to scientific knowledge construction, it was clear that in this context, and because of the model of the textbook displayed to the children, they were understood as relevant to such a purpose. As it happened, when the teacher moved to the Task Specification, signalled through a return to the use of the regulative register, she confused the issues for at least some of the students by inviting them to write a 'story'. As I indicated earlier, she was in fact much less confident about the appropriate language of the regulative register:

**Text 8.5**

> T: What I have here is a little sheet I'd like you to take back with you to your seat. On this little sheet, when you look very very closely, you may not be able to see it from the front [*sic*]. When you look closely, you'll find there are pictures, Belinda (addressed because inattentive), of all the stages that a little chick goes through before it is born.
> Stephen: Can you put second, third, fourth, and sixth?
> T: (Ignoring Stephen) Now, what you have to do is this. First thing you've got to sort out which order the pictures go in.
> Joel: I reckon the mother hen would go first.
> T: Then I'll want you to paste them into your scrapbook in the correct order, and then I want you to write a little story about this little chick, how it grew and how it hatched into a chicken. (The children here chorus 'chicken' along with the teacher.) Well let's see if someone can tell me which picture would be the first picture in this little story. Jeffrey, which one do you think?
> Jeffrey: The hen on the egg.

The difficulty with the regulative register is that it points the students in two directions. On the one hand, the advice to write a 'story' predisposes the students towards narrative construction. On the other hand, the series of pictures and the talk of sequencing these, modelled as it is in a simplified way on the textbook used to guide talk, predisposes the students to write a factual text. There is an important lesson here to do with the limitations of the regulative register and with the manner in which the two registers might usefully converge. To judge from the overall organization of the lesson, the pedagogic goals of the curriculum genre are to develop in the students oral capacity to construct sustained explanation in a manner valued for the purposes of school learning, and to develop literacy skills. These two goals are to be achieved by engagement with the instructional field. But the particular literacy tasks selected for any genre should involve some attention to the type of literate behaviour most suited to dealing with the selected instructional field. In this sense, while the classroom talk generated by the teacher was in many ways very effective, there was a loss of clearly thought out purpose with respect to the direction to develop literacy skills.

As it was, a number of the students wrote pieces that showed how confused they were by the regulative direction to write a 'story'. One example will serve to illustrate the point:

**Text 8.6**

> Once upon a time a hen lay a egg inside the egg a chicken was being born the chick eats the yolk it make(s) a little hole now the chick is making a crack.

This piece begins as story, as instanced in the Circumstance of time in marked Theme position *once upon a time*, and in the use of the past tense. Then it changes to more factual writing, as the child takes up the simple present tense with the clause *the chick eats the yolk . . .*, and the model of factual writing is sustained for the rest of the piece. This is not a successful piece of writing, since it fails both as a story and as a factual explanation.

A more successful piece was provided by a child who wrote a text that represented a reasonably adequate explanation genre. The child actually used the structure of an explanation genre. (See Christie *et al.* 1992 for accounts of the target explanation genre involved.) Though she had received no formal advice about how to structure such a genre, it seems she selected this as one implicitly available to her from the classroom talk about the book on chickens. The text, showing elements of structure, is set out here:

**Text 8.7**

**Phenomenon**
This is how a chicken grows
**Explanation sequence**
First a Mother hen lays eggs then the chicken inside gets bigger then the chick starts to crack a dotted line around the shell then the chick pushes out and when it has dryd (dried) it gets yellow and fluffy

This is an instance of an explanation, albeit a rather rudimentary one. The opening sentence establishes the Phenomenon to be explained. The subsequent element, the Explanation sequence, sets out in a series of temporally related clauses at least some of the steps in the progress from the laying of the egg to the emergence of the chick from the broken shell. The transitivity choices successfully realize aspects of the stages, involving material processes to start with (*the mother hen lays eggs, the chick pushes*) while at least one later process realizes an aspect of the chick after it has emerged from the shell (*it gets yellow and fluffy*). Finally, the tense choice is present, befitting such an explanation genre.

The child who wrote the text was successfully apprenticed into the relevant pedagogic subject position. She was, incidentally, not alone in writing as she did, but she was judged more successful than most others in the class, a view shared by both teacher and researcher. Most other children produced less coherent pieces. The regulative register, as realized in the teacher-directed talk, had operated to direct the children's discussions of the chick's development towards scientific explanation writing, even though the teacher directions regarding the actual task as we have seen were somewhat confusing.

To return for the moment to my opening observations to do with the need for teachers to think through goals in teaching, I suggest that where the language of the regulative register is focused, the directions towards the tasks the students are to achieve will be correspondingly clear. The very clarity of the directions at those critical points in lessons where pedagogic goals are being established, will ensure that students receive unambiguous information about the steps to take to achieve those goals. In an activity of the kind discussed here, the goal was to produce a written text about the instructional field of the development of chickens. While some good work went into building an understanding of the instructional field knowledge, the work of building the regulative knowledge about the act of writing was less successful. Certainly in the case of one young child this work was successful: the measure of that is that she produced a reasonably coherent explanation genre. Such a written text emerges as successfully expressing the instructional field. Yet its very success depends on the tacit operation of the regulative register which has served to predispose the child to write as she has done. As I noted much earlier in this discussion, the most important measure of the success of the regulative register is that it will disappear in the discourse, while its tacit operation ensures the success of the overall educational activity.

## 8.4  A genre in junior secondary schooling

I want now to turn to an instance of one curriculum genre chosen from the junior secondary geography classroom. I have selected it because it offers some contrast with the early childhood text, partly because the group of students involved are much older, partly because the instructional field is so different.

The genre is drawn from a very substantial macrogenre (Christie 1996). It involved a unit of work on World Heritage consisting of seventeen lessons taught over six weeks. In the first lesson, after some preliminaries, the teacher turned to the whiteboard and wrote *World Heritage*, joking about his initial misspelling:

**Text 8.8**

T:  Ooh! Try the spelling! (writes on the whiteboard) Ah, it's about a six week unit more or less. Um, with a broad title of World Heritage. It's a fairly big title, but we'll come back to that in a moment. Um, we really need to get into these key geographic ideas and the two things I want you to do is to remember the three that we are using: location, distribution and a fairly big one, a fairly new one we call spatial interaction. There are nine ideas and I've got three here. Um, and the second thing I want you to be able to do as you go through is to use those words um, frequently, accurately, correctly.
Gordon:  What's that third word . . .
T:  I'll go through each of those. OK, first thing we'll look at is simply the location of different heritage sites:
S-I-T-E-S, places. (Spells this out as he annotates on the board: his writing is often hard to read. Next to location, writes: 'of heritage sites') Now, the sum total of all that location is what we call distribution. So we'll look at the

distribution of sites within um, particular countries. (Next to distribution, adds: 'of sites within a country'.) Some are spread all over the place, some are concentrated. We'll look at where and why. And the third one, spatial interaction – I-N-T-E-R-A-C-T-I-O-N. And here, because of the nature of what World Heritage means, we have to look at the interaction between people and the effect that they have on sites. And often that effect, unfortunately, is a fairly negative one. And because of that we come back to the idea of control. (Next to *spatial interaction* writes: *between people and sites (negative ──▶ control)* We'll see how that works ah, as we go through. So, hopefully you're following the pattern of, I've used already three colours, you should have used at least three [for taking notes]. Ah, now we've only got a fairly ah, small, little screen (the whiteboard is small) here so ah, 'cos there's a bit of writing I'll be rubbing it off at fairly frequent intervals, so the moral of the story Michael is keep up!

Here the two registers converge in the manner that I suggested earlier is important if students are both to engage with the instructional information to be dealt with and also to understand the tasks to be completed with respect to that information.

In Text 8.8, the first and second order registers are both involved. We will consider the regulative register first.

With respect to mode and the textual metafunction, we can note that the text extract above is:

1. teacher monologic;
2. makes use of some teacher textual Themes helping to point directions: *and, okay, now;*
3. makes use of written language on the board as well as oral language, setting a trend that remains throughout the greater part of the total sequence.

With respect to Mood and Modality and the interpersonal metafunction, we can note:

1. The teacher makes use of the first, second and third persons (*Ah, I'll just give you a quick introduction. . .* and *but we'll come back to that in a moment*) as he directs and marshalls the students towards work;
2. declarative Mood and in speech function terms, he is giving information;
3. some high Modality, albeit metaphorically realized (e.g. *we really need to get into these key geographic ideas,* or *the two things [[ I want you to do.]].....* which means 'the two things you must do').

With respect to field and the experiential metafunction, we can note:

1. lexis such as *a six week unit more or less,* or *a fairly big title,* building aspects of the field;

2. numbers of process types that realize aspects of desired behaviours e.g. *we really <u>need to get into</u> these key geographic ideas* (material process) or *we'<u>ll</u> look at the distribution of sites* (behavioural process);
3. two identifying processes that establish major tasks for the unit, where in both cases the embeddings also realize aspects of the second order or instructional field:

    *and the two things  [[I want [you to do]] is [[to remember the three [[that we are using: location, distribution]] and a fairly big one, a fairly new one [[we call spatial interaction]].*

    *Um, and the second thing [[I want [you to be able to do [[as you go through]] ]] is [[to use those words um, frequently, accurately, correctly]]';*
4. other process types which realize teacher behaviour to direct student learning: *I'll go through each of those* (refers to matters listed on the board).

To consider the instructional register:

The second order or instructional register is realized mainly through Transitivity, normally in a Participant role but sometimes within a Circumstance:

*Um, we really need to get into these key geographic ideas* (Circumstance)

and the two things [[I want you to do]] is [[to remember the three [[that we are using: location, distribution and a fairly big one, a fairly new one [[we call spatial interaction]] ]] (here found within an identifying process)

OK, first thing [[we'll look at]] is simply the location of different heritage sites: S-I-T-E-S, places. (here also found in an identifying process)

*Now, the sum total of all that location is [[what we call distribution]].* (here found within both Participant roles in the identifying process)

*So we'll look at the distribution of sites within um, particular countries.* (Range)

*Some are spread all over the place, some are concentrated.* (in these two clauses, the complete processes realize the second order field.)

*And the third one, spatial interaction – I-N-T-E-R-A-C-T-I-O-N.* (here there is an implicit identifying process: 'the third one (is) spatial interaction')

*And here, because of the nature of [[what World Heritage means]],* (within Circumstance) *we have to look at the interaction between people and the effect [[that they have on sites]].* (within Range)

*And often that effect, unfortunately, is a fairly negative one.* (an attributive process)

*And because of that we come back to the idea of control.* (the Circumstance establishes some important field information in the nominal group *the idea of control*).

Subsequent classroom talk devoted to the instructional field led to a lengthy discussion of the term *World Heritage* and what it meant, followed by further talk of *natural* and *human* instances of World Heritage matters. Natural examples included *the environment*, where this included *the unique flora, fauna, landscape,* while *human* examples were *the flag, the type of*

*government, traditions and cultures and a way of living.* Discussion of the
World Heritage logo and its significance led to a review of the sites in Australia which are on the World Heritage list and then to the first task, completion of which led to a closure, while there would be a subsequent
activity leading to another task and closure. We will consider only the one
task and its closure. The task involved preparing a map of Australia, dis-
playing any five of the nine sites in the country. I have selected this for
some examination, coming as it did towards the end of the first genre.

The teacher's directions were partly as follows:

**Text 8.9**

(* indicates deletion of part of text)
OK, first thing then, mark in and name the World Heritage Sites here, you
should be familiar with them. ..........* Then for any five, go around your map,
so I would advise you probably to pick Great Barrier Reef, Lord Howe, Tasmania, Shark Bay and Kakadu or Uluru. They seem to be the ones spaced out.
Write out the size, location and the World Heritage features.

Here the two registers converge, though the regulative register is to the
fore, evident for instance in the Transitivity choices, most of which realize
aspects of the students' behaviour: *mark in and name the World Heritage sites;
go around your map; write out the size, location.* The instructional register is
realized mainly in nominal groups that function in associated Participant
roles: *Great Barrier Reef, Lord Howe, Tasmania, Shark Bay, size, location.*

The teacher directions were explicit, providing fairly precise guidelines
for the students' behaviour and hence the pedagogic subject positions
they were to adopt. The students and teacher engaged in subsequent talk
about such matters as the positioning of the map on the page, the merits
of writing or printing in labelling the map, and what the teacher referred
to as the need *to improve our map techniquing.*

**Text 8.10**

Susan: Sir, do you have to print it?
T: I would always print it. You never write on a map.
Sally: Well, I've written on a map.
T: Well, you haven't. (It isn't clear whether T means she has never in the past
    written on maps, or whether, having looked at her present unfinished
    effort, he considers she hasn't used writing)
Another student: Is that wrong sir? Like that, is it OK?
T: That's great. (addresses class) Ah, could you go back to some basic things.
    You must always print on a map, never write, and in this case, your printing
    should be fairly small and you should try as a final point, aim for unifor-
    mity. That is, if you've got a certain style, stay with it.

The collective effort that went into establishing the appropriate procedures to follow is too long to reproduce. I have sampled part of it because it demonstrates the operation of the regulative register, and hence also suggests something of the ideal pedagogic subject position at issue here. For the purposes of this genre at least, the directions to the students were so precise as to set obligatory requirements upon the students for the satisfactory completion of the task. The particular conception of doing geography, or related ones, has been challenged by some (e.g. Gilbert 1988, van Leeuwen and Humphrey 1996) for a variety of reasons, some to do with developing a more 'socially critical orientation to teaching geography' (Singh 1990: 8), some to do with an alleged masculinist ideology in conventional school geography (Lee 1996).

The issues are interesting, pointing to a tension in curriculum theorizing that is not new and that finds expression in discussions of many areas of the curriculum. It is to do with whether the object of the teaching programme should be to teach things 'as they are' or as they might or could be if a more critical stance were adopted. Veel (1997) has provided a related discussion to do with the science curriculum. He has considered the manner in which science genres that offer causal explanation (building reasons why things occur) are more valued by teachers than those that offer sequential explanation (telling the order things occur). He has also suggested that argumentative genres are most valued of all, because they indicate a writer who can challenge scientific positions, even proposing alternatives. Yet Veel is also able to show that the capacity to write and read sequential explanations, as well as such genres as procedures, recounts and reports (all less privileged by many science teachers as genres) is essential developmentally before students can move on to those genres which argue science in challenging ways. It seems that learning science 'the way things are' is a necessary step towards developing the capacity to challenge the ways things are and to propose alternatives.

As I suggested earlier, pedagogic discourses function in such a way that instructional discourses are taken from a primary source in which the discourses are located and then relocated for the purposes of school learning. The processes of relocating the discourses are a feature of the apprenticeship that is actually involved. The geography discourses in the macrogenre considered here were drawn from other sources, most immediately the Victorian state curriculum documentation, but also other sources of geographical learning, most notably in universities and various government agencies involved in manipulating and using geographical information. The type of geographical knowledge, including the capacity to use and interpret a map as well as to demonstrate an understanding of the *key geographic ideas* (a term used in discussions in Victorian of the geography curriculum, Geography Teachers Association of Victoria 1995: 8) is apparently relevant to the models of geography from which they are drawn, even if in the process the models have changed character to some extent. The teacher had reason to induct the students into an understanding of these things. Such an induction does not in itself involve developing individuals who will henceforth be unwilling or unable to challenge the geographical knowledge concerned. Rather, it involves developing individuals who will potentially be able to challenge geographical knowledge, because they will be aware of the principles and procedures by which it is constructed.

I have reproduced one map, produced by a student called Timothy (Figure 8.1). He displayed the map in the centre, writing relevant notes about five sites around it in boxes. What is the pedagogic subject position involved here?

Our answer to that takes us most fundamentally to the mode of constructing geographical knowledge. The ideal pedagogic subject position is that of one who constructs the relevant knowledge in a map and written text, where the relationship of the two is very intimate. Later in the macrogenre, the teacher was to talk often of the need to make *links* between image and verbal text and to state that successful use of *links* would be one matter he would evaluate highly. In the SF tradition (e.g. Hasan 1980, 1984) some language uses have been recognized as 'ancillary' to picture or activity. On occasions there is no doubt the relationship can be so conceived. But the notion of being ancillary carries a sense of subservience and it is clear that the relationship here cannot be characterized in such a way. The knowledge constructed depends upon both written text and image, and I have termed the relationship one of *synergy,* for a close cooperative action of the two is involved.

The central significance of the map to the knowledge construction is apparent both from its size and its dominating position in the centre of the page. Capacity to manipulate a drawing that depicts the continent of a country involves capacity to think of the land rather differently from the sense one carries in walking about on that land. A particular cognitive predisposition is involved in using maps in this way and it has consequences for the pedagogic subject position. The written notes, linked as they are to the various sites, represent the student's attempt to summarize main points. These notes are constructed mainly in elliptical clauses, where the transitivity processes are left out, and only participants remain, realizing aspects of the instructional field: e.g. *spectacular scenery with unique flora and fauna.* Finally, of the three key geographic ideas introduced by the teacher, two are represented – *location* and *distribution.* The locations of the sites are identified, and their distribution is revealed through their display on the map. Later work in the macrogenre would take the students into consideration of spatial interaction.

Timothy, in common with many others in his class, was successfully inducted into the required pedagogic subject position. The regulative register, realized through teacher directions and guided talk about the activity, led the student to produce the map as displayed. As in other examples of the operation of the pedagogic discourse, it will be apparent that it is the instructional register that is foregrounded while the

AUSTRALIA'S WORLD HERITAGE AREAS

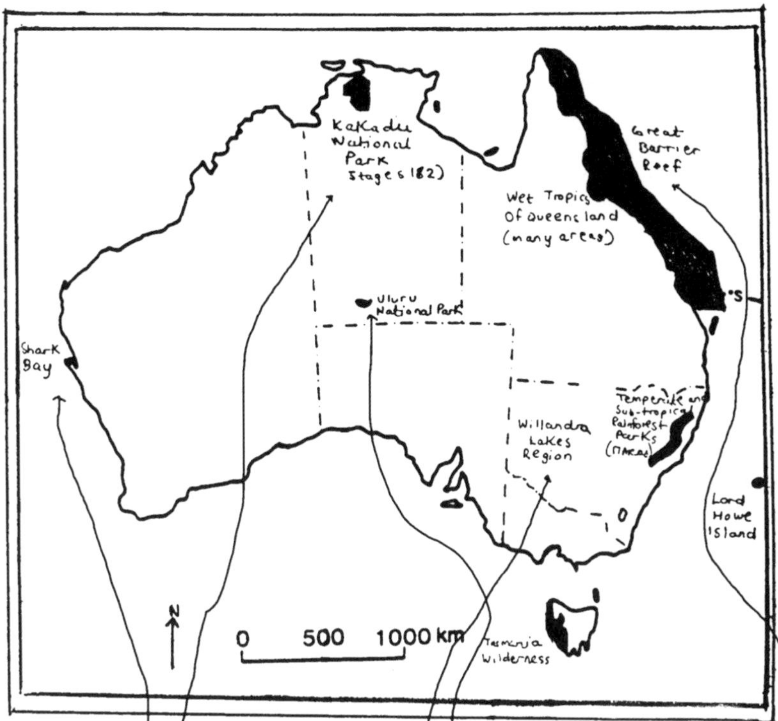

| NAME | SIZE & LOCATION | WORLD HERITAGE FEATURE |
|---|---|---|
| Great Barrier Reef | 34787 million hectares, 2000km Length. Queensland Coast | Largest coral reef system in the world. more than 1500 species of fish. |
| Kakadu National Park | 307,340 hectares of an area. Northern Territory north | Spectacular scenery with unique flora & fauna, and Aboriginal art explore their culture. |
| Uluru National Park | 132,566 hectares of area. Northern Territory, west. | Only rock so large (Ayers Rock) in the world. Cave paintings by Aborigines |
| Shark Bay | 2,320,000 hectares of area Western Australia, bay. | Unique flora and fauna on landscape and marine fauna and flora (Dolphin) |
| Willandra Lake Region | 600,000 hectares of area. New South Wales, south-west. | Earliest Known sites for Homo sapiens Sapiens (modern humans) in the world. outstanding evidence of the life and culture of early Aboriginal societies. |

**Figure 8.1** Map

regulative register is silent. But its influence remains and the measure of that is the success of the student in manipulating the instructional register as required.

## 8.5 Conclusion

I began the chapter with some observations about the nature of the pedagogic discourse of schooling and the operation of two registers, regulative
and instructional, each involved in building the pedagogic discourse. I
argued that the two work in patterned and predictable ways for the realization of pedagogic goals, though there is variation, depending upon the
age of students, the subject and the style of the teacher. I argued further
that, where the two registers work well, the regulative register serves to
point directions and define goals with respect to the 'content' being
taught as a feature of the instructional register. In other words, students
are effectively inducted into an understanding of a particular body of
instructional information in pedagogically valued ways. Close attention to
the operation of the two registers allows us to see how and where the regulative register is foregrounded, where the two registers converge, and
where the instructional register is foregrounded. It will be a measure of
the overall success of the discourse that the regulative register eventually
disappears.

## Note

1. It should be noted that in Bernstein's account of the matter, pedagogic relationships and discourses embrace relationships and discourses that are much
   wider than those found in schools. The relationships of doctor and patient, of
   architect and client, of social worker and client are all in his terms pedagogic.
   This discussion, however, is devoted only to the pedagogic discourses of schooling.

## References

Bernstein, B. (1971) *Theoretical Studies Towards a Sociology of Language. Class Codes
   and Control, Vol. 1.* London: Routledge & Kegan Paul.
Bernstein, B. (1990) *The Structuring of Pedagogic Discourse. Class, Codes and Control,
   Vol. 4.* London: Routledge.
Bernstein, B. (1996) *Pedagogy, Symbolic Control and Identity: Theory, Research, Critique.*
   London: Taylor & Francis.
Christie, F. (1989) Curriculum genres in early childhood education: a case study
   in writing development. Unpublished PhD thesis, University of Sydney.
Christie, F. (1995a) The teaching of literature in the secondary English class.
   Report 1 of a Research Study into the Pedagogic Discourse of Secondary
   School English. A study funded by the Australian Research Council. University
   of Melbourne.
Christie, F. (1995b) The teaching of story writing in the junior secondary school.
   Report 2 of a Research Study into the Pedagogic Discourse of Secondary
   School English. A study funded by the Australian Research Council. University
   of Melbourne.
Christie, F. (1995c) Pedagogic discourse in the primary school. *Linguistics and
   Education,* 3(7): 221–42.

Christie, F. (1996) Geography. Report of a Research Study into the Pedagogic Discourse of Secondary School Social Sciences. A study funded by the Australian Research Council. University of Melbourne.

Christie, F. (in press) Science: Report of a Research Study into the Pedagogic Discourse of Secondary School Social Sciences. A study funded by the Australian Research Council. University of Melbourne.

Christie, F. (1998) The pedagogic device and the teaching of English. In F. Christie (ed.), *Pedagogy and the Shaping of Consciousness: Linguistic and Social Processes*. London: Cassell, 156–83.

Christie, F. (1997) Curriculum macrogenres as forms of initiation into a culture. In F. Christie and J. R. Martin (eds), *Genres and Institutions: Social Processes in the Workplace and School*. London: Cassell, 134–60.

Christie, F. (1998) Science and apprenticeship: the pedagogic discourse. In J. R. Martin and R. Veel (eds), *The Language of Science*. London: Routledge, 152–77.

Christie, F., Gray, B., Gray, P., Macken, M., Martin, J. R. and Rothery, J. (1992) *Language: A Resource for Meaning. Explanations*, Books 1–4, and *Teacher Manual*. Sydney: Harcourt Brace Jovanovich.

Geography Teachers' Association of Victoria (1995) *Geography in the Curriculum and Standards Framework*. Melbourne: Geography Teachers' Association of Victoria.

Gilbert, R. (1988) Language and ideology in geography teaching. In F. Slater (ed.), *Language and Learning in the Teaching of Geography*. London: Routledge, 151–61.

Halliday, M. A. K. and Martin, J. R. (1993) *Writing Science: Literacy and Discursive Power*. London: Falmer.

Halliday M. A. K. (1994) *An Introduction to Functional Grammar* (2nd edn.). London: Arnold.

Hasan, R. (1980) What's going on? A dynamic view of context in language. In J. E. Copeland and P. W. Davis (eds), *The Seventh LACUS Forum*. Columbia, SC: Hornbeam Press, 106–21.

Hasan, R. (1984) The nursery rhyme as a genre. *Nottingham Linguistic Circular*, 13: 71–102.

Lee, A. (1996) *Gender, Literacy, Curriculum: Rewriting School Geography*. London: Taylor & Francis.

Martin, J. R. (1994) Macro-genres: the ecology of the page. *Network*, 21: 29–52.

Martin, J. R. (1995) Text and clause: fractal resonance. *Text*, 15(1): 5–42.

Mehan, H. (1979) *Learning Lessons: Social Organisation in the Classroom*. Cambridge, MA: Harvard University Press.

Singh, M. (1990) Mapping possibilities for a critical geography. *Geographical Education*, 6(2): 8–14.

Sinclair, J. M. and Coulthard, R. M. (1975) *Towards an Analysis of Discourse: The English Used by Teachers and Pupils*. Oxford: Oxford University Press.

van Leeuwen, T. and Humphrey, S. (1996) On looking through a geographer's eyes. In R. Hasan and G. Williams (eds), *Literacy in Society*. London: Longman, 29–49.

Veel, R. (1997) Learning how to mean – scientifically speaking: apprenticeship into scientific discourse in the secondary school. In F. Christie and J.R. Martin (eds), *Genre and Institutions. Social Processes in the Workplace and School*. London: Cassell, 161–95.

Wells, G. (1993) Reevaluating the IRF sequence: a proposal for the articulation of theories of activity and discourse for the analysis of teaching and learning in the classroom. *Linguistics and Education*, 5(1): 1–38.

# 9   Exploring reading processes

*Linda Gerot*

## 9.1 Introduction

'Exploring reading processes' is a pursuit I began more than twenty years ago. As a teacher-become-linguist, the nature of reading as a process involving language has always mattered theoretically and practically. This chapter documents the evolution of my understanding of the question 'What is it to read?' and some of that question's myriad answers. This evolution is presented via references to, and abridged accounts of, several different research studies I've conducted.

To begin any research of this type, one needs a definition of reading. My operational definition grew out of Halliday and Hasan's (1980) work of the time and has changed little over the intervening years:

> The reading process inherently involves the interaction of a reader and a text. Here the reader is considered first and foremost to be a language user and text is considered to be an instance of language in use. This implies that the reader, through her linguistic ability, is capable of ascribing meaning to and interpreting meaning from text. As a person reads a text, she responds not only to the meanings mapped onto linguistic elements, but also takes into account the sociocultural context which is reconstituted through the language patterns. In so doing, she takes into account all she knows about what is going on, what part language is playing, and who are involved. (Gerot 1982: 2)

It is the context–text relationship posited by SFL that compellingly explains for me how reading comprehension is possible at all. When we compose text, we predict from context to text; when we comprehend text, we predict from text to context. Thus, when writing, we predict from context to language and when reading we predict from language to context in terms of genre, field, tenor and mode.

If you doubt this claim, then how is it that you can answer the questions posed for Text 9.1?

**Text 9.1**
We can leave you with a functioning arm,
but we'll have to fuse your shoulder.

| | |
|---|---|
| What is the topic? | field |
| What are the roles of the interactants? | tenor |
| Was the original likely spoken or written? | mode |
| From what kind of text does the snippet come? | genre |

Of the many descriptions of the reading process available, the one I have quoted from my 1982 MA thesis perhaps comes closest to paraphrasing what is meant by reading comprehension. If comprehension has taken place, then the reader will have exploited every means that the text has provided for the reconstruction of what the text is about. While acknowledging that many texts have more than one possible interpretation and different readers may have different purposes for reading the same text, I would not suggest, as some do, that readers alone, not texts, make meaning. The author of a text is making meaning via that text, and in this sense meaning resides in the text. I take the position that reader and text interact in the creation of meaning. That is why I have always seen reading as a 'languaging' process. This is not to deny a cognitive aspect, but one must ask: about what and with what do readers cognize? The answer: linguistic meanings.

As a researcher of reading processes, I never felt I could control for individual reader characteristics. But using systemic functional linguistics, I could explore reading processes in three ways: by examining the *texts* used to test reading and those used to teach 'content' in various school subjects; by examining the *questions* used to assess comprehension, either for testing or teaching purposes; and by checking readers' understandings of *how various types of text work*. Accounts of three of my research studies are presented in the remainder of this chapter.

## 9.2 Some problems in texts used in teaching and testing reading

As part of a study (Gerot 1982) of the question 'What makes one text harder/easier to read than another?' it became apparent that many of the materials used to teach and test reading, and to teach content were flawed as *texts*. The problems were identified by using discourse analysis afforded by SFL.

In the introduction to his *Introduction to Functional Grammar* Halliday makes a claim with which I absolutely agree, which I find utterly challenging and sometimes daunting!

A discourse analysis that is not based on grammar is not an analysis at all, but simply a running commentary on a text. (Halliday 1985: xvii)

My abilities as a discourse analyst were just developing at the time this research was undertaken. While I have been able to achieve more refined, rigorous and detailed analyses since then, the account in this section does show what can be done with a reasonable understanding of the context–text part of systemic functional grammar. In this section I have included some more recent texts than those analysed in the early 1980s to show that the problems and principles still apply.

It is not an exaggeration to claim that a reader will be successful to the extent that she understands the cultural/situational context encapsulated by the text and to the extent that she understands how the language used in the text functions. A reader's lack of success cannot always be blamed solely on the reader. There are instances in which the writer appears to be insensitive to or unaware of what a reader can be expected to know through or about language. As a result, the writer places stumbling blocks, albeit unintentionally, in the reader's way.

Some children may experience difficulty when their reading comprehension is being tested on a standardized test or in a classroom situation because of the unusual form of the test texts. For younger readers in particular, the texts used in reading comprehension tests (both formal and less formal) are usually short (one to three paragraphs in length) and fictional. They are atypical in as much as in the more usual, less contrived circumstances for reading, texts are not so short or abrupt, or indeed leached dry by the imposition of four or five questions!

While it is understandable that text length is a consideration, limiting reading test texts to only a few paragraphs often means readers are dealing with truncated genres. Complete narratives (stories, adventures), for example, start with an orientation stage in which the characters and the setting of the story are introduced. This is followed by a complication stage, in which something goes wrong. In complete narratives, this is followed by a stage in which the problem is resolved. In reading tests, however, it is not unusual to find narratives starting not with an orientation but jumping straight in at the complication stage. Text 9.2 comprises only a complication; the orientation and resolution stages are missing.

**Text 9.2**

(1) Billy kept on walking. (2) There was nothing to be seen but trees and he began to worry. (3) Where was the road? (4) When he looked for the sun to find which way he should go, he saw that the sky had become very dark and cloudy. (5) It looked as though a storm was coming, and Billy was a little scared. (6) He must get home before it rained. (7) He started to run.

(ACER, 1972)

In this text, the young reader has to infer the whole orientation; 'Billy kept on walking' implies that he has already been walking for some time. From this and the second, third and fourth sentences the reader must infer that Billy is lost. Piecing this together involves the reader assimilating the shift of focus (Hasan 1964) from the narrator's viewpoint in sentence 2 to Billy's in sentence 3. Sentence 6 also involves a shift of focus from narrator to Billy. Interestingly, the questions accompanying this text demand that these focal shifts and inferences be made:

Question:         What happened to Billy in this story?
Right answer:     He got lost.
Question:         Billy was worried because
Right answer:     He could not see the road.
Question:         When Billy saw the stormy sky
Right answer:     He ran for home.

This last answer provides a happy resolution, but contradicts the text itself!

The following example from the same period is a complete text, but as a 'controlled text' suffers nonetheless. 'Controlled readers' are those which are designed to restrict the range of vocabulary and types of sentence structure and to include a good deal of repetition of words, phrases and sentences. The Endeavour Reading Programme (1975) was based on this premise.

> The sentence structures are carefully controlled but mirror the patterns the child is already using in his everyday speech. The progressive use of regularly patterned words assists the child to develop positive word attack skills.
>
> (Johnson *et al.* 1975: 7)

This programme is based on behaviourist psychological views of reading, views which, more than twenty years on and despite current curriculum documents, remain entrenched in the folklore of teaching. The programme creators appear to have had little understanding of language as text as opposed to language as word and sentence; certainly the nature of spoken language is not understood.

Each individual sentence in Text 9.3 is fine, but taken together result in a very stilted *text*. In its effort to keep sentence structures simple, to repeat certain structures and sound patterns, and to control vocabulary, textual features of conjunction and the more usual choices and development of topical Themes are ignored. The texture of the text, such as it is, depends entirely on the abnormally high number of lexical repetitions and varying referents of 'it'.

**Text 9.3**

> One Saturday, Dad took Andrew fishing. Sue did not go with them. They went fishing in the dam near the back paddock. Andrew dropped his line into the water. On the line was a hook.

Soon there was a pull on Andrew's line. It was a fish. Andrew could not see it. It was under the water. He pulled the line in. He pulled the line in fast. A big yellow fish was on the hook. Dad helped him to take it off the hook. Then Andrew put it in the fishing bag. Andrew got eight fish that day.

(Johnson *et al.* 1975)

Controlled readers are still with us today, for example in the materials used in Marie Clay's (1993) Reading Recovery program. And many of the much loved, much used 'big books', for example those in 'The Story Box' series (Shortland Publications), are also controlled readers. Text 9.4, written by Cowley (1983) as a big book in The Story Box series, is a version of a well-known children's story designed to limit variation in vocabulary and language structures consistent with other texts written specifically for the series.

**Text 9.4**

| | |
|---|---|
| Lamb went to the horse. | Lamb went to the bull. |
| 'Horse, Horse, | 'Bull, Bull, |
| will you be my mother?' | will you be my mother?' |
| 'I am a horse,' | 'I am a bull,' |
| said the horse. | said the bull. |
| 'I can't be your mother.' | 'I can't be your mother.' . . . etc. |

(Cowley 1983)

It seems ironic that the language of learning-to-read materials is so carefully controlled when the language of reading-to-learn materials is not, as can be seen in Text 9.5 from a mathematics book for learners of the same age as Texts 9.2, 9.3 and 9.4.

**Text 9.5**

Read the number.
Colour that number of beads on the string.
Count the balls.
Colour 1 red, 2 green and 3 blue.
Draw lines to match each label with the correct jars.

(Burnett 1994: 8)

An interesting study could be designed to find out how teachers and their students reconcile the use of such controlled vocabulary and sentence structures for reading instruction and such field-driven vocabulary and sentence structures for mathematics, science and art.

### 9.3 Questions used to check comprehension

When questions are used to check comprehension, the reader's success depends not only upon her ability to interpret meaning from and ascribe meaning to texts, but also to interpret and answer questions. To be successful, the reader must be at home with the language both of the texts and of the questions. What is at stake is the interaction between the reader, the text and the questions used.

Nearly fifty years ago Lorge (1949) was alluding to such an interactive view when he suggested that the relative ease or difficulty of a reading comprehension task is a function not only of the difficulty level of the text itself (as had previously been assumed) but also of the questions. Lorge made this interesting and insightful observation, then dropped it, leaving his successors with two questions:

1. What kinds of questions are asked in comprehension tests?
2. What makes a question easy or difficult?

The first demands a descriptive answer, the second an explanatory one. The answers are clearly related.

Obviously, what makes a question easy or difficult depends on what the reader has to know in order to answer that question. What the reader has to know in a reading test is typically (but not always) encoded in the text. However, the specific encoding of the needed information is subject to variation. Some questions ask about what is explicitly encoded, others ask about what is implicit or implied. Moreover, the answer to a given question may require that the reader integrate information presented in single lexical items, or a sentence, consecutive sentences, a paragraph or from sources throughout the whole text.

By describing questions in terms of the way in which the answers required are encoded in the language of the text, it seemed possible to develop a theory explaining in similar and related terms why one kind of question is more difficult to answer than another. This was the object of my first major research study in this area (Gerot 1982).

The first step in this study was to adopt or adapt an existing classification or taxonomy of question types, or to devise a new one. The extant taxonomies paid scant attention to the interaction of question and text; that is, they did not specifically relate the question to the text which supposedly provides the answer. Instead, most were based on some *decontextualized* notion of *cognitive process*.

Of these, the taxonomies of Bloom (1956) and Barrett (Clymer 1968) were, and remain influential. In fact, what these authors have claimed about questions has become taken for granted in teaching.

Bloom did not set out to develop a classification scheme for questions; he was attempting to develop a taxonomy of educational objectives. These goals or objectives were stated in cognitive behavioural terms and were said to be ordered in complexity, with the more complex behaviours subsuming the simpler ones. Because the objectives were exemplified through questions, the taxonomy was adopted as a classification scheme of questions.

Bloom was at pains to distinguish between the category 'knowledge'

which emphasized the psychological process of remembering from higher
level skills and abilities. This distinction served as the basis for positing low
and high level questions, which in turn were said to elicit low or high levels
of thinking and, by extension, lower and higher levels of attainment.
Throughout the relevant pedagogic literature, low level questions equate
with those requiring 'mere factual recall' to supply the correct answer.

While widely accepted, the claims made for cognitive level have never
been proved and remain problematic. Many teachers and educators seem
to think that 'how' and 'why' questions are necessarily better than 'who',
'what', 'when' and 'where' ones because the 'how' and 'why' require
'high level thinking skills', and the rest 'only low level mere recall' (Gerot
1989). This belief is understandable, given the arguments of Bloom and
his successors.

Bloom's work, and much of that which followed, was flawed because it
ignored the role of context. When context is considered, the arguments,
and with them teachers' beliefs about various question types, are easily
refuted. Consider, for example, the following: A student might not be
able to answer the question 'Why do reptiles bury their eggs in the
ground?' if asked out of the blue. The student, however, might be able to
infer the answer (a so-called higher cognitive order process) if the preceding statement was something like 'Reptiles lay leathery shelled eggs.
So why do they bury their eggs in the ground?' However, if the preceding
text had gone something like 'Reptiles lay leathery shelled eggs which
must be kept moist and warm, so they bury them in the ground' the original question becomes one of 'mere factual recall', a low-level question.
Whether the question is high level or low level depends on the surrounding text, and whether or not the question is being asked for the first or
the fifteenth time in a unit of school work.

The notion of 'cognitive level' remains an attractive but problematic
construct. For those concerned with 'cognitive levels' of questions, questions are discussed in terms of the 'cognitive response' they 'elicit'. Dillon
(1982), however, suggests that questions are better viewed as requests for
information. In Dillon's view, questions are seen as 'requesting', not 'eliciting', and what is required is information rather than cognition. This is a
viewpoint for which I have a great deal of respect (Gerot 1992a), but it is
one that was not available to Barrett.

Barrett's work (Clymer 1968) drew on the work of Bloom. He based his
'Taxonomy of Cognitive and Affective Dimensions of Reading Comprehension' on the type of cognitive process required to answer a particular question. Barrett's 'Taxonomy' is familiar to many teachers, if not by its rightful
name, being frequently cited in the literature on the teaching of reading.

Barrett's 'Taxonomy' (Clymer 1968: 19–22) consists of five categories:
literal, reorganization, inferential, evaluation and appreciation.

> Literal comprehension focuses on ideas and information which are explicitly
> stated in the selection.

Reorganization requires the student to analyze, synthesize, and/or organize ideas or information explicitly stated in the selection. To produce the desired thought product, the reader may utilize the statement of the author verbatim or he may paraphrase or translate the author's statements.

Inferential comprehension is demonstrated by the student when he uses the ideas and information explicitly stated in the selection, his intuition, and his personal experience as a basis for conjectures and hypotheses . . . Inferential comprehension is stimulated by purposes for reading and teachers' questions which demand thinking and imagination that go beyond the printed page.

Evaluation: purposes for reading and teacher's questions, in this instance require responses by the student which indicate that he has made an evaluative judgment by comparing ideas presented in the selection with external criteria provided by the teacher, other authorities, or other written sources, or with internal criteria provided by the reader's experiences, knowledge, or values.

Appreciation . . . deals with the psychological and aesthetic impact of the selection on the reader. Appreciation calls for the student to be emotionally and aesthetically sensitive to the work and to have reaction to the worth of its psychological and artistic elements.

This five-category system applies equally to learning-to-read and reading-to-learn materials, and is said to be graded in difficulty. Clymer (1968: 18), who first introduced the previously unpublished 'Taxonomy', states that

. . . the five major categories have been ordered to move from easy to difficult in terms of the requirements each category appears to demand.

Unlike many question taxonomies, Barrett's is at least concerned, up to a point, with text–question interaction. However, I did not adopt this taxonomy for my research for three reasons:

1. The system did not seem to be delicate enough to account for all of the questions in my data base.
2. The claims for its hierarchical stucture were not substantiated.
3. I did not know how to use these categories with reference to my enquiry since I could not discover any explicit linguistic criteria by which Barrett's distinctions could be made, especially within the category 'reorganization', and for the categories 'evaluation' and 'appreciation'.

I therefore developed my own taxonomy of question types based not on the level of cognitive processing involved but on how the information leading to the expected answer was linguistically encoded in, and so was recoverable from, the text.

How information leading to the expected answer is linguistically encoded is subject to variation. Five hundred questions accompanying four different standardized reading tests in use at the time, three books of reading comprehension exercises and three reading schemes were analysed as a basis for devising my taxonomy.

This analysis revealed that some answers could be retrieved only from outside the text, typically a dictionary or the reader's own knowledge. In cases where the needed information was encoded in the text, some questions were about what was explicitly encoded while others were about what was implicit or implied.

Halliday and Hasan's (1976) work on cohesive devices provided a way to plot various questions along a cline of fully explicit, implicit and implied. Their work on lexical cohesion provided insights for positing two 'explicit' question types: replicative and echoic. Their work on reference, substitution, ellipsis and conjunction provided insights for positing an 'implicit' question type which I termed synthesis. Beyond these cohesive relations were questions whose answers were implied by one bit of the text or by the (con)text as a whole. This insight provided the basis for positing two 'implied' question types which I termed oblique and surmise.

The taxonomy I devised consists of five categories: replicative, echoic, synthesis, oblique and surmise. These categories characterize the relationships which exist between the answers and the bits of text the reader has available for reconstructing the answers. In other words, the categories provide means for describing the relationship of the language of the answer to the language of the text.

The category 'replicative' applies when the question–answer sequence replicates or repeats the text word for word, or with only minor alterations in tense, voice, number or person. My taxonomy of comprehension question types is illustrated for Text 9.6 (ACER 1972).

### Text 9.6 The Creature

At the bottom of the cliff, a little to Dick's left, was a low, dark hole – the entrance to a cave perhaps. And out of this two thin wisps of smoke were coming. And the loose stones just beneath the dark hollow were moving (that was the noise he had heard) just as if something were crawling in the dark behind them.

Something was crawling. Worse still, something was coming out. The thing that came out of the cave was something he had never even imagined – a long lead coloured snout, dull red eyes, no feathers or fur, a long body that trailed on the ground, legs whose elbows went up higher than its back like a spider's cruel claws, bat's wings that made a rasping noise on the stones, metres of tail. And two lines of smoke were coming from its nostrils. He never said the word Dragon to himself. Nor would it have made things any better if he had.

Replicative Question:

Did the thing that came out of the cave have a long snout and dull red

eyes?
Echoic Question:

Did the creature's wings make a scraping sound on the stones?

The answer echoes the text. The answer and text differ lexico-grammatically but are semantically near equivalents. Lexical items are recoded as synonyms, near synonyms, superordinate terms or (co)hyponyms (x is a kind of y).

Synthesis Question:

Did the smoke that Dick saw come from a fire inside the cave?

Cohesive ties link one bit of information to another.

Oblique Question:

Was the creature's tail short and stumpy?

The answer is implied in some one bit of the text.

Surmise Question:

Was Dick trapped with the Dragon?

The information is inferable from diffuse clues throughout the text as a whole.

Influenced as I was by claims about the differential difficulty levels of questions in extant question taxonomies, I hypothesized that my taxonomy too was ordered in difficulty, with replicative the least and surmise the most difficult. I based this hypothesis on the notion 'integrative work' rather than cognitive level or process. Integrative work refers to the degree of reconstruction the reader must do in order to supply the correct answer. In answering reading comprehension questions, a reader has to perform different types of tasks. These differ specifically in how the required information is to be retrieved. As we have seen, in some instances this may involve the relatively simple operation of pairing an expression with its paraphrase; in others it may involve putting together bits of information from separate parts of the text. It was hypothesized that each category in my taxonomy involved more integrative work than the one before and therefore would prove more difficult. The nature of integrative work for each category is outlined below:

*Replicative*: readers have only to take note of the fact that the expression of some meaning in the text is replicated word for word in the question–answer sequence.

*Echoic*: readers have not only to locate the answer in the text but also to recode that answer; in doing so, they have to be cognizant of the semantic relation existing between the lexical item(s) used in the answer and the text.

*Synthesis*: readers interpret meaning explicitly encoded and also explicate implicit cohesive devices in the process of connecting, integrating and conflating information.

*Oblique*: readers make an inference from some one clue in the text; the reader has to single out that bit of the text which through its implied meaning leads her to the correct answer. This involves an understanding of the literal/dictionary meaning of the items in the text; at the same time, it calls for the ability to answer the question 'What follows from this?'

*Surmise*: readers must make an inference. The answer must be reconstructed from the diffuse clues throughout the text and from what the readers know about the context of situation which is reconstituted by the language patterns of the text.

Three hundred children – one hundred each in Grade Two, Grade Four and Grade Six – read five texts appropriate for their grade level. I took the texts from the ACER Primary Reading Survey Tests (1972), because it was used in the primary feeder schools of the secondary school where I was a reading resource teacher, and the test was already standardized.

Each text was accompanied by five questions: replicative, echoic, synthesis, oblique and surmise. As many of the original test questions as possible were used, but some were re-cast as yes–no–can't tell questions to avoid problems with the multiple-choice format brought to light during the pilot study; new questions, written by the researcher, were added so that all five types were represented. Inter-judge reliability for classifying the questions was 0.99 using the Spearman rank correlation coefficient. Before the final version was given to the three hundred children in the major study, three separate pilot studies were conducted using other schools to check the validity of the notion 'integrative work', the effects of the multiple-choice format and the robustness of the final version of the test instrument.

Bailey's (1978) programme CONECT was used to analyse the results. This programme provides a way to calculate the 'facility index' (the percentage of readers getting the answer right) of each question; facility index is. It also determines whether the differences in the facility indices are great enough to be statistically significant. CONECT was the first test of hierarchy to provide this.

This analysis indicated that replicative questions were easier than all the rest. There was no fixed, much less a linear ordering for the remaining four categories. Some echoic questions were more difficult than the oblique and some were easier; some synthesis questions were easier than the oblique and some were harder. In short, there was more variation *within* the categories echoic, synthesis, oblique and surmise than *between* them.

Given the similarity of my taxonomy to Barrett's first three categories, it is doubtful that his categories are in fact ordered to move from easy to difficult.

Even though my taxonomy was not hierarchical, the classification scheme and notion 'integrative work' still have application as diagnostic tools for checking what languaging strategies readers are or are not using when answering reading comprehension questions. Moreover, they provide one way of making explicit what is meant by text–question interaction in contexts of comprehension checking.

## 9.4  Testing understanding of how texts work

The study to be described in this section was inspired by the then new interest in and concern for the place of genre in the teaching of writing. I was curious about the role of genre understandings in reading. In this study (Gerot 1992b), I drew on my earlier belief that to comprehend a text readers had to be able to reconstruct the genre, field, tenor and mode of that text. I suggest that without this ability, readers have no basis for making sense of what is being read and for predicting what will happen.

To operationalize the notions register and genre, a 'genre-sorting' activity was devised. From a story book (narrative text) *Cully Cully and the Bear* (Gage 1983) and non-fiction book (report), *Polar Bears* (Baker 1990) key words and phrases were selected and printed on cards, one item per card. These items were selected on the basis that the differing purposes and generic structures of narratives and reports are realized through the distinctive language features of each of these genres.

In narratives the focus is on individual participants (Cully Cully, the bear, he, a bearskin, I), whereas reports focus on generic participants, that is groups or classes of things (polar bears, the Eskimo people, Inuit villages, noses, large rumps). Reports use many relational processes. These express the parts and qualities of the generic class discussed (*are* very large, *have* shiny black noses, can *be* very dangerous). Narratives use many material processes, mainly in the past tense (shot, went hunting), as well as some mental (thought) and verbal processes (said, tells). The key words and phrases are shown in Figure 9.1.

A Grade Four class from a primary school participated in the study. The class had begun some work with the procedure genre, but had had no specific instruction in narrative or report genres. The children had not read *Cully Cully and the Bear* or *Polar Bears*.

Working with one child at a time, the researcher asked the child to read each card in turn from the shuffled set of 28 cards and sort the cards onto paper headed 'Cully Cully and the Bear' and 'Polar Bears'. It should be noted that none of the children had any difficulty decoding the cards.

After all the children had completed the task the researcher asked the

| Narrative | Report |
|---|---|
| *Cully Cully and the Bear* | *Polar Bears* |
| a good hunter | are covered in thick fur |
| 'By jingo' | are dangerous |
| He | are very large |
| Cully Cully | attack and kill people |
| I | hungry bears |
| need a bearskin | live in the Arctic |
| once there was a | long necks and big rumps |
| said | polar bears |
| shot an arrow | raid Eskimo villages |
| tells a story | shiny noses |
| the bear | short legs |
| thought | tells facts |
| trying to take a nap | they have |
| was uncomfortable | |
| went hunting | |

**Figure 9.1** Key words and phrases from narrative and report texts

class teacher, who had worked with the children for nine months, to indicate on a class list the 'good readers', 'average readers' and 'below average readers'. The researcher did not define 'reading' for the teacher, but the teacher made clear she was evaluating the students' reading in terms of reading comprehension, not oral reading fluency.

Readers ranked 'high' or 'excellent' by their teacher made an average of 1.85 errors in the sorting task. Readers rated 'average' made an average of 6 errors, while 'poor' readers made an average of 17 errors as shown in Table 9.1.

**Table 9.1** Results of 'genre-sorting' activity

| Teacher's rating | Average number of errors | Range |
|---|---|---|
| high, excellent | 1.85 | 1–4 |
| average | 6.00 | 2–9 |
| poor | 17.00 | 14–24 |

These results strongly suggest that competent readers were able to use the language characteristics of each text to determine the purpose of that text and to reconstruct its situational context.

These conclusions are further supported in the reasons children gave for sorting the cards as they did. The competent readers such as Jamie, who made only one error, were able to articulate their reasons in terms of their understandings of generic purpose and linguistic characteristics (Text 9.7) whereas the poor readers such as Karen, who made fourteen errors, had great difficulty in explaining her choices (Text 9.8).

**Text 9.7 Interview with Jamie**

L: Hi Jamie.

J: Hi.

L: OK, these are the titles of two different books, 'Polar Bears' and 'Cully Cully and the Bear'. What I want you to do is read what's on the card and put it in that pile or that pile. (Jamie does sort)

J: Can I wait with this one?

L: Yup, put it on the bottom if you like or put it off to the side and come back to it at the end. (Jamie continues) OK, well, you did that really well. Can you tell me why you put these here under 'Polar Bears' and those cards there under 'Cully Cully and the Bear'?

J: Uh, 'Cully Cully and the Bear' – that's the name of a like, it's a story that one. 'A good hunter' – he probably was a good hunter in the story or something. 'Was uncomfortable' – he was uncomfortable, probably Cully Cully or the bear. 'Once there was' – that's the beginning of a story.

L: Uh huh.

J: 'By jingo' – that's, they usually kinda say things like that in stories, like Cully Cully, or in a story a bear could say something like that. 'Shot an arrow' – maybe at the bear.

L: Poor bear!

J: Uh, 'tells a story' – Polar bears is probably about facts. 'Thought' – the bear probably thought something. Cully Cully probably seems like 'I'. 'The bear' like the bear they say Cully Cully and the Bear. So that's 'the bear'. 'Trying to take a nap' – polar bears in facts books don't say it's trying to take a nap or anything. Cully Cully probably said 'he', the bear, or he someone. 'Hungry bears' [Jamie's only error] – like they might all be hungry and they wanted to eat something, or something like that. He went hunting to get something. And ooh. (much hesitation) In the story they might raid, might have raided, uh . . .

L: Could that one fit here too? (pointing to Polar Bears)

J: Yeah, I reckon. I think I did a mistake there.

L: You think you made a mistake? OK, that was the first one you did so maybe you weren't ready yet or weren't used to what was coming. Right, OK, what does this book tell about?

J: Seems to me like it's telling the facts or something. Like, they raid Eskimo villages. Probably it's telling you something; it's not just making it up. It's about polar bears. They live in the Antarctica. That's a fact. It tells facts. 'Shiny noses' – like they're probably saying polar bears have shiny noses. They're saying they have short legs and they say they have short legs and long necks and big rumps.

L: OK, great. So with the polar bear one it seems like maybe what they look like,

J: Yeah, and what they do

L: Yeah, and what they do and maybe where they live. Ok, that's great Jamie. That was a simple game for you. You made easy work of it.

J: Yup.

L: OK, thanks very much for helping me.

**Text 9.8  Interview with Karen**

K: I don't know. Well, this is here cause those two went (hunting). This should be here cause the bear has a shiny nose and in that story. And this bear lives in the Arctic. The hunter goes looking for the hungry bears. I don't know this one. Tells a story. I don't know. The bear's got very long legs. They need a bearskin. And . . . I'm not sure. Uh, I don't know.

L: OK, how about this side?

K: The 'polar bears' is in the title. They got long necks. They need a good hunter. They shot an arrow. I don't know that one.

L: Don't know about 'said', OK.

K: The polar bear was very uncomfortable. And polar bears have short legs. And the polar bear was trying to take a nap. I don't know.

L: Not sure about 'tells facts'? OK.

K: . . . .

L: Are covered in thick fur.

K: They are. That's a fairy tale.

L: That's a fairy tale, is it – 'once there was a'?

K: Well, this has to be in the polar bear story cause it says Eskimo. The hunter went looking for the bear. Then the bear gets found. And they have to try to catch it.

L: OK, Karen, thank you for your help.

Additional support for the above claims was provided by Rita's response to the task. In her first attempt Rita was able to classify only eight of the twenty-eight cards. Of the eight, four were wrongly classified. To help Rita save face, the researcher told her that the book called 'Cully Cully and the Bear' was a story about a hunter who needed a bearskin to sleep on, and 'Polar Bears' was a book of facts about polar bears, where they lived and what they looked like. On her second attempt Rita classified all twenty-eight cards, making only seven misclassifications.

It would seem that competent readers are able to quickly construe the genre and register of a text from the language patterns, and to use these as a basis for prediction. Unsuccessful readers appear unable to do this. Given this inability and the evidence provided in the study, the following practices are suggested.

Less successful readers should be explicitly told the purpose and context of a text before they are asked to read it independently. Knowing the purpose, the nature of the goings on and participant relationships, and the language used, provides the foundation for prediction that otherwise is lacking. The reader has a much better chance of 'making sense'.

The ultimate goal, of course, is that children become independent readers. To this end, the teacher could design and implement a programme to make explicit the purposes, generic structures and associated linguistic features of various genres. Reading can be fully integrated into a genre-based writing programme (e.g. Christie *et al.* 1990).

As the teacher and children together build a shared understanding of a field of enquiry, as they discuss the purposes, structures and language features of various texts, and as they jointly negotiate the writing of a text, textual understandings needed for both successful reading and writing are made explicit. Following such recommendations, readers would have the opportunity to see (1) that they are expected to understand that reading is a meaning-making activity, (2) what kind of sense they are supposed to be making, and (3) how sense is (to be) made.

While this study has been replicated (Knobel and Lankshear 1995, Gerot and Knobel 1995), it would be interesting to repeat the study with larger numbers of students, half of whom have now been instructed using genre-based pedagogy for several years of their schooling and half who have had no formal exposure to genre-based pedagogy. Moreover, it would be instructive to assess knowledge of genres other than narrative and report. Such a study would help us evaluate the effect of genre-based instruction on reading. Do good readers 'pick up' knowledge of how texts work regardless, or does genre-based pedagogy make a significant and measurable difference to all readers?

## 9.5 Future directions

In the twenty years that I have been involved in the research of reading processes, knowledge of language as text has increased dramatically. We are in the fortunate position to be able to use this knowledge to further enhance our understandings of what it is 'to read'.

At policy level, conservative forces have (again) begun to push reading-as-decoding (sounding out, word attack skills) to the forefront. In such a climate, using SFL to continue exploring reading as a process of making meaning of text becomes a critical counter-balance.

In this chapter I have hinted at several possibilities for further research, the questions that SFL can help us answer.

1. How does the language of controlled readers and subject texts compare? If there are significant differences (and there are, but the nature of these differences needs to be made explicit), how do teachers and/or their students reconcile the use of these differing texts?
2. I have speculated that my question taxonomy and the notion 'integrative work' can provide useful diagnostic information. Can it? Does the classification need to be expanded or altered to provide more useful information concerning a reader's languaging strategies? Do good and poor readers differ in their ability to answer the five kinds of questions? With what implications for teaching?
3. Again using this or another documented question taxonomy, what can we learn about students' reading/languaging strategies by asking them to explain their reasons for their answers? How do students' preferred answers compare to the teacher's or tester's preferred answers? What do students say about what makes a reading task easy or difficult? How

do their perceptions compare with those of adult inventors of supposedly hierarchical question taxonomies?
4. What role has reading in genre-based pedagogy? What impact, if any, does genre-based pedagogy have on reading? Does genre-based pedagogy lead to improved reading? For all readers? When genre-based pedagogy is not used, how do readers pick up knowledge of how texts work? Is there a developmental sequence in knowledge of how the text types work?

There are, of course, many questions exploring reading processes and reading pedagogy that warrant the attention of researchers. In this chapter, I have shown the usefulness of SFL in following up some of these questions and how SFL can be used as a research tool by beginning researchers to obtain informative results from practical projects.

## References

Australian Council for Educational Research (1972) *ACER Primary Reading Survey Tests, Part 2: Comprehension*. Melbourne: A.C.E.R.

Bailey, M. (1978) The analysis of sequential structures in educational data. Unpublished doctoral dissertation. Macquarie University, Sydney.

Baker, L. (1990) *Polar Bears*. Sydney: Doubleday.

Bloom, B.S. (1956) *Taxonomy of Educational Objectives: Handbook I: Cognitive Domain*. New York: Longman, Green.

Burnett, J. (1994) *Queensland Maths Links: Student Workbook 1*. Queensland: Mimosa Publications.

Christie, C. (ed.) (1990) *Literacy for a Changing World*. Hawthorn: ACER.

Christie, F. *et. al.* (1990) *Language: A Resource for Meaning*. Sydney: Harcourt, Brace Jovanovich.

Clay, M. (1993) *Reading Recovery: A Guidebook for Teachers in Training*. Portsmouth: Heinemann.

Clymer, T.C. (1968) What is reading?: some current concepts. In H.M. Robinson (ed.), *Innovation and Change in Reading Instruction*. Sixty-seventh Yearbook of the National Society for the Study of Education. Chicago: University of Chicago Press.

Cowley, J. (1983) *Who Will Be My Mother?* The Story Box. Auckland: Shortland Publications.

Dillon, J.T. (1982) The effect of questions in education and other enterprises. *American Educational Research Journal*, 19(4): 540–51.

Gage, W. (1983) *Cully Cully and the Bear*. London: The Bodley Head.

Gerot, L. (1982) A question of answers in reading comprehension. Unpublished MA(Hons) thesis. Macquarie University, Sydney.

Gerot, L. (1989) The question of legitmate answers. Unpublished doctoral dissertation. Macquarie University, Sydney.

Gerot, L. (1992a) *Questions of Choice in Classroom Discourse: Paradigms, Realisations and Implications*. Occasional Papers in Applied Linguistics, No 1. Centre for Studies of Language in Education. Darwin: Northern Territory University.

Gerot, L. (1992b) Towards a text-based theory and practice of reading. Paper presented at the 19th International Systemic Functional Conference.

Macquarie University, Sydney.

Gerot, L. (1998) *Making Sense of Reading*. Gold Coast: Antipodean Educational Enterprises.

Gerot, L. and Knobel, M. (1995) Children's understandings of language purposes and functions in reading. In M. Tickoo (ed.), *Reading and Writing: Theory and Practice*. RELC Anthology Series 35. SEAMEO Regional Language Centre.

Halliday, M.A.K. (1985) *An Introduction to Functional Grammar*. London: Edward Arnold.

Halliday, M.A.K. (1994) *An Introduction to Functional Grammar* (2nd edn). London: Edward Arnold.

Halliday, M.A.K. and Hasan, R. (1976) *Cohesion in English*. London: Longman.

Halliday, M.A.K. and Hasan, R. (1980) *Text and Context: Language in a Social-Semiotic Perspective*. Sophia Linguistia VI. Publication of the Graduate School of Languages and Linguistics. Sophia University: Tokyo.

Hasan, R. (1964) A linguistic study of the contrasting features in the style of two contemporary English prose writers. Unpublished doctoral dissertation, University of Edinburgh.

Johnson, F.C., Berkley, G.F., Hamilton, R., Moore, D.B. and Scott, E. (eds) (1975) *Endeavour Reading Programme* (3rd edn). Sydney: Language Arts Associates/ Jacaranda Press.

Knobel, M. and Lankshear, C. (1995) *Learning Genres: Prospects for Empowerment*. Brisbane: NLLIA Ltd Child/ESL Literacy Research Network Node (Queensland).

Lorge, I. (1949) Reading and readability. *Teachers College Record*, 51: 90–7.

# 10 Interpreting literature: the role of APPRAISAL

*Joan Rothery and Maree Stenglin*

## 10.1 Introduction

Throughout their primary and secondary schooling, students are regularly asked to respond to a range of story texts constructed in a variety of modes. The nature of this response varies, but rarely does it focus solely on the experiential meanings of the text. Even in their first years of schooling students are asked to respond interpersonally to texts by talking about the part they 'liked best' and giving reasons to support their choice, or by focusing on the interpersonal response of a character to events in the text and referring to events in the story to 'explain' the character's response. The first type of response, the personal, has been strongly foregrounded in educational contexts in Australia from the middle years of this century (Rothery 1990). It is derived from a Leavisite approach to studying literature, an approach which emphasized the role of the personal response of the reader in understanding the values constructed in literature. Until recent years, this approach has been a dominant one in studying literature at the tertiary level. A significant aspect of it is that there is no explicit focus on the structure of language or the text. Students are asked to respond to meanings but the language system, the resource for constructing meaning, remains invisible.

The second type of response, where students are asked to give reasons for a character's reaction to events, introduces students to the view that an important reason for reading literature is to interpret meanings in the text. The following excerpt from a transcript of a kindergarten lesson clearly shows this focus. In the transcript James, a student, is talking with his teacher about the book *There's an Alligator Under My Bed* by Mercer Mayer (1988) which he has just read.

> J: There's an alligator under my bed.
> There's an alligator under my bed. I'm walking up on wood so he doesn't get me.
> T: That's a good idea.
> J: And he's looking but he can't see me.

T: Why is the boy so happy?

J: Because the crocodile he's trapped him there . . . and he's going back walking up the stairs.

By asking about a character's response to events, the teacher is telling James, albeit implicitly, that focusing on the reactions of characters to events and the reasons for their reactions is an important aspect of reading and interpreting stories.

These two strands of response to story continue into the secondary years but they have not been clearly distinguished by teachers, partly because the majority of secondary school teachers have not been introduced to a study of text in a systematic way. As students enter the middle and final years of their secondary schooling, interpretation responses are sought and highly valued in classroom and examination tasks. The personal response may still be asked for orally but it is the interpretation which is most valued (Macken and Rothery 1990). More is expected of students than simply giving reasons for a character's reactions. They are asked to articulate the theme(s) of the work or, presented with the theme in the wording of the question, students are asked how it has been constructed in the text. It is this response genre, identified as interpretation (Rothery 1990), which will be the focus of this chapter.

By the end of the middle years of schooling in New South Wales secondary schools, some students do not distinguish between personal and interpretation responses when asked to write about story texts (Macken and Rothery 1990). Text 10.1, a personal response, was written in a public examination to answer a question that asked why a story ended in the way that it did. No mention was made of the type of response text expected to answer the question successfully. In Text 10.1 words indicating an emotional response to the story the student has read ('CLICK') are underlined.

**Text 10.1 Response to 'CLICK' – grade E −**

The author has intentionally written the ending this way to create the effect that she wanted. I felt eerie and isolated after reading the ending – 'like a padlock snapping open' sounded so lonely and made me feel so afraid.

I also felt very empty after reading the passage. It has such a depressing ending that it made me feel afraid and scared. The way 'CLICK' is written by itself in a sentence and in capital letters, added to the emptiness. I can really imagine the exact sound it makes, the way it 'sounded through the room.' 'Sounded through the room' is another example of how the author creates the feeling of isolation so carefully displayed. It sounds hollow and dead and creates fear in your mind.

This is what makes the passage so effective – the way the mood of the characters is portrayed so clearly. I enjoyed this passage immensely. The ending was very clear and well written.

The response was given an E− grade because it did not articulate the theme of the story. The students who wrote interpretations received A or B grades. Text 10.2 exemplifies the interpretation response, and again, words indicating an emotional response to the story are in italics.

**Text 10.2 Response to 'CLICK' – grade A+**

'Click. The television switch sounded through the room like a padlock snapping open.' Click by Judith Stamper is a very <u>didactic</u> short story, the <u>moral</u> of which the ending of the story and its title convey to the reader. Click is about a young girl who has run away from <u>reality</u> and its unhappiness and the death that it confronted her with.

She was unhappy with her family life; she was lonely because her parents and herself lived their lives apart. They had <u>a very distant relationship</u>. Jenny recognised <u>this</u>, but instead of facing <u>it</u>, and making what she could out of <u>it</u>; or trying to rectify *it*, she chose to hide from <u>it</u>. Her hiding place was the <u>fantasy, make-believe</u> world of television. Jenny only went out to investigate the accident because there was a television commercial on. When she arrived, the girl was already dead and Jenny, when she looked into the dead girl's face was shocked back into <u>reality</u>.

'It seemed <u>more real</u> than anything . . .' 'cut through the cloud in her mind.' As <u>it</u> hit her, Jenny's reaction was to 'switch the channel', to escape; to hide from <u>reality</u>. Jenny realised when she went back inside that the world of television no longer gave her protection from <u>reality</u>.

Once she had been jolted back into consciousness, the <u>make believe</u> world seemed too <u>fake</u>. This whole experience: the dead girl's face, the shock of *reality* awoke Jenny. The conclusion, 'Click the television switch sounded through the room like a padlock snapping open' was symbolic. The padlock was Jenny's mind and it's snap was the awakening of <u>reality</u> in that mind. A realisation that it couldn't run away.

This response articulates a dominant message in the story that facing up to reality is a more worthwhile behaviour than living a life of illusion. It is a message which confirms a value widely held in Western societies.

## 10.2  Identifying and writing response genres in English

Personal response and interpretation, the two genres noted in the introductory section, are the ones foregrounded in the study of English in school contexts. They are not the only response types in English. For a more comprehensive exploration of genres in school English see Rothery (1995).

The Leavisite approach has had wide-ranging implications for the study of literature, beyond that of emphasizing personal response. For example, the focus on texts as discrete, creative products is assumed to be a 'natural' way of working with them. As a consequence, texts are culturally and historically decontextualized. Students are denied the opportunity to perceive different patterns of intertextuality across and within story types.

More importantly, they are denied tools for working with texts. Not only the study of language and texts, but literary criticism is seen to have no place in the study of English literature in New South Wales schools – another consequence of Leavis's influence.

> Any sophisticated concept of literary criticism is here unhelpful. The first perceptions of a text need to be validated by further experience of it, and by close attention of its detail. (Board of Senior School Studies 1982: 2)

To *write* an interpretation successfully, students need tools which will help them to articulate an emotional response to the text; make moral or ethical evaluations of the main characters, their attitudes, their relationships and their behaviour; and evaluate the aesthetic quality of the literary work being studied. SFL provides teachers and students with tools for working with story and response genres. These tools enable teachers to analyse the interpretation response and articulate what students are expected to do in writing such a text. They also enable teachers to see how little students can do in such writing when they are deprived of knowledge about historical and cultural contexts for literature and theories of literary criticism. First let us analyse the structure of the interpretation genre from an SFL perspective.

### 10.2.1  The social purpose of interpretation

The social purpose of an interpretation is to articulate the dominant or culturally conventional message(s) in a literary work (novel, poem, play, thematic narrative, etc.) and demonstrate to the reader how this message is realized through the events and/or the characterization of the text. It should also be noted that a text may be given multiple readings. However, it is clear from reading successful responses to literature by both junior and senior secondary school students that students do not challenge culturally conventional readings of literature. Anecdotal evidence from teachers marking responses to literature written by senior secondary school students in public examinations affirms the rarity of a response that challenges a conventional reading. When such a response is received markers are confused about how to evaluate it. They have no guidelines for marking such a text. Examiners expect and reward a culturally conventional reading of a thematic narrative. A conventional reading of a short story is demonstrated in analyses by Rothery and Veel (1993). We would argue it is important for teachers and students to have an explicit understanding of what is valued and rewarded in response to literature. Such an understanding is the first step in denaturalizing conventional readings and thus seeing them as a particular orientation to interpreting meaning rather than the 'natural one'.

## 10.2.2 The generic structure of interpretation

An analysis of the generic structure of the interpretation genre reveals differences between junior and senior secondary interpretations. For instance, junior secondary interpretations move through the following stages (Rothery 1995):

Text Evaluation ^ Text Synopsis ^ Reaffirmation of Text Evaluation ^ (Reaction).

The function of the Text Evaluation stage is to articulate the message of the literary work. It is this articulation which gives the work a particular sociocultural value. The function of the Text Synopsis stage is to show how the events of the text are crucial for realizing or constructing the message. Event recontextualization involves a selective retelling of the narrative to show how the structure of the narrative conveys the message. One way of doing this is to show how the main character changes psychologically and 'grows' as a result of being involved in the events of the narrative. This type of recontextualization also stems from the influence of Leavis as it is seen to be evidence of the reader responding sensitively to the text. It is the epitome of the 'personal growth' orientation to teaching English (Leavis 1962, 1967, Dixon 1967).

The Text Synopsis focuses on selection and selective retelling. This is a deliberate choice as students have few tools of literary criticism which would enable them to deconstruct the text rather than selectively retell it. Students are also expected to include quotes in this stage. These quotes are regarded as the evidence supporting the judgements they have made about the main character's 'growth' and inner change.

The next stage is the Reaffirmation of the Text Evaluation. It involves restating the significance of the message of the text more forcefully and elaborating on it in terms of the symbolism in the text and the values it endorses. The final and optional stage is the Reaction stage. In this stage the writer makes a personal response to the text. This personal response may be to the message, the events or the characters. On the basis of reading a large number of interpretations, the Reaction stage seems to be included only infrequently.

In senior secondary interpretations, the question makes different demands on the students as it either explicitly states the message of the literary work for the student or strongly points students towards it. Students are asked to discuss how the writer has dealt with the theme or aspects of it. As already noted, students lack the tools for a technical discussion of the construction of the work. They thus fall back on a focus on characterization. The justification for the students' reading of the text comes from quotes and by citing evidence from events in the text.

At the senior secondary school level, each stage of the interpretation requires a more intensive, and extensive, exploration of the literary work being appraised. In the Text Evaluation stage, for instance, students are also expected to establish a character-oriented struggle or dichotomy which will be supported and developed further in the Text Synopsis stage. This struggle is often between two opposing ethical/moral values such as good and evil, which are represented by particular characters in a text. This struggle is made manifest both through external events and the inner psychological struggle of the main character(s). To write successfully about these oppositions and struggles, students need to preview, through macro-Themes (Chapter 2), the way their interpretation will be developed. An example of this is shown below:

> The negative value given to television as the world of illusion, as opposed to the positive value of reality represented by the accident is questionable. (Rothery 1995: 171)

This macro-Theme states the message which can be read from the narrative 'CLICK' and thus points to events in the narrative which will support this reading. At the same time, the macro-Theme challenges a conventional reading of 'CLICK' and thus alerts the reader to the fact that the conventional reading will be challenged further in this response.

The Text Synopsis stage in interpretations at the senior secondary school stage still focuses on selective retelling but through character recontextualization. The character-oriented dichotomy which is established in the Text Evaluation is further elaborated on in the Text Synopsis stage. Characters become tokens for values. That is to say they represent values dominant in the society. A significant issue here is that values can and do change over time and what was mainstream in certain periods of history may be marginalized in others. These values are foregrounded in the hyper-Themes of the Text Synopsis and supported by events from the text. Thus, although character recontextualization is the main focus of this stage, students are still required to selectively retell the events of the text. Their criteria for selection, however, are the evidence which these events present to support the students' judgements of characters' qualities.

Text Evaluation

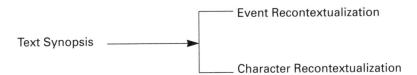

Reaffirmation of Text Evaluation

**Figure 10.1** The generic structure of interpretations at the senior secondary school level

## 10.3 Analysing generic structure in an interpretation response

In the remainder of this chapter we will examine closely an interpretation written in the final public examination for English in secondary schools in New South Wales (Board of Studies NSW 1994). According to the examiners it is an example of the 'Typical Excellent' Higher School Certificate (HSC) response. The question the student answered is printed first.

'It is the darker side of human nature which fascinates the audience in these tragedies of blood.'

Choose ONE of the plays set for study and discuss the ways the dramatist has explored and exploited this fascination.

The response is reproduced as Text 10.3, with the stages marked. The paragraphs are also numbered for ease of reference in working through the analyses.

### Text 10.3 Duchess of Malfi interpretation: Typical Excellent response

*Text Evaluation*
1. John Webster's The Duchess of Malfi does indeed explore and exploit man's fascination with the darker side of human nature. This is done via the powerful characterisation of infinitely evil characters such as the Cardinal and Ferdinand, in contrast with examples of pure human virtue such as the Duchess and Antonio. The animalistic imagery and the themes of rottenness which pervade the play also assist our appreciation of this 'darker side' as does the strongly ritualistic element of the work.

*Text Synopsis*
2. In characters such as Ferdinand and the Cardinal we find an evil which seems to know no bounds – each is guilty of hypocrisy, lust and ambition, yet at the same time they are two very different characters. Webster's characterisation and portrayal of Ferdinand is one of the most powerful in the play. This man is shown to be extremely passionate and is constantly surrounded by animalistic imagery such as 'howling like a wolf' and 'traps his prey'. The extremes of his emotion are shown through the hot and cold images which also pervade his words: 'burnt in a pit', 'heated fury'.

3. The Cardinal contrasts with Ferdinand in that he is far more controlled and cold. He shows no remorse for his many evil actions yet never succumbs to the fearful rage which Ferdinand does. Webster uses the human fascination with the darker side of our nature to entice us into his play by creating creatures as ultimately dark as the Cardinal and Ferdinand. The Cardinal is far removed from the world of God, he has stepped totally outside the macrocosmic rationality of this Christian world. His poisoning of the Bible to poison murder Julia is a powerful image as through his committing this sin he poisons the works of the whole Church. The Cardinal is

also shown to be a sinner in the fact that he has Julia, a married woman, as his lover and in that he has bribed his way into the church.

4. Webster has filled the play with images which many find to be grotesque and unnecessary. Yet these serve to fascinate and intrigue the audience. Late in the play, as Ferdinand imposes many tortures upon the Duchess, we see a live presentation of the horror which exists within Ferdinand's mind, the mind of a mad and irrational thinker. These images may be too barbarous for some to accept on a naturalistic level yet they in fact reflect the barbarous nature of the society and of Ferdinand's mind.

5. We meet the dancing madmen who symbolise the state of decay in which Ferdinand's mind exists. They show the confusion of his feelings towards the Duchess as does his uncontrollable rage when imagining the 'lusty widow' in the sexual act with another. The torture sequence allows us insight into Ferdinand's mind. We note that the hand of supposed love and reconciliation which he offers to her is in fact dead, thus demonstrating that there is no purity or love within him. His desire to meet the Duchess only in darkness is representative of the fact that he lives his life in darkness, that he is far removed from the reality of this world. The horror of the presentation of the dancing madmen, the dead hand and the wax figures all allow the dramatist, Webster, to pander to the Elizabethan/ Jacobean audience's fascination with the macabre, whilst at the same time contributing to a further understanding of the evils which exist in Ferdinand's mind.

6. As Ferdinand is the head of State and the Cardinal is the head of the Church, their evil permeates throughout the society. However, there must be flaws in the other characters in the society which allow this evil to take hold. When we first encounter the world of Malfi it is totally removed from the macrocosmic rationality, each man acts for himself. There seems to be no harmony and few act within the Christian humanistic ideal of working for the good of mankind. Webster uses this scene of moral decay as the perfect setting for a struggle of divine and almost satanic forces as each attempts to gain control of the world. So destroyed is the moral fabric of this society that the world is open to penetration by other forces, which is seen in the symbolic invasion of the Swiss.

7. Bosola is a character in whom there is a contradiction of opposing forces. Good and evil are juxtaposed within him and each struggles to take hold of him. Webster uses this struggle to entrance the audience as we observe Bosola's hubris, his ambition, allowing him to move further and further from human integrity. Antonio introduces the underlying goodness in Bosola with his words:

'Tis a pity
He is thus neglected. I've heard him to be
very valiant. This foul melancholy
will poison all his goodness . . .

and Delio speaks of Bosola as a 'fantastical scholar.' We are intrigued as
Bosola's ambition tragically causes him to fall from grace.

8. Bosola, like Ferdinand and the Cardinal, cannot control the darker side of
his nature though unlike these two, he recognises this fact. He laments his
role in the world, proclaiming:

> O, that to avoid ingratitude
> for the good deed you have done me, I must do
> All the ill that man can invent . . .

and Webster capitalises upon this internal conflict showing Bosola's role as
a continual struggle between his darker side and his good reason. We know
that he recognises the brothers as evil for he describes them as 'plum
trees . . . that grow crooked over standing pools' and that he respects the
Duchess whose nobility 'gives majesty to adversity'. Yet it is to Ferdinand he
proclaims 'I am your creature.'

9. Bosola does sink to the pits of despair and suffers both self pity and fear.
However, he ultimately rises above his hubris and overcomes this through
catharsis. After the death of the Duchess, he becomes resolved to act as an
agent of divinity in seeking revenge yet it is not until he has accidentally
slain Antonio, 'the man I would have saved 'bove my own life' that he is
powerful enough to act. We see this change in Bosola, the definite self
recognition of his inner integrity, in the Cardinal's ability to deflect him
from his purpose which promises wealth and his words:

> I stand like one
> That long hath done a sweet and golden dream
> I am angry with myself now that I awake.

He has come to recognise the futility of pursuing earthly greatness and has
overcome the darker side of his nature.

10. That the audience is intrigued by this change and Bosola's cathartic potential moralises upon us, like Antonio and the Duchess, he comes to symbolise the heights to which mankind can eventually rise. In this way, Webster
uses the destruction of the darker side of human nature to satisfy his audience.

11. Each author of a Revenge Tragedy is concerned with different aspects of
the work, yet for each, the form is a highly ritualistic convention. Webster
takes advantage of this in that he exploits these rituals in an often grue-
some and bloody fashion. Although the Duchess' death is one of grace and
serenity, the death of those who have succumbed to the evil side of their
nature (Ferdinand and the Cardinal) is presented almost as a mad joke.
Webster's final presentation of these two characters shows them as totally
degraded elements. Ferdinand descends into the ultimate form of bestial-
ity by becoming a wolf. This is because he has stepped far beyond the
Christian humanistic vision of the world and attempted to execute

Revenge himself. In his selfish belief that he is capable of doing the work of God without his guidance, Ferdinand suffers from the madness he intended to inflict upon his sister. He is reduced to mutterings about 'strangling' and finally murders his own brother and co-conspirator whilst in a delusionary state fearing he is the enemy. Here Webster dramatises the depths to which man is capable of sinking and through Ferdinand's final decayed state we have a full examination of the darker side of human nature.

12. This 'tragedy of blood' is indeed filled with ritualistic murders for at the end, Antonio, the Duchess, Cariola, Ferdinand, the Cardinal, Bosola and a servant all lay dead. Each has suffered due to the decay of the society. Webster uses Antonio and the Duchess to emphasise the destructive nature of the penetration of the evil side of human nature in that their lives must be sacrificed before the avenger, Bosola, can achieve the unity of purpose to destroy the evil forces which will allow a restoration of society to take place.

*Reaffirmation of Text Evaluation*
13. An overview of the Duchess of Malfi shows that it is indeed a tragedy of the blood. Innocent children are murdered due to their uncle's incestuous desire for their mother and his inability to control his passions. It is twists such as these which show Webster to be a true master of the macabre with a talent for exploiting our fascination with human nature's dark side. The severed hand, the murder of a lover by a 'melancholy churchman', the dead figures made of wax and the dancing madmen are powerful representations of what succumbing to our darker side may lead to, and although these shock the audience, they also thrill to it.

14. Thus we see through his rich characterisation of the evil existing within the Cardinal and Ferdinand and of the inner struggle Bosola experiences, Webster has explored and exploited our fascination with the human capacity for evil. Webster has also used rich visual and sensuous imagery to convey the horrors of which the human mind is capable and in doing so has held his audience spellbound. His grotesque presentation of the rituals of Revenge Tragedy has not detracted from the moralistic and didactic message yet has added much colour and interest.

## 10.4 Analysing the student's interpretation

The opening sentence of the Text Evaluation stage endorses and affirms the general thematic statement quoted in the question and thus naturalizes the examiner's reading of the play:

> John Webster's The Duchess of Malfi does indeed explore and exploit man's fascination with the darker side of human nature.

It is very clear from this opening statement that the student accepts, unquestioningly, the examiner's reading of the themes of the play.

The second part of the question asks students to specify how the dramatist has explored and exploited the human fascination with the darker side. In other words they are being asked to demonstrate how this message has been constructed by the playwright. This student addresses the second part of the question in the remainder of the Text Evaluation by foregrounding the characterization in the play:

> This is done via the powerful characterisation of infinitely evil characters such as the Cardinal and Ferdinand, in contrast with examples of pure human virtue such as the Duchess and Antonio.

In the Rheme of this clause the student is demonstrating his/her explicit awareness that in order to answer the second and main part of the question successfully, character recontextualization is required. Moreover, the qualifier of characterization, the Head of the nominal group in the Rheme above, establishes a strong dichotomy between good and evil and instantiates this dichotomy by making the characters tokens for the values in the play. Evil is thus represented through the characters of Ferdinand and the Cardinal while goodness and virtue are instantiated by the Duchess and Antonio.

The strength in establishing this dichotomy and instantiating it is twofold. At a textual level, it signals that this dichotomy will become the organizing principle of the student's Text Synopsis stage. The student can then justify his/her 'appraisal' of these characters by selectively retelling the events of the play. At a deeper level it indicates a strong awareness, on the part of the student, of the social purpose of thematic narrative. Thematic narratives are vehicles for dealing with the inner change of characters or participants. These changes are the consequence of the resolution of conflict between mainstream ethical values which are held in the culture. They are driven by conflict and characters are often pitched against one another (Rothery and Veel 1993, Rothery 1995, Rothery and Stenglin 1997). Establishing such a clear dichotomy signals that this student is aware of the driving force which underlies all narratives: the struggle to overcome adversity.

The final sentence in the Text Evaluation also identifies the imagery, themes and ritualistic elements of the literary genre of Revenge Tragedy as crucial elements contributing to the playwright's construction of the message:

> The animalistic imagery and the themes of rottenness which pervade the play also assist our appreciation of this 'darker side' as does the strongly ritualistic element of this work.

Thus the second half of the Text Evaluation not only answers the question in a nutshell, it also serves as the macro-Theme for the remainder of the interpretation.

As signalled by the macro-Themes in the Text Evaluation, the Text

Synopsis in this interpretation develops the dichotomy between good and evil. It does this through character recontextualization. Ferdinand and the Cardinal are established as the tokens for evil; Bosola is recontextualized as the character who is struggling to overcome the evil forces within him and the Duchess and Antonio are instantiated as the tokens for good in the play. The values of good and evil which each character represents are clearly and explicitly foregrounded to the reader in the hyper-Themes of the text. For instance:

> In characters such as Ferdinand and the Cardinal we find an evil which seems to know no bounds . . .

> The Cardinal contrasts with Ferdinand in that he is far more controlled and cold.

> Bosola is a character in whom there is a contradiction of opposing forces.

The student supports these character judgements through the selective retelling of events from the play. Such selective retelling is not the only means s/he uses to do this; quotations are also used. Thirteen quotations from the play have been included in this interpretation and it is important to note that all of them fall within the Text Synopsis stage. This student is thus using quotes from the play as evidence to support the character judgements s/he is making.

Another strength of the Text Synopsis stage, is the writer's ability to establish the theme of the 'darker side of human nature' as a superordinate term, define it more precisely as constituting 'evil', then specify the qualities that represent evil in the play: 'hypocrisy, lust and ambition'. These qualities are then exemplified and developed through character instantiations. For instance, in the opening of this stage, the evil characters Ferdinand and the Cardinal are both established as tokens for hypocrisy, lust and ambition. They are then contrasted. Ferdinand is shown to further instantiate evil through lexical items and selective quotes associated with heat: 'passion', 'rage', 'animalistic imagery', 'barbarousness', etc. Whereas the Cardinal is shown to instantiate evil through lexical items associated with coldness through his capacity to commit murder, i.e. he experiences no remorse, is never fearful and never succumbs to rage.

By breaking down the superordinate term 'the darkness of human nature' into parts, the writer also avoids the undue repetition of the term 'darker side'. In fact, there are only ten references to 'the darker side' of human nature throughout this entire text: two in the opening stage, two in the closing stage and the others scattered through the Text Synopsis.

In order to address the construction of the play and further develop the macro-Theme of the Text Evaluation, the final two paragraphs of the Text Synopsis shift to address some of the conventions used by writers of Revenge Tragedy. Throughout this stage of the interpretation, the student effectively utilizes hyper-Themes to clearly signal the shifting focus of the Text Synopsis to the reader: from character recontextualization to text construction. For example in paragraphs 2 and 3 in the Text Synopsis, the hyper-Themes are characters in the play:

> In characters such as Ferdinand and the Cardinal we find an evil which seems to know no bounds – each is guilty of hypocrisy, lust and ambition. . .

> The Cardinal contrasts with Ferdinand in that he is far more controlled and cold.

Whereas in paragraphs 4 and 5, the hyper-Themes signal a shift to a focus on the construction of the play:

> Webster has filled the play with images which many find to be grotesque and unnecessary.

> We meet the dancing madmen who symbolise the state of decay in which Ferdinand's mind exists.

The final strength of the Text Synopsis stage is the writer's ability, at a key point in the interpretation, to go beyond the play and explicitly point to the evil symbolized by the characters and the imagery in the play as a metaphor for the evil in the society at large:

> These images may be too barbarous for some to accept on a naturalistic level yet they in fact reflect the barbarous nature of the society and of Ferdinand's mind.

This student also extends Bosola's struggle and eventual catharsis to a metaphorical level which extends beyond the play:

> That the audience is intrigued by this change and Bosola's cathartic potential moralises upon us, like Antonio and the Duchess, he comes to symbolise the heights to which mankind can eventually rise.

The final stage of the text, the Reaffirmation of Text Evaluation, not only restates the theme but also evaluates the worth of the play and the skill of the playwright by appraising the imagery in the play and the effectiveness of Webster's characterization. It is interesting to note in the final sentence of the text, that this student has an explicit awareness of the broader sociocultural purpose of thematic narrative:

> His grotesque presentation of the rituals of Revenge Tragedy has not detracted from the moralistic and didactic message yet has added much colour and interest.

## 10.5  A resource for interpersonal meaning: the APPRAISAL network

Whenever we use language to interact, we are establishing a relationship between the speaker and listener or reader and writer. At the level of register (that is, field tenor and mode) Martin (1994) construes tenor as being influenced by the relative status of, and contact between, participants. Martin has also located some systems for making interpersonal meaning as part of discourse semantics – linguistic resources for constructing text. One of these systems is the APPRAISAL system network made up of the subsystems of AFFECT, JUDGEMENT, APPRECIATION and AMPLIFICATION. These discourse semantic resources are shown in Figure 10.2.

Martin first introduced this system network at a presentation to SYLC (Sydney Linguistics Circle) at Macquarie University on 3 June 1994. This, and further development by Martin (in press) is the basis of the analysis undertaken in this chapter. The APPRAISAL system network is set out in Figure 10.3.

Each system will be described briefly. The system of MODALITY will not

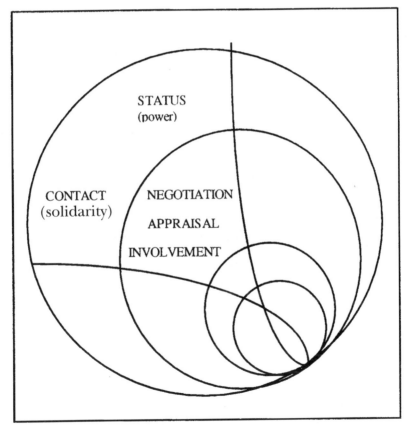

**Figure 10.2** Resources for interpersonal meaning in discourse semantics

be described as it has not been used in the analysis of Text 10.3. Only those networks recently developed will be described as these provided the principal tools for the analysis (Martin 1995, 1997a, 1997b, in press).

### 10.5.1 The system of JUDGEMENT

JUDGEMENTS involve an explicit evaluation of other people and their actions and are made by reference to socially determined expectations regarding behaviour. It should be noted therefore that this is a highly culturally specific domain of analysis. Martin (1994) proposes five major subsystems of JUDGEMENT, each with either a positive or negative value: propriety, veracity, tenacity, capacity and normality. Each subsystem will now be elaborated. Some instances of the lexical items that realize each subsystem have also been included.

#### 10.5.1.1 The subsystems of JUDGEMENT

*Propriety*
Propriety involves assessing one's compliance or defiance with the social system. If one complies, one is often judged positively. Instances of positive ethical JUDGEMENTS include 'moral, good, upright, ethical, kind', etc. Instances of negative ethical JUDGEMENTS include 'immoral, evil, corrupt, wicked, sinful, mean, damned', etc.

*Veracity*
Value JUDGEMENTS relating to veracity concern integrity and falsity. Instances of positive veracity JUDGEMENTS include attributes such as 'honest, credible, real, genuine, trustworthy', etc. Instances of negative veracity JUDGEMENTS incorporate values such as 'dishonest, deceitful, hypocritical, deceptive', etc.

*Tenacity*
Tenacity is construed by reference to inner mental or emotional states rather than external moral regulation. Instances of positive tenacity include values such as 'brave, reliable, flexible, careful, dependable', etc. Instances of negative tenacity include 'cowardly, weak, unreliable, stubborn, obstinate, reckless' etc. These JUDGEMENTS are based on the writer/speaker's evaluation of the participants' emotional disposition or state of mind.

*Capacity*
The subsystem of capacity assesses the person or actions with reference to an assessment of their ability: whether or not the individual has the capacity to perform some action or achieve some result. Positive JUDGEMENTS of capacity include 'clever, gifted, talented, sound, sane, educated, literate, accomplished', etc. Negative JUDGEMENTS include 'slow, stupid, thick, dull, insane, unwell, inexpert, foolish, illiterate, ignorant', etc.

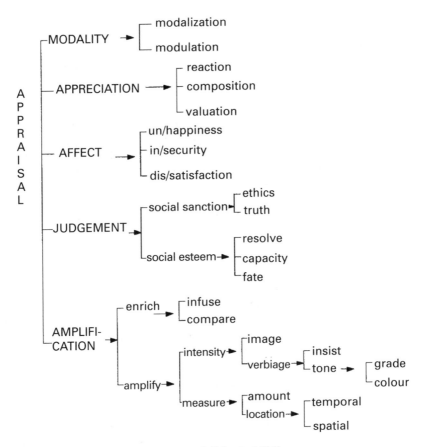

**Figure 10.3** The APPRAISAL system network (Martin 1994)

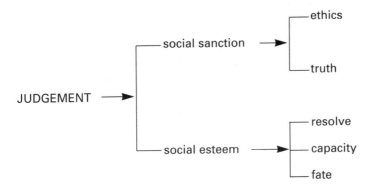

**Figure 10.4** The subsystems of JUDGEMENT

*Normality*
The final subsystem of JUDGEMENT is normality. Positive evaluations of normality include 'lucky, fortunate, predictable, fashionable'. Negative evaluations include 'tragic, obscure, unexpected, peculiar, odd, doomed', etc.

*Social Sanction and Social Esteem*
The five subsystems of JUDGEMENT discussed so far, fall into two more general groupings termed 'social Esteem' and 'social Sanction'. Normality, capacity and tenacity make up 'social esteem' while veracity and propriety make up 'social sanction'. The main reason behind this subdivision is a meaning difference. Normality, capacity and tenacity are subcategories of social esteem because positive values from all three increase one's esteem in the public eye while negative values decrease it. Veracity and propriety, on the other hand, fall into the domain of right and wrong which constitutes the social system of moral regulation or social sanction.

### 10.5.2   The system of APPRECIATION

The system of APPRECIATION involves the speaker/writer's evaluation of the worth of a text or process in a culture. It is made up of three subsystems: reaction, composition and valuation. Each subsystem is aligned with one of the three metafunctions of language: experiential or ideational meaning, interpersonal meaning and textual meaning.

#### 10.5.2.1   The subsystems of APPRECIATION

*Reaction*
Reaction is interpersonally tuned. It describes the emotional impact of the work on the reader/listener/viewer. Positive reactions include evaluations such as 'captivating, absorbing, engaging, stunning, fascinating, moving, entertaining, dramatic', etc. Negative reactions include 'dull, boring, tedious, dry, uninviting, flat, predictable, monotonous', etc.

*Composition*
Composition is textually tuned. It describes the texture of a work in terms of its complexity or detail. Positive evaluations of composition include terms such as 'harmonious, well proportioned, simple, elegant, intricate, rich, detailed, precise', etc. Negative evaluations of composition include such terms as 'ornamental, discordant, irregular, disproportionate, extravagant, simplistic', etc.

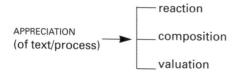

**Figure 10.5** The subsystems of APPRECIATION

*Valuation*

Valuation is ideationally tuned. In visual arts and literature it relates to a proclamation of the 'message' of the work. Positive valuations include terms such as 'challenging, significant, profound, provocative, inspiring, universal, unique', etc. Negative valuations include lexical items such as 'shallow, insignificant, banal, uninspiring, disturbing, sentimental, irrelevant, conservative, reactionary', etc.

### 10.5.3  The system of AFFECT

The system of AFFECT involves the speaker/writer's evaluation of the mental state of the participant(s).

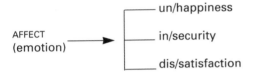

**Figure 10.6**  The subsystems of AFFECT

### 10.5.3.1  The subsystems of AFFECT

AFFECT is made up of three subsystems and each has a positive and negative value: happiness/unhappiness, security/insecurity, satisfaction/dissatisfaction. Each subsystem is further divided according to whether it is an emotion that is felt by the participant or an emotion that is directed at someone.

### 10.5.4  The system of AMPLIFICATION

The AMPLIFICATION network has to do with lexical items which intensify meanings.

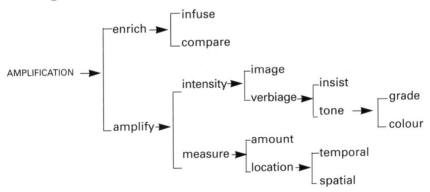

**Figure 10.7**  The subsystems of AMPLIFICATION

10.5.4.1 The subsystems of AMPLIFICATION

The subsystems of AMPLIFICATION distinguish between explicit intensification and infused intensification. Explicit intensification uses scalable lexical items such as adjuncts (adverbs) which grade and intensify meanings (really, very); repetition and a taboo set of meanings, e.g. 'fuck'. It also draws on items which measure amount, e.g. 'heaps' and temporal and spatial location (e.g. 'immediately, urgently; nearby, far, here'). Infused intensification is more implicit, for the meaning of a word is intensified by infusing a circumstance of manner with a process. Thus instead of saying 'ran quickly' we can infuse them and select one word such as 'sprinted' or 'bolted' which has a 'stronger' interpersonal connotation. Another choice for infused intensification is that of metaphorical comparison, e.g. 'ran like a bat out of hell', 'man of steel', 'iron lady', etc.

### 10.5.5 Double codings

Some terms may require a double coding or a double layered interpretation of their interpersonal meaning for they often draw on more than one subsystem of the APPRAISAL network. Thus a number of meanings may be assigned to any APPRAISAL item. This is where this system plays a vital part in helping us to understand how readers coming from different positions in a culture can understand a work differently. Some may only make one coding; others may make several. For instance, in an interpretation of a self-portrait by the Australian artist Heather Dorrough (Board of Studies 1990), the writer frequently uses 'aging' to describe the representation of the female figure. Some students may 'read' aging as 'JUDGEMENT: negative capacity', while others may 'read' it as 'AFFECT:insecurity/apprehension'. Thus we can see how different people may interpret the same text differently, depending on their sociocultural positioning, age and gender. This method of analysis thus illuminates reading position and enables us to see how the same text can have different meanings for a range of readers.

   The interpersonal meanings drawn from the resources of the APPRAISAL system network can be expressed in almost all classes of words and grammatical structures, as well as through rhythm, stress and intonation in spoken language and typographical conventions in written language such as capital letters and exclamation marks. APPRAISAL is most often coded by explicit lexical items in a text, e.g. 'shame'. Competent writers and speakers are able to distribute both explicit and implicit interpersonal meanings through the whole text so that the audience is 'positioned' toward a particular point of view or interpretation of the content. The rhetorical effect of this distribution of interpersonal meanings is that the interpretation or point of view of the speaker/writer will seem 'natural' to the reader. It is in this way that the diffused rhetorical patterning of interpersonal meanings in a text positions the reader or listener to regard the events being written about in a particular way.

## 10.6 The results of an analysis of APPRAISAL in an interpretation response

The analysis of APPRAISAL in Text 10.3, the 'Typical Excellent Response', was undertaken in the following way: First lexical items instantiating APPRAISAL were noted. Next the person doing the appraising was identified. Then the instantiation was identified in respect of a subsystem of APPRAISAL. Finally who/what was being appraised was identified (Stenglin 1996). Table 10.1 shows the number of choices in each system for each stage in the generic structure of the interpretation. Table 10.2 shows the choices from the JUDGEMENT system in each stage of the text and the total number in the text.

**Table 10.1** The global distribution of APPRAISAL in the interpretation

| Generic Structure | AMPLIFICATION | APPRECIATION | JUDGEMENT | AFFECT |
|---|---|---|---|---|
| Text Evaluation | 8 | 3 | 8 | 0 |
| Text Synopsis | 84 | 47 | 157 | 44 |
| Reaffirmation of Text Evaluation | 7 | 18 | 18 | 3 |
| Total | 99 | 68 | 183 | 47 |

**Table 10.2** Distribution of the JUDGEMENT subsystems

| | Social Esteem | | | Social Sanction | |
|---|---|---|---|---|---|
| Generic Structure | Fate | Capacity | Resolve | Ethics | Truth |
| Text Evaluation | 0 | 2 | 0 | 6 | 0 |
| Text Synopsis | 12 | 27 | 17 | 100 | 1 |
| Reaffirmation of Text Evaluation | 1 | 4 | 2 | 12 | 0 |
| Total | 13 | 33 | 19 | 118 | 1 |

Table 10.1 shows the distribution of APPRAISAL in the interpretation response in relation to the generic structure of the text. The predominant choices throughout the text are for JUDGEMENT. One would expect this to be the case as the Key Learning Area of English is about propriety, and ethical values, which are part of the JUDGEMENT system. The next set of choices which predominate are for AMPLIFICATION. At first sight the extent of these choices is unexpected. The reader is not immediately conscious of the significant role they have in the interpretation in building a strong case for the writer's character APPRAISALS. This finding highlights the value of an SFL analysis because it reveals trends which otherwise may go unnoticed. Almost at the bottom of the scale come choices relating to APPRECIATION. One would actually expect more choices from this system, given the fact that students were asked to discuss the ways in which the dramatist has explored and exploited the fascination with the darker side

of 'human nature'. One would expect the student to discuss, in detail, strategies and techniques used by the dramatist for this exploration. The linguistic resources for this kind of discussion fall within the realm of the subsystems of APPRECIATION (reaction, composition, valuation). The system with the least number of instantiations throughout the interpretation is AFFECT. This is an interesting finding given the foregrounding that the personal, affectual response to literary works is currently being given in syllabus documents at both junior and senior secondary levels.

The breakdown of JUDGEMENT choices in Table 10.2 shows there are 118 instantiations of propriety in the text and only one for veracity. This finding concurs with Rothery's research into junior secondary English (1995) in which she argues that English as a school subject is primarily about apprenticing students into cultural values and a socioculturally determined ethical system of behaviour.

The number of choices for AMPLIFICATION is interesting; it is second only to JUDGEMENT in the number of instances chosen. Presenting an interpretation of a creative work in strong terms is highly valued in writing in school English. It seems to be 'read' as indicating the strength of the writer's conviction and also works to make the writer's interpretation of the text seem 'natural' or agreed.

Given the question the student was set, which focuses on how the dramatist has explored and exploited the audience's fascination with the darker side of human nature, the reader would expect the choices for capacity to be numerous, thus indicating an intensive exploration of the writer's techniques and strategies for constructing such a drama. In the absence of tools enabling such deconstruction, however, the writer has chosen a traditional path for interpreting literature, recontextualizing the characterization in the play in terms of an ethical struggle, for it is through the recontextualization of this struggle that they are then able to articulate the message of the literary work, even though this was not asked for explicitly.

Again, in light of the question set, the reader would expect the writer to draw on linguistic resources from the subsystem composition in APPRECIATION. Although there are 31 instances of choices for composition in the text, these are few in comparison to the choices for propriety. The relatively few choices for composition indicates that the student does not have access to technical/cultural/historical knowledge of text construction either from a linguistic or literary criticism perspective. The principal resource for writing about literature is the subsystem of JUDGEMENT within the APPRAISAL system network.

## 10.7 Teaching literature in educational contexts

The analysis of the student writer's response to the question about Revenge Tragedy and the use of APPRAISAL choices used to construct the text, immediately raise questions about the role of English in educational curricula and the pedagogies employed to teach it. At present it is likely, on the basis of the evidence given in the New South Wales Higher School Certificate examination responses, that literature is taught in school contexts in such a way that it 'naturalises' conventional sociocultural practices and values. With no other tools than those of the APPRAISAL system students have little opportunity to develop a critical literacy. The resources of SFL offer students the opportunity to develop a critical awareness of how a school subject such as English deals with texts considered significant in the culture, and how these texts are themselves structured to convey themes (Rothery and Veel 1993). This awareness is the first step towards students developing a critical literacy which enables them to challenge the practice of English and the conventional interpretation of texts that are studied. It is an approach that could be allied with Critical Theory (Cranny-Francis 1996, Cranny-Francis and Martin 1993), thus giving students a sociocultural and historical literary perspective on the works they read as well as a linguistic one.

## 10.8 Future research directions

The traditional focus in school contexts on experiential meanings gives us only a partial understanding of the language requirements of school learning. The use of interpersonal meanings in learning a range of school subjects such as history, visual arts, geography and English is crucial. In all these areas students are expected to assess and evaluate field knowledge. This chapter has addressed only one area of English, that of response to literature in respect of the use of APPRAISAL. It has not taken account of the use of APPRAISAL in story genres which are read and written by students, although some work has been done in this area by Macken-Horarik (1996) who has also analysed APPRAISAL choices in interpretations written by junior secondary students. This chapter has not touched upon a pedagogy for teaching the use of this most important resource in educational contexts. This is another challenging area for educators to investigate. The chapter has, however, taken another step in making explicit to teachers and students the literacy requirement of school English in respect of response to literature.

## References

Board of Senior School Studies (1982) *Years 11 and 12 2/3 Unit Related English Syllabus.* Sydney: NSW Board of Studies.

Board of Studies New South Wales (1994) *Sample HSC Answers English 3 Unit.* Sydney: NSW Board of Studies.

Board of Studies New South Wales (1990) *Sample HSC Answers Visual Arts 2/3 Unit.* Sydney: NSW Board of Studies.

Cranny-Francis, A. (1996) Technology and/or weapon: the discipline of reading in the secondary English classroom. In R. Hasan and G. Williams (eds), *Literacy in Society.* London: Longman.

Cranny-Francis, A. and Martin, J. R. (1993) Making new meanings: literary and linguistic perspectives on the function of genre in textual practice. *English in Australia*, 105: 30–44.

Dixon, J. (1967) *Growth Through English.* London: National Association for the Teaching of English and Oxford University Press.

Leavis, F. R. (1962) *The Great Tradition.* Harmondsworth: Penguin Books.

Leavis, F. R. (1976) *The Common Pursuits.* Harmondsworth: Penguin Books.

Macken-Horarik, M. (1996) Construing the invisible: specialised literacy practices in junior secondary English. Unpublished PhD thesis, University of Sydney.

Martin, J. (1994) Beyond exchange: APPRAISAL systems in English. Paper given to the Sydney Linguistics Circle, NCELTR, Macquarie University, 3 June.

Martin, J. R. (1995) Reading positions – positioning readers: Judgement in English. *Prospect*, 10(2): 27–37.

Martin, J. R. (1997a) Analysing genre: functional parameters. . In F. Christie and J. R. Martin (eds), *Genres and Institutions: Social Processes in the Workplace and School.* London: Pinter, 3–39.

Martin, J. R. (1997b) Register and genre: modelling social context in functional linguistics – narrative genres. In E. R. Pedro (ed.), *Proceedings of First International Conference on Discourse Analysis.* Lisbon: Colibri/Portuguese Linguistics Association. 1997, 305–44.

Martin, J. R (in press) Beyond exchange: appraisal systems in English. In S. Hunston and G. Thompson (eds), *Evaluation in Text: Authorial Stance and the Construction of Discourse.* Oxford: Oxford University Press.

Mayer, M. (1988) *There's an Alligator Under My Bed.* London: Macmillan.

Rothery, J. (1990) Story writing in primary school: assessing narrative type genres. Unpublished PhD thesis, University of Sydney.

Rothery, J. and Macken, M. (1991) Developing critical literacy: an analysis of the writing task in a year ten reference test. *Issues in Education for the Disadvantaged Schools Program:* Monograph. Sydney: Metropolitan East.

Rothery, J. and Stenglin, M. (1997) Exploring experience through narrative. In F. Christie and J. R. Martin (eds), *Genres and Institutions: Social Processes in the Workplace and School.* London: Pinter.

Rothery, J. and Veel, R. (1993) Exposing the ideology of literature. *English in Australia*, 105: 16–29.

Stenglin, M. (1996) Unpacking the interpersonal demands of literary criticism. Unpublished MA dissertation, Macquarie University, Sydney.

# 11 Investigating subject-specific literacies in school learning

*Len Unsworth*

## 11.1 Introduction

From the perspective of SFL, developing knowledge and understanding in school subject areas and developing control of the linguistic resources that construct and communicate that knowledge and understanding are essentially the same thing (Hasan 1996). Furthermore, in SFL research and in research from a variety of other theoretical perspectives (Richards 1978, Applebee 1981, Street 1984, Davies and Greene 1984, Gee 1990) it has been shown that subject areas have their own characteristic language forms and hence entail distinctive literate practices. In contributing to the explication of differences in literate practices across subject areas, SFL – because it is premised on the complete interconnectedness of the linguistic and the social – also contributes a resource for developing students' awareness both of the fundamentally social nature of the literate practices they are engaged in and of how they are socially positioned by these practices.

The challenge in this short chapter is to sketch the breadth of relevant SFL work showing the scope of research possibilities, and to provide some detailed illustration of how SFL has been used in investigating subject-specific literacies. One strategy will be to confine the detailed discussion of linguistic analyses to grammatical metaphor and Theme, as indicated in Section 11.2, 'Focusing on the written medium'. Section 11.3, 'An outline of SFL research across school subject areas', notes the curriculum areas that have been addressed and illustrates the nature of the work by describing some key aspects of the research in school history and science. 'Resourcing apprenticeship and resistance to subject-specific literacies' (Section 11.4) also draws on school history and science to provide some evidence both for the necessity of the grammar of the written medium for the construction of subject area knowledge and for its distinctive deployment in different subject areas; and to show that SFL research is concerned with the development of critical social literacies in school subject areas. Section 11.5, 'Renovating written explanation in school science', illustrates the application of analyses of grammatical metaphor and Theme from a study comparing explanations of the same phenomena in different junior secondary school science books. The chapter concludes with 'Dimensions of further subject-specific literacy research'.

## 11.2 Focusing on the written medium

As students progress through the upper primary school to the secondary school and beyond, the linguistic resources that construct and commmunicate the increasingly specialized knowledge of discipline areas are those of the written medium. It is through their engagement with written texts that students gradually reconstitute their lexicogrammar in the more abstract written mode, providing the discursive means for the construction of what Vygotsky refers to as 'scientific concepts' and the development of the 'higher mental functions' (Wells 1994). The question is: What are the distinctive linguistic structures of the written as opposed to the spoken medium that are essential to subject-specific literacies? There is, of course, a range of grammatical differences (extensively documented) between spoken and written language (Perera 1984, Halliday 1985, Hammond 1990). The focus here is on the extensive use of 'grammatical metaphor' in written texts (Halliday 1985, 1993a, b, Martin 1992, 1993b, c), which Wells (1994: 82) has drawn attention to.

Grammatical metaphor refers to

> . . . a substitution of one grammatical class, or one grammatical structure by another; for example, <u>his departure</u> instead of <u>he departed</u>. Here the words (lexical items) are the same; what has changed is their place in the grammar. Instead of the pronoun <u>he</u> + verb <u>departed</u>, functioning as Actor + Process in a clause, we have determiner <u>his</u> + noun <u>departure</u>, functioning as Deictic + Thing in a nominal group. (Halliday 1993a: 79)

Where a verb ('results in') or a noun ('the result') substitutes for a conjunction (because), this metaphorical realization of conjunctive relations is referred to as logical metaphor. For example, instead of 'He failed because he was lazy', this could be expressed metaphorically as 'His failure was the result of his laziness' or 'His laziness resulted in his failure'. (For further discussion and accounts of other types of grammatical metaphor see Halliday (1994a, b), Martin (1992) and Halliday and Matthiessen (in press).)

## 11.3 An outline of SFL research across school subject areas

The most extensive SFL research on subject-specific literacies has been in the areas of history, science and geography, with an emerging body of work in mathematics, media studies and visual arts. The impetus for much of this work has been the research of J.R. Martin and his colleagues at the University of Sydney, which was followed by extensive collaborative research through the *Write it Right* project with the Metropolitan East Disadvantaged Schools Program within the New South Wales Department of School Education. Christie (1984a, b, 1989a, b) has also investigated writing in primary school curriculum areas and in collaboration (Christie *et al.* 1990a, b, 1992) has published curriculum materials focusing on literacy development across curriculum areas. (For further SFL work on literacy in primary school curriculum areas see Derewianka 1990a, b, 1995, Derewianka and Schmich 1991.) Lee (1996) locates her work in geography at the literacy/curriculum intersection in school geography within a framework of feminist and post-structuralist analyses. Although she takes issue with the work of Martin and his colleagues 'her principal approach is to selectively use the lexicogrammatical analysis of systemic functional linguistics . . . (xiii)'. Extensive work in the subject area of English (Macken and Slade 1993, Macken-Horarik 1996, Martin 1996, Rothery and Macken 1991a, b, Rothery 1993, 1996) is taken further by Rothery and Stenglin in Chapter 10. What follows is a sketch of some key aspects of SFL research in history and science.

The initial work on history (Eggins *et al.* 1992) indicated that the genres that were privileged in school history (as reflected in assessment contexts) were those of explanation and argument rather than narrative. The role of history is to arrange, interpret and generalize from the events of the past. This involves distancing language from the then-and-there, and is largely achieved through marshalling the resources of grammatical metaphor. 'The "Story of people" serves only as the point of departure in this process of distancing the recoverable past' (Eggins *et al.* 1992: 96).

The results of the subsequent *Write It Right* study of the language of school history are reported in a resource book for teachers (Coffin 1996). The book is mainly organized around a typology of the principal genres identified in the writing of school history as summarized in Table 11.1.

Each genre is discussed in terms of its social purpose and role in school history writing. Examples of the genres are described in terms of generic structure, discourse semantic and lexicogrammatical features. These linguistic descriptions are presented as a resource for developing students' comprehension and composition of history texts and for incorporating a critical perspective on the construction of history in such texts. There is not the space here to even review this detailed account and its implications for teaching; however a useful digest of some of the key aspects has been reported by Veel and Coffin (1996). They discuss examples of four text types: autobiographical recount, historical recount, historical account and analytical exposition. Their analyses include lexical density (proportion of lexical items, or content words, per clause), grammatical metaphor, proportion of personal/individual and abstract/institutional participants, as well as temporal and causal relations. As the genres shifted from chronicling history to reporting history to explaining history and then to arguing history, there was a progressive increase in lexical density, grammatical metaphor,

**Table 11.1** Overview of key written genres (text types) in school history

| | Text type | Social purpose | Stages |
|---|---|---|---|
| **Chronicling history** | Autobiographical Recount | to retell the events of your own life | Orientation Record of Events (Reorientation) |
| | Biographical Recount | to retell the events of a person's life | Background Record of Events (Evaluation of person) |
| | Historical Recount | to retell events in the past | Background Record of Events (Deduction) |
| **Reporting history** | Descriptive Report | to give information about the way things are or were | Identification Description (Deduction) |
| | Taxonomic Report | to organize knowledge taxonomically | Classification Description of types or parts |
| | Historical Account | to account for why events happened in a particular sequence | Background Account of Events (Deduction) |
| **Explaining history** | Factorial Explanation | to explain the reasons or factors that contribute to a particular outcome | Outcome Factors Reinforcement of Factors |
| | Consequential Explanation | to explain the effects or consequences of a situation | Input Consequences Reinforcement of con-sequences |
| **Arguing history** | Analytical Exposition | to put forward a point of view or argument | (Background) Thesis Arguments Reinforcement of Thesis |
| | Analytical Discussion | to argue the case for two or more points of view about an issue | (Background) Issue Arguments Position |
| | Challenge | to argue against a view | (Background) Arguments Anti-Thesis |

abstract/institutional participants and causal relations. From the results of their analyses Veel and Coffin (1996: 216) were able to argue that

> in studying school history successive forms of consciousness [realised in language] both assume and subsume earlier forms of consciousness; each form stands on the shoulders of the preceding one, both developing and re-interpreting the social order it represents.

However, they also problematize the apparent 'natural' sequencing of these genres, pointing out that, although the sequence may be linguistically sound, the historical recount and historical account genres privilege the 'grand narrative' tradition of history, which from a Foucaultian view (Foucault 1972, 1978), has significant limitations. A balance must be maintained between the necessity to provide students with linguistically responsible preparation for reading and writing expository texts which challenge commonly held views, and the need to view the use of grand narrative texts with suspicion. Veel and Coffin suggest that explicit teaching about language – teaching genre, grammar and discourse – as an integral part of school history, can help students to develop a critical orientation through an understanding of the 'constructedness' of texts. Understanding how language is used to construct meanings helps students to see not only what is being emphasized and privileged and whose point of view is being conveyed, but also how this is accomplished. Some exemplification of the grammatical analyses of school history texts in relation to these issues is given in Section 11.4.

A substantial body of SFL research on the language of school science has emerged over the last decade, notably studies by Lemke (1990) on talking science and Halliday and Martin (1993) on writing science. The latter, which includes accounts of the generic structure, lexicogrammatical and discourse semantic features of school science books, formed the basis for further research in this area in the *Write it Right* project. Some aspects of this work are reported by Veel (1997). The principal genres found in the school science texts are summarized in Table 11.2.

Veel points out that an account of the language of school science must do more than catalogue genres and grammatical features. He notes that the kind of language encountered and used by students in school science makes possible some ways of thinking about the world and at the same time prevents or marginalizes others. Developing literacy in science, then, is not just a matter of acquiring certain mechanical skills but actually of being apprenticed into a particular world view. The pathways associated with this kind of apprenticeship, Veel suggests, need to be questioned in relation to issues such as: Do/should the ways of making meaning in school science reflect the practices of 'adult' science? What kind of social subjects does the language of science produce? He then describes the 'idealised knowledge path' in school science as constructed by the form of school science texts. This involves a progression from genres concerned with 'doing science' (procedure, procedural recount) to those concerned with 'organising scientific information' (descriptive and taxonomic reports), then 'explaining events scientifically' (sequential, causal, theoretical, factorial, consequential explanations and explorations) and ultimately 'challenging science' (exposition and discussion). There is a concomitant shift in this genre progression from the grammar of spoken medium to the grammar of written medium. This is illustrated by analyses of examples of sequential, causal, factorial and theoretical explanations in terms of lexical density, nominalization, temporal and causal relations and internal/external conjunctive relations. The results show increasing lexical density, greater use of nominalization, more frequent occurrence of causal relations and increased use of internal conjunction. The kind of

**Table 11.2** Genres in secondary school science books

| Genre | Social purpose | Stages |
|---|---|---|
| procedure | To enable scientific activity, such as experiments and observations, to occur | Aim^<br>Materials needed^<br>Steps |
| procedural recount | To recount in order and with accuracy the aim, steps, results and conclusion of a scientific activity | Aim^<br>Record of Events^<br>Conclusion |
| sequential explanation | To explain how something occurs or is produced – usually observable sequences of activities which take place on a regular basis | Phenomenon identification^<br>Explanation sequence (consisting of a number of phases) |
| causal explanation | To explain why an abstract and/or not readily observable process occurs | Phenomenon identification^<br>Explanation sequence (consisting of a number of phases) |
| theoretical explanation | To introduce and illustrate a theoretical principle and/or to explain events which are counter intuitive | Phenomenon identification/<br>Statement of theory^<br>Elaboration [1-n] |
| factorial explanation | To explain events for which there are a number of simultaneously occurring causes | Phenomenon identification^<br>Factor [1-n] |
| consequential explanation | To explain events which have a number of simultaneously occurring effects | Phenomenon identification^<br>Effect [1-n] |
| exploration | To account for events for which there are two or more viable explanations | Issue^<br>Explanation 1^<br>Explanation [2-n] |
| descriptive report | To describe the attributes, properties, behaviour, etc. of a single class of object | General statement^<br>Description |
| taxonomic report | To describe a number of classes of thing in a system of classification | General statement^<br>Description |
| exposition | To persuade the reader to think or act in particular ways | Thesis^<br>Arguments 1-n^<br>Reinforcement of Thesis |
| discussion | To persuade the reader to accept a particular position on an issue by presenting arguments for and against the issue | Issue^<br>Dismissal of opponent's position^<br>Arguments for |

knowledge construed in the texts by specialized technical discourse is increasingly removed from the kind of knowledge construed in the here-and-now of everyday life. Veel concludes by examining options for reforming and/or increasing access to the hegemonic discourses of school science.

## 11.4  Resourcing apprenticeship and resistance to subject-specific literacies

This section recapitulates some aspects of the work of Halliday and Martin (1993) to  illustrate how accessing subject area knowledge and accessing the grammatical forms of the written medium are inextricably linked. The first move will be to show how the resource of grammatical metaphor is integral to the construction of technicality in science. Grammatical metaphor is also crucial to the construction of the discourse of history – but an abstract rather than a technical discourse.

The centrality of grammatical metaphor to the construction of scientific knowledge has been demonstrated extensively by Halliday (1993e, f) and Martin (1993b, c, d). Martin (1993b: 225) notes that the major semiotic resource for the translating process from commonsense to scientific knowledge is elaboration, which, at the clause rank, is constructed through the relational identifying clause (Halliday 1994a: 122–30). In this clause type an identity relation between two participants is constructed. More specifically, introducing technical terms means placing a Token in relation to its Value. The technical term is the Token. What is being defined by this technical term must be grammaticalized as a Thing, even if semantically it is not. In the following examples quoted in Martin (1993c: 178), 'weathering' and 'erosion' are defined as technical terms. This relies on the event sequences they summarize being nominalized as participants so that they can be equated with the pseudo-things, 'weathering' and 'erosion'.

| The production of rock waste by mechanical processes and chemical changes | is called | weathering |
|---|---|---|
| Value | Process | Token |

| The destruction of a land surface by the combined effects of erosion and removal of weathered material by transporting agents | is called | erosion |
|---|---|---|
| Value | Process | Token |

The active role of language in constructing scientific understanding by means of the resources of grammatical metaphor is illustrated by Martin's (1993e) analysis of the following segment from a secondary school science textbook:

> (a) As far as the ability to carry electricity is concerned, (b) we can place most substances into one of two groups. (c) The first group contains materials with many electrons that are free to move. (d) These materials are called conductors (e) because they readily carry or conduct electric currents. (f) Conductors are mostly metals (g) but also include graphite. (h) The second group contains materials with very few electrons that are free to move. (i) These materials are called non-conductors (j) and are very poor conductors of electricity. (k) Non-conductors can be used to prevent charge from going where it is not wanted. (l) Hence they are also called insulators. (m) Some common insulators are glass, rubber, plastic and air. (n) There are a few materials, such as germanium and silicon, called semiconductors. (o) Their ability to conduct electricity is intermediate between conductors and insulators. (p) Semiconductors have played an important role in modern electronics. (Heffernan and Learmonth 1983: 212).

Martin draws attention to the role of grammatical metaphor in the realization of the criterion used to classify substances – 'the *ability* to carry electricity'.

> This kind of coding involves the nominalisation of potentiality, which in the spoken language would typically be coded as the modal verb (as in substances can/can't carry electricity) . . . the nominalised rendering of the criterion, 'the ability to conduct electricity', opens up a semantic space for substances which are *partially* able to conduct electricity. This space is not available in the more spoken coding since one of the peculiarities of potentiality, as far as modality is concerned, is the fact that it is not gradable. With potentiality realised as a modal verb, substances either can or can't conduct electricity; there's nothing in between. Potentiality contrasts in this respect with other modalities, like those of probability or obligation (following Halliday, 1985: 334–40). (Martin 1993e: 95)

Martin goes on to point out that once nominalized, potentiality becomes gradable ('A low/medium/high ability to conduct electricity'). This expanded meaning potential is used to establish a category of substances whose 'ability to conduct electricity is intermediate between conductors and insulators'. In other words the construction of this uncommonsense, scientific knowledge

> depends on the grammar of writing – on a process of nominalisation which makes available meanings that are not readily available in the spoken form. (Martin 1993e: 95)

As well as its functionality in construing the taxonomic structure of scientific knowledge through the linguistic realization of definition and classification, grammatical metaphor is also a crucial resource in scientific argument, facilitating the development of a chain of reasoning. In order to lead on to the next step you have to be able to summarize what has gone before as 'the springboard for the next move' (Halliday 1993b: 131). By expressing a series of events as a Thing, those summarized events can then assume a participant role in the next part of the explanation. You can see this in Figure 11.1, which shows an analysis of the explanation of 'bending light' in a science book for primary school students (Taylor 1989). Here events initially realized as processes are subsequently summarized and realized through nominalization as participants.

So 'travels more slowly' becomes 'this slowing down'; the 'Thing' ('this slowing down') is what makes the light change direction. Similarly, the verbal structure 'change direction' becomes a Thing in the nominal group, 'The bending of light'. This is equated with another Thing, 'refraction', and this 'makes your legs look shorter than they really are'.

This development of a chain of reasoning can be described from the perspective of the grammatical resources for realizing textual meaning. In written language familiar information, or the Given, tends to be conflated

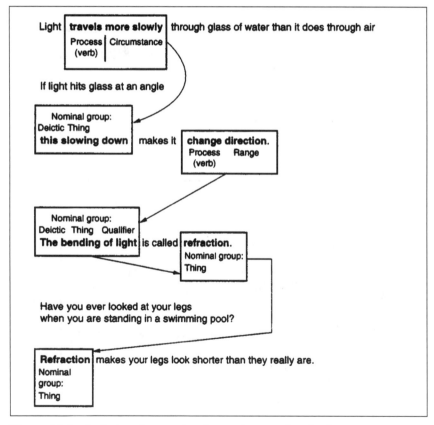

**Figure 11.1.** A chain of reasoning in a primary school science text

with Theme. The information that is being introduced, or the New, occurs in the Rheme at the end of the clause. The New, introduced rhematically, is compacted by nominalization and hence 'packaged' in a form that allows it to be located in Theme position as the Given in the subsequent clause. This also occurs in the 'bending light' text and is further illustrated in the segments from two books for primary school students shown in Figure 11.2.

In the language of school science grammatical metaphor is central as both a FIELD oriented resource for the construction of technicality and a MODE oriented resource for the effective texturing of recursive shifts from familiar to New to familiar information in the progession from everyday to scientific understanding. Nevertheless, as Halliday points out, the forms of scientific English can 'take over', with writers getting locked into unnecessarily complicated language patterns even where there is not motive for it (Halliday 1993a: 70). In any case, nominalization frequently entails ambiguity, especially for those who are relative novices in the field. Halliday (1993f) showed that the following clause has 128 possible interpretations:

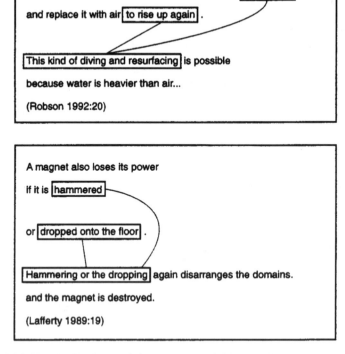

**Figure 11.2** Nominalization and the texturing of Given and New information in two science texts

The growth of attachment between infant and mother signals the first step in the development of the child's capacity to discriminate amongst people.

But beyond the notion of 'innocent ambiguity' Halliday (1993a: 23) points out that

> ... as our linguistic construction of experience becomes more and more elaborated, and its grammar increasingly remote from its origins in everyday speech, the high prestige, elitist discourse which it engenders becomes available for ideological loadings of all kinds.

Grammatical metaphor, then, is also one aspect of syndromes of grammatical features which conspire to construe reality in certain ways. Explicit attention to the nature and functioning of grammatical metaphor is one strategy for developing a critical perspective on such construals. (For a discussion of grammatical conspiracies promoting ideologies of 'growthism' and 'classism' see Halliday (1993a) and for discussion of grammatical metaphor and ideology in ecology and environmentalism in school science see Veel (1998).)

While the language of subjects like science and geography is characterized by the development of technicality, Martin (1993b: 226) points out that the discourse of history, by contrast, is not essentially technical.

> Aside from a small set of terms referring to periods of time (the Middle Ages, the Dark Ages, the Renaissance, etc.) and possibly some distinctive -isms (e.g. colonialism, imperialism, jingoism, etc.), relatively few technical terms are used; and where they are used they tend to be borrowed from other disciplines rather than established by the historical discourse itself (e.g. socialism, capitalism, market forces, etc.).

However, as Martin goes on to explain, the fact that the discourse of history is not technical does not make it any easier to read. The language of history can be very abstract and it is the use of grammatical metaphor which constructs this abstraction. As Veel and Coffin (1996) show, as students move from the genres which chronicle history (biographical recount, historical recount) to genres which explain and interpret history (historical account, factorial explanation, consequential explanation, analytical exposition) the presence of people as participants is effaced. Instead of people involved in processes, these event sequences are nominalized and, as abstract participants, are related to other abstract participants. This can be seen in the following excerpt from a secondary school history text analysed by Martin (1993b):

> The enlargement of Australia's steel-making capacity, and of chemicals, rubber, metal goods and motor vehicles all owed something to the demands of war. (Simmelhaig and Spenceley 1984: 172)

Notice that the nominalizations here ('the enlargement of Australia's steel-making capacity' and 'the demands of war') are not technical terms, but in realizing events metaphorically as pseudo-Things, any mention of human involvement is removed and an abstract version is constructed. This can be easily seen if you try to 'talk out' this text into the grammar of spoken language.

> Australians made  more steel, chemicals, rubber, metal goods and motor vehicles than they had before partly because they needed more of these goods to fight the war.

To get this back to the concrete, lived experience of the time, you would have to add in more of the subsumed events like 'built more factories', 'employed more women', 'worked longer hours'. But Martin points out that the abstraction of the written version also involves what he calls 'buried reasoning', or the metaphorical realization of cause–effect relations. In spoken medium logico-semantic relations, such as cause–effect, are most commonly realized by conjunctions. In the 'talked out' version of the text, the reasoning is realized by the conjunction 'because'. In the written version this is 'buried' in the process 'owed'. This metaphorical realization of conjunctive relations by processes like 'results in' and 'depends on', and nominal groups like 'the effect', 'the reason' and 'the result', are more frequent in written medium and are characteristic of genres which explain and challenge in history.

The functionality of grammatical metaphor as a tool for organizing texts that explain and challenge history was demonstrated by Martin (1993b) in his analysis of the text from which the excerpt above was taken (Simmelhaig and Spenceley 1984: 172). He indicates that grammatical metaphor is strongly associated with Theme in the second paragraph. What are introduced rhematically as New events at the end of one clause are summarized through nominalization and restated as familiar information, or Given, in Theme position as the point of departure in the next clause (Figure 11.3). In the third paragraph, however, grammatical metaphor is more strongly associated with New (Figure 11.4).

Martin draws attention to the first clause in Figure 11.4 to show how the deployment of grammatical metaphor in the New is essential to the appropriate distribution of textual meanings. He notes that a more congruent realization would be a projected clause complex with its own Given and New structure, where the New falls on 'revealed' and 'inadequate':

> The war had also revealed
> that Australia's scientific and research capabilities were inadequate.

But this is not appropriate since 'Australia's scientific and research capabilities' is introduced to the text for the first time and hence should be located as New. It is the use of grammatical metaphor in the written

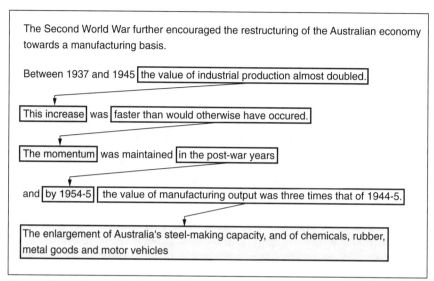

**Figure 11.3.** Nominalization and Rheme/Theme progression in a history text

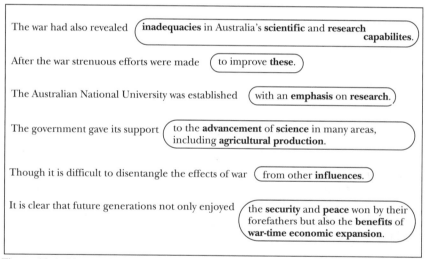

**Figure 11.4.** Nominalization and the locating of New information

version which enables this appropriate texturing to be achieved. Martin (1993b: 244) goes on to indicate how Theme and New make different contributions to the organization of text.

> Theme in a sense provides the text's angle on its field; it is the peg or two on which the rest of the text's meanings are hung. New, by contrast, elaborates the field, developing its meanings – fleshing out the construction of experience with which the text is concerned. Looking upwards to context, Theme is

genre-oriented, angling a text in relation to its social purpose; New, on the other hand, focuses on field, developing the institution at hand.

Grammatical metaphor is also central to the construction of particular interpretive perspectives on history. History deals with the accumulation of events over long periods of time, so it tends to bundle such sequences of events together and package them as if they were a 'thing'. Hence we have the use of nominalization realizing periods of time like 'the Depression', 'the Gold Rush', 'the Chinese Revolution', etc.

> This makes it possible for a whole series of separate events, for example attacking, burning, destroying, fighting, and resisting, to be condensed into a single Nominal Group such as 'this period of Black resistance'. (Coffin, 1996: 91)

The particular nominalization selected to do this condensing of events is strongly linked to the ideological and cultural perspective of the writer of the history. Compare the following possible nominalizations, all condensing events over the same time span:

> this period of Black resistance
> this period of early conflict
> this period of Black lawlessness
> this period of Black violence
> this period of violent suppression of Blacks

As nominalizations these periods of time can participate in a process as in the following example:

> The period of violent suppression provided a catalyst for organised resistance.

And periods of time as noun groups can become the Appraiser – time and events themselves are responsible for proving, demonstrating and showing. In this way the role of the historian/writer as interpreter is obscured and what is really an interpretation becomes naturalized as fact and therefore unquestionable. For example:

> The period of Black resistance showed how strongly Aboriginal people resisted the invasion.

Deductions of this kind can be further abstracted from the writer responsible for them by choosing a grammatical structure which avoids verbs like 'showed', 'demonstrated' or 'proved'. Instead a less straightforward way of grammaticalizing deduction is to use a noun like 'sign' which can then be qualified by 'good', as in the following example:

Joining the League of Nations was a clear <u>sign</u> that the country wanted to be part of the rest of the world.

By effacing the writer as interpreter of events and disguising deductions as facts, grammatical choices are made to position the reader to accept an interpretation as unproblematic and indisputable. By alerting readers to these techniques, we make it possible for them to resist such positioning. To do this we need the kind of grammatical knowledge that can be deployed as a tool for critical reading. (For more on grammar as a tool for critical literacy see Fairclough 1992, 1995, Macken-Horarik and Rothery 1991, Martin 1989, 1995, 1996, 1997.)

This brief exploration of grammatical metaphor in school science and history certainly does not exhaust the discussion of its significance in these subject areas, and, of course, it has a major role in the construction of distinctive discourses in other subject areas. (See, for example, Humphrey 1996 in relation to geography; Veel 1998, on the role of nominalization in the language of mathematics education.) Grammatical metaphor is also just one parameter, albeit a crucial one, of functionality and distinctiveness in the language of school subject areas. The studies cited here explore a range of parameters, their interrelationships and implications for teaching and learning.

## 11.5  Renovating written explanation in school science

The development of students' science learning throughout their schooling entails a gradual apprenticeship to the distinctive linguistic forms of scientific English (Lemke 1989, 1990, Halliday 1993a). As previously discussed, these forms extend well beyond the obvious issue of technical vocabulary to distinctive selections from the grammatical forms that characterize written rather than spoken language (Lemke 1990, Halliday 1993a). As shown earlier, these forms are functional in actually constructing scientific understanding rather than simply expressing it, and hence cannot simply be replaced by more familiar grammatical patterns of everyday language use (Martin 1993a, b, c, Halliday 1993a). Furthermore, the language experience of many students does not include a strong orientation to these 'written' grammatical forms. Explicit pedagogic support is required to develop students' familiarity with them (Lemke 1990, Wells 1994). While the importance of 'hands on' investigative work, observation and negotiation of understanding through associated talk cannot be underestimated in science teaching, it is also clear, according to Wells (1994), that effective use of science texts and the development of students' writing have a very significant role. The quality of the writing in science textbooks in terms of supporting students in 'gradually reconstituting their lexicogrammar in the more abstract written mode' is a crucial factor.

The purpose of this section is to show how specifying grammatical differences can indicate the relative usefulness of school science texts in apprenticing students to the distinctive grammatical forms used in constructing scientific understanding. The site for analysis is the explanation of sound waves in junior secondary school textbooks. The texts examined were part of a larger study of the semiosis of recontextualization of science explanations in the upper primary and junior secondary school science books commonly used in Australia (Unsworth 1995, 1997). Only two of the analyses undertaken can be discussed in the space available here: the role of grammatical metaphor in the construction of technicality and the role of the Theme/Rheme and Given/New analyses in revealing the texturing of familiar and new information as the texts develop. The schematic structure for Text 11.1 (Chapman *et al.* 1989) and Text 11.2 (Heffernan and Learmonth 1990) is shown in Figure 11.5.

### 11.5.1 Grammatical metaphor and the construction of technicality

The linguistic construction of technicality in these explanations is achieved through a series of reconstruals. Initially, the phenomenon of sound waves is realized using grammatical metaphors which are fairly familiar in everyday language use, for example:

> 15 Figure 15.1 shows a vibrating object [[producing sound waves]].
> (Text 11.1)

The nominal group 'a vibrating object' is a metaphorical realization of 'an object vibrates'; 'producing' is a logical metaphor for a series of causal relations, congruently realized by conjunctions such as 'so', 'because' and 'thus'. These metaphorical realizations are progressively 'unpacked' in the text. The first step here is to unpack the nominal group 'a vibrating object' as a clause (16) realizing a commonsense, observable event (Text 11.1)

> 16 As the object moves to the right

The second step begins a cline of technicality with clause 17 congruently realizing the first of a chain of invisible technical events:

> 17 it pushes or compresses the air particles next to it.
> 18 The compressed air particles then push on the particles to their right
> 19 and compress them.

But the next move is to a higher level of technicality:

> 20 As each air particle pushes on the next one to its right
> 21 the compression travels through the air.

Here the congruently realized technical events in clause 20 are 'repacked'

| | TEXT 11.1 | TEXT 11.2 |
|---|---|---|
| ORIENTATION | | |
| Phenomenon Identification Link | What causes and transmits sounds?<br>01 [[To make sounds]] requires vibrations [[which disturb the air]].<br>02 Small vibrations cause soft sounds.<br>03 Large vibrations disturb the air more<br>04 to produce loud sounds.<br>04a Vibrating materials produce sound | Sound waves<br><br>01 You have just seen a number of sources of sound,<br>02 many being produced in a way similar to musical instruments.<br>03 In each case a vibration was needed<br>04 to produce the sound |
| Analogic Account | 05 Vibrating materials send sound waves through the air<br>06 As the materials vibrate<br>07 they disturb the air particles near them.<br>08 These air particles disturb other air particles and so on.<br>09 Just like a long chain of dominoes, the disturbance or sound wave is passed on from air particle to air particle.<br>10 Unlike the dominoes, the air particles spring back to their original position.<br>11 Sound waves travel through gases, liquids and solids<br>12 because they all contain particles [[which will carry or transmit disturbances]].<br>13 However, sound waves will not travel through a vacuum<br>13.1 which is an empty space:<br>14 without particles [[to transmit the disturbance from a vibrating object]], sound waves cannot be formed. | |
| PHENOMENON EXEMPLIFICATION | 15 Figure 15.1 shows a vibrating object [[producing sound waves]]. | 05 If we look at how a tuning fork produces sound<br>06 we can learn just what sound is. |
| IMPLICATION SEQUENCES | 16 As the object moves to the right<br>17 it pushes or compresses the air particles next to it.<br>18 The compressed air particles then push on the particles to their right<br>19 and compress them.<br>20 As each air particle pushes on the next one to its right<br>21 the compression travels through the air.<br>22 When the vibrating object moves back to its left<br>23 the air particles next to it are no longer being pushed. | 07 By looking closely at one of the prongs<br>08 you can see that it is moving to and fro (vibrating).<br>09 As the prong moves outwards<br>10 it squashes, or compresses the surrounding air.<br>11 The particles of air are pushed outwards<br>12 crowding against and bashing into their neighbours<br>13 before they bounce back.<br>14 The neighbouring air particles are then pushed out<br>15 to hit the next air particles and so on. |

**Figure 11.5** Schematic structure of the explanation of sound in two secondary school textbooks

|  |  |  |
|---|---|---|
|  | 24 They spread out<br>25 or are stretched apart.<br>26 As a compression travels through the air<br>27 it is followed by the stretching apart of air particles.<br>28 Because the vibrating object continually moves back and forth<br>29 a series of compressions and stretchings of air particles is sent out from the object. | 16 This region of slightly squashed together air moving out from the prong is called a compression.<br>17 When the prong of the tuning fork moves back again<br>18 the rebounding air particles move back into the space that is left.<br>19 This region where the air goes thinner is called a rarefaction<br>20 and also moves outwards.<br>21 The particles of air move to and fro in the same direction in which the wave moves<br>22 and do not move along with the compression. |
| CLOSURE<br>Conclusion<br><br>Extension<br><br><br><br><br><br><br><br><br><br>Generalization/<br>Application | 30 These compressions and stretchings make up a sound wave<br>31 The vibrating object focuses most of the sound waves in the general direction of its vibrations.<br>32 However, bending of the edges of the sound waves has the effect of sending them out in all directions around the vibrating object.<br>33 This is shown by the top view of the vibrating object in figure 15.1.<br>34 The same process can occur with the particles in a liquid or a solid<br>35 so that they will also transmit sound. | 23 Thus sound is a compression wave that can be heard. |

**Figure 11.5** (continued)

using the grammatical metaphor 'the compression' in clause 21, so we have a more metaphorical reconstrual, as a 'macro' technical event. Finally, the recursive macro technical events are metaphorically construed as a Thing – 'a series of compressions and stretchings of air particles' – which is a participant in a 'meta' technical event, and identified with the original common-sense metaphor 'sound waves', as shown in clauses 29 and 30.

> 29  a series of compressions and stretchings of air particles is sent out from the object.
> 30  These compressions and stretchings make up a sound wave.

In Text 11.1 different types of grammatical metaphor are involved with each progression along the cline of technicality. The deployment of grammatical metaphor initially involves the shift to quality. In Text 11.1 the ten instances of grammatical metaphor, involving a Material process functioning as a Classifier, are made up of seven occurrences of the structure 'vibrating object', two of 'vibrating materials' and one of 'compressed air particles'. The reconstrual of technical events as macro technical events then necessitates the shift to Thing. Hence the Process^Medium structures 'compresses air particles' (clause 17) and 'compress them' (clause 19) become the metaphorical Thing, 'compression' (clause 21). This Thing is then a participant in the next stage in the reconstrual of the implication sequence as a macro event: 'the compression travels through the air' (clause 26). The concomitant movement back of the air particles when the object moves back to the left is also metaphorized as a Thing ('the stretching apart of air particles'), but avoids the technical nominalization, 'rarefaction'. Further reconstrual of these macro technical events also necessitates the resources of grammatical metaphor because it is the recursive macro event complex which needs to be reconstrued as a metaphorical Thing so that it can be a participant in the technical meta event. It is therefore the logical relation involved in recursion, i.e. temporal succession, which is metaphorized to construct the metaphorical Thing 'a series of compressions and stretchings of air particles' (clause 29). Through presuming demonstrative reference ('These') in clause 30, this metaphorical Thing is equated with the more familiar 'sound wave'. The development of the grammatical metaphor in Text 11.1 and the cline of technicality are shown in Figure 11.6.

In Text 11.2 there are problems in the deployment of metaphors involving a shift to Thing in order to effect reconstrual of technical events as macro technical events. There is no use of logical metaphor in their further reconstrual as a meta technical event.

The deployment of grammatical metaphor involving shift to Thing, which is necessary to the reconstrual of technical events as macro events, is not well managed. The first clause relevant to this shift to the macro event is 16:

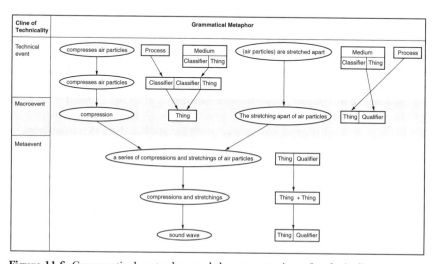

**Figure 11.6** Grammatical metaphor and the construction of technicality

16 This region of slightly squashed together air moving out from the prong is called a compression.

The metaphorical form of 'This region of slightly squashed together air moving out from the prong' causes a good deal of confusion, especially the Qualifier 'moving out from the prong', because, in fact, there is no actual movement of air. There is no concrete participant which is actually transferred away from the prong. This is an abstraction from a series of event sequences which occur contiguously at fixed locations radiating from the vibrating object. It is the technical event of air particles compressing adjacent air particles which is appropriately condensed metaphorically as the Thing 'compression'. At the next level of technicality this metaphorical Thing can be a participant in a macro technical event, i.e. moving out from the prong. Part of the problem with this text is that 'compression' does not function as a participant in a macro event. 'Rarefaction' does function as an ellipsed participant in clause 20:

19 This region where the air goes thinner is called a rarefaction
20 and also moves outwards.

But again the problem is that the nominalized Value ('The region where the air goes thinner'), for which 'rarefaction' is the Token in clause 19, constructs a technical term which names a concrete participant, i.e. 'This region where the air goes thinner'. It is difficult to understand 'rarefaction' as a reconstrual of an implication sequence because in the metaphorical form of the Value, the invisible event is downranked as a Qualifier ('where the air goes thinner') of the nominal group 'This region'. Clause 20 seems to realize the actual transference of a concrete participant ('This region') rather than the occurrence of an abstract event. The notion of the reconstrual of technical events as macro events at a higher level of abstraction is lost. In Text 11.2 there is no realization of a macro event complex and no use of the logical metaphor which reconstrues the recursive macro event complex as a Thing as in clause 29 from Text 11.1:

29 a series of compressions and stretchings is sent out from the object.

So, in Text 11.2, this recursive macro event complex is not reconstrued as a participant in an event at a higher level of technicality, i.e. sound wave. Instead sound is defined as 'a compression wave that can be heard' (23). Now, if the participant 'wave' is actually constituted by a series of alternating compressions and rarefactions, it is difficult to understand the use of the metaphorical Thing 'compression' as a Classifier of 'wave'. At this stage of the explanation of the phenomenon this Classifier^Thing structure seems to be an inappropriate conflation of two different levels of the metaphorical construal of technical events. The deployment of grammatical metaphor does not support the reconstrual of unobservable events at progressively higher levels along a cline of technicality as was achieved in Text 11.1.

Further analyses (Unsworth 1995, 1997) showed that Text 11.1 included two discrete text segments (Link, Analogic Account) as preliminary/preparatory 'passes' at the semiotic reconstrual described, thus foreshadowing the deployment of grammatical metaphor in the third 'pass', which is the Implication Sequences stage. What is being provided here at the level of genre is a sequence of 'advance organisers' to scaffold the progressive increase in technicality. These 'graduated shifts' from the more familiar commonsense perspectives towards a more systematic scientific view are not matched in Text 11.2. In it there is more of a 'melding' of commonsense and scientific orientations at the level of lexicogrammatical realization through lexical selection of commonsense items and the use of (frequently anthropomorphic) lexical metaphors.

### 11.5.2 Theme: texturing the flow of familiar and New information

The Theme analyses are based on those discussed in Chapter 2 except that, in this study, dependent clauses occurring before their main clauses are also analysed as *marked* Themes. In such cases the Theme is not then analysed in the subsequent main clause (Martin 1992). The Theme analysis follows Martin (1992) to show the 'method of development' of the text.

The Implication Sequences stages of Texts 11.1 and 11.2 are compared below to show very different patterns of Theme selection. Here again it will be argued that Text 11.1 provides a texturing of the flow of familiar and New information that is much more helpful to students.

### 11.5.2.1 Theme in Text 11.1

The Theme analysis for Text 11.1 is shown in Figure 11.7. The Themes are located on the left of the diagram; marked Themes are shown in italics.

The predominance of marked Themes in the Implication Sequences is a central resource in the development of this text element. The role of the thematic dependent clauses is to update what can be regarded as familiar ('Given', Halliday 1994a) information as the text progresses. Part of this is to track the component events in the commonsense, observable implication sequence, i.e. the movement back and forward of the vibrating object. These component events as marked Themes in clauses 16 and 22 are accumulated as a marked Theme in clause 28 (Figure 11.7). But, in addition, the marked Themes in clauses 20 and 26 pick up the New information from previous clauses, located in the Rheme. (See Halliday 1994a on the relation between Rheme and New.) This unfamiliar technical information first appears as New information in the Rheme, but subsequently is located in the Theme position since it can be regarded as

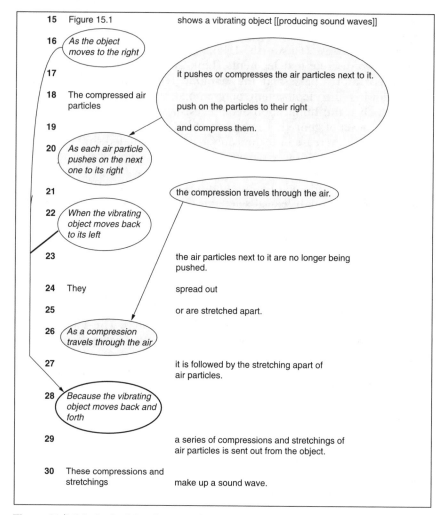

**Figure 11.7** 'Method of development' in the Implication Sequences of Text 11.1

familiar. In this way the familiar (Given) is updated as a point of departure for the further introduction of New information in the subsequent rhematic independent clauses. While the marked Themes in 16 and 22 are constituent events in the sequence realized in 28, the marked Theme in 20 is in a constituency relation to 26. The method of development is progressively moving the point of departure from constituent events to macro events in terms of both commonsense and uncommonsense Implication Sequences (Figure 11.7).

But it is in the progression of New information in the rhematic independent clauses where the events in the technical implication sequences are condensed and reconstrued at higher levels of abstraction. This reconstrual necessitates nominalization and hence deployment of this form of grammatical metaphor must be introduced through the Rheme. So the new information, progressively introduced and distilled rhematically through nominalization, is finally accumulated as Hyper-New (Martin 1992) in clause 30, which functions as the Conclusion in the Closure element of the structure (Figure 11.8).

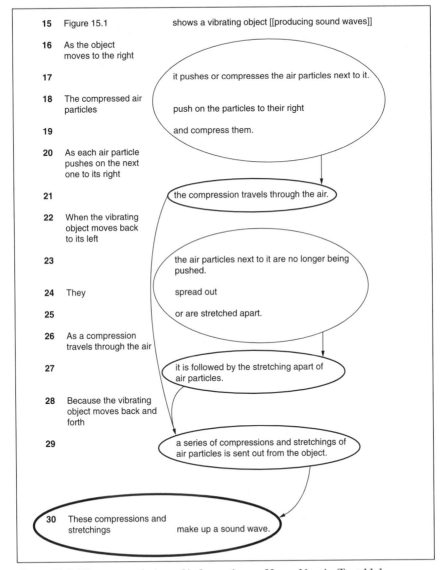

**Figure 11.8** The accumulation of information as Hyper-New in Text 11.1

11.5.2.2 Theme in Text 11.2

Text 11.2 has fewer marked Themes than Text 11.1. What is similar in the method of development is the progression through the Theme of the component events of the commonsense activity sequence (the vibration of the object), with each movement of the object realized in a thematic dependent clause. But in Text 11.2 these are not accumulated in a subsequent marked Theme realizing the whole of the observable event sequence. (In fact the whole event is introduced rhematically in clause 8, prior to the component events.) In addition, although the Theme selections do update Given information about the technical Implication Sequences as the text progresses by picking up New information developed and distilled through the Rhemes, there is no cumulative effect as in Text 11.1 (Figure 11.9).

The Theme analysis indicates that Text 11.1 manages the relationship of what is known to the progressive development of New information in a much more clearly discernible pattern than 11.2.

In Text 11.1 a particular co-patterning of grammatical choices, including grammatical metaphor, effectively explains sound waves as a series of reconstruals of technical Implication Sequences. In Text 11.2 the absence of this grammatical co-patterning produces ambiguity and distortion in the explanation. Further, the co-patterning with selections for Theme and New also distinguishes Text 11.1 from Text 11.2 in terms of effective texturing of the flow of familiar and New information as the texts develop.

The analyses discussed here indicate that effective explanations in school science are identifiable and amenable to specification. Further research identifying the nature of the effectiveness of such texts (whether in books, on CD-ROMs or on Web sites) when used by different groups of science students for a variety of purposes may well lead to a practical agenda for the reform of secondary science explanations.

## 11.6 Dimensions of further subject-specific literacy research

This is an expansive and expanding research area. Here we will simply note some lines of relevant innovative enquiry to encourage you to explore the potential of SFL for your own study. Expansion of SFL description of language is itself stimulated in accounting for the nature of subject area literacies. The initial approach to identifying genres, for example, involved locating texts in distinct categories on the basis of how they were different (typology). More recently (Lemke 1995, Martin 1997, in press) genres have been described in terms of the extent of shared features or proximity along particular linguistic parameters (topology). Lemke (1995) points out that this is not to argue against teaching 'ideal' canonical genres, which he sees as good teaching practice in introducing students to a particular genre. Nevertheless Lemke also points out that these 'ideal' canonical genres are relatively infrequent in teaching

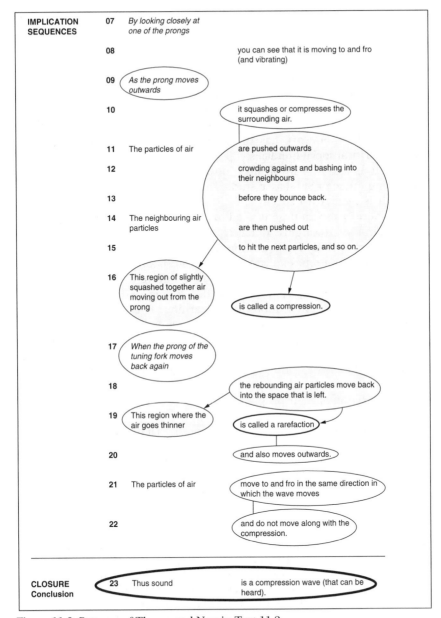

**Figure 11.9** Patterns of Theme and New in Text 11.2

materials. A topological perspective takes account of this and in addition provides a pedagogical resource for supporting students' progression in the learning of additional genres and for encouraging them to produce more variant versions of genres in response to functional tasks. Further research is needed on topological accounts of genre in subject areas.

There is also the concern to develop critical literacies (Coffin 1996, Humphrey 1996), which has drawn on Martin's recently developed description of APPRAISAL systems in English (Martin 1995, 1996, 1997). These systems augment SFL descriptions of resources for realizing interpersonal meaning and indicate how choice of lexis can 'colour' representations of experience with particular forms of affect, judgement and valuation as well as grades of personal perspective and degrees of amplification (see Chapter 10 for the application of APPRAISAL analyses to English teaching). Further work has the potential to enhance pedagogies oriented to critical social literacies.

As well as research involving innovative SFL descriptions, there is an increasing range of SFL-based studies in subject-specific literacies. Further research is needed to specify the literacies of additional school subject areas. There is also an urgent need for research into the literacy practices entailed in the growing use of electronic and multimedia learning materials (Large *et al.* 1995, The New London Group 1996, Lemke 1998). Much remains to be done in explicating the semiosis of recontextualizing subject area knowledge in texts for learners at different school levels (Cross 1995, Unsworth 1995, 1997) and in developing pedagogies for critical social multiliteracies in school subject learning. There is a growing, albeit tacit, recognition of the contribution to be made by SFL. This is reflected in a recent article in the *Harvard Educational Review* where ten educationalists from the United Kingdom, the United States and Australia, calling themselves the New London Group[1] set out an agenda for a pedagogy of multiliteracies which draws significantly on SFL concepts. They described a key foundation of their proposal as

> an educationally accessible functional grammar; that is, a metalanguage of that describes meaning in various realms. These include the visual, as well as the multi-modal relations between different meaning-making processes that are now so critical in media texts and the texts of electronic multi-media. (New London Group 1996: 77)

## Note

1. Courtney Cazden (Harvard, USA); Bill Cope (University of Technology Sydney, Australia); Norman Fairclough (Lancaster University, UK); Jim Gee (Clark University, USA); Mary Kalantzis (James Cook University of North Queensland, Australia); Gunther Kress (University of London, UK); Allan Luke (University of Queensland, Australia); Carmen Luke (University of Queensland, Australia); Sarah Michaels (Clark University, USA); Martin Nakata (James Cook University of North Queensland, Australia).

## References

Applebee, A.N. (1981) *Writing in the Secondary School.* Urbana: National Council for the Teaching of English.

Chapman, B., Perry, L., Stead, K. (1989) *Science 9.* Mitton, Queensland: Brooks Waterloo.

Christie, F. (ed.) (1984a) *Children Writing: Reader.* Geelong: Deakin University Press.

Christie, F. (ed.) (1984b) *Children Writing: Study Guide.* Geelong: Deakin University Press.

Christie, F. (ed). (1989a) *Writing in Schools: Reader.* Geelong: Deakin University Press.

Christie, F. (ed.) (1989b) *Writing in Schools: Study Guide.* Geelong: Deakin University Press.

Christie, F., Gray, P., Gray, B., Macken, M., Martin, J. and Rothery, J. (1990a) *Language: A Resource for Meaning – Exploring Reports (Teachers' Book).* Sydney: Harcourt Brace Jovanovich.

Christie, F., Gray, P., Gray, B., Macken, M., Martin, J. and Rothery, J. (1990b) *Language: A Resource for Meaning – Exploring Procedures (Teachers' Book).* Sydney: Harcourt Brace Jovanovich.

Christie, F., Gray, P., Gray, B., Macken, M., Martin, J. and Rothery, J. (1992) *Language: A Resource for Meaning – Exploring Explanations (Teachers' Book).* Sydney: Harcourt Brace Jovanovich.

Coffin, C. (1996) *Exploring Literacy in School History.* Sydney: Metropolitan East Disadvantaged Schools Program, New South Wales Department of School Education.

Cross, M. (1995) The textual representation of knowledge for novice learners. Paper presented at the Australian Systemic Functional Linguistics Conference, University of Melbourne.

Davies, F. and Greene, T. (1984) *Reading and Learning in the Sciences.* Edinburgh: Oliver and Boyd.

Derewianka, B. (1990a) Rocks in the head: children writing geology reports. In *Knowledge About Language and the Curriculum: The LINC Reader,* Hodder and Stoughton, London.

Derewianka, B. (1990b) *Exploring How Texts Work.* Sydney: Primary English Teaching Association.

Derewianka, B. (1995) Using functional grammar in the classroom. In J. Murray (ed.), *Celebrating the Differences, Confronting literacies: Conference Papers from the Australian Reading Association National Conference Sydney July 1995.* Melbourne: ARA.

Derewianka, B. and Schmich, M. (1991) Factual texts in the upper primary school. In E. Furniss and P. Green (eds), *The Literacy Connection.* Melbourne: Eleanor Curtain.

Eggins, S., Wignell, P. and Martin, J. R. (1992) The discourse of history: distancing the recoverable past. In M. Ghadessy (ed.), *Register Analysis: Theory and Practice.* London: Pinter.

Fairclough, N. (1995) *Critical Discourse Analysis: The Critical Study of Language.* London: Longman.

Fairclough, N. (ed.) (1992) *Critical Language Awareness.* London: Longman.

Foucault, M. (1972) *The Archaeology of Knowledge.* Trans. A. M. Sheridan Smith. New York: Pantheon.

Foucault, M. (1978) *Introduction: The History of Sexuality,* vol 1. Trans. Robert Hurley. Harmondsworth: Penguin.

Gee, J. P. (1990) *Social Linguistics and Literacies: Ideology in Discourses.* London: Falmer Press.

Halliday, M. A. K. (1985) *Spoken and Written Language*. Geelong: Deakin University Press.

Halliday, M. A. K. (1985) *An Introduction to Functional Grammar*. London: Edward Arnold.

Halliday, M. A. K. (1993a) The act of meaning. *Applied Linguistics Association of Australia Occasional Paper* (13): 42–61.

Halliday, M. A. K. (1993b) The analysis of scientific texts in English and Chinese. In M. A. K. Halliday and J. R. Martin (eds), *Writing Science: Literacy and Discursive Power*. London: Falmer.

Halliday, M. A. K. (1993e) On the language of physical science. In M. A. K. Halliday and J. R. Martin (eds), *Writing Science: Literacy and Discursive Power*. London: Falmer Press, 54–68.

Halliday, M. A. K. (1993f) Some grammatical problems in scientific English. In M. A. K. Halliday and J. R. Martin (eds), *Writing Science: Literacy and Discursive Power*. London: Falmer Press, 68–85.

Halliday, M. A. K. (1994a) *An Introduction to Functional Grammar* (2nd edn). London: Edward Arnold.

Halliday, M. A. K. (1994b) Metaphor as semogenic process. Paper presented to the Workshop on Scientific Discourse, University of Sydney.

Halliday, M. A. K. and Martin, J. R. (eds) (1993) *Writing Science: Literacy and Discursive Power*. London: Falmer Press.

Halliday, M. A. K. and Martin, J. R. (1993a) General orientation. In M. A. K. Halliday and J. R. Martin (eds), *Writing Science: Literacy and Discursive Power* London: Falmer.

Halliday, M. A. K. and Martin, J. R. (1993b) The model. In M. A. K. Halliday and J. R. Martin (eds), *Writing Science: Literacy and Discursive Power*. London: Falmer.

Halliday, M. A. K. and Matthiessen, C. (in press). *Construing Experience Through Meaning: A Language-Based Approach to Cognition*. Sydney:

Hammond, J. (1990) Is learning to read and write the same as learning to speak? In F. Christie (ed.), *Literacy for a Changing World*. Hawthorn: Australian Council for Educational Research.

Hasan, R. (1996) Literacy, everyday talk and society. In R. Hasan and G. Williams (eds.), *Literacy and Society*. London: Longman.

Humphrey, S. (1996) *Exploring Literacy in School Geography*. Sydney: Metropolitan East Disadvantaged Schools Program, New South Wales Department of School Education.

Large, A., Behesti, J., Breuleux, A. and Lenaud, A. (1995) Multimedia in primary education: how effective is it? *School Quarterly*, 24(1): 19–25.

Lee, A. (1996) *Gender, Literacy, Curriculum: Re-Writing School Geography*. London: Taylor and Francis.

Lemke, J. (1989) Making text talk. *Theory into Practice*, 28: 136–41.

Lemke, J. (1990) *Talking Science: Language, Learning and Values*. Norwood, NJ: Ablex.

Lemke, J. (1995) Typology, topology, topography: genre semantics. *Network*, 22:

Lemke, J. (1998) Multiplying meaning: visual and verbal semiotics in scientific text. In J. R. Martin and R. Veel (eds), *Reading Science*. London: Longman.

Macken, M. and Slade, D. (1993) Assessment: a foundation for effective learning in the school context. In Bill Cope and Mary Kalantzis (eds), *The Powers of Literacy: A Genre Approach to Teaching Writing*. London: Falmer.

Macken-Horarik, M. (1996) Literacy and learning across the curriculum: towards a model of register for secondary school teachers. In R. Hasan and G. Williams (eds), *Literacy and Society*. London: Longman.

Macken-Horarik, M. and Rothery, J. (1991*) Developing Critical Literacy: A Model for Literacy in Subject Learning*. Sydney: Metropolitan East Disadvantaged Schools Program.

Martin, J. R. (1989) *Factual Writing: Exploring and Challenging Social Reality*. Oxford: Oxford University Press.

Martin, J. R. (1992) *English Text: System and Structure*. London: Benjamins.

Martin, J. R. (1993a) Genre and literacy – modelling context in educational linguistics. *Annual Review of Applied Linguistics*, 13: 141–72.

Martin, J. R. (1993b) Life as a noun: arresting the universe in science and humanities. In M. A. K. Halliday and J. R. Martin (eds), *Writing Science: Literacy and Discursive Power*. London: Falmer.

Martin, J. R. (1993c) Literacy in science: Learning to handle text as technology. In M. A. K. Halliday and J. R. Martin (eds), *Writing Science: Literacy and Discursive Power*. London: Falmer.

Martin, J. R. (1993d) Technicality and abstraction: language for the creation of specialized text. In M. A. K. Halliday and J. R. Martin (eds), *Writing Science: Literacy and Discursive Power*. London: Falmer.

Martin, J. R. (1993e) Technology, bureaucracy and schooling: discourse resources and control. *Cultural Dynamics*, 6(1): 84–130.

Martin, J. R. (1994) Macro-genres: the ecology of the page. *Network*, 21:29–52.

Martin, J. R. (1995) Reading positions/positioning readers: JUDGEMENT in English. *Prospect: A Journal of Australian TESOL*, 10(2): 27–37.

Martin, J. R. (1996) Evaluating disruption; symbolising theme in junior secondary narrative. In R. Hasan and G. Williams (eds), *Literacy in Society*. London: Longman.

Martin, J. R. (1997) Analysing genre: functional parameters. In F. Christie, and J.R. Martin (eds.), *Genres and Institutions: Social Processes in the Workplace and School*. London: Cassell.

Martin, J.R. (in press) A context for genre: modelling social processes in functional linguistics. In R. Stainton and J. Devilliers (eds), *Communication in Linguistics*. Toronto: GREF.

Martin, J. R., Wignell, P., Eggins, S., and Rothery, J. (1986) Secret English: discourse technology in a junior secondary school. In L. Gerot, J. Oldenburg and T. van Leeuwen (eds), *Working Conference on Language in Education: Language and Socialization: Home and School*. Sydney: Macquarie University, 143–73.

New London Group (1996) A pedagogy of multiliteracies: designing social futures. *Harvard Educational Review*, 66(1): 60–91.

Perera, K. (1984) *Children's Reading and Writing*. Oxford: Blackwell.

Richards, J. (1978) *Classroom Language: What Sort?* London: George Allen and Unwin.

Rothery, J. (1993) *Exploring Literacy in School English*. Metropolitan East Disadvantaged Schools Program, Erskineville, NSW.

Rothery, J. (1996) Making changes: developing an educational linguistics. In R. Hasan and G. Williams (eds), *Literacy in Society*. London: Longman.

Rothery, J. and Macken, M. (1991a) Developing critical literacy through systemic functional linguistics: unpacking the 'hidden curriculum' for writing in junior secondary English in New South Wales. Monograph produced by Metropolitan East Disadvantaged Schools Program, Erskineville, NSW.

Rothery, J. and Macken, M. (1991b) Developing critical literacy: an analysis of the writing task in a year 10 reference test. Issues in Education for the socially and economically disadvantaged. Monograph 1. Metropolitan East Disadvantaged Schools Program: Erskineville, New South Wales.

Street, B. (1984) *Literacy in Theory and Practice.* Cambridge: Cambridge University Press.

Unsworth, L. (1995) How and why: recontextualizing science explanations in school science books. Unpublished PhD thesis, Department of Linguistics, University of Sydney.

Unsworth, L. (1997) Sound explanations in school science: a functional linguistic perspective on effective apprenticing texts. *Linguistics and Education,* 9(2): 199–226.

Veel, R. (1997) Learning how to mean – scientifically speaking: apprenticeship into scientific discourse in the secondary school. In F. Christie and J. R. Martin (eds), *Genres and Institutions: Social Processes in the Workplace and School.* London: Cassell, 161–95.

Veel, R. (1998) The greening of school science: ecogenesis in secondary class-rooms. In J. R. Martin and R. Veel (eds), *Reading Science: Functional and Critical Perspectives on the Discourses of Science.* London: Routledge.

Veel, R. (1999) Language, knowledge and authority in school mathematics. In F. Christie (ed.), *Pedagogy and the Shaping of Consciousness: Linguistic and Social Processes.* London: Cassell.

Veel, R. and Coffin, C. (1996) Learning to think like an historian: the language of secondary school History. In R. Hasan and G. Williams (eds), *Literacy in Society.* London: Longman, 191–231.

Wells, G. (1994) The complementary contributions of Halliday and Vygotsky to a language-based theory of learning. *Linguistics and Education,* 6(1): 41–90.

## School texts

Chapman, B., Perry, L. and Stead, K. (1989) *Science 9.* Milton, Queensland: Brooks Waterloo.

Heffernan, D., Learmonth, M. (1983) *The World of Science,* vol. 4. Melbourne: Longman Cheshire.

Heffernan, D. and Learmonth, M. (1990) *The World of Science,* vol 3 (2nd edn). Melbourne: Longman Cheshire.

Lafferty, P. (1989) *Hands on Science: Wind to Flight.* London: Gloucester Press.

McClymont, D. (1987) *Water.* London: Macdonald.

Robson, P. (1992) *Water, Paddles and Boats.* London: Franklin Watts.

Simmelhaig, H. and Spenceley, G.F.R. (1984) *For Australia's Sake.* Melbourne: Nelson.

Taylor, B. (1989) *Science Starters: Bouncing and Bending Light.* London: Franklin Watts.

Taylor, B. (1991) *Science Starters: Air and Flying.* London: Franklin Watts.

# 12  Close reading: functional linguistics as a tool for critical discourse analysis

*J. R. Martin*

## 12.1  Critical discourse analysis

Critical discourse analysis (CDA) is an approach to discourse analysis which focuses on inequality in society and the ways in which texts are used to realize power and ideology. CDA is concerned not only with analysing texts to investigate power, but also with finding ways of redressing inequalities. The leading figures in CDA have involved themselves in issues such as racism, sexism, colonialism and environmentalism (Caldas-Coulthard and Coulthard 1996, Chilton 1985, Fairclough 1995a, Fairclough and Wodak 1997, Lemke 1995, van Dijk 1991, Wodak 1987a, b, Wodak *et al.* 1990). They have also addressed issues in the field of language in education, where questions of inequality and how to redress inequality are always present (Cope and Kalantzis 1993, Fairclough 1992a, Giblett and O'Carroll 1990, New London Group 1996, Walton 1996, Wodak *et al.* 1989).

CDA and systemic functional linguistics (SFL) have been closely associated since the pioneering work of critical linguists at East Anglia (Fowler *et al.* 1979, Fowler 1996). Fairclough (1995a: 6–10) notes that SFL is a congenial theory for CDA because it is multifunctional, well adapted for text analysis and concerned with relating language to social context. Australian theorists have used and adapted SFL to gain a critical perspective on texts in a wide range of registers (e.g. Hasan 1996, Kress 1985/1989, Martin 1986, Melrose 1996, Schirato and Yell 1996, Thibault 1991, Threadgold 1997), including work of special educational significance (Christie 1999, Christie *et al.* 1991, Lee 1996, Martin 1985/1989, 1990).

For many, one of the real strengths of SFL in the context of CDA work is its ability to ground concerns with power and ideology in the detailed analysis of texts as they unfold, clause by clause, in real contexts of language use (including the analysis of multi-modal texts involving pictures and diagrams, e.g. Kress and van Leeuwen 1996, O'Toole 1994). SFL provides critical discourse analysts with a technical language for talking about language – to make it possible to look very closely at meaning, to be explicit and precise in terms that can be shared by others, and to engage in quantitative analysis where this is appropriate (Nesbitt and Plum 1988, Plum and Cowling 1987; cf. Biber 1988).

In this Chapter I'll take the multifunctionality dimension (see Chapter 2) which Fairclough (1995a) finds attractive as an organizing principle for the chapter, and exemplify some of the ways in which SFL enables a critical perspective on discourse which addresses a number of CDA concerns.

## 12.2  Constructing power (ideational meaning)

To begin I'll look at some work by Ruth French, Joan Rothery and Geoff Williams on gender relations in infant and primary school. Ruth, a primary school teacher, was working with two of Australia's key language in education specialists on functional grammar in relation to gender and genre. The text they were working with was *Piggybook*, a picture book and feminist narrative for young readers (Browne 1989).

From the perspective of ideational meaning we are interested in how a text of this kind constructs power (especially gender roles). In the experience of CDA analysts one relevant part of language is TRANSITIVITY; its puporse is to construct processes, the participants involved in them and the circumstances in which they take place. In the English language (Halliday 1994, Matthiessen 1995) the most critical variable has to do with whether or not a process is brought about by an impending agency. When we say, for example, that someone is sitting, or singing, or thinking, or reading, there is an ongoing activity undertaken by someone. But when we say that someone sat the baby up, or sang the baby to sleep, or taught the child to read, we have an activity that is undertaken by someone (sitting, sleeping, reading) and made possible by someone else (who enabled them to sit, sleep, read). Halliday refers to the participant who undertakes an activity as Medium, and the participant who brings about the undertaking as Agent. So, Mediums act or get acted on, and Agents act themselves on Mediums. The causal relation between Agent and Medium is outlined in Figure 12.1.

Clearly this dimension of meaning is central to the analysis of inequality and power in discourse. It allows us to ask questions about who is acting, what kinds of action they undertake, and who or what if anything they act upon. If we consider Mrs Piggott's role in *Piggybook*, clause by clause,[1] we arrive at an analysis such as that outlined in Table 12.1. From this we see that at the beginning of the story Mrs Piggott is very agentive inside the home, acting on domestic things. Then we enter a phase of the story where she stops acting on domestic participants, a role she maintains until the last line of the story where she becomes an Agent again, but this time on something outside not inside the home – the family car.

**Figure 12.1** The relation of Agent to Medium

**Table 12.1** Mrs Piggott's Activity in *Piggybook*

| Agent (Actor acting on things) | Process [Range] (what happens) | Medium (Actor acting or Goal being acted on) | Circumstance (when and where) |
|---|---|---|---|
| | was | his wife | inside the house |
| [Mrs Piggott] | hurry up with | the breakfast | |
| [Mrs Piggott] | hurry up with | the breakfast | |
| Mrs Piggott | washed | all the breakfast . . . | |
| [Mrs Piggott] | made | all the beds | |
| [Mrs Piggott] | vacuumed | all the carpets | |
| | went | [Mrs Piggott] | to work |
| [Mrs Piggott] | hurry up with | the meal | |
| [Mrs Piggott] | hurry up with | the meal | |
| Mrs Piggott | washed | the dishes | |
| [Mrs Piggott] | washed | the clothes | |
| | did the ironing | [Mrs Piggott] | |
| | cooked | [Mrs Piggott] | some more |
| | 's | Mum (Mrs Piggott) | where |
| | was | Mrs Piggott | the . . . day; not there |
| | coming home | Mum (Mrs Piggott) | when |
| | walked in | Mrs Piggott | |
| | come back | [Mrs Piggott] | |
| | stayed | Mrs Piggott | |
| | was happy | Mum (Mrs Piggott) | |
| she (Mrs Piggott) | mended | the car | |

On the other hand, if we consider Mr Piggott and the boys we find a complementary pattern of roles. In the first part of the story they do things and say things, but don't act directly upon anything in the home; and the circumstances of their activities have to do with things outside the home – work and school. Then Mrs Piggott leaves and they have to open the envelope containing her good-bye note. Subsequently they are forced to try (not very successfully) to act on domestic things, after which they more or less give up trying to behave as people and snuffle around like pigs, rooting for scraps on the floor. Once Mrs Piggott returns they turn back into people and act successfully on domestic things while Mrs Piggott mends the car.

**Table 12.2** Mr Piggott and the boy's Activity in *Piggybook*

| Agent (Actor acting on things) | Process [Range] (what happens) | Medium (Actor acting or **Goal being acted on**) | Circumstance (when and where) |
|---|---|---|---|
| | lived | Mr Piggott | with his two sons . . . |
| | called | he (Mr Piggott) | every morning |
| | went off | he (Mr Piggott) | to his . . . job |
| | called | Simon & Patrick | |
| | went off | they (Simon/Patrick) | to their . . . school |
| | left the house | they (Mr/Simon/Patrick) | |
| | called | the boys | every evening |
| | came home | they (the boys) | from their . . . school |
| | called | Mr Piggott | every evening |
| | came home | he (Mr Piggott) | from his . . . job |
| | had eaten | they (Simon/Patrick) | |
| | got home | the boys | one evening . . . |
| | demanded | Mr Piggott | |
| | got home | he (Mr Piggott) | from work |
| Mr Piggott | opened | it (the envelope) | |
| | are pigs | You (Mr/Simon/Patrick) | |
| | shall . . . do what | we (Mr/Simon/Patrick) | |
| | said | Mr Piggott | |
| they (Mr/Simon/Patrick) | had to make | their own meal | |
| they (Mr/Simon/Patrick) | had to make | their . . . breakfast | next morning |
| Mr P, Simon & Patrick | tried to look after | themselves (Mr/boys) | |
| they (Mr/Simon/Patrick) | (never) washed | the dishes | |
| they (Mr/Simon/Patrick) | (never) washed | their clothes | |
| | squealed | the boys | after . . . meal |
| | should know | I (Mr Piggott) | how |
| | grunted | Mr Piggott | |
| | became . . . grumpy | they all (Mr P/boys) | |
| | have to root around | we (Mr P/boys) | |
| [Mr P/boys] | find | some scraps | |
| | snorted | snorted Mr Piggott | |
| | come back | [Mrs Piggott] | |
| | snuffled | they (Mr P/boys) | |
| Mr Piggott | washed | the dishes | |
| Patrick and Simon | made | the beds | |
| | did the ironing | Mr Piggott | |
| | helped | they (Mr P/boys) | with the cooking |
| | enjoyed it (cooking) | they (Mr P/boys) | |

I have glossed over the details of this analysis here (for support in undertaking analysis of this kind see Chapter 2 and Martin *et al.* 1997). But what I
have offered does, I think, indicate something of the detail, precision and
explicitness of a close reading of power in relation to agency and the gendered relations it enacts. Alongside this, the analysis digitalizes the meanings
involved so that they can be counted if one wants to approach questions of
language and in/equality from a quantificational perspective. We can say
just how many times a participant is involved in processes in just what kinds
of ways; once we've analysed enough examples, we can perform statistical
analyses to check the significance of differences between female and male
protagonists and what they act upon, from one stage of the story to another.
Usually, to get enough examples, we have to analyse more than one text.

This brings us to the problem of the social, since when we bring in more texts we want them to be comparable – and comparability has to be stated with respect to a model of the social context in which texts occur. In SFL, social context is modelled as systems of register (field, mode and tenor) and of genre (see Chapter 1). These social systems are seen as realised through language. This means that linguistic analyses such as transitivity (Tables 12.1 and 12.2) can be related to social analyses through the concept of realization. When we say that language realizes register and genre we mean that language construes, is construed by, and over time reconstrues the social. Power in other words is not a fixed variable; it shifts around, as texts unfold (as in text 12.1), as social subjects develop and as communities evolve.

Ruth French and her class were mainly concerned with the way in which grammar construed gender and genre in *Piggybook*. Working together they came up with the following summary of their analyses. The students involved were in Year 6 when this text was negotiated. In Text 12.1 they refer to Mediums acted on by Agents as Goal, and the Agents acting on them as Actors (see Chapter 2).

**Text 12.1. *What we learnt about the grammatical patterns of Piggybook.***

**Beginning**
All the Goals Mrs Piggott did were to do with housework.
   Only Mrs Piggott had Goals. This shows she is the only one doing something TO something else.
   Mr Piggott and the boys only did things for themselves; they did not do work in the home. This is shown by the fact that they didn't have any Goals. They were the only characters that talked. They told Mrs P to hurry up.

**Resolution**
At the end, everyone did an action to something – to benefit the whole family, not just themselves. Everyone had Goals at the end.
   Now the Goals for Mrs Piggott included more than housework.

[*She mended the car.* – displayed as an Actor Process Goal diagram]

The Goals had a big role in structuring the narrative. The pattern of Actors and Goals changes at the end. This makes the Resolution.

The inspiration for critical orientations to literacy teaching of this kind goes back of course to work by critical linguists at East Anglia (see especially Trew's (1979) canonical deconstruction of media discourse in relation to British colonialism in Zimbabwe). For a richer analysis of social actors than those illustrated above see van Leeuwen (1996). Poynton (1985) addresses gender relations from the perspective of SFL; her work is nicely complemented from the perspective of critical theory by Cranny-Francis (1990, 1992) (see also Cameron 1990, 1992, Coates 1996, Kothoff and Wodak 1997, West *et al.* 1997, Wodak and Schulz 1986). Kress (1996)

suggests that deconstructive activities such as those illustrated should lead
to productive activities which renovate gender relations if CDA is to fulfil
its ambition of redressing inequalities (see also Janks and Ivanič 1992 on
emancipatory discourse). This challenge is taken up in part in an educational context by Cranny-Francis (1993) and Lee (1996); see also Walton
(1996) for a critical review of critical social literacy programs and the
research that informs them.

## 12.3  Enacting power (interpersonal meaning)

In this section, I'll draw on some work I did with one of Australia's leading cultural theorists, Anne Cranny-Francis, when we were members of
the Newtown Semiotic Circle (during the time it met in Sydney in the late
1980s and early 1990s to exchange ideas across the frontiers of SFL and
critical theory). Anne and I were working on popular culture at the time,
looking in particular at the ways in which popular music could be
deployed to challenge power (Cranny-Francis 1994, Cranny-Francis and
Martin 1991). One of the multimodal texts we looked at in some detail
was U2's 'Sunday Bloody Sunday', a song about the troubles in Ireland.
The group performed the song for several years in the 1980s (up to their
1988 Rattle & Hum tour); ever controversial, it was banned by Mrs
Thatcher in Northern Ireland, and the group apparently wore out their
welcome in a number of pubs in the south. During one of their final per-
formances of the song, included on their Rattle & Hum tour video collection, Bono phased the following rap (Text 12.2) into the song; as Bono
points out in the introduction to the performance on the video, the band
was in a state of shock because of an IRA bomb blast in Enniskillen which
had killed eleven people and injured several others earlier that day.

### Text 12.2

I'm going to tell you something. I've had enough of Irish Americans who
haven't been back to their country in 20 or 30 years, come up to me and talk
about the resistance, the revolution back home, and the glory of the revolution, and the glory of dying for the revolution. Fuck the revolution! They don't
talk about the glory of killing for the revolution. What's the glory in taking a
man from his bed and gunning him down in front of his wife and children?
Where's the glory in that? Where's the glory in bombing a Remembrance Day
parade of old age pensioners, their medals taken out and polished up for the
day. Where's the glory in that? To leave them dying or crippled for life or dead
under the rubble of the revolution that the majority of the people in my country don't want. No more. Say 'No more.' No more. – No more. No more. – No
more. . . .

From the perspective of interpersonal meaning we are interested in how a
text of this kind enacts power. How does it position some 50,000 American fans in the debate over Ireland, and Britain's ongoing control of the

northern counties? The most relevant part of English clause grammar in this case is MOOD (see Chapter 2). Its purpose is to position speakers in relation to listeners as stating, questioning, commanding or exclaiming. The four choruses of 'Sunday Bloody Sunday' can be used to illustrate these functions, since each deploys a different mood and so positions listeners to receive information, to provide information, to perform a service or to empathize with the feeling:

**typical Statements** (declaratives): include a Subject and Finite, with the Subject coming before the Finite [Subject *we*, Finite *can* below]

   *We can* be as one tonight.

**typical Questions** (interrogatives): include a Subject and a Finite, usually with the Finite coming before the Subject, and a Wh phrase if asking for information [Subject *we*, Finite *can*, Wh *how long* below]

   *How long must we* sing this song?

**typical Commands** (imperatives): do not have a Subject or Finite

   Wipe your tears away.

**typical Exclamations** (minor): don't have a Subject or Finite (or any verb):

   Sunday, bloody Sunday.

In addition there is the possibility of a non-finite clause, which has a verb, but not one which is negotiable (see Chapter 2). Non-finite clauses, in other words, are clauses which might have been part of the argument, but have been back-grounded, to take them out of the repartee. To see how this works, consider Text 12.3 from Monty Python's first movie (text from Martin 1992).

**Text 12.3  Monty Python – argument**

I came here for a good argument.
No, you didn't. You came here for an argument.
Well, an argument isn't just contradiction.
It can be.
No it can't. An argument is a connected series of statements intended to establish a proposition.
No it isn't.
Yes it is . . .

Note how the Subject and Finite elements of clause structure are used to sustain three volleys of repartee:

1. I came . . . . – No, you didn't. . . .
2. an argument isn't . . . – it can be. – No it can't.
3. An argument is . . . – No it isn't. – Yes it is.

Non-finite clauses simply remove this dialogic potential by eliminating the meaning which makes a clause negotiable – its finiteness. There are two types of non-finite clause: the realis or imperfective, realised by the -ing form of the verb, and the irrealis or perfective, realised by the infinitive (with to). Note how the responses below negotiate the meaning of the preceding finite clause, not the non-finite one (even though the non-finite clause, small caps, is closer).

It was always controversial, SINGING THIS SONG.
– Was it?

They have decided NOT TO SING THE SONG ANY MORE.
– Have they?

On the basis of these distinctions we can analyse the way in which Bono positions and repositions his audience in his rap (Subject and Finite underlined throughout). He begins with declarative mood, giving information:

[declarative]
I'm going to tell you something.
I've had enough of Irish Americans who haven't been back to their country in 20 or 30 years, [who] come up to me and [who] talk about the resistance, the revolution back home, and the glory of the revolution, and the glory of dying for the revolution.

He then switches to imperative, to dismiss the way in which he feels some Irish Americans glorify the revolution:

[imperative]
Fuck the revolution!

This is followed by a declarative clause, giving information about the acts of killing the revolution has involved:

[declarative]
They don't talk about the glory of killing for the revolution.

This is followed in turn by four interrogative clauses which ask the audience for information about the existence or location of glory in two kinds of killing. The information the audience has been positioned to provide is of course impossible to provide, since glory is not a value we naturally associate with killing a father in front of his family or bombing elderly war veterans. For this reason Bono's four queries would be referred to in traditional terms as 'rhetorical questions' and would be heard not as asking for information but as giving the information[2] that glory is not to be associated with such activity.

[wh interrogative]
What's the glory in taking a man from his bed and gunning him down in front of his wife and children?
Where's the glory in that?
Where's the glory in bombing a Remembrance Day parade of old age pensioners, their medals taken out and polished up for the day.
Where's the glory in that?

Bono continues with a non-finite clause[3], which includes as an embedding the controversial declaration that the majority of people in Ireland don't want the revolution:

[non-finite]
To leave them dying or crippled for life or dead under the rubble of the revolution that the majority of the people in my country don't want.

This non-finite clause, itself non-negotiable, contains within it a deeply embedded clause qualifying *the revolution* which itself qualifies *the rubble* which complements the preposition *under* in a circumstance of location in an agentive relational clause. This embedded clause (*that the majority of the people in my country don't want*) contains a proposition that in a sense clinches Bono's argument – since if it is the case that Irish people don't actually want a revolution, then Irish-Americans ought not to be supporting one (for non-finiteness and embedding, see Chapter 2) I'm not acquainted with the poll on which this proposition is ultimately based or how controversial Bono's reading of that poll might turn out to be. But rhetorically, the proposition has been placed in a next-to-unassailable position, since embedded clauses, although finite, are not really arguable,[4] and the clause into which it is so deeply embedded has no finiteness to negotiate.

At this point Bono uses a minor clause to construct his anguished plea for an end to the carnage:

[minor; Command]
No more.

And follows with an imperative instructing the audience to join him in his plea:

[imperative]
**Say** 'No more.'

They take up the invitation, with Bono leading the chant:

[minor; Initiation^Response]
No more.
– No more.

[minor; Initiation^Response]
No more.
– No more. . . .

This is a very compelling piece of rhetoric. It sends shivers up and down my spine each time I watch it on the video, and must have been absolutely electrifying live. The music of the song is very much backgrounded throughout the rap. The lighting is subdued, with a spotlight on Bono who has moved away from the rest of the band to the left of the stage. It is the wording, voice quality and body language that take advantage of his charismatic speaking position in front of an audience of adoring fans to drive the message home.

What seems crucial to this interpersonal enactment of Bono's power is not just the number or type of mood selections he makes, but the manner in which he moves from one selection to the next (alongside the ideational meanings he positions listeners to interact about). His goal is to align the audience with his position, a significant objective given the amount of funding for the IRA donated by Irish expatriates in America. He pursues this by first tabling a proposition about the glory of the revolution, then dismissing it (*Fuck the revolution*), then subverting it (*Where's the glory . . .*), then undermining it (*the revolution that the majority of the people in my country don't want*), then pleading for an end to the violence (*No more*), and closes by aligning the audience to plead with him, chanting in response to his cue. This positioning harmonizes with the lyrics of the song proper, in which Bono refuses violence and calls for a Christian resolution to the troubles (*The real battle's yet begun, to claim the victory Jesus won, on Sunday bloody Sunday*) without involving an appeal to Christianity, which in the context of rock music is likely to alienate as many listeners as it aligns.

In this section we've looked at one of the ways in which interpersonal meaning is used to enact power, and drawn attention to the importance of looking closely at the way in which meanings unfold in a text. The contingency of one choice in relation to the next is critical to understanding the way in which texts position readers and listeners. It's important to remember in research that the rhetoric of this contingent unfolding is lost once we start counting choices, aggregating them, doing statistics and looking for global patterns across texts and their speakers.

It's also important to note that enacting power is not necessarily a bad thing. Speaking for myself, I don't begrudge Bono taking advantage of his role as a performer to argue against violence. To my mind, popular music gives a very public voice to people from a range of marginal positions who might not otherwise be heard. When Billie Holiday recorded 'Strange Fruit' in 1939 it was banned from American radio, since the United States was not ready for a song about lynching (especially one that used such a disturbing metaphor for the bodies of lynched African Americans hanging dead in trees). But the record was released and the song performed. It still resonates throughout the civil rights movement in America and elsewhere in the world. Her power to enact; what haunting courage, what incisive verve! The price she paid . . .

For work on other interpersonal systems in relation to power, see Martin (1995b) (on modality) and Martin (1999b) (on evaluative language). Related work on interpersonal meaning from a functional perspective is found in Kress (1985) and Poynton (1985). From the perspective of CDA, Wodak (1996) looks at interaction in doctor/patient consultations, school committee meetings and therapeutic communication; Coulthard (1996) considers police interviews. Eggins and Slade (1997) provide a general SFL framework for looking at conversation, interpreted locally as interaction and globally as genre.

## 12.4  Naturalizing power (textual meaning)

Finally, let's look at some research reported in Chapter 10 by Mary Macken-Horarik and Joan Rothery, who worked innovatively for several years with the New South Wales Disadvantaged Schools Program. Mary and Joan were investigating the discourse of secondary school English, looking at narrative genres, and at the critical responses students were expected to write on examinations (Macken-Horarik and Rothery 1991, Rothery 1994, Macken-Horarik 1996). At one end of the marking scale for responses they found texts like 10.1, which respond emotionally to the short narrative under consideration; at the other end of the scale they found texts like text 10.2, which retell the story as an abstract psycho-narrative in which the protagonist wrestles with morality (in the case of this response, the ethical issue has to do with facing reality and avoiding the fantasy world of TV).

From the perspective of textual meaning we are interested in how texts naturalize power by weaving together meanings into an apparently seamless whole in order to position readers and listeners in particular ways. Essentially this has to do with the way in which the writers texture ideational and interpersonal meaning – the way they phase these strands together to form a coherent response. Texts 10.1 and 10.2 are both coherent in this respect; but they establish complementary reading positions, which examiners may treat in different ways.

Let's explore this complementarity from the perspective of Theme and

New as outlined by Halliday for the English clause (see Chapter 2). In English, Theme is realized through first position. New is realized through a major pitch movement on what is known as the tonic syllable, and tends to be realised clause finally. We can simplify the analysis for writing by looking at the information in first and final position. Theme realizes a text's method of development – the angle or perspective the text takes up with respect to the information it constructs. New realizes a text's point – it constructs an expanding pool of information as the subject matter of a text.

In Text 10.1, the main patterns of Theme selection have to do with the student writer and the text the student is responding to:

Method of development of Themes (in finite, ranking, non-branched clauses)

| student critic: |
|---|
| I<br>I<br>I<br>I |

| the text: |
|---|
| it (the passage)<br>The way 'Click' is written by itself in a sentence and in capital letters<br>this (the way the mood of the characters is portrayed so clearly)<br>the ending |

| quotations from the text: |
|---|
| 'like a padlock snapping open'<br>'Sounded through the room'<br>it ('sounded through the room') |

etc.
    The author

As far as New is concerned, the overwhelming pattern has to do with the student's emotional response to the text, with the author's technique as a supporting motif:

Point of News (in ranking clauses):

| emotional response: |
|---|
| eerie and isolated<br>so lonely |

so afraid
empty
a depressing ending that made me feel scared and afraid
the emptiness
another example of how the author creates the feeling of
isolation . . . displayed
hollow and dead
(fear) in your mind
(enjoyed) . . . immensely

| author's technique: |
| --- |

this way ( . . . like a padlock snapping open)
the effect that she wanted
the exact sound it [= CLICK] makes
the way it sounded through the room

| technique evaluation: |
| --- |

so effective
so clearly
very clear and well written

| text: |
| --- |

the ending
the passage

Overall, the most general pattern is for the student and the narrative to be positioned as Theme in relation to emotional response as New.

In Text 10.2, on the other hand, the overwhelming choice for Theme is the narrative's main protagonist, Jenny, with the text and the TV switch as minor motifs:

Method of development (Unmarked Themes in ranking clauses)

| Jenny: |
| --- |

she
she
because her parents and herself
they
Jenny
she

> her hiding place
> Jenny
> and Jenny
> when she
> Jenny's reaction
> Jenny
> when she

the text:

> Click by Judith Stamper
> Click
> The conclusion 'Click ... television switch sounded ... the room ... a padlock snapping open'

the switch:

> the television switch
> [the padlock]
> [and it's snap]

TV world:
> that the world of television
> the make believe world

etc.
> this whole experience; the dead girl's face; the shock of reality
> the girl
> because there

As far as patterns of New are concerned, the dominant pattern has to do with the morality of the narrative (fantasy vs reality), with the nature of Jenny's family relations and the accident as supporting motifs.

Point (News in ranking clauses)

fantasy vs reality:

> a young girl ... run away from reality and ... unhappiness and death ... confronted her ...
> the fantasy, make-believe world of television
> back into reality
> to 'switch the channel', to escape; to hide from reality
> protection from reality
> too fake
> realised
> the awakening of reality in that mind
> a realisation that it couldn't run away

| family problems: |
| --- |

with her family life
lonely
apart
a very distant relationship
recognised this (= having a very distant relationship)
hide from it (= the distant relationship)

| accident: |
| --- |

outside
the accident
already dead
into the dead girl's face
back inside

etc:
a ... didactic short story, the moral ... the ending ... story, and ...
   title conveys to ... reader
symbolic
Jenny
Jenny's mind
a television commercial on
like a padlock snapping open

Overall, the most general pattern is for the story's protagonist to be positioned as Theme in relation to ethical response as New.

In sum then, the reading position naturalized by Text 10.1 would be filled by an examiner interested in how the student reacted emotionally to the story (since the angle on the story is the student and the point is her feelings). The reading position naturalized by Text 10.2, on the other hand, would be taken up by an examiner looking for the student's understanding of the moral of the tale (since the angle on the story is its heroine and the point is how to live – fantasy vs reality). In New South Wales there are certainly teachers who read both texts compliantly outside of the context of public examination. But as Mary's and Joan's research revealed, under examination conditions Text 10.1 is read resistantly, and given the lowest possible grade (E−), whereas Text 10.2 is read compliantly, and celebrated as an outstanding response (A+). In teaching and in the syllabus, both texts are referred to as involving a 'personal response'. In the absence of explicit teaching about which kind of reading position to naturalize in exams, it's up to the students to figure out the difference and recognize which contexts place value on one or the other. In other words the secondary English curriculum is a canonical hidden curriculum, which deploys what Bernstein (e.g. 1975) refers to as an invisible pedagogy to enfranchise certain groups of students and disenfranchise others (Chouliarki 1997/1998, Christie 1999).

From these examples we can see that power is a context-specific variable. What works in one situation may not work in another, and inequality has as much to do with knowing when to say something as learning how to say it. At the same time, it's important to remember that if we are interested in redressing inequality, we have to focus attention on the way in which texts can be designed to align readers and listeners; otherwise we don't have a model of discourse which we can use to renovate our social world.[5] The flow of meanings in a text naturalizes a reading position for that text, a position which speakers and writers design because of the ways in which they want to act on others.

Not all texts naturalize a single position; sometimes voices[6] in a text contest with one another. One good example of a seamful text of this kind is the following exchange (Text 12.5) between Frank and Rita in the movie *Educating Rita* (Cranny-Francis and Martin 1994) in which teacher and student clash over the value of Frank's poetry (evaluation underlined):

**Text 12.4  From the film *Educating Rita* – Frankenstein scene, abridged**

R:  . . . This is <u>brilliant</u>. You have got to start writing again, Frank. It is <u>brilliant.</u> It's it it's <u>witty</u>; it's <u>profound, full of style</u>.

F:  Oh tell me again, and again.

R:  No, it is, Frank. It's not just me that thinks so. Me and Trish sat up and read them last night and she agrees with me. Why did you stop? Why did you stop working when you can produce work like this? Uh, now what did Trish say? 'It's <u>more resonant than purely contemporary poetry</u>. It has in it, like, it has in it a <u>direct line through to the 19th century traditions of em like wit and classical allusion</u>.

F:  Oh, that's marvellous, Rita. It's fortunate I never gave this to you earlier. Just think if you'd have seen this when you first came here.

R:  Oh, I would never have understood it.

F:  You would have thrown it across the room and dismissed it as <u>total shit</u>, wouldn't you?

R:  I know. But, I mean, I could never have understood it then. I wouldn't have been able to, you know, recognise or understand <u>the allusions</u>.

. . .

F:  <u>This clever pyrotechnical pile of self-conscious allusion is worthless, talentless shit</u>. There is <u>more poetry in in the telephone directory and probably more insight</u>. However, this has <u>one advantage over the telephone directory</u>. It is <u>easier to rip</u>. It's <u>pretentious, characterless and without style</u>.

R:  It's not.

. . .

Here we find a different pattern of information again to that in Texts 10.1 and 10.2. In Text 12.4 Frank's poetry is a predominant choice for Theme, and choices for New have to do with its value. Rita values the work highly:

... This is *brilliant*.
It is *brilliant*.
It's it it's *witty*;
it's *profound, full of style*.
'It's *more resonant than purely contemporary poetry*.
It has in it, like, it has in it *a direct line through to the nineteenth century traditions of em like wit and classical allusion*.
I wouldn't have been able to, you know, recognise or understand *the allusions*.

Frank, does not agree:

and dismissed it as *total shit*, wouldn't you?
*This clever pyrotechnical pile of self-conscious allusion* is *worthless, talentless shit*.
There is *more poetry in in the telephone directory and probably more insight*.
However, this has *one advantage over the telephone directory*.
It is *easier to rip*.
It's *pretentious, characterless and without style*.

This kind of response to text was not entirely absent[7] in Text 10.1:

This is what makes the passage so effective
– the way the mood of the characters is portrayed so clearly.
the ending was very clear and well written.

But there it was overwhelmed by emotion; in Text 12.4 it is the aesthetic value of the poetry which is at stake.

The disagreement in Text 12.4 seems more like the argument the client thought he'd paid for in the Monty Python skit exemplified (Section 12.3). But in the film it soon degenerates into volleys of name calling as Frank and Rita hurl insults at one another. Difference explodes into verbal violence of a deeply hurtful order:

**Text 12.5** continued ...

R: Yeah, Yeah. Well, eh, I'll tell you what you can't bear, Mr Self-pity and Piss-artist. What you can't bear is that I'm educated now. I've got what you have and you don't like it. I mean, good god, I don't need you. I've got a room full of books. I know what wine to buy, what clothes to wear, what plays to see, or papers and books to read and I can do it without you.

F: Is that all you wanted? Have you come all this way for so very very little.

R: Oh yeah, it's little to you, Frank, who squanders every opportunity and mocks and takes it all for granted.

F: Found a culture have you, Rita? Found a better song to sing. No, you found a different song to sing and on your lips it is shrill and hollow and tedious. Ah Rita, Rita.

R: Oh ho ho ho, Rita. Nobody calls me Rita but you. I dropped that pretentious crap as soon as I saw it for what it was. Rita. Nobody calls me Rita.

F: What is it now then, eh? Emily or Charlotte or Jane or Virginia?

As Texts 10.1 and 12.4 exemplify, the consequences of resisting the reading position being naturalized by the person you are interacting with can
be severe: for the person you are resisting (the examination candidate in
Text 10.1) or for the person resisting you (the stinging repartee in Text
12.4). One of the key tasks in applied linguistics research has to be that of
making understandings available as to the consequences of assuming one
reading position or another. For example, in the Australian secondary
English curriculum you have to know the differences among a 'personal'
response, Leavisite criticism and New Criticism (Belsey 1980). As far as
textual meaning is concerned the key differences in these responses are
outlined in Table 12.3.

**Table 12.3** Information flow in relation to types of criticism

| response type: | Theme | New |
| --- | --- | --- |
| Personal | I (= writer) | emotion [AFFECT] |
| Leavisite | hero | ethics [JUDGEMENT] |
| New Criticism | text | aesthetics [APPRECIATION] |

In general terms, personal responses takes the writer as point of departure and the writer's emotional response as news; Leavisite response takes
the hero of the story as point of departure and the ethics they engage
with as news; New Criticism takes the text as point of departure and the
aesthetic value placed on it as news. In New South Wales, a personal
response suits many English teachers in classrooms, but for purposes of
public examination students would be well advised to write a Leavisite
response for narrative and a New Critical response for poetry.

For helpful discussions of the English curriculum placed under the
microscope here, see Hunter (1994) and Cranny-Francis (1996). Detailed
work on Theme across a range of registers is found in Ghadessy (1995);
for fairly technical discussions of textual meaning see Halliday and Hasan
(1976) and Martin (1992). Alternatives to disenfranchising pedagogy are
outlined in Christie (1999), Cope and Kalantzis (1993), New London
Group (1996) and Martin (1999). For related CDA work on texture in
relation to reading position, see Fairclough (1996) on the technologiza-
tion of discourse and Fairclough (1995b) and Wodak (1996) on media
discourse.

## 12.5  Dissembling power: a note on nominalization (ideational metaphor)

One of the regions of analysis where CDA and SFL have contributed most
fruitfully to each other has been the interpretation of nominalization,

involving what Halliday (1985) calls ideational metaphor (Chapter 2). Halliday's work in this area begins with the notion of grammar and semantics in what he calls a 'natural' relation with each other.

**Text 12.5  Took the Children Away, by Archie Roach**

One dark day on Framingham
Came and didn't give a damn
My mother cried go get their dad
He came running fighting mad
Mother's tears were falling down
Dad shaped up he stood his ground
He said you touch my kids and you fight me
And they took us from our family
Took us away
They took us away
Snatched from our mother's breast
Said this was for the best
Took us away

In Text 12.5 (Roach 1990), meanings map onto wordings directly.[8]

Participants come out as nouns (*Framingham, My mother, their dad, He, Mother's tears, Dad, he, He, you, my kids, you, me, they, us, our family, us, They, us, our mother's breast, us*).

Processes come out as verbs (*Came, cried, go get, came running, were falling, shaped up, stood, said, touch, fight, took, Took, took, Snatched, Said, was, Took*).

Qualities come out as adjectives (*mad*). And logical relations come out as conjunctions (*and, and, and*).

This kind of direct mapping of meanings onto wordings is associated by Halliday (e.g. 1985) with spoken language, and is representative of the language used by Aboriginal people to recount their experience as children of being taken from their families by government officials to be raised in institutions and foster homes, isolated from their native language and culture. As I revise this paper in June 1999, the Australian government continues to refuse to apologise to Aboriginal people for this shameful policy. The language of their refusals is very different from that used by Archie Roach to document the genocide. Here's an example (from Manne 1998: 55).

**Text 12.6**

The Prime Minister acknowledges and thanks you for your support for his personal apology to indigenous people affected by past practices of separating indigenous children from their families. However, the government does not support an official national apology. Such an apology could imply that present generations are in some way responsible and accountable for the actions of earlier generations, actions that were sanctioned by the laws of the time, and that were believed to be in the best interests of the children concerned. [Senator Herron writing on behalf of the Prime Minister, John Howard, to Father Brennan in late 1997]

In language of this kind the mapping of meaning onto wording is no longer direct. Processes are regularly realized as nominal groups instead of verbs, as if they were things, not actions: *your support, his personal apology, past practices of separating . . ., an official national apology, an apology, the actions, actions*. One effect of this is that logical relations are realized not by conjunctions connecting clauses but by prepositions and verbs connecting nominalised actions (e.g. *for your support, for his personal apology, for the action; affected by past practices, such an apology could imply*). The result is a radical retexturing of what in typical spoken language would have sounded rather different. Here's a version of what Text 12.6 might have sounded like without this kind of indirect mapping of semantics and grammar:

**Text 12.6A**

The Prime Minister received your message and he thanks you because you supported him because he apologised personally to indigenous people because government officials took their children away from them. But the government will not apologise officially on behalf of the nation, because if it does, then people might argue that indigenous people can blame present generations and make them explain why government officials took their children away; but they took them away because the laws of the time approved and allowed them to take them away, and the government thought the children would benefit more if the officials took them away than if they left them with their families.

Note that at certain points in our translation we have had to fill in material that was not made explicit in Senator Herron's reply: Who was it that took the children away? (government officials); Who might hold current generations responsible? (indigenous people). This highlights the way in which nominalized language allows writers to manipulate agency. In Text 12.6A there are nine Agents, all but one of them people acting on other people (Agents underlined below):

because <u>you</u> supported him
because <u>government officials</u> took their children away from them.
that <u>indigenous people</u> can blame present generations
and <u>indigenous people</u> make them explain
why <u>government officials</u> took their children away;
but <u>they</u> took them away
and <u>the laws of the time</u> allowed them to take them away,
if <u>the officials</u> took them away
than if <u>they</u> left them with their families.

In Text 12.6 on the other hand there are only four Agents, none of them specific individuals (Agents <u>underlined</u> below):

> . . . affected <u>by past practices of separating indigenous children from their families</u>.
> <u>the government</u> does not support . . .
> <u>Such an apology</u> could imply . . .
> . . . were sanctioned <u>by the laws of the time</u>

Alongside this issue of manipulating agency, nominalized language also enables writers to reframe arguments in their own terms. In Text 12.6A for example, there are eighteen ranking clauses to argue with; the Mood elements of these clauses (Subject and Finite) are listed below:

| *Subject Finite* | |
|---|---|
| The Prime Minister received . . . | did he? |
| and he thanks . . . | does he? |
| because you supported . . . | did I? |
| because he apologised . . . | did he? |
| because government officials took . . . | did they? |
| But the government will not . . . | won't they? |
| because if it does . . . | might it? |
| then people might argue . . . | might they? |
| that indigenous people can blame . . . | could they? |
| and indigenous people make . . . | would they? |
| why government officials took . . . | did they? |
| but they took . . . | did they? |
| because the laws of the time approved . . . | did they? |
| and the laws of the time allowed . . . | did they? |
| and the government thought . . . | did they? |
| the children would . . . | would they? |
| if the officials took . . . | did they? |
| than if they left . . . | did they? |

In Text 12.6 on the other hand there are only four ranking clauses[9] to dispute. The first two are in effect performatives (acknowledging and thanking), so there is nothing to challenge. This leaves two clauses, one having to do with the government not supporting an apology and the other with what such an apology could imply:

| *Subject Finite* | |
|---|---|
| The Prime Minister acknowledges . . . | does he? |
| and (he) thanks . . . | does he? |
| However, the government does not . . . | doesn't it? |
| Such an apology could . . . | could it? |

This shifts the debate away from the facts of the matter (who did what to who and who will hold who accountable as in Text 12.6A) and over to the abstract legal niceties of whether or not an apology will lead to claims for compensation, which is what the government is really worried about. At this point in Australian history, leadership means not having to say you're sorry.

Re-reading early work by critical linguists (e.g. Trew 1979) one has the impression that nominalization is treated as a bad thing because it distorts reality. Contemporary critical theory would probably prefer to argue that although Archie Roach and Senator Herron are very differently positioned in this debate, both use language to construct agency and arguability in terms that contest power. Halliday's work on ideational metaphor provides an ideal lens for unpicking the texture of discourse in highly charged contexts like that of the stolen generations in Australia or the troubles in Ireland (cf. Bono's use of nominalisation in Text 12.3). This lens can also be applied to the somewhat less sensational struggle over the English curriculum outlined for Texts 10.1 and 10.2. (Note the degree of nominalisation involved in writing *Click is about a young girl who has run away from reality and its unhappiness and death that it confronted her with.*) For recent work on 'nominalized' texture, see especially Christie and Martin 1997, Halliday and Martin 1993, Martin and Veel 1998.

### 12.6 Integration

Space precludes an illustration of my point here, but in closing I would like to emphasize the need for the integration of analyses in critically oriented research. Halliday's metafunctions are the most powerful technology we have for factoring out the complementary meanings of a text and relating them systematically to their social context. But just as a functional grammar is a resource for reconciling ideational, interpersonal and textual meanings in the clause, so our theory of discourse has to address the integration of different kinds of meaning in text. Beyond this, we have to consider the relation of language to other systems of meaning (e.g. music, image, kinesics) and interpret texts across a range of cooperating semiotic modalities. I suspect that genre theory will continue to have a key role to play in theorizing the integration of meanings, across modalities (see Christie and Martin 1997, Martin and Veel 1998).

I would also stress the need for better descriptions of social context to guide and motivate the linguistic analyses we undertake. These will prove most useful where context is modelled as a social semiotic (after Halliday 1978) – that is, as a system of meanings. This has been the project of Sydney-based systemic linguists now for more than a generation (e.g. Eggins and Slade 1997, Fries and Gregory 1995, Hasan and Williams 1996, Martin 1992, 1999a, Poynton 1985, Ventola 1987); it involves treating context as an inter-discursive resource of social actions. As this project unfolds, the precise relation of particular linguistic choices to social parameters will become increasingly clear – we'll have both a semiotic theory of the social and a social theory of language to work with. It is such a functional linguistic perspective on intertextuality that this book invites researchers to help construe.

Finally I'd like to encourage researchers to focus more attention on emancipatory discourse, which Janks and Ivanič (1992: 305) describe as 'using language, along with other aspects of social practice, in a way which works towards greater freedom and respect for all people, including ourselves'. For example, as I write, in Australia one burning issue has to do with land rights for Aboriginal people; another relates to the generations of Aboriginal children taken from their families – the 'stolen generations' (Section 12.5). I don't think we can participate productively as critical linguists in these debates without considering more carefully the discourses that other disenfranchised groups have used to contest practices which disempower them. This will allow us to understand how changes have been achieved and to take heart from the achievements of others. We have to spend less time looking at discourses which oppress and more time looking at discourses which challenge, subvert, renovate and liberate – and celebrate those discourses as enthusiastically as we can. Otherwise our analysis is too negative and too depressing. We need some celebratory discourse analysis alongside our critique!

## Notes

1. In Table 1, the Process column includes Halliday's Range function – nominal expressions which function as expansions of the process rather than as distinct affected or effected participants

2. Technically speaking, what we have here are interpersonal metaphors of mood (Halliday 1985 and Chapter 2) – statements realized as interrogatives rather than declaratives (examples of what are referred to as 'indirect speech acts' in speech act theory).

3. It is tempting to read this clause as a continuation of the previous sequence, with *Where's the glory* implied. But in that case, it should be imperfective (*in leaving . . .*), not perfective (*to leave*).

4. Note that the tag and elliptical response in an exchange such as *They support a revolution that the majority of the people in my country don't want, don't they? – Do they?*, it's the main clause, not the embedded clause which is negotiable.

5. I accept of course that social subjects make different readings of texts (tactical, resistant or compliant) depending on their reading position; but I insist on the notion that text can naturalize a reading position – since, without this notion, agency (our ability to act on the social) is effaced and without agency we cannot challenge power.

6. I'm concerned here with contesting voices, which I've referred to elsewhere as contratextuality (Cranny-Francis and Martin 1991), not simply with heteroglossia.

7. Following Bakhtin, some theorists would thus refer to the play of critical voices in Text 10.1 as involving dialogism (or heteroglossia, after Kristeva); others might even refer to Text 10.1 as a mixed genre on such grounds. I wouldn't myself use the term genre in this way, but have no objection in substance as

long as room is made for the notion of a text naturalizing a reading position with one or another voice, or genre, foregrounded by the global trajectory of meanings in the text.

8. There are in fact three exceptions to this in this stanza of the song: *give a damn* (process as verb + noun), *fighting mad* (process as intensifier) and arguably *for the best* (quality as head of a nominal group). Note that in each case, however, the indirect mappings are 'fossilised' in lexicalized phrases.

9. The clause following *imply* is taken as an embedded fact, not a projection, in this analysis: *Such an apology could imply [[that present generations are in some way responsible and accountable for the actions of earlier generations, actions that were sanctioned by the laws of the time, and that were believed to be in the best interests of the children concerned]].*

## References

Beaugrande, R. de (1997) Society, education, linguistics and language: inclusion and exclusion in theory and practice. *Linguistics and Education*, 9(2): 99–158.

Beaugrande, R. de (in press) Performative speech acts in linguistic theory: the programme of Noam Chomsky. *Journal of Pragmatics*.

Belsey, C. (1980) *Critical Practice*. London: Methuen

Bernstein, B. (1975) *Class, Codes and Control Vol. 3: Towards a Theory of Educational Transmissions*. London: Routledge & Kegan Paul.

Bernstein, B. (1990) *The Structuring of Pedagogic Discourse: Class, Codes and Control, Vol. 4*. London: Routledge.

Bernstein, B. (1996) *Pedagogy, Symbolic Control and Identity: Theory, Research, Critique*. London: Taylor & Francis.

Biber, D. (1988) *Variation Across Speech and Writing*. Cambridge: Cambridge University Press.

Browne, A. (1989) *Piggybook*. London: Little Mammoth.

Caldas-Coulthard, C. and M. Coulthard (1996) Preface. In Caldas-Coulthard and Coulthard, xi–xii.

Caldas-Coulthard, C. and M. Coulthard (eds) (1996) *Text and Practices: Readings in Critical Discourse Analysis*. London: Routledge.

Callow, J. (1996) *The Action Pack: Environment (Activities for Teaching Factual Writing)*. Sydney: Metropolitan East DSP (Language and Social Power Project).

Cameron, D. (ed.) (1990) *The Feminist Critique of Language: A Reader*. London: Routledge.

Cameron, D. (1992) *Feminism and Linguistic Theory*. London: McMillan.

Carter, R. (1996) Politics and knowledge about language: the LINC project. In Hasan and Williams, 1–28.

Chilton, P. (1985) *Language and the Nuclear Arms Debate*. London: Pinter.

Chouliarki, L. (1997) Regulation in 'progressivist' pedagogic discourse: individualised teacher-pupil talk. In E. R. Pedro (ed.) *Proceedings of First International Conference on Discourse Analysis*. Lisbon: Colibri/Portuguese Linguistics Association, 47–72. *Discourse and Society*, (1998) 9(1): 5–32.

Christie, F. (ed.) (1999) *Pedagogy and the Shaping of Consciousness: Linguistic and Social Processes*. London: Cassell.

Christie, F., B. Devlin, P. Freebody, A. Luke, J. R. Martin, T. Threadgold and C. Walton (1991) *Teaching English Literacy: A Project of National Significance on the Preservice Preparation of Teachers for Teaching English Literacy*. Vols 1–3. Canberra:

Department of Employment, Education and Training; Darwin: Centre for Studies of Language in Education, Northern Territory University.

Christie, F. and J. R. Martin (eds) (1997) *Genres and Institutions: Social Processes in the Workplace and School*. London: Cassell.

Coates, J. (1996) *Women's Talk*. Oxford: Blackwell.

Coates, J. and D. Cameron (eds) (1988) *Women in Their Speech Communities: New Perspectives on Language and Sex*. London: Longman.

Cope, W. and M. Kalantzis (eds) (1993) *The Powers of Literacy: A Genre Approach to Teaching Literacy*. London: Falmer.

Coulthard, M. (1996) The official version: audience manipulation in police records of interviews with suspects, 166–78.

Cranny-Francis, A. (1990) *Feminist Fiction: Feminist Uses of Generic Fiction*. Cambridge: Polity Press.

Cranny-Francis, A. (1992) *Engendered Fictions: Analysing Gender in the Production and Reception of Texts*. Sydney: New South Wales University Press.

Cranny-Francis, A. (1993) Gender and genre: feminist subversion of genre fiction and its implications for critical literacy. In Cope and Kalantzis, 90–115.

Cranny-Francis, A. (1994) *Popular Culture*. Geelong, Vic.; Deakin University Press.

Cranny-Francis, A. (1995) *The Body in the Text*. Melbourne: Melbourne University Press.

Cranny-Francis, A. (1996) Technology and/or weapon: the discipline of reading in the secondary English classroom. In Hasan and Williams, 172–90.

Cranny-Francis, A. and J. R. Martin (1991) Contratextuality: the poetics of subversion. In F. Christie (ed.), *Literacy in Social Processes: Papers from the Inaugural Australian Systemic Linguistics Conference, Deakin University, January 1990*. Darwin: Centre for Studies in Language in Education, Northern Territory University, 286–344.

Cranny-Francis, A. and J. R. Martin (1993) Making new meanings: literary and linguistic perspectives on the function of genre in textual practice. *English in Australia*, 105: 30–44.

Cranny-Francis, A. and J. R. Martin (1994) In/visible education: class, gender and pedagogy in *Educating Rita* and *Dead Poets Society*. *Interpretations: Journal of the English Teachers' Association of Western Australia*. 27(1): 28–57.

Cranny-Francis, A. and J. R. Martin (1995) Writings/readings: how to know a genre. *Interpretations: Journal of the English Teachers' Association of Western Australia*. 28(3): 1–32.

Eggins, S. and J. R. Martin (1977) Genres and registers of discourse. In T. A. van Dijk (ed.), *Discourse as Structure and Process*. London: Sage, 230–56.

Eggins, S. and D. Slade (1997) *Analysing Casual Conversation*. London: Cassell.

Fairclough, N. (1989) *Language and Power*. London: Longman.

Fairclough, N. (ed.) (1992a) *Critical Language Awareness*. London: Longman.

Fairclough, N. (1992b) *Discourse and Social Change*. Cambridge: Polity Press.

Fairclough, N. (1995a) *Critical Discourse Analysis: The Critical Study of Language*. London: Longman.

Fairclough, N. (1995b) *Media Discourse*. London: Edward Arnold.

Fairclough, N. (1996) Technologisation of discourse. In Caldas-Coulthard and Coulthard, 71–83.

Fairclough, N. and R. Wodak (1997) Critical discourse analysis. In van Dijk, 258–84.

Fowler, R. (1996) On critical linguistics. In Caldas-Coulthard and Coulthard,

3–14.

Fowler, R., B. Hodge, G. Kress and T. Trew (1979) *Language and Control.* London: Routledge & Kegan Paul.

Fries, P. and M. Gregory (eds) (1995) *Discourse in Society: Systemic Functional Perspectives.* Norwood: Ablex.

Ghadessy, M (ed.) (1995) *Thematic Development in English Texts.* London: Pinter.

Giblett, R. and J. O'Carroll (eds) (1990) *Discipline – Dialogue – Difference: Proceedings of the Language in Education Conference, Murdoch University, December 1989.* Perth: 4D Duration Publications, School of Humanities, Murdoch University.

Halliday, M. A. K. (1978) *Language as a Social Semiotic: The Aocial Interpretation of Language and Meaning.* London: Edward Arnold.

Halliday, M. A. K. (1985) *Spoken and Written Language.* Geelong, Vic.: Deakin University Press.

Halliday, M. A. K. (1993) *Language in a Changing World.* Canberra: Applied Linguistics Association of Australia.

Halliday, M. A. K. (1994) *An Introduction to Functional Grammar.* London: Edward Arnold.

Halliday, M. A. K. and R. Hasan (1976) *Cohesion in English.* London: Longman.

Halliday, M. A. K. and J. R. Martin (1993) *Writing Science: Literacy and Discursive Power.* London: Falmer (Critical Perspectives on Literacy and Education).

Hasan, R. (1990) Semantic variation and sociolinguistics. *Australian Journal of Linguistics,* 9(2): 221–76.

Hasan, R. (1996) *Ways of Saying: Ways of Meaning.* London: Cassell.

Hasan, R. (1998) The disempowerment game: language in literacy. *Linguistics and Education,* 10(1): 25–88.

Hasan, R. and G. Williams (eds) (1996) *Literacy in Society.* London: Longman.

Hunter, I. (1994 )*Rethinking the School.* Sydney: Allen & Unwin.

Janks, H. and R. Ivanič (1992) CLA and emancipatory discourse. In Fairclough, 305–31.

Kotthoff, H. and R. Wodak (1997) *Communicating Gender in Context.* Amsterdam: Benjamins.

Kress, G. (1985) *Linguistic Processes in Socio-cultural Practice.* Geelong, Vic.: Deakin University Press.

Kress, G. (1996) Representational resources and the production of subjectivity: questions for the theoretical development of Critical Discourse Analysis in a multicultural society. In Caldas-Coulthard and Coulthard, 15–31.

Kress, G. and T. van Leeuwen (1996) *Reading Images: The Grammar of Visual Design.* London: Routledge.

Kutz, E. (1997) *Language and Literacy: Studying Discourse in Communities and Classrooms.* Portsmouth, N.H.: Boynton/Cook.

Lee, A. (1996) *Gender, Literacy, Curriculum: Re-writing School Geography.* London: Taylor & Francis.

Lemke, J. (1995) *Textual Politics: Discourse and Social Dynamics.* London: Taylor & Francis.

Macken-Horarik, M. (1996) Literacy and learning across the curriculum: towards a model of register for secondary school teachers. In Hasan and Williams, 232–78.

Macken-Horarik, M. and J. Rothery (1991) *Developing Critical Literacy: A Model for Literacy in Subject Learning.* Sydney: Metropolitan East Region Disadvantaged Schools Program (Issues in Education for the Socially and Economically Disadvantaged Monograph 2).

Manne, R. (1998) The stolen generations. *Quadrant* No. 343. 42(1–2): 53–63.

Martin, J. R. (1985) *Factual Writing: Exploring and Challenging Social Reality.* Geelong, Vic.: Deakin University Press.

Martin, J. R. (1986) Grammaticalising ecology: the politics of baby seals and kangaroos. In T. Threadgold, E.A. Grosz, G. Kress and M.A.K. Halliday (eds), *Semiotics, Ideology, Language.* Sydney: Sydney Association for Studies in Society and Cultur,e 225–68.

Martin, J. R. (1990) Language and control: fighting with words. In Walton and Eggington, 12–43.

Martin, J. R. (1991) Critical literacy: the role of a functional model of language. *Australian Journal of Reading,* 14(2): 117–32.

Martin, J. R. (1992) *English Text: System and Structure.* Amsterdam: Benjamins.

Martin, J.R. (1993a) Genre and literacy: modelling context in educational linguistics. *ARAL,* 13: 141–172.

Martin, J. R. (1993b) Technology, bureaucracy and schooling: discursive resources and control. *Cultural Dynamics,* 6(1): 84–130.

Martin, J. R. (1995a) Reading positions/positioning readers: JUDGEMENT in English. *Prospect: A Journal of Australian TESOL,* 10(2): 27–37.

Martin, J. R. (1995b) Interpersonal meaning, persuasion and public discourse: packing semiotic punch. *Australian Journal of Linguistics,* 15(1): 33–67.

Martin, J. R. (1997a) Analysing genre: functional parameters. In Christie and Martin, 3–39.

Martin, J. R. (1997b) Register and genre: modelling social context in functional linguistics – narrative genres. In E.R. Pedro (ed.), *Proceedings of First International Conference on Discourse Analysis.* Lisbon: Colibri/Portuguese Linguistics Association, 305–44 .

Martin, J. R. (1997c) Linguistics and the consumer: theory in practice. *Linguistics and Education,* 5(4): 411–448

Martin, J. R. (1999a) Mentoring semogenesis: genre-based literacy pedagogy revisited. In F. Christie, 123–55.

Martin, J. R. (1999b) Modelling context: the crooked path of progress in contextual linguistics (Sydney SFL). In M. Ghadessy (ed.), *Context: Theory and Practice.* Amsterdam: Benjamins, 25–61.

Martin, J. R. (in press) Beyond exchange: APPRAISAL resources in English. In S. Hunston and G. Thompson (eds) *Evaluation in Text.* Oxford: Oxford University Press, 142–175.

Martin, J. R., C.M.I.M. Matthiessen and C. Painter (1997) *Working With Functional Grammar.* London: Edward Arnold.

Martin, J. R. and R. Veel (1998) *Reading Science: Critical and Functional Perspectives on Discourses of Science.* London: Routledge.

Matthiessen, C.M.I.M. (1995) *Lexicogrammatical Cartography: English Systems.* Tokyo: International Language Sciences Publishers.

Melrose, R. (1996) *The Margins of Meaning: Arguments for a Postmodern Approach to Language and Text.* Amsterdam: Rodopi.

Nesbitt, C. and G. Plum (1988) Probabilities in a systemic functional grammar: the clause complex in English. In R.P. Fawcett and D. Young (eds), *New Developments in Systemic Linguistics. Vol. 2: Theory and Application.* London: Pinter, 6–38.

New London Group (1996) A pedagogy of multiliteracies: designing social futures. *Harvard Educational Review,* 66(1): 60–92.

O'Toole, M. (1994) *The Language of Displayed Art.* London: Leicester University Press.

Plum, G. and A. Cowling (1987) Some constraints on grammatical variables: tense choice in English. In R. Steele and T. Threadgold (eds), *Language Topics: Essays in Honour of Michael Halliday. Vol. 2.* Amsterdam: Benjamins, 281–305.

Poynton, C. (1985) *Language and Gender: Making the Difference.* Geelong, Vic.: Deakin University Press.

Roach, A. (1990) Took the Children Away. *Charcoal Lane.* Sydney: Mushroom Records (Produced by P. Kelly and S. Connolly)

Rothery, J. (1994) *Exploring Literacy in School English (Write it Right Resources for Literacy and Learning).* Sydney: Metropolitan East Disadvantaged Schools Program.

Shirato, T. and S. Yell (1996) *Communication and Cultural Literacy: An Introduction.* Sydney: Allen & Unwin.

Thibault, P. (1991) *Social Semiotics as Praxis: Text, Social Meaning Making and Nabakov's Ada.* Minneapolis: University of Minnesota Press.

Threadgold, T. (1997) *Feminist Poetics: Poiesis, Performance, Histories.* London: Routledge.

Trew, T. (1979) 'What the papers say': linguistic variation and ideological difference. In Fowler *et al.*, 117–56.

van Dijk, T. (1991) *Racism and the Press.* London: Routledge.

van Dijk, T. (ed.) (1997) *Discourse as Social Interaction.* London: Sage.

van Leeuwen, T. (1996) The representation of social actors. In Hasan and Williams, 32–70.

Ventola, E. (1987) *The Structure of Social Interaction: A Systemic Approach to the Semiotics of Service Encounters.* London: Pinter.

Walton, C. (1996) *Critical Social Literacies.* Darwin: Northern Territory University Press.

Walton, C. and W. Eggington (eds.) (1990) *Language: Maintenance, Power and Education in Australian Aboriginal Contexts.* Darwin, NT: Northern Territory University Press.

West, C., M. M Lazar and C. Kramarae (1997) Gender in discourse. In van Dijk, 119–43.

Wodak, R. (1987a) Kommunikation in Institutionen. In U. Ammon, N. Ditmar and K. Mattheier (eds), *Sociolinguistics – Soziolinguistik.* Amsterdam: de Gruyter, 800–20.

Wodak, R. (1987b) And where is the Lebanon? A socio-psycholingusitic investigation of comprehension and intelligibility of news. *Text,* 7(4): 377–410.

Wodak, R. (1996) *Disorders of Discourse.* London: Longman.

Wodak, R. and M. Schultz (1986) *The Language of Love and Guilt.* Amsterdam: Benjamins.

Wodak, R., F. Menz and J. Lalouschek (1989) *Sprachbarrieren: Die Verständigungskrise der Gesellschaft.* Vienna: Edition Atelier.

Wodak, R., P. Nowak, J. Pelikan, H. Gruber, R. de Cillia and R. Mitten (1990) '*Wir sind alle unschuldige Täter': Diskurshistorische Studien zum Nachkriegsantisemitismus.* Frankfurt: Suhrkamp.

# Index

# Open Linguistics Series

*Series Editor*
Robin Fawcett, University of Wales, Cardiff

This series is 'open' in two senses. First, it provides a forum for works associated with any school of linguistics or with none. Most practising linguists have long since outgrown the unhealthy assumption that theorizing about language should be left to those working in the generativist-formalist paradigm. Today large and increasing numbers of scholars are seeking an understanding of the nature of language by exploring one or other of the various cognitive models of language, or in terms of the communicative use of language in social contexts – or both. This series is playing a valuable part in re-establishing the traditional 'openness' of the study of language. The series includes many studies that are in – or on the borders of – various functional theories of language – and especially, because it has been the most widely used of these, systemic. functional linguistics. The general trend of the series has been towards a functional view of language, but this simply reflects the works that have been offered to date. The series continues to be open to all approaches – including works in the generativist-formalist tradition.

The second way in which the series is 'open' is that it encourages studies that open out 'core' linguistics in various ways: to encompass discourse and the description of natural texts; to explore the relationships between linguistics and its neighbouring disciplines such as psychology, sociology, philosophy, and cultural and literary studies; and to apply it in fields such as education, language pathology and law.

Relations between the fields of linguistics and artificial intelligence are covered in a sister series, *Communication in Artificial Intelligence*. Studies that are primarily descriptive are published in a new series, *Functional Descriptions of Language*.

*Recent titles in the series*: